James Duncan

The Dynasty of David, or Notices of the Successive Occupants of the Throne of David

With questions at the end of each reign

James Duncan

The Dynasty of David, or Notices of the Successive Occupants of the Throne of David
With questions at the end of each reign

ISBN/EAN: 9783337248147

Printed in Europe, USA, Canada, Australia, Japan

Cover: Foto ©ninafisch / pixelio.de

More available books at **www.hansebooks.com**

Yours truly,
James Duncan.

THE DYNASTY OF DAVID:

OR,

NOTICES OF THE SUCCESSIVE OCCUPANTS OF THE THRONE OF DAVID.

With Questions at the end of each Reign.

BY

REV. JAMES DUNCAN,

BAYFIELD, ONT.,

WITH MEMOIR BY THE REV. JOHN LOGIE.

His name shall endure for ever.—Psalm lxxii.

TORONTO:
JAMES CAMPBELL & SON.
1872.

PRINTED BY HUNTER, ROSE & CO.
TORONTO.

CONTENTS.

	Name.	Page.	Character.
I.	DAVID	1	Modest and ministerial.
II.	SOLOMON	23	Ungrateful and unfaithful.
III.	REHOBOAM	46	Haughty and humiliated.
IV.	ABIJAM	69	Enlightened, but unworthy.
V.	ASA	91	Eminent, but retrogressive.
VI.	JEHOSHAPHAT	113	Wisely-solicitous, but weak.
VII.	JEHORAM	137	Wicked and woe-submerged.
VIII.	AHAZIAH	160	Misassociated and misled.
IX.	JOASH	182	Highly-favored, but recreant.
X.	AMAZIAH	205	Ambitious and most wilful.
XI.	UZZIAH	226	Distinguished but dishonored.
XII.	JOTHAM	247	Undistinguished and **inefficient**.
XIII.	AHAZ	268	Outrageous and unrepentant
XIV.	HEZEKIAH	289	Illustrious but unguarded.
XV.	MANASSEH	311	Flagitious, but penitent.
XVI.	AMON	333	Impious and unloved.
XVII.	JOSIAH	354	Pious and progressive.
XVIII.	ZEDEKIAH	376	Unteachable and deeply chastized.

* * * *

XIX.	IMMANUEL-JESUS.	387	Transcendant, effulgent, and abiding.

PREFACE.

It may seem mistaken and presumptuous to place a volume of small pretensions before the public; also, it may seem unnecessary, if not somewhat childish, to add questions to each reign.

To these anticipated objections we answer :—

1st. All minds are not of the highest grade, nor yet are all minds equally developed. If only books of the highest stamp were published, the general mind could not have the benefit or the enjoyment of reading. There must be provision for the mass as well as for the refined and the speculative; and we hope there may be some among the various grades who may find these pages not unprofitable.

2ndly. We fancy that the added questions may be found useful to some parents who wish to carry forward the Bible-education of their young people, beyond the ordinary catechisms. The questions in the ordinary catechisms are necessarily general and dogmatic, and meant to be committed to memory; these questions are to a great extent personal and biographical, and meant—not to be committed to memory, but simply to aid converse between parents and their young people concerning the characters in question. While the parent who sees them need not confine himself wholly to them, he may yet find them useful in the way of suggestion—enabling him more fully and more easily to impress important truth on the heart of those he loves, than he could without their aid.

We mistake if there is not some intermediary books wanting between catechisms and treaties.

J. D.

PREFATORY NOTE.

In laying this volume before the public, it is only just to state that not one half of the book was prepared for the press by the author himself. The eighth sermon was not completed when he was called away.

From the manuscripts first used in the pulpit, the remaining discourses have been prepared with as great care as possible; but those by whom the work has been accomplished, are keenly conscious of what has been its difficulty; the exact meaning even may not always have been apprehended, and there may be some things necessarily left unchanged, which the author's own careful hand would have better adapted to the present purpose. Earnestly requesting that such flaws found in the later pages may be accounted, not to him who penned the sermons, but to those who have timidly and carefully attempted to prepare them for publication, the volume is submitted to the prayerful perusal of those who love, or would love, to find God and his teaching in every part of the word of Life.

MEMOIR.

The Rev. James Duncan, the author of this volume of sermons, was born on the 18th of April, 1803, at Alnwick, County of Northumberland, England. His parents, William and Eleanor Duncan, were members of the Secession congregation there—the same congregation in which Dr. Kerr, now of Glasgow, laboured for some years. With reference to his parents, he too could well say:

> My boast is not that I can trace my birth
> From loins enthroned, or rulers of the earth,
> But higher far my proud pretensions rise
> The son of parents passed into the skies.

By the blessing of God on the pious training under their parental care, and the ministrations of the sanctuary, two of the members of the family were led to devote themselves to the office of the Christian ministry. William, the younger brother, a few years ago "finished his course" in Australia; and James, the elder, the subject of this memoir, rested from his labours, at the commencement of the present year, in Canada.

With a view to the office of the ministry, James entered the University of Edinburgh, pursued with marked success his literary and philosophical studies under the distinguished men who at that time filled their respective chairs. He next entered the Divinity Hall of the then United Secession Church, and passed through the Theological course with highest credit and promise. A short time after he was duly licensed a preacher of the gospel, and spent a few months labouring in several of the vacant congregations of the church.

He accepted a call from the small and recently formed congregation of Warkworth, a quiet and rather pleasant village on the banks of the Coquet River, about eight miles distant from his native town. His ordination took place in the month of June 1836.

The entire period of his ministry in England from 1836 to the year 1854, when he left for Canada, was devoted to the advancement of the spiritual interests of this small but interesting congregation. It has been well said, "that nation is happy that has no history"—understanding by *history* what has too often passed under that name—a record of factions in the government, of intrigues and immoralities in the court, of civil broils and foreign wars. It is no less true of many of the most faithful and honoured ministers of Christ, they have been happy in having no such history. This happiness was pre-eminently Mr. Duncan's during the eighteen years of his ministry in Warkworth, there were no quarrels in the session, no factions in the congregation, not even one solitary appeal in complaint to any of the church courts of the denomination. It could be truly said of them, "How good and how pleasant it is for brethren to dwell together in unity."

The village itself in its quiet simple beauty (one of the

many lovely villages of old England) its homes clustering around the venerable ruins of the castle of Warkworth, one of the ancient seats of the Percy family, often referred to in the writings of Shakespeare,—this lonely and peaceful village is no inapt representation of the peaceful labours and results of Mr. Duncan's ministry among them, or rather, they resembled the gentle form of the river which glided past—but a few yards from his Church and Manse—on its way to the German Ocean. So passed peacefully along his quiet untiring labours, with their blessed fruits to the great ocean of eternity.

Sabbath after Sabbath you find him in the pulpit " a scribe well instructed in the mysteries of the kingdom of God," " striving (and not unsuccessfully, through God's grace) to approve himself unto God a workman that needeth not to be ashamed." You meet him beside the bed of the sick and the dying, pouring the balm of Christian consolation into suffering souls, dispelling gloom, cheering the drooping, inspiring with the spirit of Christian resignation many a troubled soul, leading them quietly to feel and say, " It is the Lord," " He doeth all things well," " Even so Father, for so it seemeth good in thy sight." He fails not to visit all the families of his flock, and he is there, as in the pulpit, the man of God. No trifling gossip, no frivolous questions does he discuss.

The blessing of the Master rested on the labours of the servant. The congregation, for the most part belonging to the humbler classes of the village and immediate neighbourhood, crowded around him Sabbath after Sabbath to receive from his hand " the bread of life," looking up to him with an admiring affection and respect we have never seen surpassed.

Happy above most in his domestic relations, he had married the eldest daughter of Mr. John Jobson, a gentleman living in the immediate neighbourhood. And as Mr. Duncan's family increased, great care was bestowed in their education, which was carried on entirely under the parental roof. This notice of his labours in Warkworth, may be closed by referring to a statement once made to the writer by a very intelligent young man belonging to the village, and whose connections at that time lay with the Church of England. It certainly was one of the finest compliments I ever heard paid to a minister of Christ. This young man, though otherwise intelligent and amiable, had spoken and acted in such a way as to lead his fellow-villagers to cherish the belief that he was an unbeliever in Christianity. In conversation with him one day, I asked him if it was true that he had lost faith in Christianity. After a momentary pause he replied, "Not altogether, Mr. Duncan—the Presbyterian minister—stands between me and infidelity. From what I see and know of that man, I cannot believe that Christianity is a lie." On inquiry, some years afterwards, about this young man, I learned with pleasure, that he became altogether a Christian on the best grounds, joined the fellowship of Mr. Duncan's congregation, and after adorning the doctrine of his God and Saviour, died a short time ago in the faith and hope of the gospel.

More than ordinarily attached to his family, as they advanced towards manhood, he saw and felt as a matter of simple duty, that remaining in England, they must be scattered. To prevent this, his thoughts were turned to emigrating to one or other of the colonies, and thus secure a home for them on a farm. He at **last** resolved on coming **to** Canada, and forthwith resigned his charge in Warkworth amid mutual regret. He found a home for his family not far from the shore of Lake Huron, in the neighbourhood of the village of Bayfield, and only **a short** distance from of one of our congregations, then under **the** pastoral care of Mr. Logie. A few months after his arrival, the minister of Bayfield Road congregation, on account of the extent of this field of labour, felt himself compelled to resign his charge of the congregation into the hands of the Presbytery. Having abundant opportunity of learning the ministerial gifts of Mr. Duncan, **a** unanimous call was tendered to him, which after **mature** deliberation was accepted.

The year **1854** saw him inducted into the pastorate of this congregation. His labours were pursued in their midst with the same quiet diligence on his part, and the same unity and peace, the same affectionate respect and confidence on the part of the congregation as in England. After a ministry of sixteen years in Canada, increasing infirmity constrained him **in** June 1870, to resign his charge. For many years he had suffered from a painful affection in his eyes, so much so, at one time, as to lead to the interruption of his studies, when attending the University, and more or less he continued **to** feel this weakness to the close of his life. **A few** years ago he was afflicted with a partial failure of memory, which caused him to lay aside his former habit of preaching from notes, and write his sermons fully out, and read them to his people. This was followed no long time after, with a tendency to asthma, accompanied with such bodily weakness as almost entirely to unfit him for active exertion.

Six months only had elapsed from his resignation when the great summons came, and the time and the manner most singularly in accordance with his previously expressed desires. In conversation, not long before, on death and the well grounded hopes of the Christian in connection with that event, among other remarks he stated that now, since his work and usefulness were well nigh over, he had a desire that his release might come speedily, as he was anxious not to prove a burden to the loved members of his family, through helplessness from the increasing infirmities of age. He remarked also his desire to be exempted from the sufferings of a protracted death-bed, as he had always shrunk with peculiar sensitiveness from pain, but he quickly added—"These are my weaknesses, the will of the Lord in this, as in all else be done." The loving Saviour sympathized with the weakness of his servant, and granted him the desires of his heart.

On Sabbath, the 8th January, 1871, he was worshipping with the church below before the dawn of another day he was worshipping with the church above. On returning to his home he made no complaint, seemed in his usual health, discharged the ordinary duties of the Christian father, and retired to bed at his usual hour. Towards midnight he appeared to have been seized with an attack of asthma. He was in the act of rising to secure some medicine to relieve his breathing. Mrs. Duncan persuaded him to remain in bed till she went for the medicine desired, first helping to support him, with the aid of pillows, in a sitting position, as more easy for his breathing, and so calm was he and seemingly unconscious of what was just at hand, noticing that Mrs. Duncan, in her haste to bring relief, was neglectful of herself, his last words were, "put something around you, you will catch cold." On returning with the means of relief she noticed that his head had fallen to the one side. He was dead—thus passed away without a struggle without even the consciousness of the presence of death this servant of the Lord. How appropriate the words of the hymn.

"Servant of God, well done!
Rest from thy loved employ,
The battle fought, the victory won,
Enter thy Master's joy.

The voice at midnight came,
He started up to hear,
A mortal arrow pierced his frame,
He fell, but felt no fear.

His spirit with a bound,
Left its encumbering clay;
His tent at sunrise on the ground,
A darkened ruin lay.

Soldier of Christ—well done,
Praise be thy new employ,
And while eternal ages run,
Rest in thy Saviour's joy.

The physician called in—pronounced disease of the heart the cause of his death. Three of his brethren in the ministry took part in the funeral service, held in the church, amid the sorrowing family, the members of the congregation and many sympathizing friends from the localities around. To the members of the bereaved family, these promises of God have come near, "I will be a husband to the widow, and a father to the fatherless,"— and those words of richest comfort, "Sorrow not even as others which have no hope," may they be enabled to lay hold of them. To the congregation this scripture demands practical application, "Remember them that have the rule over you, who have spoken unto you the word of God, whose faith follow, considering the end of their conversation, Jesus Christ, the same yesterday, to-day, and for ever."

On meeting Mr. Duncan for the first time, a look of intelligence, the prominent brow, the massive head, conveyed to the thoughtful observer the impression, this must be a man of no ordinary mental endowments. This impression was confirmed on listening to his conversation, it ripened into conviction on hearing him in the pulpit, or from the platform. As a student he carried off some of the highest literary honours of the University of Edinburgh—among others, the first prize for poetry—original and translated. In the Divinity Hall his exercises called forth the warm encomiums of his professors. By his fellow students he was looked up to as possessed of high mental ability. They anticipated for him the highest prospects in the future as a light in the church, and a credit to the denomination. In a conversation, many years ago, with one of his fellow students now well known in the Christian world, and well qualified to judge—Dr. Eadie, of Glasgow—remarking on the disappointment often expressed in connection with young men; some from whom little was expected, in after years becoming distinguished, filling their old friends with agreeable surprise, others from whom you expected great things, being never afterwards heard of. He referred to Mr. Duncan, than minister at Warkworth, as the most remarkable example of this second class that had come under his observation. "We all," he said, " regarded him as a man of highest promise, of superior mental abilities and gifts, that he would yet be heard of in the church ; now he has sunk into obscurity, he is never heard of."

It is just to state, in this connection, that the church to which Mr. Duncan belonged was not in fault (if fault there was) for his comparative obscurity, in the village of Warkworth. His distinguished ability as a man, and attainments as a minister of Christ, were known and appreciated in the highest quarters of that church, and persistent efforts were put forth to induce him to leave his village charge. At one time the greatest pressure was exerted in urging him to take charge of one of the large and influential congregations of the denomination in the city of Edinburgh. All in vain, his resolution was inflexible to remain where he was.

In proof of the high regard in which he was held as a man and a Christian minister, it may not be out of place here to present some extracts from the public testimony borne to his many excellencies. The first is **taken** from **a** biographical sketch that appeared in one of **the** newspapers **of his** native country, England, since his death. It was written, we believe, by one of his former members **in** Warkworth congregation.

"**Mr.** Duncan was minister of the United Presbyterian Church at Warkworth, for eighteen years. He was **a** beautiful character, full of manly tenderness and strength, humble, unassuming, **an** eloquent preacher, and a man of rare culture. By his people he **was** greatly beloved, to all he was a sympathizing father and able counsellor. **He walked** very closely with God, and perhaps all his people were not able to **keep** pace with his brightening spirituality. No doubt **he** sometimes outsoared their highest flights. But it was his delight to point sinners to Jesus, **and this he even** did in the simplest and most persuasive manner. He possessed **a** fine poetic genius, and a literary taste almost unerring. He carried off several prizes for poetry during his college course, and we have seen notes of high approval appended by the late celebrated Professor Wilson, (Christopher North) to some of his translations of Homer. He published a few sermons and poems during his residence at Warkworth; but only those who heard his voice Sunday after Sunday could form a just opinion of his powers—of the exhaustless freshness of his mind, and the dignity and splendour of diction which he could command." Yet another brief extract from the same sketch. "During his college career he was laid aside for about a year, **his** sight having almost entirely left him, and it was at **one time** doubtful whether he would ever be able to **re-**

sume his studies. A circumstance occurred in this connection worth noting, evincing as it does Mr. Duncan's strict adherence to principle. A gentleman who knew his worth offered him the office of postmaster of Berwick-upon-Tweed, with a salary of three hundred pounds sterling a year. After deliberation he declined the tempting offer because it would have entailed upon him some Sunday duty." We extract from another sketch of his life, published in the paper of his native town, the following:—
"He passed through the literary and philosophical classes of the University of Edinburgh, and the theological course of the Secession Church with great distinction. In Professor Wilson's class he gained the first prize for poetry; and his essay on conscience was pronounced the best of the session. A few sermons and poems have been published by him, but they form no adequate representation of his mental power. The news of his death will be received by his old friends with great regret. He was much esteemed among them for his abilities and the genial kindness of his disposition." I may also refer to the testimony borne by his brethren of the Presbytery of Huron, at the period of his resignation, extracted from Minutes of Presbytery.

"The Presbytery, in accepting Mr. Duncan's resignation of his pastoral charge, desire to place on record their sense of the loss sustained by the causes which, in the Providence of God, have led to this step. Throughout the period of his connection with this Presbytery, Mr. Duncan had won, in ever increasing measure, the confidence and love of his brethren; and they cannot allow his official connection with them to cease without expressing their gratitude to the Great Head of the Church, that one so distinguished for his ability, and attainments, depth of piety, and singleness of purpose in the work of the ministry, should have been so long spared in the service of the Church. They would express their deep sympathy with him in the present state of his health, their hope that a cessation from public duty may tend to his improvement in physical energy, and their prayer that his declining years may be crowned with the richest manifestations of the Master's presence and favours."

The question may naturally arise in the mind of the reader who, probably for the first time, may have heard that there was such a gifted Brother in our Canadian Church. How came he to remain in such obscurity? furnishing another illustration to the truth:

> Full many a gem of purest ray serene,
> The dark unfathomed caves of ocean bear;
> Full many a flower is born to blush unseen,
> And waste its sweetness on the desert air.

This obscurity arose partly from his meekness, he was one of the most unassuming of men. We never think of him in this light without having the testimony borne of Moses irresistibly suggested to our mind: "Now the man, Moses, was very meek above all the men which were upon the earth," and, but for the divine hand that pushed Moses to the front, he would have passed the remainder of his days in the obscurity of the land of Midian. It arose also partly from physical causes, the weakness of his eyes, which at one time threatened him with blindness and interrupted his studies for a whole year—an excessive sensibility **that led** him to shrink from the excitement of a more active life. He could seldom be induced to preach out of his **own** pulpit, except by great pressure, and then only in a few churches in his immediate neighbourhood. His non-attendance in the Church Courts may also in some measure help to account for his being almost unknown to the church at large. Once calling his attention to this, his quiet reply was, "I have no gift and no inclination that way, I feel grateful that so many of my brethren can make themselves useful in the public business of the church, and supply the place of a sleeping partner like myself." A young brother of the Presbytery of Newcastle once called the attention of the Court to Mr. Duncan's non-attendance. Mr. Pringle, of Newcastle, then one of the most active and public spirited members of Presbytery, arose and said, "Let Mr. Duncan alone, he is a man *sui generis*, notwithstanding his non-attendance, we ought, as a Presbytery, to feel grateful that such a man is among us."

And after all, may he not have accomplished in his comparative obscurity, more true service for the Master than had he occupied a place in the front rank? May his meekness, coupled with his eminent gifts and graces, not now serve "to point a moral." In these days, when ambition is the besetting sin of many a Christian minister, as they are seen jostling each other in their eager rush for the uppermost seats of the synagogue, is it not refreshing to turn away from the unseemly sight to see *this* brother quietly taking his place in the lowermost seat, **preferring the** small, struggling congregation in the obscure village, to the large and influential one in the capital of Scotland. When he left behind him, on the eighth of January last, one of **the** lowermost seats in the Church Militant, may he **not, on reaching the** Church triumphant, have heard **from the** lips of the great Master the joyful salutation, "Come up hither." "**He** that humbleth himself shall **be exalted."**

Many ministers, excelling their brethren **in** mental power, have **yet** been greatly deficient in the gifts of **persuasive** eloquence. **It was** not so **with** Mr. Duncan, his gift in this respect **was** equal to his intellectual ability. **On** reading, several years ago, for the **first** time, the memoir of the Rev. Mr. Toller, of Kettering, England, by Robert Hales, in a very interesting passage of that memoir to which reference is made by the late Rev. Mr. James, of Birmingham, in his "Earnest Ministry," **a** description is given of the remarkable power of persuasive eloquence possessed by Mr. Toller.

I was then much struck with the resemblance to what **I** had seen and felt **under Mr.** Duncan's ministry in Warkworth. It was our privilege to spend **a** year **in** that neighbourhood, about twenty-five years ago. The remembrance of those Sabbaths, worshipping in **that** humble chapel, rises **up** before us like a beautiful vision of the past calling forth our grateful thanks for the high privilege we then enjoyed along with our fellow worshippers. Truly "we joyed when it was said unto us, go ye **up** into the house of the Lord." We had listened in our native Scotland **to** the ministrations of many of the most gifted and eloquent of her ministers, but never before had we seen the cross so lifted up as in that pulpit in Warkworth; never had we listened to such clear and impressive exhibitions of the grand doctrines of Christianity; never had we witnessed such effects on an audience. **It** is to say little, that we **were awed** with the beauty and grandeur of the thought, lifted to highest admiration at the elevation and dignity of the language. We were at times as if spell-bound under the sway of the preacher's power, at one time thrilled with rapture **as** he dwelt on the character of **God, on** the manifestation of his mercy and love in the gift of his Son, on the beauties of holiness, on the joys **of the** blessed, and again melted into tears as the evils of sin were portrayed, or the humiliations and sufferings of the Saviour passed before the view. The heart and conscience were appealed to in a manner so tender, so melting, so irresistibly moving, I can only say it was to us like a new revelation of the power of human speech, it was sometimes felt to be almost overwhelming.

I may just point out one or two features in this wondrous power of the preacher.

The remark has been made **in** reference to the power possessed by the eloquent Whitefield, that from the very manner in which he pronounced "Mesopotamia" he could make you either laugh or weep. On listening to Mr. Duncan, we were struck with this very peculiarly, even in his very utterance of **a** sentence of Scripture which you may have heard a thousand times, without being specially impressed with its beauty or its force. As it fell from his lips it seemed to possess a new beauty, to have a new

depth and width of meaning, a more convincing power. His very utterance of the sentence, "In him dwelleth all the fulness **of the** God-head bodily," came home to the mind with such clearness and power that it seemed impossible to doubt the divinity of the Saviour. It seemed as if the very utterance of the words had sent a flood of light upon the understanding and an overwhelming tide of impression on the heart. Another example we can never forget, on repeating the words, "Behold I come quickly," **the tone and** emphasis was **such** that the effect on the audience, and ourselves was electrical; it seemed to break **upon** the soul like the living voice of the Lord, authority, warning, summons to instant preparation, appeared to blend together in arousing and startling the hearer.

Another characteristic feature of his preaching was the power of concentrating the attentive of his hearers on one fixed point, whether a Bible character, an event in Scriptural history, a doctrine, or a divine precept, placing it before you till the attention of his audience was secured, and then **he** surrounded it with such a flood of light, that it stood before **you** afterwards in almost visible distinctness, literally haunting you for weeks and months afterwards, as haunts the traveller some special sights, which have most impressed his mind.

But the excelling feature of his power was earnestness. Many circumstances lent a charm to his address, his striking intellectual appearance; a voice of great sweetness and compass; a diction slightly tinged with the poetic, and peculiarly his own; the silvery accent of his fine English voice, these combined exerted no little influence in favour of the speaker. But overtopping them all, and in a brief space sweeping them all out of sight, was that earnestness, which seemed to infuse the soul of the speaker, beneath his glowing words and burning periods, into the very hearts of his hearers. It was the remark of a brother, on returning from listening to one of his addresses from the platform, "Is it not a pity that such a man should be addressing an audience like this, that cannot appreciate him." So far as the intellectual side of his address was concerned there may have been some truth in this—doubtless the humblest of his audience may have failed to comprehend some of his language or grasp the elevation of his thoughts, but the humblest failed not to catch the spirit of the speaker—a sight of their faces set all doubts at rest; there, on every face, was enthroned the excited interest, the rapt delight, no doubt mingled here and there with a trace of bewilderment. One of these plain hearers, on hearing just such an address, remarked to the writer, "I never heard the like of that before, long as I have been in the world."

As a man and a Christian, to know him was to love him; as a husband, affectionate and sympathizing; as a father, blending the gentle and the firm; he ruled well in his own house; as a ruler in God's house, faithful, yet drawing by a singular power of attraction the hearts of his people towards him; in the community around the object of universal respect and esteem. A little incident will explain the secret of this general esteem. Meeting an individual one day on the highway, the name of Mr. Duncan was incidentally mentioned. "I never heard him speak, but one thing **I know**," said he, "he **is a** very pleasant man **to** pass **on** the road." A friend in Warkworth, in a communication on hearing of his death, remarks, "**I** enjoyed the pleasure of his acquaintance, from **the** autumn of **1840** till he **left** for America; **we** were attached friends, no one could know him and not love him, he was always so humble, so kind in disposition, so amiable in his manners, that he possessed in no ordinary degree the power of making himself beloved by all who knew him. His mental endowments were of a high order, I can truly say that I have met with few, if **any,** possessed of a clearer head, and a more loving heart than Mr. Duncan."

He was held in the highest respect and love by every one of his brethren in the ministry who enjoyed his friendship. He was uniformly kind and courteous, and, in reference to his brethren, he seemed only to have an eye for their excellencies, none **for** their weaknesses; indeed of all the fathers and brethren with whom we have had personal acquaintance, we know of none that surpassed him in drinking the spirit of these lovely Scriptures: "Let the same mind be **in you** which was in Christ Jesus." "Charity suffereth long and is kind, vaunteth not itself, is not puffed up, thinketh no evil, beareth all things, believeth all things, hopeth all things." Put on, as the elect of God, holy and beloved, bowels of mercies, kindness, humbleness of mind, meekness, long suffering, **let** the peace of God rule in your hearts, be thankful.

Noticing his strong attachment to the endearments **of** of his peaceful home, and shrinking from the excitements of publicity; the inference would be altogether incorrect, that absorbed in his own little world, he looked with something like indifference on all that was passing in the world without. On the contrary, no man more sympathized with the maxim of the ancient philosopher, "Whatever concerns man concerns me." Foremost of all, he ever manifested the deepest interest in all that concerned the interest of that "kingdom which is not meat and drink, but righteousness and peace, and joy in the Holy Ghost." And the constant tendency of his mind, was to look at all other movements going on in the world in their bearing on the higher interests of the kingdom of Christ. In a volume recently published on the History of Alnwick, his name is honourably mentioned as one of the most celebrated of the young men that led to the formation in that town of the first "Literary Society." We well remember the lively interest he took in England, in what was then called the Voluntary Controversy, or the Spiritual Emancipation of the Church of Christ, from State controul. We have lying besides us a lecture on the Independence of the Kingdom of Christ, published at the request of the Young Mens' Voluntary Association of Alnwick.

He showed also a deep interest in the Temperance reformation, then at its commencement; indeed, I notice in the sketches of his life published in his native county of Northumberland, that the friends of temperance there claim him as the founder of many of their societies. We have beside us two publications, in poetry, entitled "Daniel," and "Timothy," "For the sober and the

Young," written expressly to promote the cause of temperance. That interest remained unabated in Canada. As a token of his deep and intelligent interest in all that was going on in the world, I may mention that the last time we were privileged to meet he manifested high expectations from the French and German War, then going on, and occupying the general attention. Like many of the thoughtful, he regarded the Providential mission of Prussia as a great one; her origin, sprung from the bosom of the reformation; her rapid progress to her present commanding position; the need of some power in Central Europe to keep in check the Popish nations, Austria and France; he dwelt with animation on the probable benefits to Christendom from a United Germany applying this vigorous check; these were some of the topics on which he dilated with interest.

The publication of this volume of his sermons will be received with favour by the many friends who enjoyed his friendship, had often profited from his ministrations, and admired the grace of God in him through these sermons, "though dead to them he may yet speak."

The thought is a pleasing one, that Heaven is being enriched with the spoils of earth, and as the shadows of evening are felt gathering around many of us, and the solemn announcement is ever reaching us, "Your fathers, where are they? and the prophets, do they live for ever?" it yields the highest encouragement to look up, and there, along with patriarchs, prophets, apostles, confessors, and martyrs, to see the ever increasing number of the loved fathers and brethren, who but yesterday lived and laboured at our side, **and** thus seeing and feeling ourselves encompassed **with** so great a cloud of witnesses. How impressive and stimulating comes **to us the** sacred summons, "**Lay** aside every weight, **the sin that doth** so easily beset, run with patience the **race set** before you, looking unto Jesus the author and finisher of your faith, who for the joy **set** before them, endured the cross, dispising the shame, **and is set** down at the right hand of the throne **of** God."

NOTE.—The foregoing brief Memoir of the Rev. James Duncan (save a few additions) is taken from the July number of the "Record of the Canada Presbyterian Church," as furnished by the Rev. John Logie, Mr. Duncan's predecessor in the congregation of Bayfield road.

I. DAVID.

"And David perceived that the Lord had established him King over Israel, and that He had exalted His Kingdom for His people Israel's sake."—II. Samuel v., 12.

MEN are little able to anticipate the future, either for good or for evil. Blessings spring up in the path of the wise, which they never could have dreamt of in the earlier stages of their being: and sorrows and agonies assail the consciousness of the unwise, which they could not have believed possible in the sweet hours of their youth and inexperience.

How little David imagined, while yet a shepherd boy, the wonderful history he was to work out, and the lofty honours that were to attach to his name! He was to be the founder of a royal dynasty: he was to be the sweet singer of a recovered world: he was to be the type and progenitor of a Shepherd King, more glorious and more potent than aught of glory or of potency ever known among men: and yet he went in and out of his father's house wholly unconscious of his lofty destiny. There was nothing apparently to distinguish him from other boys, and yet what an unusual splendour was in due time to crown his name and his memory.

His greatness, however, was not sudden; it grew upon him gradually, and it had not attained its full development even when he was summoned to the Unseen. His renown is extending in the earth at the present hour. Linked with the Divine, his name will go down with honour to the latest posterity.

There is much to be said concerning this illustrious individual, as you very well know; but we would confine your attention, on the present occasion, to three things suggested by the words of our text, viz., his modesty, his enlightenment, and his fidelity.

I. His modesty in relation to his own greatness.

He had now reached the summit of human ambition. He was undisputed King in Israel: his capital was fixed: his palace was built: his kingdom was established. There was no tribe now in revolt: there was no rival to dispute his royalty; and neighbouring kings sent messages of recognition and friendship. He was secure in the heights of Zion, and nothing formidable or perturbing presented itself at any point of his horizon.

What, in such circumstances, might we expect the sentiments of David to be? Why, judging according to the general course of things, we would expect him to be imperious and self-centred. We would expect him to be full of his achievements, and bent on making everything subservient to his own aggrandisement. It was so with Nebuchadnezzar at Babylon, when he found himself undisputed master in Chaldea; and, as he walked in his hanging-gardens, looking over the mighty city which he ruled, and in which thousands of warriors and artizans were ready to do his bidding—whether in the way of conquest or of construction, he exclaimed, "Is this not great Babylon, that I have built for the house of the kingdom, by the might of my power, and for the honour of my majesty?" You see the lofty bearing of the man. It is by his own power (as he supposes) that he hath achieved his greatness, and himself is the end of it all. And it is not otherwise with successful aspirants after royalty in every age, though they may not express themselves so clearly or so proudly. They recognise no unseen Power or Providence. They are the artificers of their own greatness (such at least is their assumption), and they are their own end. All the resources of the community must be thrown into their coffers. All the genius of the gifted must be employed to show forth their greatness. All the skill of the skilful must be engaged in decorating their palaces or their persons. It **is** well if they content themselves with legalised exactions. In too many casses they display a spirit **of** caprice and cruelty. I need but remind you of Nero and Tiberius, Emperors of Rome. Of the latter it has been said: "He lived in the dreadful privacy of some fabled deity, and was only felt **at the** farthest ends of his Empire by the unhappiness he **occasioned.** By his murders and imprisonments, **and every** species of suffering, men's hearts and minds **were bowed** down beneath this invisible and irresistible oppressor."

In the light **of these** examples mark **the** modesty of David :—

First. "**He** perceived that God had made him **King**." It **was not** by his own prowess, nor yet **by** his own **wisdom,** that **he** had been enabled to overcome the many obstacles that lay in his way to supreme power. True, he had proved himself both courageous and prudent as the servant of King Saul, but these excellencies had only intensified the hatred of his master toward him. These very excellencies had thus rendered his life more **precarious,** and his possible elevation more unlikely. **The** truth is, it was a higher hand **than** his that had put aside all rivals. It was a mightier will than his that had controlled the jealousies of the tribes, and conciliated their regards toward himself. He **was** not, therefore, the architect of his own fortunes, but the favoured and honoured one of an unseen Providence. If it be said, that he could have less excuse than Nebuchadnezzar for attributing his elevation to his own power, seeing that he was anointed **to** the office of King while yet a youth, we answer **in the first** instance, that Nebuchadnezzar **was** the son of a king, and had thus a starting point for royalty independently of his own agency. This to him amounted to a designation as decided as that given to David. Then, in the second place, the agency of David had interwoven itself for years with the Divine purpose and Providence, just **as** in the case of Nebuchadnezzar. You will remember that it is natural and easy for the heart of man to overlook, or **to** forget altogether, the unseen Providence of God, and to estimate all things by the visible agency by which that Providence works. Thus Nebuchadnezzar estimated his own fortunes; and thus the kings of earth usually estimate their own aggrandisements and advantages. **But not so** David. He perceived the hand **of** God in his elevation. He was **not** content to account **for** his advancement by attributing it to his own abilities, **or** to his own political sagacity. His achievements **as a** warrior, and his skill in administration, **had no** doubt contributed to the result; but a wider wisdom than his **had** furnished the theatre, and controlled the elements **of** opposition, and lent facilities, without which he never could have reached the **stable** royalty **in** which he now found himself:—" He perceived that the Lord had established him King over Israel!" **And** he had a further perception still. It was,—

Second, that his royalty was ministerial and not ultimate. In the words of our **text, he** perceived "that the Lord **had** exalted his kingdom **for** His people Israel's **sake."** It **was** not simply, **you** perceive, that David might shine among men. It was not simply for David's personal aggrandisement. This, of course, would arise by his royal distinctions, and in the progress of his royal administration, but this was not the ultimate purpose **of** his success and glory. It could not otherwise be but **that** he would become famous and illustrious **as** the reigning monarch of **a** successful and a united people, but this his glory was rather incidental to his elevation than the end aimed at in his elevation. He, as King of **Israel,** was, under God, **what** Joseph was under Pharaoh,—**he** was exalted for the good of the kingdom. Pharaoh **took** his ring from his finger, and authorised Joseph to act with **a** view **to** the preservation of the people during the coming famine; and God, in effect, took a ring from His finger, and authorised David to care for Jacob His people and Israel His inheritance. And David knew it. He perceived the intention of God in the establishment of His kingdom,—It was for Israel's sake.

With such **a** conviction, David could not consistently

abuse his position to selfish ends. He could not make war merely to gratify his own ambition. He could not force contributions from his subjects merely to please his own vanity. In one word, he was not at liberty to prefer his own wishes to the interests of his kingdom. He was a responsible official. King though he was in relation to men, he was still a servant in relation to the unseen Power that had elevated his kingdom, and he must use his **royal** power in the interests of that kingdom. He must combine its resources and its chivalry to free the inheritance assigned to it by God from enemies and intruders: he must see to it, that the worship of **the** God of Israel was duly attended to: he must gather, as far as he could, the tribes to one centre of devotion, in conformity with the unity of Jehovah. The polytheistic nations might have many shrines, but the people whose God was one must have only one central shrine, and David must see to this. He must promote, too, justice, and education, and temperance, and all other excellencies among the people, so far as his example and his royal influence extended.

Such was the modest position and modest perceptions of David in the height of his prosperity. He was King because God had made him so. It was not by usurpation on his part, nor yet by superiority in him, but by the will and power of God. And he was King, not for his personal gratification, but to subserve the interests— the liberty, the unity, and the advancement of Israel. Other Kings may walk loftily; David could not, so long as he retained and cherished these convictions. Other Kings **may abuse** their power, and pervert the resources of their kingdom to selfish aggrandisement; David could not, so long as he remembered his ministerial position. So far from his elevation causing pride or strengthening selfishness in him, it could only, with these convictions, give modesty to his thoughts, and righteousness to his government. And here allow me to observe, that this modest and ministerial style of feeling ought to characterise all successful men. Success **in** any undertaking, or in any acquisition, requires and implies more than merely activity, or ability, or perseverance on the part of the successful party. There is a permissive or a favouring Providence involved in that success. An unseen hand hath withheld opposition, or removed hindrances. Many things beyond the control of the successful party have contributed to the result; and the recognition of this fact is calculated to make, or to keep, the successful one humble and modest. It is often otherwise, we know. Too many, in every walk of activity, are disposed to feel if not to speak in the style of Nebuchadnezzar. They recognise only their own agency in their good fortune, and overlook the concurring and favouring agencies or circumstances that made their success possible. They are proud in consequence, and take far more credit to themselves than they are entitled to. Instead of gratitude to an unseen and combining Providence, they boast of their own skill or sagacity, and forget their ministerial responsibility. Their acquisitions are their own, as they suppose, and these acquisitions are to be spent or employed solely for their own gratification or aggrandisement. They fail to see that God, in His Providence, hath made them rich or powerful that they may subserve the purposes of His government, by soothing the disappointments of the less fortunate, or by ministering to the maintenance or the extension of Divine truth in the earth. So far as an unseen Providence is concerned, and so far as the higher purposes of loving intelligence in relation to humanity are in question, they are as little awake as the inferior creation. They live to themselves alone. They enter not into the thoughts of God. They never think of the ministerial character of their prosperity; and they fail, therefore, to consecrate their resources by an enlightened and devout use of the same. 'Tis pity that it should be so; for they lose thereby an opportunity of ennobling themselves and of mitigating the evils that affect their race. In the language of Scripture,—"They sow to the flesh, and not to the Spirit," and they, you know, who sow to the flesh shall of the flesh reap corruption. Their riches will perish with them. These riches, having ministered to their pride, and selfishness, **and** estrangement from God, can have no ulterior benignant influence on their history. Had these riches been employed in the interests of Heaven—had their successful possessor **sowed to the Spirit**, and **not to** the flesh, then they had eventuated **in a joyous** ingathering—even in immortal **life and honour:** for, "He that soweth to the Spirit **shall of the** Spirit reap life **everlasting!**" O that **men would be** reminded of their **true** wisdom **in the** matter of earthly success! It **is not to** pride themselves **in that** success, **nor yet to spend the resources** thereby **gained** for their personal gratification. It **is,** on the **contrary, to** recognise **the** gracious Providence that has **blessed their** efforts, and to **use** their acquisitions in **concurrence** with the higher purposes of that Providence. **It is to** recognise the fact, that they are stewards **of** the All-Controlling **One, and** to help on, as His willing and intelligent servants, **His** rectifying and healing operations in the earth as fully **and** as far as their resources will permit. This, this, **is** true nobility! This is to enter into the thoughts of God—to rise above self and decay—to concur in the grand purposes of the universe—to find a lofty joy now—and to prepare the **way** for a larger and loftier joy hereafter!

But this leads me **to** notice concerning David :—

II. This enlightenment in relation to the purposes **of God** *in* **the** *earth.*

He **knew** that **God** had chosen **a** people from among the nations **to** subserve some worthy and Divine purpose. This appears in his conviction concerning the ministerial character of his established kingdom. It was for "His people Israel's sake." All peoples were God's **in** the light of creation, but all were not His by miraculous interposition and covenant. This honour belonged to the children of Israel. They were **a** chosen generation —a peculiar people—an holy nation. David recognised this fact: and he knew, besides, that Israel, **as** God's people, were a blessed people, and that they were not only blessed themselves, but designed to be, in some way, the means (or medium) of blessing to mankind. The truth is, David was not unmindful of the promise made to Abraham: "In thee and in thy seed shall all the nations of the earth be blessed." How this purpose was to be wrought out, he might not see, but the promise was to him reliable and gladdening notwithstanding.

God then had a people in the earth, and David apprehended the fact: and God had shown the profoundest interest in that people, and David knew it. He had raised up Moses in their behalf. He had brought them from their Egyptian bondage under that leader, and with a high hand. He had legislated for them—minutely and appropriately. He had shown to them something of His august majesty at Mount Sinai, and obtained from them their consent to be His. He had led them through the wilderness, and placed them in Canaan—spite of armed and apparently unconquerable opposition. He had raised up deliverers for them from time to time, and now He had enthroned David in the heights of Mount Zion in their interests. David recognised it all, and ruminated on the wondrous history continually. His Psalms are full of these themes. And he knew further, that God had ulterior agencies in reserve in relation to the accomplishment of His purposes in and by that people. He knew that what had already been done was but a preparation for far greater things that were yet to be done. He anticipated the enthronement on Mount Zion of a King; whose power would be irresistible, and whose favour would be the very highest felicity. This King would dash His implacable enemies in pieces like a potter's vessel, and would bless beyond thought all those who put their trust in Him. He sang of this King as " the Lord of glory," whose coming would be a matter of transcendent joy, thus, " Lift up your heads, O ye gates, and be ye lifted up, ye everlasting doors, and the King of glory shall come in." Nay more, he spake of this wondrous One as seated at the right hand of the Majesty on high, and as addressed by the Supreme Ruler, as "a priest for ever after the order of Melchizedek." And all nations, he knew, would feel in some way the influence of this King of glory and this priest of enduring power. It was not Israel alone that would be benefited by these Divine evolutions, but the entire world.

Such were the apprehensions and convictions of David. He saw a meaning in history higher and more significant than the thoughts of men. He entered, as it were, into the thoughts of God on a national and world-wide scale, as well as in relation to himself. And this is what we call his enlightenment; and this enlightenment accounts for his modesty in relation to his own greatness. He felt himself to be but the servant of a higher will than his own. Nay, Israel itself was not ultimate; its advancement and higher fortunes were to be made to bear on the interests of the world. And if Israel itself was not ultimate, much less his own royal glory—seeing that he was exalted for Israel's sake—even for the consolidation and exaltation of God's people. He was but one of a succession of agents, employed by God to carry forward a Divine purpose in relation to Israel, and to the world through Israel. Moses and Samuel had preceded him, and how many might follow him before the advent of the Lord of glory he could not tell. His throne he clearly saw was subservient, and his glory only incidental. The supreme matter was the purpose of the God of Israel, who established his throne, and who used him, in common with many more, to secure results of which he had, and could have, no adequate conception.

This state of mind and thought is very different, as you must at once perceive, from the state of mind and thought among ordinary kings. Read the history of any of them, from Alexander to Napoleon, and find if you can any traces of the enlightenment of which we speak. They recognise not the all-embracing Providence of Heaven. They enter not in their policy into the thoughts of God. They recognise not the fact that God hath a peculiar people among men; nor do they shape their policy with an eye to the liberty and safety of that people. God moves in history, but they do not seek to walk in the same line with Him. In many cases, they overlook the fact of God's Providence and purposes altogether: nay, sometimes they set themselves in direct opposition to the Supreme will. Instead of remembering and consenting to the purposes of God by His people, they persecute that people, and even seek to annihilate that people. And, when they find they cannot succeed in this, they seek by bribes to subordinate the Divine element in human society to their own earthly and crooked ways. The fact is, they are so beclouded in mind as to be wholly unconscious of any thing like ministerial responsibility. They live for themselves alone, as we have already said. They tax the resources of the nations and the industry of the industrious for their own earthly aggrandisement, and think only to gratify their own pride, and to follow out the dictates or caprices of their own irresponsible will. Hence their oppressions at home, and, when opportunity offers, their invasions abroad. Might with them is right, and subjection to a commanding and unseen purpose in history is a thing they never dream of. This is a matter deeply to be regretted. It is the fruitful and endless source of oppressions, revolts, conflicts, invasions, and barbarous executions from age to age. Millions have suffered in consequence, and millions are even now suffering in many parts of the earth. Were rulers generally enlightened, like David, in relation to their ministerial and subservient character, they could not tyrannise as they do; and were they aware that a Divine purpose runs through the ages, and shapes itself by the agency of a chosen people, they would not dare to oppress or labour to extinguish, as they do, or to pervert, the sacred association.

But this subject again belongs to ordinary men as well as to kings. It admonishes us, and all, of things higher and more important than the ordinary interests of life. It reminds us of God's purpose, and of God's people; and we ought to remember, that we have better means of knowing that purpose, and of tracing the action of that people on the institutions and progress of the world, than David himself had. We are not unfamiliar with the name of the illustrious Leader of God's people in these later ages. We hear of Him continually—even of Immanuel, *the Incarnate One*—His disciples in our own day are every where. They are found in all latitudes, and they speak all languages. They are scattered far and near, but they are all one in their glorious Chief. They constitute the spiritual Israel. They are God's people, and God's agents for the enlightenment of mankind. Their existence and their undertakings are of far more consequence to human society than is the policy of the mightiest nation among men. They are scattering the seed of divine Truth through all lands even now—seed that will yet spring forth in a harvest of righteousness and joy over all the earth. Their agents are on all continents, and on very many of the islands of the sea. Then, their influence at the Court of Heaven is availing, and their petitions before the Throne are perpetual. Their prayers, indeed, are but the echoes in heaven of the words and breathings of the Spirit of love in their hearts on earth. God from His throne touches them on His footstool, and they from the footstool send their grateful response back to the throne. God wakes them to prayer that He may put forth His strength in answering their prayers. Their petitions are but an index to His purposes. They labour and pray that all the world may be turned from idols to the living God, and all the world shall accordingly be turned from idols to the living God. The days of benediction are advancing apace. The promise to Abraham shall yet be amply fulfilled,—that in him, and in his seed, all the world should be blessed. The special seed of Abraham, we know, is the Son of God in human nature, and His true and loving disciples constitute in and with Him heaven's consecrated host for the emancipation and harmonisation of long-enthralled and dissociated humanity.

Now, to know this is to be enlightened with the enlightenment of David, and to enter into the thoughts of God. Alas, how many do not! Alas, how many have no apprehension beyond the visible interests of this passing life! Like the kings in their palaces, very many private men think only of their own advancement, or of how they may most effectually gain advantage against their neighbours. They have no conception that there is a divine interest interweaving itself with human things—a divine interest which demands consideration and regard. They may know that there is such an association as the Church, but they never dream of it as a remedial agency for the rectification of the world. They regard it rather as a refuge for the timid or the penitent, where personal safety may be sought. Even in this light, they concern themselves little about it so long as they are in health and able to prosecute the prizes of earth; but to regard true Christians as the people of God—as a consecrated agency for the outcarrying of divine purposes among men—of this they have no apprehension. Still less do they perceive, that it is their duty to strengthen the heavenly agency by joining the Church, and by entering into its purposes. If you talk to the prosperous in the spirit of our text—saying that they have been made prosperous, or established in their prosperity, for God's people's sake—they would stare or sneer at you as fanatical. But why should it be so? If men were as enlightened as David it would not be so. Is not the purpose of God pressing through the ages as certainly now as in the times of the son of Jesse? Hath not God a people—an Israel—a prayerful host—now as surely as He had then? If that Israel-people is more spiritual and more scattered than formerly it is only that it may be more effective and more extensively influential. If God enunciated and conserved His Truth in ancient Israel, He seeks to spread it by His modern Israel; and if David's throne was established for God's Israel's sake, why should the prosperous not reckon that their prosperity hath been given, or established, in the same interest? If they do not, it is because they stand aloof from the sacred people, which is their dishonour, or because they are unenlightened or apathetic in relation to God's purposes of mercy toward the **earth.** It **were** well that the prosperous should reconsider their prosperity in the light of this subject, and that all, whether prosperous or not, should remember that their history ought to be ministerial rather than self-terminating—in other words, every intelligent man should seek to help on **as** he may, the work of God in the earth—a work which **we** repeat runs through the ages. The agency of each may be small—may be infinitesimal—but it ought to **run** in the line of the divine purposes.

And this leads me to notice, **in** relation **to David :—**

*III. His fidelity in relation to the kingdom in the interests of which **his** throne had been established.*

Here observe, **that** the bent of a man's mind **will be seen** by his first solicitude when he finds himself **at** leisure or in possession of power. So long as circumstances control him you cannot determine decidedly what he supremely wishes; but let him, by the acquisition of wealth, or by the removal of checks and hindrances, be free to choose, and you will forthwith have indications of his true character. **If** vicious, he will speedily throw himself into vicious pursuits and vicious companionships. If virtuous, he will seek virtuous associations, and turn to some appropriate undertaking or pursuit. More particularly, if he delight in pictures, or in books, or in landscape gardening, he will take immediate steps to furnish his gallery, or his library, or to have his parks and pleasure grounds improved or extended, as the case may be. This, then, is one way by which we learn to know what a man is. Another way is, to mark his history, and to notice what is the ever-recurring and persistent purpose of his heart. He may often seem to act inconsistently. He may even be forced out of his chosen channel from time to time, but ever he will find his way back again, and press on in one direction. There may be eddies in his progress, and unexpected turns, as **in** the case of a river, but still the stream of his history moves on, and is **not** to be per manently altered by obstacles lying in his way. When, therefore, we can perceive some ever-recurring solicitude in any man's history, we thereby understand his character, even though that character may have much about it that is, on a limited inspection, inconsistent with itself; that is to say, persistency manifests character as well as a first free and voluntary act. A third way of judging of character is—the arrangements a man makes at his death. These, if in harmony with his previous history, indicate very decidedly the supreme solicitude of his heart. Of course, a man may make arrangements in relation to his property at his death very different from the complexion of his life. In that case, the arrangement only indicates fear, or superstition, or interested influence over him by others; but when the arrangement is spontaneous, and in accordance with the life-history, it gives further evidence of the state of the heart.

Now, judge of David's fidelity to the interests of Israel, and to his sense of the ministerial character of his royalty, by these tests, and you will find, we fancy, something both to be admired and imitated.

In the *first* place: What was his immediate solicitude on finding himself securely enthroned on the heights of Zion? What was the first public care that occupied him when his rivals of the house of Saul were removed and his persistent enemies, the Philistines, effectually subdued? Was it some selfish gratification, or some personal ambition? Was it some grand display to dazzle the mind of his subjects, and to impress upon them his own glory and greatness? Not at all! It was the upbringing of the Ark of God from Baale (or Baalah) of Judah (or *Kirjath-jearim*). Now that his capital was fixed, he would, as the first exercise of his undisputed royalty, have the symbol of the Divine presence enshrined there. For this purpose, he gathered together the chivalry of Israel—even thirty thousand men—and they commenced the procession with sacred gladness and varied music: "All the house of Israel played before the Lord on all manner of instruments made of fir wood—even on harps, and on psalteries, and on timbrels, and on cornets, and on cymbals." True, he and they were arrested by the sudden death of Uzzah, who, for irreverence and unpermitted liberties with the sacred sign, was smitten of the Lord, and died by the ark; but that did not vitiate the intention of David. It checked his zeal, but it did not falsify his loyalty. It was meant, too, to remind him of an oversight, but not to disown his service. In the engrossments of public affairs he had overlooked the special directions given by God Himself as to the manner of carrying the ark. It was set on a new cart, when it ought to have been borne by the Levites. Still, the intention of David was loyal. He meant to honour the God of Israel; and he meant to unite the tribes of Israel around the symbol of the Divine presence, as well as around his own throne. He was willing to have his own royalty overshadowed by the presence of a higher royalty; nay, he was desirous of merging his own glory as king in the greater glory of the God of Israel. An earthly-minded and self-seeking king would have preferred to leave the ark in obscurity while he gathered the glory of the tribes around himself; or, if he brought the ark to his capital at all, it would have been to increase his own glory by subordinating its ordinances and ministrations to his policy. But it was not thus with David. He acknowledged his elevation to be of God, and in the interests of God's people; and while he wished to associate the ark of God with his throne and capital, it was in acknowledgment of the supremacy of the God of Israel, and of the subordination and ministerial character of his own government. Here then was one decided evidence of his fidelity. We have a

Second, In his persistency as to purpose. Though turned for the moment from his undertaking—by the death of Uzzah, he was not permanently so. So soon as his mind recovered its tone after that startling event, he resumed his purpose. He made new arrangements for having the ark brought to Jerusalem, and placed in the tabernacle which he had prepared for it. And the

up-bringing was a joyous as well as a solemn occasion.—
It is said that "David and all the house of Israel brought
up the ark of the Lord with shouting and with the sound
of the trumpet." Nor did he attempt to make capital
out of the occasion in the way of securing honour to himself. Instead of this, he actually danced before the ark,
as an humble attendant, girded with a linen ephod. A
self-centred monarch would have been himself a conspicuous object in the procession—drawing as much attention and admiration from the excited multitude as
possible, but David was content to be nothing on the
occasion, that the entire interest might gather around the
ark of the God of Israel; nay, he was content to minister
himself in a humble position to the glory of the Lord.

Then, his solicitude concerning the ark of the Lord did
not stop here. Having secured its presence in his capital,
he was struck with the disparity between its accommodation and his own. "I dwell," said he to Nathan, "in a
house of cedar, but the ark of God dwelleth within curtains." This, to the mind of David was unseemly and
incongruous. Had he felt himself to be first and the ark
second, it had been proper enough, but he felt rather that
his throne was subordinate while the symbol of God's
presence was preeminent. His next solicitude was, therefore, to build an house for the ark of the Lord, surpassing and outshining his own palace, as far as he possibly
could make it. He was checked in this purpose, as you
know; but, did he thenceforth dismiss the thought of
any further honour to the ark of the Lord? Not at all.
If he could not build the house, he could make preparations for its erection. Informed that his son would
build it, he set aside the spoils of his wars and the surplus
of his revenue with a view to the great undertaking. A
worldly minded ruler would have accumulated the treasure
for its own sake, or spent it for his own glory; but David's
supreme solicitude was to honour God, and to subserve
the purposes of God's grace among men, and therefore he
consecrated his wealth to the undertaking—which he might
not himself accomplish. But for his pre-eminent de-

votedness, he would have left Solomon to find the means of building the Temple himself. You see thus that he was faithful to the God of Israel, by whom his throne had been established. His devotedness was neither temporary nor discontinued. His deviations from rectitude might be (were indeed) serious, but the bent of his history was heavenly and disinterested. **And** the third test is equally decisive: That is,

Thirdly, the arrangements he **made a year** or two before his death. These were still in keeping with his lifelong solicitude concerning the ark of the Lord. **He called** Solomon, his **son and** successor, and, having **enjoined** on him to attend to the statutes and judgments which the Lord charged Moses with concerning Israel, he delivered himself thus:—"Now, behold, in my trouble **I have** prepared for the house of **the** Lord an hundred thousand talents of gold, and **a** thousand thousand talents of silver; and of brass and iron without weight; for it is in abundance: timber also and stone have I prepared; and thou mayest add thereto. **Moreover** there **are** workmen with thee in abundance, hewers and workers of stone and timber, and all manner of cunning men for every manner of work. Of the gold, the silver, and the brass, **and the** iron, there is no number. Arise therefore, and be doing, and the Lord be with thee." (1 Chron. xxii., 14—16.)— The King commanded the Princes also to help Solomon in the great and pious undertaking.

See, then, how completely the zeal and fidelity of David are vindicated:—his first solicitude after the establishment of his throne was for the honour of God—his persistent solicitude through life was for the honour of God—his latest solicitude and directions were still for the honour of God. He wished, with a view to this honour, for "the building of a house for the ark of the Lord which should be exceeding magnificent, of fame, and of glory, throughout all countries," and he devoted *millions of wealth* for the purpose, as well as employed workmen to prepare stones and other materials for the undertaking. David had his faults, and they were serious faults too;

but half-heartedness in the service of God was not one of them. There are who obtrude his faults on observation; but they, who do so, are careful to forget all the evidence his history furnishes of true loyalty to the interests of Israel and of Heaven: and such, we fancy, will be found wanting when brought into comparison with him before the great white throne. Will they, think you, be found to have subserved the purposes of Heaven, as David did? Will they be found to have thrown all their solicitudes into the advancement and establishment of God's kingdom in the earth, as David did? Will they be found to have thrown all their wealth and accumulations into the treasury of God, as David did? Will they be found to have manifested a supreme and persistent regard to the unity and glory, and piety of Israel, as David did? We fear not. Nor will it be better in this respect with many who are content to merge David's faults in his excellences, and who claim him as a fellow-servant. It will be seen concerning them also, that they have not ministered of their means, or of their abundance, either to the unity of God's people, or to the extension of His truth—(not, at least, in any full stream of loving-concurrence)—after the manner of David.

Nor let it be said, that David's case was peculiar. There are similar cases in modern times. Two strike us now. Carey, the great missionary, had an ample income from Government, as Professor at Fort William. He took a small pittance for his own maintenance, and devoted all the rest to the cause of God. It was not with him, a trifle to the cause of God and the rest for self, but, a trifle for self and the rest for the cause of God. Thomas Gouge again, who lived in the seventeenth century, gave two-thirds of his income, as well as his personal exertions, to the advancement of education in Wales. He had £300 a year: he gave £200 of it in the service of Heaven and humanity. But the whole matter lies in the state of the heart—he that loveth little will give little, while he who loveth much will not be content with small givings!

QUESTIONS ON DAVID.

To what eminence did David ultimately attain?
> He became undisputed master in Israel. He fixed his capital on Mount Zion, and all the tribes gathered loyally around his throne.

What was the sentiment of Nebuchadnezzar when he found himself undisputed master in Babylon?
> Pride and self elation. "Is this not great Babylon," said he, "which I have built for the house of the kingdom, by the might of my **power,** and for the honour of **my** majesty."

Is it not very generally with the Royal **and the** Imperial as it was with Nebuchadnezzar?
> History seems to say so:—Whether Persian, Macedonian, Roman or Modern.

But **was** it so with David **in** the heights of Mount Zion?
> No: his convictions were those of a man who recognised a power higher than his own.

What did he perceive concerning his royalty?
> That it **was** of God and not merely by his own prowess or genius.

Had not his **own** prowess and prudence contributed to the result?
> Certainly: but he **saw** at the same time, that **a** wider wisdom than his own had made the necessary combinations and secured success to his agency.

And what did he understand to be the object **of God** in making him king?
> To promote the interests of Israel: "He perceived that God had made him king for His people Israel's sake.

Was his reign in accordance with this perception?
> For the most part it was:—He fought the battles of Israel—he arranged according to divine direction the worship of Israel—and he made it his supreme care **to** prepare for the erection of a superb Temple as a centre of worship for **the** sacred tribes of Israel.

What are the lessons which this style of feeling and acting on the part of David when crowned with success should teach to successful men?
> A modest estimate of their own agency in relation to their success, and a desire to understand how God would have them use their acquisitions in His service.

THE DYNASTY OF DAVID.

Is it usually thus with successful men ?

We fear not : too many such attribute their success to their own skill or sagacity, and, forgetting their ministerial responsibilities, employ their acquisitions for the gratification of their own humours or ambitions.

What in that case is the effect of their success on their nature and history ?

It re-acts disastrously upon both. It debases the one and darkens the other. In the language of Scripture, "They sow to the flesh, and of the flesh they reap corruption."

What on the other hand is the effect, or re-action, of prosperity, when successful men regard themselves as servants and stewards of God ?

The use they make of their wealth in that case ennobles their nature and brightens their history : "They sow to the spirit, and of the spirit they reap life everlasting."

To what extent was David enlightened as to the purposes of God ?

He knew that the Holy One had chosen a people from among the nations with a view to ulterior proceedings. He knew most of the miraculous history of the people, and he ruminated upon the miraculous history continually. He knew also, that an illustrous Priest and king was yet to arise among that people to bring about the times of universal benediction promised to Abraham : "In thee and in thy seed, shall all the nations of the earth be blessed."

What is noteworthy in this enlightenment on the part of David ?

That he entered thereby into the thoughts of God—not only in relation to his own royalty, but also in relation to the people over whom he ruled, and to the entire world indeed through that people.

Is such enlightenment common among Rulers now ?

Far from it : Rulers generally overlook the fact that God hath a people in the earth, and that through that people He is seeking to prepare the nations for their higher destinies.

What is that too, in relation to their office, which Rulers very generally forget ?

Its ministerial and responsible character : they very generally think that the resources of the nation are for their aggrandisement, and not that their office is for the good of the nation.

What are some of the sad consequences of this mistake on the part of Rulers?

Oppression, exaction, revolt and cruel wrongs. **If Rulers were aware, like David, that a divine purpose runs through the ages, and that that purpose shapes itself in some measure by the agency of a chosen people, would they persecute or seek to bribe that chosen people, as they so often do?** No indeed: they would not dare **to** interfere with so important and so sacred an agency.

Does this subject of enlightenment as to the purposes of God belong to ordinary men as well as to kings?

Certainly: it is important that all should know **that** God hath a peculiar people among men—that the tribes of that peculiar people are led by Immanuel—that the influence of that people at the court of Heaven is availing—and that that people constitute, in connexion with their great chief, God's consecrated host for the rectification **of** the world.

And is it enough merely to know that **there is** such a people?

No: every man to whom the testimony of God comes is under obligation to join this people, and to help on their great purpose.

Is it necessary for the poor and **the** uninfluential **as** well **as** for the ruling and the successful to do so?

Yes: every intelligent being, however humble, ought to help on as **he** may the work of God in the earth.

How did David show his zeal for the cause of God on his finding himself established in his kingdom?

By his prompt attempt to bring up the **ark** of God to his capital thus, marking the subordination of his throne to the God of Israel.

He failed in the attempt, as you know. How did he further show his devotedness?

By renewing the attempt soon after: and especially **by** his humble and worshipful bearing on the occasion.

How next did he manifest his enlightened zeal for God's purposes in Israel?

By proposing to build a Temple **of** unusual magnificence for the ark.

When **arrested in** this by Nathan, how did **he** still **more** strikingly manifest his supreme and persistent solicitude for the honour of God and the unity of the tribes?

By putting aside all the spoils of **his** conquests, and by making other large and long preparations for the building of the Temple by his son.

While **we** deplore David's faults, **is** it right to overlook **the** evidence of his prevailing fidelity and devotedness?

Assuredly **not**; they do injustice to **him who** obtrude his faults while they merge his disinterestedness and un**wavering zeal for** God.

Are there any similar cases of unstinted devotion **to the cause of God** in modern times?

Yes: Carey, for example, in the **last age, and** Thomas Gouge in **the** 17th century.

What chiefly determines the rate of giving to the cause of God?

The **state of the heart.** They **who love** much will give accordingly.

What in few words are the **lessons to be** learned from this **view** of David's **sentiments and** character?

That success is of God—and **that the successful ought to use** their acquisitions in the **interests of God's Israel.**

II. SOLOMON.

"And the Lord was angry with Solomon, because his heart was turned from the Lord God of Israel, which had appeared to him twice, and had commanded him concerning this thing that he should not go after other gods: but he kept not that which the Lord commanded. Wherefore the Lord said unto Solomon, 'Forasmuch as this is done of thee, and thou hast not kept my covenant and my statutes, which I have commanded thee, I will surely rend the kingdom from thee, and will give it to thy servant.'"—(I. Kings, xi., 9, 11.)

IT is not **safe to judge of** men, **or of their** happiness, by appearances. This **every one knows in** words, but very many disregard it in fact. The young, especially, fancy that the rich must **be** happy, and happy because of their riches. They forget or overlook the **unseen** elements that belong to the question, **and attach an** undue importance to the one element **that** addresses itself to their observation.

Solomon **is a** striking instance of this. He was distinguished in his day by his wisdom, and by the splendours of his court. Kings and chiefs came from all the regions around Palestine, (or sent their ambassadors) to behold his grandeur, and **to** listen to his utterances. His palaces were superb; the Temple of Jehovah, built by him, was pre-eminent among human erections, for its golden beauty and magnificent site. He had added ornamental buildings besides all around his capital (to say nothing of Tadmor in the wilderness); and all his appointments, **as to** shields and thrones, and drinking vessels, and horses and chariots, **were** of the most costly description. His, indeed, would seem to have been the golden age, and himself the most sumptuous of monarchs.

If riches and splendour could secure happiness, then Solomon must be regarded as happy; and, viewed from a human point of sight, he was really pronounced to be so by his contemporaries. The Queen of Sheba gave utterance to the conviction of his numerous visitors when she exclaimed in his presence, "Happy are thy men (O King!) and happy are these thy servants, which stand continually before thee, and that hear thy wisdom!" This was but an indirect and delicate way of saying, "Happy art thou, O Solomon!"

Such was this prince as seen to the eye; he was the greatest and happiest of men: and yet at the very time an unseen cloud rested upon him. The frown of Jehovah darkened all his glory. If men, dazzled by the visible, and but partially informed, pronounced him happy, the enlightened servant of the Divine judged and decided otherwise. The grand essential of happiness was not then his. The complacency of the Eternal was not resting like sunshine upon his heart. On the contrary, "The Lord was angry with Solomon." It is not pleasant to live under the anger of a fellow-mortal, how much less pleasant—(nay, how positively painful!) to live under the frown of the Almighty! The admiration of the Queen of Sheba, was a small set-off against the displeasure of God. Pity for Solomon! We would have expected better things concerning him, had we known only of his conduct and prayer at the dedication of the Temple. And how weak is human nature, when so wise and so promising a king should have so far forgotten himself as to incur the anger and disapprobation of his father's Almighty Friend.

In further noticing this prince, we shall remind you of the reasons of God's displeasure with him—of the sad consequences of his folly—and of the use of his story to us.

I. *The reasons of God's displeasure with Solomon.*

These were, in general, the countenance and encouragement he gave to Idolatry. He not only tolerated idolatrous worship in Jerusalem (and this had been bad enough), he actually engaged in such worship himself. "He went after Ashtoreth, the Goddess of the Zidonians, and after Milcom, the abomination of the Ammonites:" Nay, more, "He built an high place for Chemosh, the abomination of Moab, in the hill that is before Jerusalem, and for Moloch, the abomination of the children of Ammon: and likewise did he for all his strange wives, which burnt incense and sacrificed unto their gods." I suppose he would think this was liberality on his part, and a proof of that superior wisdom for which he was famed. It is thus at least with many would-be-wise ones in our own day. They put truth and error on the same footing, and cry out against those who object to their action as bigoted and narrow-minded. They pride themselves in being free from what they regard old-fashioned prejudices, and fail to perceive that their fancied liberality in relation to error, is really injustice and treason in relation to truth. The earth-born has no right to be put upon the same footing with the heaven-descended, and Solomon at least was in circumstances to know the difference. He knew very well that the God of Israel was the true God, and that no god could confer benefits or answer prayer save Jehovah Himself alone. He knew this, not merely theoretically and historically: he knew it by personal experience as well: and, therefore, he was the more inexcusable in his defection. He built high places for false gods in the very presence of the Temple of the true God, and thereby diminished the glory that ought to have been supreme in Jerusalem; and, thereby also prepared the way for division and confusion, and every evil work, where only unity and harmony, and the fruits of righteousness, ought to have been found. No wonder that God was angry with him. Even as an individual, apart from the responsibilities of his position, his conduct was unworthy and base; but it becomes far more reprehensible, and even abominable, when you consider his position, his privileges, and his distinctions.

Think *first*, of his obligations as the favoured one of

God. "God had appeared to him **twice.**" God had departed in his favour from His ordinary style of dealing with men. Only endeavour to realise the fact: the August One who **dwelleth not in** temples made with hands, **and whose** over-flowing glory **is such,** that the heavens of heavens cannot contain **it,—this** great and August One had actually deigned **to commune** with Solomon individually. He appeared **to Solomon in** Gibeon, **in a** dream by night, and **said, " Ask** what I shall give **thee !"** and when Solomon asked wisdom to rule, He said, **" Behold, I have done according** to thy words. Lo, I **have** given thee **a wise and** an understanding heart, **so** that there **was** none like thee **before thee,** neither after thee shall any arise like unto thee : and I have also given **thee** that which thou hast not asked, both riches and **honour : so that** there shall not be any among the kings **like unto thee all** thy days." **Such** was God's first **appearing to** the favoured king : **and he** appeared a second **time to** him **after** the dedication of the Temple, and assured **him of His** continued regard : and the Lord said **unto** him, " I have heard thy prayer and thy supplication, that thou hast **made** before **me : I have** hallowed this house which thou hast built, to put my name there for ever : and mine eyes and my heart shall be there **perpetually."**

Now, what might be **expected** from Solomon after this ? **was it** a meet return **on his** part that he should become **indifferent to the** Temple, where God had promised **to have His eyes** and His heart continually ? Still more, **was it a** meet return to build opposing shrines in the very presence **of** that Temple ? Was it not rather ingratitude—shameful, indescribable ingratitude ? Though God had bestowed on him no such kindness, and no such distinction, **as** that of appearing to him personally, **it** had **been** ungrateful **in** him to have acted so, considering what **God** had done for his nation and for his father's house; but, when you add his personal obligations to his national and ancestral obligations, you cannot but perceive his enormous ingratitude. Why should he of all men prove recreant and forgetful in relation to divine condescension and kindness? Why should he, the most favoured man of Old Testament times, be unmindful of his heavenly Benefactor? O, why should Solomon insult God? One would have thought that such conduct would have been impossible in his case. Listening to him in his earlier and better days, when he so gracefully and devoutly dedicated the Temple in the midst of his loyal and rejoicing people, we would have thought that the absurdities and abominations of Idolatry could never have appeared to him other than repulsive and offensive! And we would have expected, and especially in view of God's special kindness and condescension to himself, if tempted to patronise the shrines of idols, he would have exclaimed, in the language of Joseph, "O, no! Other men may listen to you in this matter, but for me, so fully informed of the truth, and so specially favoured and honoured by the God of Israel, the thing is impossible! While memory lasts, I can never forget the visions and the promises of the Almighty: and, so long as these remembrances fill my consciousness, you ask in vain from me any thing that would dishonour His name. He is my God, and I am His servant-king; and no shrine shall arise in my kingdom, so long as I rule, to dim the glory of His Temple! I can never honour Him enough for His distinguishing goodness to me, and I would not be found ungrateful for His mercies."

This, I say, we might have expected in the case of Solomon: but what instead do we find? Why, base and senseless defection,—shameful forgetfulness!—inexcusable trifling! His heathen wives wish one thing, and his divine Benefactor wishes another: he yields to his wives, and forgets his Benefactor! Without benefiting his wives, he dishonours his matchless Friend, and lays himself open to the charge of dark and inexcusable ingratitude. The heathen, who know God's eternal power and glory only by creation, are said to have been *without excuse* when they sought false divinities, what then can be said in extenuation of Solomon's Idolatry, who not only knew God as revealed to Moses, and in the history of his nation, but who also knew Him by personal intercourse and inexpressible favours? No language can express the turpitude of his defection, or adequately represent all his criminality. But think—

Secondly, of the charge committed to him as the king of God's people. In this capacity (I mean as king in Israel), he had two important things to care about ;— the one was the honour of God, who had chosen him to the kingdom ; and the other was the peace and harmony, and improvement of his subjects. In relation to the first of these, viz—the honour of God, he must steadily keep in view the peculiarity of the kingdom over which he presides. It is the kingdom of God as distinguished from all the kingdoms of men. It is a kingdom meant by Him who selected and located it, to be a protest against the Idolatry and unrighteousness of all surrounding and contemporary kingdoms. It is a kingdom meant to reveal to men the supremacy, the holiness, and the mercy of the true God. Nay, it is a kingdom meant to prepare for the illumination of all nations and all times! A kingdom whose ultimate purposes were the incarnation of the Son of God, as a divine and competent Saviour, and the utter and absolute abolition of Idolatry and unrighteousness from all the continents and islands of the earth! All this Solomon knew, in a measure, from the writings of Moses, and from the sacred compositions of his father—compositions in perpetual use in the worship at the Temple ; and all this he ought to have kept before his mind. And accordingly, knowing this, his first great solicitude, as king of this kingdom, ought to have been to keep his kingdom entirely and sacredly free from Idolatry. Then, his second great solicitude ought to have been the peace, the harmony, and the religious improvement of his people. It was by these that the immediate purposes of the kingdom were to be brought about. It was by these that the nations were to be taught the beauty and the superiority of true religion. It was by the exemplification of unity and heavenly virtue that blinded nations were gradually **to be won** from the degradations and miseries of Idolatry. **These** blinded and idolatrous nations could not themselves **attain** to unity, for they had lords many, and gods many; but Israel had one only, all-sufficient, almighty centre, and therefore might be expected to furnish an illustration of religious and social unity, and **so** of virtue and excellence; **the** blinded and idolatrous nations could never attain **to** these, seeing that their very gods **were** the patrons **of** immorality and defilement: but the people of the true God might attain to no small degree of excellence under **the** heavenly and quickening influences **to** which, as the people of the one true God, they **were** subjected. And it was for Solomon to see to this **matter**; and that, not only in the interests **of** Israel, but also in the interests of the world. He must promote, as far as he possibly could, that exemplification of true religion and righteousness which was meant to enlighten the darkened, divided, and wandering tribes of men.

You see thus the charge committed to Solomon **as** king of God's people; he must use his authority to keep Idolatry out of the kingdom; and he must use his influence and resources as king to promote the **unity and** religious progress **of** his people.

Now, how did **he** discharge **those duties?** Was he faithful or was he unfaithful in relation to them? He was unfaithful in the very highest degree. Instead of attending to the honour of God, and maintaining God's exclusive rights in Israel, he actually himself became **an** idolator, as already stated; and, not satisfied **with** going after other gods, he used his royal resources to build for these other gods shrines **in** the sacred territory. He taxed the people of God to build altars for the enemies of God. He used the resources of the sacred kingdom **in** the interests of **the** very irreligion which that kingdom was meant **to** oppose. His fault was no common fault, you perceive. It was not simply a case of unfaithfulness; it was unfaithfulness doubled and complicated. It was using the resources placed at his disposal as king, to subvert the very purposes of his royalty. No wonder that God was angry with him! Any man would be deeply angry with a favoured servant, who not only disregarded his master's interests, but actually stole his master's money to give to his master's enemies, that these enemies might be the better able to subvert his master's most cherished purposes! Any man would frown upon a trusted subordinate who proved himself not only indifferent to the peace and unity of the family of his superior, but who actually gave himself to practices which necessitated the disunion and dishonour of that household. And this Solomon did in relation to Israel. He gave himself to Idolatry, and that on a scale that is perfectly astounding. It was not merely one idolatry that he countenanced; it was many. He built shrines for the abomination of the Zidonians—for the abomination of Ammon—for the abomination of Moab —and for other strange gods. Wonder it is that he did not, among all his sacred erections, build an altar to Dagon, the fish-god of the Philistines. It was no want of complaisance on his part if he did not. It only arose from the fact that he had not got a Philistine princess among his wives. O, but he was strangely and indescribably unfaithful to the charge committed to him in relation to God!

And he was not less unfaithful in relation to his subjects. Instead of studying to promote their unity and improvement, he took the most effectual way to divide and degrade them. Instead of gathering them around the Temple, that they might exert an enlightening influence on surrounding Idolatry, he actually brought Idolatry into their midst—thus weakening their power of testimony, and destroying their influence for good.

Besides, instead of using the resources of the kingdom, which as king he was enabled to gather from all the tribes, for the good of Israel, he spent these resources on himself. He cared only for his own aggrandisement. He gathered around him a disproportionate and extravagant court. He multiplied to himself wives, and horses, and all manner of luxurious equipments. **He acted as if** Israel were nothing, and himself everything,—or rather, as if Israel had been made for him, and for him alone. Instead of endeavouring to fill worthily the righteous throne of David, he became the selfish and oriental despot. He laid heavy taxes on his people to maintain his extravagance. Instead of pressing lightly on his subjects, as any wise ruler would do, and securing their loyalty by consideration and moderation, he had them, at the period of his death, at the very point of rebellion by his excessive exactions. What think you of the wisdom of this wisest of men? Surely you must acknowledge that his self-love had turned it into folly: and you cannot **wonder that** God, who gave him that wisdom for the best of purposes, should have been grieved and angry with him when He saw His precious gift so shamefully perverted! But think,

Thirdly, **of** his privileges as to religious knowledge. He was fully instructed, or, at least, he had the means of being fully instructed, in the mind and will of God— whose king he was. He had the writings of Moses, and he was under obligation, as king, to make a copy of these writings for himself, to read them continually, and **to** regulate all his ways by their directions, and according **to** their spirit. And he was not unreminded of his duty in this respect. His father David, when dying, urged him **to** " keep the charge of the Lord, to walk in His ways, to keep His statutes, and His commandments, and His judgments, and His testimonies, as these were written in the law of Moses," that he might make his way prosperous and transmit **a** stable throne to his son : and God, the great God Himself, had condescended to urge the **same** course when He appeared to him the second time—assuring him besides, that if he proved self-willed and disobedient, he would even bring about the expulsion of Israel from their pleasant inheritance, and the overthrow of the beautiful Temple which he had been honoured to build. Solomon was thus most impressively reminded of the law which was to guide him, and of the unspeakable importance of his attending to it. His dying father urged it; and the condescending and unsearchable Almighty did so as well. What more powerful influences could have been brought to **bear upon** him? And there was nothing **to** prevent **his converse** with that **written** law: he was neither unlettered **nor** unintellectual. **He** was, on the contrary, **a** student **and a keen observer**: and he had ample leisure **to** attend **to the** sacred and important writings.

Now, he either read these writings **or** he did **not**. If he **did not**, how inexcusable and wicked **his** indifference and neglect. If **he did read** them, and yet flatly and habitually disobey them, how monstrous his presumption! We may almost surely assume that he did read them, and yet dared to treat them as if they were mere idle talk. **In some** things, **nay**, in many things, he might obey them, **because** they crossed **not** his inclinations or his pride; but where his own humour was concerned, he violated them without scruple. He acted as **if** he had **a** dispensing power, **or,** as if the law had been made for others and not for him. As king, he felt in his **pride** that he was above the law—that he was an exception to the common herd— **and** that he might consult his **own** glory even in opposi**tion to** the divine directions. **God** had said expressly **and** earnestly by Moses, that **there was to be no** intermarrying between His covenanted **people and the** worshippers of idols: and yet Solomon, **in the face of** this interdiction, **loved** many strange wives—women of the Moabites, Ammonites, Edomites, Zidonians, and Hittites! Yea, even "of the nations concerning which the Lord said unto the children of Israel, ye shall not go in to them, neither shall they come in unto you; for surely they will turn away your heart after other gods. Solomon clave **unto** these in love! And he had seven hundred wives, princesses, **and** three hundred concubines! How dared he, I wonder, in the face of such **a** prohibition, accumulate such a harem, and of such materials? And how enormous his egotism, as well as his presumption, in gathering around him such **an** establishment! How blinded by pride and vain ostentation must have become, in his latter years, this once wisest of men!

Such was the exceeding unworthiness of **Solomon**. He was ungrateful to a most condescending and unsearchable Benefactor! He was unfaithful in a position of loftiest trust: and he was disobedient in relation to the very highest authority! No wonder, I repeat, that God was angry with him! Any one of these faults was enough to justify displeasure; but when all were combined, and that in the case of the most favoured of men, we can find no words to express our conviction of his folly, or of the amount of displeasure to which he laid himself open. And that folly will yet more fully appear as we notice its effect on the house of David, and on the people of Israel. God, indeed, threatened to dismember the kingdom, and to cast His people out of His sight, and to overthrow the Temple, if Solomon and his sons should act disobediently: and it might seem at first sight that these things would accrue *from without,* as it were, in the way of penalty and punishment; but the truth is, they arose from within, that is, from the very folly of Solomon itself. And this leads me to notice—

II. The sad Consequences of Solomon's Conduct.

See *First,* the case of his people. They were in a state of bitter dissatisfaction at his death, and ready for revolt, as already observed. That dissatisfaction had been growing for years, and it could no longer be repressed when Rehoboam ascended the throne. The ten tribes especially demanded, in unmistakable terms, a relaxation of their burdens. The truth is, the old jealousy of Ephraim against Judah had been thoroughly awakened by the selfish and extravagant administration of Solomon. It took David seven years to harmonise the tribes, and to gather them into one homogeneous people; but Solomon undid all the labour, and all the patience, and all the magnanimity of his father in this matter. For the sake of his own selfish aggrandisement, and for the gratification of an inordinate love of display, he overtaxed his subjects, opened up old jealousies, and aroused resentful and rebellious feelings. It was the glory of David to gather the tribes into one : it was the dishonour as well as the crime of Solomon to divide them into two. By conciliation and consideration David won upon the jealous tribes and left a consolidated empire : by pride and oppression Solomon dissolved the bonds that bound the tribes into unity, and left the kingdom in a state of dislocation and dismemberment. David won his triumph in the face of many hostile and obstructive influences: Solomon brought about his dishonour in spite of every conceivable influence in his favour. Yes ; though his father's name was to him a tower of strength—though his own surpassing wisdom as a ruler in the first years of his administration was the joy and boast of his subjects—though the magnificent Temple he had been enabled to build surrounded his name with glory, and furnished a brilliant centre of union for the tribes—though all these things were in his favour, he failed to leave a united and a satisfied people when he died. His extravagance and his selfishness had ruined all. Thus with his kingdom : Then think—

Secondly, of his son. Instead of a spirit of conciliation, Rehoboam manifested a spirit of haughtiness and pride. When asked to relax the burdens which his father had imposed, he threatened to increase them. One might have expected something like modesty, and a wise regard to the voice of his subjects, in a young ruler just taking possession of his throne ; but there was no such thing with Rehoboam. He treated his people as if they had no rights ; and he felt concerning himself as if he had "a right divine to govern wrong." He had no idea of a right of judgment, or of interference with his administration, on the part of his subjects : they had simply to contribute toward his grandeur without complaint—no matter how excessive the imposts he might cause to be levied upon them. The possibility of any of the tribes renouncing their allegiance never seemed to enter his mind : and when ten of them declared themselves to this effect, he set himself to reduce them to subjection by force. He was arrested in this, as you know, but his action, so far as it went, only embittered the seceded tribes the more, and confirmed the dismemberment of his kingdom. What pity, we cannot help exclaiming, that he did not listen to the counsel of the old men, and use gentle words to the dissatisfied tribes! He might thus have prevented the schism; and then, by a conciliatory and economical administration, he might have undone the mischief which his father's folly had occasioned, and brought the tribes again into unity and loyalty.

But while we grieve for his conduct, we can scarcely wonder at it when we think of his father's administration. He had seen how Solomon treated and estimated his subjects. He had seen how the wealth of the nation had been collected for years to swell the pomp of his father's establishment. He had learnt from his father's example to consider himself everything, and the nation nothing. It had been strange if he had learnt moderation in the ostentatious court in which he had been brought up: and still more strange had it been, if he had learnt to think of the throne as established for the good **of** the community. O, no! The community was out of the question altogether—except as a means of sustaining the throne, and pouring the results of its labour into the lap of him who sat upon it. Solomon himself might have some lingering notions of right in this matter—notions of his better years not yet fully extinguished, but **Rehoboam** had none such. He accepted **the** practice of his father as his rule, and not his precepts **or** theoretic utterances. This, you know, is but too common with young people. When their parents are partly wrong and partly right, they adopt the wrong and drop the right. Thus Solomon's folly and false estimate of his position reappeared in Rehoboam without any of the lingering remains of those juster views which might still cling to the elder Sovereign. In one word, the style of Solomon's court in the latter years of his reign almost necessitated that haughty and unreasonable demeanour of

Rehoboam toward his subjects which completed the dismemberment of the kingdom: that is to say, the dissatisfaction of the tribes, and the haughty selfishness of the young king, are both to be traced to the same cause: Solomon was the fault in both cases. But the consequences of his folly do not terminate here: they extend into subsequent ages. Think—

Thirdly, of his dynasty: or rather, of the dynasty of David of which he was an important member. He departed from the law of that dynasty. He introduced a new style of action into the sacred and royal family: and that, not only as to extravagance, but also as to worship,—his heart went after other gods. David's mind was single: Solomon's was not. What then might be expected in the subsequent occupants of the sacred throne? Not uniform and consistent piety surely, after the defection of so important a member of the series. Evil you know is more easily and more readily imitated than good; and what more likely than that subsequent and inferior kings should imitate the errors of Solomon rather than the piety of David? True, David was the proper type of the dynasty, but Solomon's glory had in some measure eclipsed the glory of his father: and their descendants, when disposed to Idolatry, would be very ready to take encouragement in their folly, and to excuse themselves for it, by referring to the case of Solomon. Had that prince been true to the David style of character, the joint influence of father and son might have gone far to stamp the true character on all the members of the dynasty; but, by being untrue and unfaithful, Solomon broke and weakened the influence for good, and gave encouragement to lax and inconsistent courses in his successors. And such was the result in fact. Most of his successors were tainted with the evil of Idolatry, and some of them were fully given to it:—Jehoram was so; and Ahaz, and Amon, and Zedekiah. Some one or two reverted to the David standard of piety, such as Hezekiah and Josiah; but it was only by special divine grace that it was so—grace counteracting the natural influence of Solomon's folly over the character and history of his descendants. Thus you see that Solomon injured by his inexcusable conduct not only his kingdom and his son, but also his dynasty for many ages after his death.

One more sad consequence of his defection we may just mention.

Fourthly, he prepared the way for the overthrow of the beautiful Temple which **he** had been honoured to rear. His evil example in the matter of Idolatry not only perpetuated itself from generation to generation among his successors, but the evil grew and extended itself among the tribes. With some brief and decided checks, it still continued, and even advanced in depth and in volume. At first, only a few frequented the false shrines, but, in the progress of time, the whole nation, with a few exceptions, did so. In the days of Solomon, the Temple of God still retained its ascendancy in Israel, but in the days of Zedekiah, the son of Josiah, that Temple was overshadowed and forsaken. The evil heart of Solomon had by that time become the evil heart of the nation, and God was constrained to deal with it accordingly. After four hundred and twenty-four years from its erection, God summoned the avengers of His injured honour to overthrow the sacred house which Solomon had built, and to burn **it** with fire. It had had various fortunes before that, in consequence of the evil leaven of Idolatry introduced by its builder. Thirty years from its completion, it had been despoiled by Shishak, King of Egypt; and it had been pillaged and profaned from time to time because of, or by reason of, the growing evil; but at last, the evil had assumed such dimensions as to require more decided demonstrations on the part of God. Accordingly, Nebuchadnezzar appeared before Jerusalem with his ruthless soldiery :—the city was overthrown, the temple destroyed, and the inhabitants carried away into captivity! And all this was but the consummation of the sin and folly of Solomon. I do not forget that thousands besides Solomon concurred and helped on the development, **but** Solomon nevertheless commenced the movement that spread so widely, and terminated so fatally. No wonder that God was angry with him!

I have now to notice, in the way of conclusion and improvement,

III. *The* **use of** *Solomon's story to us.*

We have not thus gone over the faults of Solomon, **and the** sad consequences of his folly, either to gratify a malignant feeling or a self-complaisant one. We do not condemn him under the flattering thought that we are better than he, or that we are incapable of such unworthy conduct. **No;** the very contrary is the fact. It is because the folly of Solomon abounds in our own day that **it is** right to review his story **as** an appropriate **warning to** ourselves. **We** can commit substantially **the same faults as he,** and myriads do commit the same faults as **he,** even **in** this nineteenth century of the Christian **era.** Only think again what his faults were:— they were, ingratitude toward the condescending Divine, unfaithfulness to the Kingdom and purposes of God, and inattention and disobedience to the written directions of heaven.

Now we affirm, in connection with his first great fault, *viz.*, ingratitude to the condescending Divine; that **God** hath been more condescending to us than He was to Solomon. Does this **seem** an unwarranted statement? It is not so: only remember *the Incarnation*. Here is **a** stretch of condescension **far** beyond that shown to Solomon. God appeared **to** Solomon twice for a few brief moments: He hath appeared to us through all the years of a human life. He appeared to Solomon in vision only: He hath appeared to us in human personality—just as men appear to each other. He appeared to Solomon as a superior asking obedience; He hath appeared to us as a companion and an example—taking us, as it were, by the hand, and offering to lead **us** through the intricacies of life with all tenderness and brotherly sympathy! O, if the condescension of God to Solomon in appearing to him **in a** vision laid Solomon under obligation—far more does the appearing of God to us in human nature lay us under obligation. The only difference in favour of Solomon is, that the appearance to him was personal and immediate, while the appearance **to us is** general and indirect. But even this is in **our** favour if rightly considered. It enables us better to understand the greatness of the kindness shown to us. Did we, each of us, **see** the Saviour in His humanity, the sight, by reason **of** our own littleness, would be-little the manifestation. We would not, and could not in that case, apprehend the thousandth part of the condescension. We could not take in all the truth. It is needful that the Divine manifestation should be seen from **a** suitable distance to apprehend something of its amplitude. Besides, there **is need** of time as well **as** distance to allow the great truth to settle into our understandings, and to assume any thing like suitable proportions in our thoughts. Even in this respect, therefore, our obligations are greater than those of Solomon; and if he was ungrateful to God **who** appeared to him twice, in forgetting the condescension and kindness shown to him, what shall we say of our ingratitude if we forget the condescension of the Incarnation? If, in the face of the fact that God, in the person of His Son, hath identified Himself with us, with a view to our emancipation from Satan, what shall be said **of** our ingratitude, or how shall it be characterised, if we still continue the willing servants of Satan? Why, then, we are worse and more ungrateful than Solomon—wicked and ungrateful though Solomon was. O, it is grievous to think that it is even thus with many professing Christians—they receive the grace of God in vain! We would warn all against the monstrous mistake. Do not forget, we would say, that God hath appeared unto you in the person of His Son! Rather live in the light of the fact, and endeavour to feel the obligation which that fact lays upon you to abide by the divine and holy! Remember daily, that though no man hath seen God at any time, yet the only begotten Son which is in the bosom of the Father—He hath declared Him! Remember further, that to see the Son is to see the Father, and see that you act **on** this conviction. Gaze in the direction of the Divine, **that** is, in the direction of the Incarnate One! Admire and love **the** Divine, **as it** effulges in the Incarnate One! And the more so, because of the manner of this revelation of the Divine. The Son of God appeared in **lowliness** that **He** might conciliate and **bless.** He shrouded **His** glory that He might not terrify or consume. We ought to love **and** admire Him for this; **and we** ought to yield **ourselves to** the constraining influence of this love and condescension!

But to revert to Solomon, his **second** fault was unfaithfulness; and I say, that God hath given to us, to every one of us, a charge to keep as well as to Solomon. We may be unfaithful in relation to that charge as he was to his; and many, very many, alas, are so. God hath not given us a kingdom to control, nor the resources of a kingdom to expend; but He has given to each of us our own nature to control, our own history to regulate, and a portion of His property to employ or to disburse. And here we might say that, though the charge committed to each of us is small **as** compared **to** that committed **to** Solomon, yet it is really not small in fact. Even if our charge were small, still fidelity can be shown in small matters as well **as** in great; but I affirm again, that our charge is not small. We have, each of us, illimitable capabilities to control in our own mysterious **nature.** We have, each of us, reason rightly to **use.** We have, each of us, mighty passions to hold in check, and to regulate in their action. We have, each of **us, a** half-creative power of imagination to watch, lest **it** become defiled and defiling. We have, each of us, a will to harmonise with the Will that is absolute and infallible. Nay more, **we** have, besides, each of us, **a** temple to build for the inhabitation of God as well as Solomon,—not, indeed, **a** material temple in the midst of an earthly kingdom, but **a** spiritual temple in our own spiritual nature. This work needs all our attention, and all our solicitude—not for seven years alone, as in the building of Solomon's Temple, but during all our earthly lives. And then, while this temple is building, we have our lives to regulate socially in all the relations in which we stand. We must live for God, and not for ourselves. We must attach ourselves to the faithful, and not to the unfaithful, and that, spite of apparent interests thereby disregarded. And we must be careful **to** exert only **a** healthful influence, right and left, and along the whole path of our earthly progress. This surely is not **a** small charge; and no one need envy Solomon because his was **to** appearance greater. Each will find his own enough, especially if he add **to** his mental responsibilities the responsibility attaching to the use **or** disbursement **of** that portion of God's property placed **at** his **disposal.** This each is under obligation to use **for** Him who gave it. Now, who **can say** that he hath been faithful in all these respects, and up to the **measure** of fidelity which God has a right to expect? Who can truthfully say that he is building a temple for the inhabitation of God in his own unseen nature? Or, that he is using his influence as **a** son, or as **a** father, or as **a** neighbour, **truly,** consistently, and lovingly for God? Or, that he is expending his earthly resources with a view **to** the purposes and approbation of the Most High? I fear that many will have to acknowledge that they are not better than Solomon;—not better as to the consecration of their own heart to God—not better as to the use of their influence —and not better as to the disbursement of their means. We blame Solomon. We are indignant with Solomon. Can we not learn to turn our blame and our indignation upon ourselves? Can we not take warning, while there is opportunity to repent, and give ourselves to faithfulness under the throne of God—faithfulness **as to** our affections, as to our influence, and as to our possessions?

But once more, Solomon was inattentive and disobedient in relation to the written revelations of God. And I remind you, that that same condescending One hath given written directions to us far more complete, and far more fully illuminated, than those given to Solomon. And how are we walking in relation to these directions? **Are** we studying them daily? **Are** we loving the law of the Lord, the completed, the luminous law of the Lord, as David loved the typical and unfinished revelation given **to** him? Can we truly say, each of us, as he said—"O how I love Thy law; it is my meditation all the day?" Or, are **we not** rather **like** Solomon, who fancied himself **so** wise as **to** render constant attention **to** the Divine writings unnecessary, and thereby allowed the truth to slip from his memory, or who fancied himself so important a personage as that he might transgress the Divine directions with impunity? Let us beware of such folly! Let us be reminded of our privileges in this respect. They are more ample than those of Solomon himself! And let us assure ourselves, that we can make our way really and ultimately prosperous, only by giving constant **attention**, earnest faith, and willing and consistent obedience **to** the word **of** the Lord! Do **not** think your own wisdom **or your own** strength sufficient, **else** you may, like Solomon, dishonour your profession, and injure the Kingdom of God among men. **You** need—we all need—Divine wisdom to guide and sustain! See that you seek these daily; and seek them, **not** only by prayer, but also by a proper and constant attention to the heaven-sent directions furnished in the sacred volume. Had Solomon attended to the directions given to him he could not have **erred** so fatally. Will you repeat his folly?

QUESTIONS ON SOLOMON.

Why was God angry with Solomon?
  Because he encouraged and practised Idolatry: "He went after Ashtoreth, the goddess of the Zidonians, and after Milcom, the goddess of the Ammonites."
How may we suppose Solomon blinded himself to his folly in this?
  He would fancy himself liberal, and free from narrow prejudices and national exclusiveness.
Are there not many in our own time who act in a similar spirit and comfort themselves with a similar self-flattery?
  Yes: very many. They place truth and error on a com-

mon footing, and fancy themselves eminently candid in doing so.

What special faults did Solomon commit by thus lending himself to Idolatry?

He showed himself to be ungrateful, unfaithful and disobedient.

How does his ingratitude appear?

By viewing his conduct in the light of God's special condescension to him: "God appeared to him twice."

How does his unfaithfulness appear?

By his violation of the duties incumbent on him as king of the sacred people: he neither guarded the honour of the God of Israel, nor yet consulted the interests of the people of Israel.

How does his disobedience appear?

By his disregarding God's express prohibition of idolatrous intermarriages: he had many strange wives.

How may we suppose him excusing this violation of the divine prohibition?

By his official elevation probably: he had gradually come to think himself as above law—an idea which is very common with the socially elevated. Such individuals think it all very right that the common people should attend to the Ten Commandments, but they think that these commandments may be liberally interpreted, or even set aside altogether for their convenience.

Apart even from divine prohibition, what appears in Solomon's accumulating so many wives, and keeping up so extensive an establishment?

Enormous and overgrown egotism.

Were the consequences of his presumption and ingratitude inconsiderable or limited?

By no means: they were serious and far-spreading.

Mention some of the parties and interests affected by his in**consistency** and folly.

His kingdom: his son: his dynasty: and the beautiful Temple which he had been honoured **to** build.

How did his folly affect his kingdom?

His burdensome court created universal dissatisfaction, awoke the old jealousy of Ephraim against Judah, and issued under Rehoboam in the dismemberment of the tribes.

How does Solomon stand contrasted with his father David **in** this?

David **by** prudence and conciliation united the tribes;

Solomon by extravagance and **love** of display divided them.

How did Solomon's unwise magnificence affect his son?
 It encouraged in him the haughty and absurd selfishness which effectually alienated the ten tribes from the house of David.

How did his Idolatry affect the dynasty **of** which **he was so** important **a** member?
 He introduced thereby a style **of** action into the sacred and royal family wholly diverse from that of David, and thus furnished his successors incitement and excuse for departing from the covenant of God.

And how did Solomon's folly affect the Temple?
 His evil example grew and extended itself through successive generations until the nation became obstinately idolatrous, and then the agencies of destruction were summoned to overthrow Jerusalem and its **sacred** edifice.

Was Solomon himself alone chargeable with all this evil?
 No, indeed; many concurred with **him** to this end, but he it was who began **the** movement which culminated in the captivity. No wonder that God should be angry with him.

Can Solomon's faults be repeated in our day?
 In substance they can: men can still be, and, alas, **too** generally are, ungrateful to God, unfaithful to the charge committed **to** them **by** Him, and disobedient to divine directions.

How has God shown His condescension **to us** in these **New** Testament times?
 Eminently, by the Incarnation.

If **Solomon** showed himself to be ungrateful by forgetting **that God** appeared to him in vision twice, will we be **free** of the charge of ingratitude if we forget that God hath appeared to us in our own nature, and that during **a** whole human life?
 It cannot be! This is a far greater stretch of condescension than the appearance **to** Solomon, and lays us under corresponding obligation.

God hath not made us kings among men, **as** he did Solomon, but hath He not given to each of us a charge to keep?
 Certainly: each hath his own nature to keep, and to employ for God—and each has some possessions committed to him to be used as God would have them.

Are men generally faithful—each to his particular charge?

No, indeed, too many, like Solomon, serve self and forget God.

Are we not as highly privileged as Solomon was in relation to divine revelation?

Far more so: we have ampler communications than he, and a fuller light thrown on these communications

What is the folly of many in modern times in relation to these communications?

It is very much that of Solomon: they think that they have outgrown these communications, and hold themselves too enlightened to need a perpetual recurrence to them.

What should be our sentiment in relation to God's oracles?

That of David when he exclaimed, "O how I love Thy law, it is my meditation all the day!"

What will be the consequence if we adopt the style of Solomon in this respect instead of that of David?

Injury to ourselves, to our connexions, to our successors, and to all the interests with which we stand connected.

What should **be** the determination of the young in this matter?

That they will seek wisdom rather than wealth, and **follow** David rather than Solomon.

What, in general, are the things which the story of Solomon ought to suggest in relation to our own circumstances and duties?

First, that the condescension of God in the Incarnation lays **us** under stronger obligations to grateful obedience than even His appearance to Solomon laid upon that prince; and *Secondly*, that our only wisdom is to abide continually by the divine directions furnished to us in the Scriptures. If even Solomon, with all his wisdom, erred when he overlooked these Scriptures, we cannot wisely assume that they are unnecessary for us. You know the difference between the sun and the stars. The stars may interest us, but we can prosecute the task of life only under the illuminations of the sun. A similar difference exists between the Book of God and all other books. You may be interested and amused by the countless volumes of man's productions that issue from the **press**, but you can safely prosecute the pilgrimage of life **only** under the illumination of revelation.

III. REHOBOAM.

And Solomon slept with his fathers, and was buried in the City of David his father; and Rehoboam his son reigned in his stead.—I. Kings xi., 43.

SOME men dream of development as the great secret of creation—of ever-advancing excellence—of a necessary progress to perfection; but the idea has small countenance from the moral history of families and nations. True, there is a providential advancement in the history of mankind, but that is, in spite of the waywardness and wilfulness of men, and by agencies which usually have to fight for footing in human society. The improvement is from without, and not from within. It comes by the interpositions of God, not by the evolution of native virtue in man. This is strikingly seen in the history of the Jewish people. Selected from the nations, and favoured with special legislation and special securities, one might have expected in them, stability in goodness, if not continual ascent toward a higher platform. But what do we find? Just perpetual decline and demoralisation! It matters not how often they are lifted from the pit of bondage and sorrow, they sink continually into it again. It matters not what warnings are given to them, or what judgments are poured out upon them, so soon as they have opportunity they are grovelling again in the mire.

And it is not otherwise in the covenanted house of David than in the general history of Israel. So long as the members of that house are merely human, so long they are perpetually sinking. Now and then a good king does arise by the special grace of Heaven, but ever the downward tendency reasserts itself. What is gained under one king is speedily lost under his successor, **and** these kings of the sacred house go, in the face of all propriety, from bad **to** worse. Though favoured in their founder, though **under** special covenant with Heaven, though honoured to be the guardians of the hope of **the** world, aye, and though every possible inducement to fidelity is brought to bear **upon** them, it is all **to no** purpose:—They give themselves to ever-increasing disobedience and folly.

Happily, the dynasty terminates **in** the divine, and then stability, and advancement, and victory, without overthrow, are secured: but until the divine is reached, we find only alternation and disappointment. Rehoboam, **for** example, was but one remove from David, and yet Rehoboam departed from the ways of David, and utterly forgot or disregarded the conditions of the covenant which made him king.

In noticing this member of the royal house, we shall remind you, of the character of his reign, of the folly of his choice, and of his utter unfitness for the typical office and honour of his dynasty.

I. The character of his reign.

That was anything but pleasing. It was, on the contrary, darkened and irritated: and that from the beginning to the end of it. (Unless you except the first three years, when the good people flocked to Jerusalem from the dissenting and misguided tribes; but even these years can scarcely be excepted.) There was not even an occasional light, or an exceptional burst of glory, during its continuance. From first to last, it was sombre and unrelieved. And this is the more noticeable when we remember that it followed the most brilliant reign probably in the world's history. Solomon's court was the resort of kings and queens. They came from all quarters to hear his wisdom, and to gaze upon his grandeur. They came because of his fame, and they returned to their respective peoples and palaces to confirm and to extend his renown. His people were rich. His reign, extending over forty years, was pacific as it was brilliant. His relations were amicable in every direction, and no rival power thought to invade his dominion, or to curtail his territory. But all this was changed in the case of Rehoboam. Instead of being a centre of glory, blazing in the eyes of admiring nations, he sunk into forgetfulness and obscurity. The lofty cavalcades, and the long retinues of the Kings of the East and of the South, no longer sought the City of Jerusalem, or climbed the heights of Zion. One might have expected that some of the glory of his father, though diminished and declining, might have attached to the reign of Rehoboam; but it was not so. The cloud had already begun to gather when Solomon died. They forthwith overspread the heavens as Rehoboam stepped into the throne; and they never lifted again during the seventeen years of his reign. More particularly,

First, the reign of Rehoboam commenced with *dismemberment*. He was not dethroned, but ten parts of his subjects out of twelve renounced their allegiance. He still held the metropolitan city, and the royal palaces of David and Solomon, but his subjects were gone, all but a fraction. A rival king now occupied a large part of the sacred territory, and he found himself shorn of the greater part of his royalty. This must have been very galling to him. How could he recover or retain the prestige of his house with so narrow a domain? Had he lost two tribes and retained ten, the evil, however disagreeable, might have been more endurable; but to lose ten out of twelve, was almost next to extinction. And then, he had calculated long on the whole dominion. For twenty years at least, that is, from the time of his own majority, he had looked forward to the hour when he would occupy the place of his father. The thought of losing a large part of what he considered his patrimony had never once crossed his thoughts; and we may well believe, **on the** other hand, that his flatterers had filled his imagination with the glories of his coming reign. With every new manifestation of the grandeur and influence of his father, his heart had swollen in **its** pride and expectation, and he had admitted no shadow or misgiving **to** darken the prospect. How confounded then—how grieved—how indignant even, he must have felt when he saw himself so hopelessly weakened and re- duced as **a** king! The glory of his father, which here- tofore had nourished his pride, now only embittered his heart. Had he been born in humble circumstances, and elevated like Jeroboam to royalty, even two tribes would have seemed to him a not unworthy kingdom; but born the son of Solomon, and the grandson of David, his diminished territory was to him small and contemptible. He felt shorn of his just rights, as he thought, and that to an unbearable degree; and that too by one whom he had known as the servant of his father, and his own inferior. As heir-apparent to the throne, while yet that throne seemed unshaken and unclouded, Rehoboam had **fre- quently** bowed graciously to Jeroboam, in common with many others, as he swept past them in royal state. Yes, he remembered the time when Jeroboam thought it honour to receive a smile of recognition from **him,** and now Jeroboam gathered around him ten of **the** twelve tribes **of** Israel! The thing seemed preposterous, out- rageous, and unendurable! But Rehoboam could not help himself. His former servant was now more than his rival, his subjects had renounced him, his territory had been torn away from him, and he was now left to make the best he could of narrowed circumstances and dimin- ished revenues. **He** could no longer hold up his head among contemporary sovereigns, nor congratulate himself upon his distinguished inheritance. But

Secondly, his people became loathsome by *defilement*. Here was another dishonour. He might not himself feel it, but history hath recorded it against him. He was not only lessened as to his royalty, but his diminished realm was also lessened as to its purity. Had he been faithful to his position, and used his influence aright, he might still have claimed the respect of mankind, and of posterity. Jerusalem was still his capital. The magnificent Temple erected by his father, and the wonder of that age, was still the centre of religious worship, and the Shechinah dwelling place of the true God. These were distinctions which Jeroboam could not share with him, and they were greater and more important than even the allegiance of the ten revolted tribes. With proper attention to these privileges, and a careful culture of piety in himself and in his people, his kingdom, small as it now was, might still have been the glory of kingdoms, and the centre of the world's admiration; but he was unfaithful, ungodly, and idolatrous. He lent no countenance to piety among his people, and he put no arrest on the heathenism and shocking immoralities that had already begun to show themselves even before the death of his father. We rather fear that he countenanced and encouraged his subjects in their neglect of God's worship, and in their devotedness to idols and immorality. Any way, here is the account given by the sacred narrative of his government in the early years of it, and we hear of no reformation under him in his late years :—

> "And Judah did evil in the sight of the Lord, and they provoked Him to jealousy with their sins which they had committed above all that their fathers had done. For they also built them high places and images, and groves, on every high hill, and under every green tree. And there were also Sodomites in the land; and they did according to all the abominations of the nations which the Lord cast out before the children of Israel."—I. Kings xiv., 22–24.

What an abasement was here ? "They did according to all the abominations of the nations which the Lord cast out before the children of Israel." These nations had been sunk in the very lowest depths of immorality, so low that they only defiled the land on which they dwelt; and yet, Israel, called to supersede them because of their vileness, had actually sunk to the same abominations—to the same low and dishonourable level—and that under the grandson of David! Surely there was small honour to the king of such a people, who resisted not, if he did not countenance, such practices, grandson of David though he was! What more of evil could the son of a heathen prince or savage have done or permitted? But a further dishonour overtook this sad reign:—

Thirdly, it became darkened by *invasion and impoverishment*. "And it came to pass in the fifth year of King Rehoboam, that Shishak, King of Egypt, came up against Jerusalem: and he took away the treasures of the house of the Lord, and the treasures of the king's house; he even took away all: and he took away all the shields of gold which Solomon had made." (1 Kings, xiv., 25, 26.) How this invasion came about does not appear. Rehoboam had made no demonstrations against Egypt, so far as we know, and **had** given no offence to that court; and yet Shishak came with an overwhelming force, and helped himself to all the remaining wealth of Solomon. We can have no doubt as to the true reason, though the proximate inducements to the **invader do** not appear. Rehoboam had forsaken God, **and God left** him to invasion and impoverishment. This is **the true** and short account of the matter. Possibly, however, Jeroboam had something to do with it in the way of incitement. He had himself dwelt at the Court of Egypt, and had agents there, **no** doubt. He might think to weaken the hands of the son of Solomon, as his own hostile neighbour, by hinting **to** Shishak that the ample stores of gold now accumulated in the Temple at Jerusalem might be an easy prey to one **so** powerful as he. And Shishak might need supplies, **as** kings generally do, and therefore might be very ready and willing **to** relieve Rehoboam of his surplus riches. Any way, the robbery by Shishak must have been very galling **to** the son of Solomon. It was taking, if I may say so, the last gleam of splendour out of his fortunes. No doubt he remembered besides, in contrast to the bearing of the Egyptian king, the days and relations of other years, and bitterly would he feel the change. He had seen the time, when an Egyptian princess was his step-mother, and proud to be so, and when the ambassadors of Egypt bowed with reverence before the throne in which his father sat, and into which himself was about to spring. He had felt then almost more than an equal even for the proud Pharaohs: and now they appropriated without scruple the wealth of his kingdom, and treated him as a powerless slave. But he had no remedy: with Jeroboam on the one side, and Shishak on the other, he could only stand by while they robbed him and feel his own bitter humiliation. We can fancy how his heart would boil with indignation as he saw the troops of the spoiler file away from his impoverished and dishonoured capital. The dismemberment of his kingdom only prepared the way for its impoverishment; and dishonour and contempt naturally fall to the lot of the impoverished when they have nothing but their riches to commend them. Such was the sad fortune of Rehoboam!

But there is yet another element of distress to be mentioned:—

Fourthly, there was continued war between Rehoboam and Jeroboam. Their rivalry and enmity never spent itself. They kept up the contest all their days. The invasion of Shishak was only in the fifth year of Rehoboam, and he reigned seventeen. Had he been at peace with Jeroboam, and cultivated friendly relations with him, he might have recovered from the grief of the loss of his wealth, and enjoyed quiet, at any rate, in his humiliated state. But no! His wounds could not be permitted to heal. The constant irritation of war and contest kept them open and sore; and for this we blame him rather than Jeroboam. That sovereign sought only the stability of his own ten shares of the kingdom. He had no thought, in the first instance, of invading Rehoboam, or of wresting from him the two remaining tribes. He would have been content with peace if only Rehoboam would have allowed it; but Rehoboam was not. He still yearned for the recovery of his lost territory. He still harassed Jeroboam, and compelled Jeroboam to harass him. In this way he fretted himself during **all his reign**, and wasted his resources, and embittered the feelings **of** the tribes toward each other. In this way, too, he showed his obstinacy and unsubmissiveness. He knew **that** God **had** determined the curtailment of his kingdom, **and he** ought to have bowed to **the** divine determination **and the** divine judgment. **But he would not;** and he only irritated and distressed himself **in** consequence. He could not unseat **Jeroboam, but he showed** his spite and dissatisfaction by unneighbourliness and hostility. True, **Jeroboam's** folly called for chastisement at the hands of God, but Rehoboam did not need to have been the instrument **of** that chastisement, unless it had suited his own insubordinate humour to be so.

Such, **then,** is the character of this sad reign : **it is** gloomy with a manifold gloom. Neither at its commencement, nor in **its** progress, **is** there anything to relieve the shadows that rest **upon it.** There was indeed a season when, it is said, things **went** well at Jerusalem, but that **was** only on the retirement **of** Shishak, **and as compared** with the distresses of overthrow and the presence **of enemies. It was** not the sunny well-going of piety **and** obedience. **It was** merely the well-going of the smitten, **made** somewhat less restive by the conviction of **the** hopelessness of resistance. Foreign pressure **was** removed, but sunshine did not return. Oh! but **the** experiences of Rehoboam were gloomy and sad! Victories cheered **the** toils of David, and uncommon honours shone upon the head of Solomon, but neither victories nor honours cheered the royal days of Rehoboam. No sunshine rested on his throne, and no flowers sprung in his path. He was conversant only with privation and bitter annoyance.

Now, it is well to mark the reason **of** this **as** well as the fact : and that reason, we think, will be found in his mistaken choice, which **we** come next to notice :—

II. The folly of his choice.

That choice is not set forth in words, as in the case of **his** father, Solomon, but we think it is clearly implied in the account given of his parentage in connexion with his sad reign. It is emphatically said, and twice within a few verses, that "his mother's name was Naamah, an Ammonitess." Now, this Naamah, the mother of Rehoboam, might be a proselyte, but we fear that, if even it were so, her attachment to Israel was only nominal, and that she retained many of her superstitions and much of the spirit of her idolatrous ancestry. Assuming this, the choice of Rehoboam was between the faith of his father and the superstitions of his mother: and he seems to have chosen the latter. He certainly wished the throne of Solomon, but not in connexion with the faith and habits of David. He would have the throne of his Hebrew father, with the traditions and licence of his idolatrous mother. He would rule for himself, and not for the good of Israel. He might give some external attention to the law of his kingdom for appearance sake, but he would have himself at liberty to follow the bent of his inclinations—recoiling from the thought of a close and continuous observance of the Mosaic ritual. It is expressly said in Chronicles, after a repetition of his Ammonitish maternity, "that he did evil because he prepared not his heart to seek the Lord." In other words, he did not choose the fear of the Lord, but evil rather. And you must see the bearing of this on his subjects. To do evil, in his royal position, and because of alienation from God, was to encourage evil in his dominions, and alienation from God among his people as well. He ought to have been a pattern of piety to those beneath him: and he ought, David-like, to have used his power and influence for God. Instead of this, he was an example of evil-doing: and he used his influence, if not his power, on the side of evil, and in opposition to the Holy One of Israel.

Now this was inexcusable in Rehoboam. He had overwhelming reasons for making a different decision between the faith of his father and the superstition of his mother. He was favoured above many in this respect. For example:—

First, he saw the Temple of God at Jerusalem in its

first beauty and unsoiled magnificence. He was a boy about nine or ten years old at its dedication. We cannot believe that he was absent on that solemn and memorable occasion. No doubt he occupied at it a position suitable to his rank, and favourable for observing and seeing all. He might not then, at his tender age, understand all the significance of the ceremonial; but he saw enough to arrest his thought and lay him under obligation to further enquiry as he grew older. He heard then the beautiful and devout breathings of his father, in the dedicatory prayer, and also the sublime songs of the sacred choristers. He heard the acclamations of the multitude, and witnessed, in part at least, the multitudinous offerings made at the altar. He saw the procession that bore the ark, the symbol of the Divine presence, to its place; and if he saw not the mystic and supernatural Shechinah cloud, he saw, at least, the crowding priests emerging in haste from the cloud-filled tabernacle, and heard, no doubt, the reason of their hasty exit. What was there in the Ammonitish Idolatry to compare with this? There might be song and gorgeous ceremonial, but no sentiments like those of his father's prayer, and no token of power like that of the ark deposited in the most holy place, and no supernatural or luminous cloud like that which filled the tabernacle! There were clearly here materials for thought and inquiry, and solemn impression, on the part and on the mind of the youthful prince; and this of itself was enough to decide his choice, as he grew older and more fully acquainted with the exercises of the Temple, and the historical past which that Temple embodied. But further,—

Secondly, he had heard the earnest and enlightened instructions of his distinguished father. Solomon could not leave his son and heir untaught, and we know the spirit of his teaching. Hear a specimen of his tender and urgent addresses:—

"My son, if thou wilt receive my words,
And incline thine ear unto wisdom,
And seek for her as thou seekest for hid treasure,
Then shalt thou understand the fear of the Lord,
And find the knowledge of God."

Again,—

> "My son, forget not my law,
> But let thine heart keep my commandments,
> For length of days, and long life, and peace, shall they add to thee."

Again,—

> "Happy is the man that findeth wisdom,
> And the man that getteth understanding."
> "All the things that thou canst desire are not to be compared to her."
> "Her ways are ways of pleasantness,
> And all her paths are peace.
> She is a tree of life to them that lay hold upon her!"

Once more,—

> "My son, attend unto my wisdom,
> And bow thine ear to my understanding,—
> That thou mayest regard discretion,
> And that thy lips may keep knowledge."

Surely such addresses, and such assurances, ought to have been irresistible in **the way of** determining the choice and inquiries of Rehoboam: and the more so, as coming from a father so exalted, and so wise, and so devoted to the God of Israel at the time of their utterance. It **was** during Solomon's best years, be it remembered, that these instructions were tendered to Rehoboam; and what could his mother, Naamah, say in opposition to them? **Or** what could she urge in favour of her idols at all to compare with the representations of Solomon concerning the power and holiness of the God of Israel? What? Just nothing **at** all; or, what was worse than nothing at all, she could only speak of cruel rites, or meaningless ceremonies, or unworthy practices, or powerless objects of worship. But further,—

Thirdly, Rehoboam must have heard of his grandfather, David. He had not known him personally, as he was but an infant of **a** few months when David died; but he must have heard of his exploits and of his victories, wrought and achieved under the guidance or in the name of the God of Israel. **He** must have heard of the overthrow of Goliath, and of David's forbearance in relation to Saul, and of his forbearance, or patience rather, in relation to the kingdom—ruling for seven years in Hebron, waiting God's time for his enthronement over all the tribes. And he must have known **how** God opened up his way at last, and made a covenant with him and his house for ever, and how he gave him Solomon to succeed him,—investing him with unusual glory, and giving to him unusual wisdom. Knowing all this, he ought to have found obligation resting on him **to** inquire after, and **to** abide by, the God of David his grandfather, and Solomon his father. What ancestry could his mother point **to as** compared to this? And what divinity could she report as compared with the God of Israel? She could only set legends against facts, and small and absurd legends against great and impressive facts. Once more:—

Fourthly, Rehoboam **must have** been acquainted with the history of his country. **He** was under obligation to copy and study the books of Moses as heir to the throne of Israel; and Solomon no doubt directed him **to** this duty. But, even though he neglected it, he must have heard the story of Abraham, and the stories of Joseph, and of Moses, and of Joshua, and of Samuel. He cannot be supposed to have been ignorant **of the** wonders in the land of Ham wrought by God in favour of Israel—of the wonders of the wilderness—of the wonders of the conquest and settlement of Canaan—or of the story of the Judges. He would learn somewhat of those things, if from no other source, from the sacred compositions of his grandfather, as used continually in public worship. And what story could his mother present as comparable to the records of Israel? Where would she find tokens of Omnipotence or of mercy in the history of the idols of Ammon at all fit to be compared with the interpositions of Jehovah? She could not: the thing was impossible; and therefore Rehoboam was under obligation to prefer the faith of his father and the knowledge of the God of his nation. He was under obligation, we say, "to prepare his heart to seek the Lord."

But this he **did** not **do.** He yielded himself to the influence of his mother, and forgot or despised the instructions of **his** father. He held loosely to the fashions of his father's court for the first three years **of** his reign, **but** he kept himself aloof from the knowledge of the true **God**: and in this you see **the secret** of the unsunny and sombre character of his administration. By turning from **God** he turned **from** the fountain of light **and** honour. **By** leaving heavenly wisdom unsought, **and** unappropriated, he failed to find the tree of life and the paths **of** pleasantness. By failing to devote himself to the service of the True, he failed to find the imperishable and the satisfying,. "Them that honour me," says God, "I will honour: while they that despise me shall be lightly esteemed." Rehoboam disregarded, if he did not despise, the God of Israel, and sunshine died out of his history in consequence. Nay, he yielded himself to other worship, and he **not** only failed in the matter of renown, but actually incurred curtailment, impoverishment, and disgrace! **It** was vain, **so far** as Rehoboam was concerned, that God dwelt in the unrivalled Temple of Jerusalem: in vain that Solomon urged and instructed: in vain that David **had** led the way to his descendants **in** a life of dependence and devotedness: and in **vain** that Moses had recorded the wondrous interpositions **of** the Most High. Rehoboam treated all **as** of no consequence, and regulated his administration, not as the vicegerent of God, but as the self-centred and independent ruler of his people. He disclaimed, in effect, his subjection **to** Jehovah, and Jehovah in righteousness left him to work out **his** own dishonour and humiliation.

Some may be disposed to blame Solomon for taking to himself an Ammonitish princess, and thus preparing the way for his son's defection and disgrace: and they do well who do so. Solomon was deeply to be blamed in this. He disobeyed God's express commandment in doing so: nay, he set aside the dictates of ordinary prudence by doing so. He ought to have known, with all his wisdom, how insidious and how powerful is the influence of **a** fanatical or superstitious mother over her children: and he ought to have known, that evil is of readier growth in the human heart than good. Let blame rest upon him accordingly, but not in extenuation of Rehoboam's conduct. The fault of Solomon belongs to Solomon's history, not to Rehoboam's. True, we may pity the Prince, so likely to be perverted by his heathenish mother, but we cannot exculpate him. Many are more unfavourably situated than he for coming to a right decision: nay, few comparatively **are** in so v ourable position. Without excusing Solomon, we must condemn Rehoboam for his choice. He rejected the true and the potent, and accepted the empty and **the** debasing: and that in the presence of **the** amplest evidence as to the value of that which he rejected and the emptiness of that which he chose. Admitting that he was more in his mother's **society** when young, that was no reason why he should disregard **facts** and conscience, when he grew to the years of discretion, and when the light of heaven was brought so fully to bear upon his nature. He should have prepared his heart to seek the Lord, and he should have sought rather to draw his mother to the right side than have allowed himself to be drawn by her to the wrong.

The truth is, the comparison of his father's earlier and later history alone ought to have decided him had there been nothing else. He had seen both. He had seen the honour and the glory of Solomon's better days ere yet his wives had drawn away his heart from God, and he had seen the obscurations, and divisions, and heart-burnings, of his idolatrous years. He had seen with his own eyes the dedication of the Temple on the one hand, and also the uprearing and consecration of the idolatrous shrines which his father had been induced to set up on the other. He had felt the dignity of the one occasion, and the debasement of the others. He knew, or might have known, the inspiriting and uniting effect of the one ceremonial on and throughout the nation, and he knew the divisive, darkening and embittering effect of the others! He ought to have determined accordingly. He ought to have emulated his father in the days of his stability and single-eyed loyalty, and not in the days of his decay and bewilderment. He ought to have dissented from, and **resisted, the current of evil, and not yielded himself to its sway:** but, instead **of** this, the probability is that he **helped it** on, and gave increasing power to it by his influence and example. **And** the evil only grew worse with **time.** Solomon escaped **away** from it by death, but Rehoboam lived to feel its distressing and darkening effects. Pity for Rehoboam! He threw himself, and that with his eyes open, into the wake of Idolatry, and he found even in this world the impoverishment and dishonour which Idolatry and ungodliness inevitably bring sooner **or** later.

We might learn a lesson here: we too are called on to make our election between God and the world—between Christ and **Satan.** Let us not be as foolish as Rehoboam **was.** There is only one right: let us embrace it. Let **us** prepare our hearts to seek God: and let us resist the influences which would draw **us** away from them. If Rehoboam had mighty inducements to choose right, we have still mightier inducements than **he.** If he was inexcusable for resisting the evidence of divine forthcoming, we will be still **more** so if we turn away from Christianity. We have not only all the preliminary history and manifestation which ought to have swayed Rehoboam, we have also actual manifestation of the divine in the human to influence and sway us. We have evidence abounding and beyond measure, that God hath spoken to us by His Son— that He seeks to detach us from all false refuges—that He is prepared to bless **us by** turning us away from our iniquities—that He seeks our confidence and labours for our good—and shall we, **or,** to change the person, will you refuse Him your attention, your faith, your gratitude, your obedience? Will you rather abide by the delusive, the debasing, and the destructive, than give yourselves to your Redeeming Creator? O, it will be infatuated and ungrateful thus to act! It will be to cast in your lot with the dishonoured Rehoboam, and to renounce the fortunes and the companionship of the divine David. Be sure that you make not this mistake. Listen not to the blandishments of society, nor yet to the prejudices of education; but give yourselves to the Truth, even to the mighty and merciful Saviour. Too many have mothers like Rehoboam—fraught with superstition and ignorance of divine things ; but the influence of such ought not to stand in the way of the demonstrations of Heaven. Let mothers be honoured, but not to the dishonour of God ! Let mothers be honoured, but let the divine Saviour be honoured more. He can do for us what our mothers cannot. He can save to the uttermost all them that come unto God by Him. If there be he who prefer father, or mother, or wife, or child to Him, they thereby show that they are not worthy of Him, and can have no participation with Him. He leads to life and honour, but they who keep aloof from Him will find themselves in the way of death, impoverishment and dishonour. He is the Light of the world, and they that follow after Him shall not walk in darkness, but shall have the light of life. Let every one beware how he neglects so great a Saviour and so great a salvation!

But to return to Rehoboam, we notice:

III. His utter unfitness for the typical offices and honour of his house.

You will remember that the royal house of David was meant to be a type and foreshadowment of the true and divine King of Israel. It was the honour of the successive kings of that house (that is, if obedient and faithful), not only to rule over their contemporaries, but also to prefigure the glorious and divine. The excellences of that glorious and divine One are manifold, and each king in his day, might have, and ought to have, foreshadowed some one or more of these excellences. No one human king could foreshadow them all, but each might contribute to the completeness of the type. David, the founder of the house did so, by his name, and by his victories. Solomon also did so, by his name, and by his Temple-building, and by the pacific and happy character of his reign. But what shall we say of Rehoboam? Did he foreshadow in himself any of the excellences of Messiah— the then to be revealed king of the Israel of God? Or did his government give any intimation of the peculiarities of God's reign upon the earth? Not any as you must clearly perceive. So far from this, he was in direct antagonism to the great anti-type of his house, and to the peculiarities of the rule of that anti-type. Rehoboam was proud, oppressive, and unpacific. He met the reasonable demands of his subjects with haughty refusal. Instead of relieving or lessening their burdens, he proclaimed it to be his purpose to augment these burdens: and instead of studying the things that make for peace, he had continual wars with his neighbour Jeroboam. How unlike in all this was he to the Prince Divine who was yet to spring from the royal family of Judah! How unlike his answer to his oppressed subjects to the invitation of Messiah addressed to the estranged and the sorrowful! "My father chastised you with whips," said Rehoboam in his pride, "but I will chastise you with scorpions!" "Come unto Me," says Messiah, "and I will give you rest. Take my yoke upon you, and learn of me: for I am meek and lowly in heart, and ye shall find rest unto your souls." Rehoboam would not redress unmerited wrong: Jesus is prepared to relieve and to remove merited sorrows. Rehoboam fancies that he has "a right divine to govern wrong," but Jesus walks righteously, tenderly and sympathisingly. Rehoboam would lay and increase heavy burdens upon his subjects; Jesus removes burdens from His, and that by taking them Himself. Rehoboam irritates and dismembers: Jesus soothes, heals, and re-harmonises. How unlike the one to the other! How little fitted was Rehoboam to foreshadow the sentiments or the reign of the Just One! His name was appropriate, and might have suggested to him a happier course. It means, as is said, "one who enlarges or gives liberty to the people." Had he listened to his subjects, and relieved their burdens, he might have justified his name, and retained his place among the royal types of his house. But he did not. He had not caught the spirit of the coming centre of salvation, unity and peace, which was yet to arise in his family. The light of the illustrious was not upon him. He sunk out of the ranks of the representatives of Messiah, and down among the unilluminated and unhonoured. No subsequent generations turn to him to note, or to watch, or to admire, the corruscations and beauties of the then unrevealed Luminary of Time. He had opportunity to have ranked with the honoured ones who caught, in their seat of elevation, the rays of the Sun of Righteousness ere yet that Sun had ascended above the horizon, but he chose otherwise, and thus forfeited the honour and the felicity of the royal and typical house to which he belonged.

And here again is a lesson for us. We cannot be of the royal sons of David, who were meant to typify the coming centre of excellence, but we may be of the royal family of God who are meant to reproduce and perpetuate in the eyes of men the excellences of that centre. David and Solomon were before Messiah as to His human manifestation : we are after Him. But the light of Messiah shines in all directions, and it is meant to be reflected from all His attendants in whatever position they occupy. If it was right and necessary that friends and attendants preceding His manifestation should foreshadow His excellences, it is equally right and necessary that His friends and attendants following that manifestation should imitate and reproduce them. If it was necessary that David and Solomon should be lovers of righteousness and lovers of peace, it is equally necessary that we should be lovers of righteousness and lovers of peace ; and if Rehoboam forfeited his honours and his privileges as a harbinger of Messiah, because of his want of conformity to Messiah, so we in like manner must not be surprised to be excluded from Messiah's retinue, if we remain unrenewed and unlike Him in spirit and purpose. He is the first born among many brethren, and He is the standard of character for them all. Every disciple must be conformed to his chief—must be like his chief (modified in each, of course, because of the fragmentary nature **of** creature life, and because that each has an appropriate place to occupy in the one harmonised and beautified mystical body of Christ), and each must be wholly separated from every thing opposed to the character and purposes of his chief. Look then to the Chief : He is meek : He relieves **the** burdened : He makes peace : and every one who truly belongs to Him must, in like manner, be meek, considerate and pacific. If **we** walk otherwise—if we **walk** in pride, if we refuse relief to the burdened when **we have** the power to help, if we selfishly perturb and irritate when we ought to soothe and **to** pacify,—then we just repeat the folly of Rehoboam, sink from the dignity and benignity of **true** discipleship, and show **to** all enlightened ones that we do not belong to the heavenly Kingdom. You would not wish to be excluded **from** heaven at **last.** You would not wish to have addressed **to** you **the** cutting words : " Depart from Me, ye workers of iniquity : I never knew you." You would not wish to **be** told by the great Redeemer, and at the threshold of glory, " You never gave any evidence of love to Me, or of sympathy with My purposes. You were self-pleasing and proud, when I wished you to take on my yoke of meekness and lowliness. You were oppressive and unkind to your fellows, when I wished you to undo the heavy burdens, and to sympathise with the sorrowful. You were restless and dissatisfied besides, when I wished you **to be** submissive and trusting. Go ! I did not ask you **to work** out a righteousness for yourself, but I did expect some evidence of your professed faith in Me. You can furnish none. Your life, you know, with all your professions **to** the contrary, was unmeek, inconsiderate, and unpacific, and you can have no part with Me !" Alas for those who are preparing for such a sentence.

If it was bitter for Rehoboam to forfeit the honours and the riches of the house of David, how much more the grief of forfeiting the honours—the eternal honours—and the riches, of the house and family of God !

QUESTIONS ON REHOBOAM.

What was the general character of this reign?
    Unsunny and irritated.
What made this the more bitter to Rehoboam?
    His remembrances of his father's reign, which was perhaps the most brilliant in the world's history.
Did **no** lingering beam of his father's glory remain to **this** prince?
    Not any: the clouds began to gather even before Solomon's death, and they never lifted again during all the years of Rehoboam's royalty.
How did the reign commence?
    By dismemberment. Ten of **the** twelve tribes were **torn** away from the house and dynasty of David.
How must the dismemberment have been regarded by the inflated mind of the son of Solomon?
    As galling and humbling in no ordinary degree.
What would make it the more grievous to Rehoboam?
    The thought of the time when Jeroboam, his successful rival, was but an officer in his father's court, and eager to receive recognition or attention from himself as heir apparent to the throne.
What was the next step in his dishonour?
    His kingdom became increasingly defiled and darkened by evil. Instead of recovering from the errors of Solomon, it only grew worse and worse. "They built high places" (it is said) "in every high hill, and did according to all the abominations of the nations which the Lord cast out before them." (This might not disturb Rehoboam, but it was his dishonour notwithstanding.)
What next embittered the life of this prince?
    Shishak, King of Egypt, invaded his territory, and took away the treasures and golden shields of the Temple, as well as the treasures of the king himself. (This might be at the instigation of Jeroboam, which would make it specially grievous: and it must have been further grievous as done by a power which had been in such friendly relations with his father.)
Besides this indignity from Egypt, was there no chronic grief or irritation affecting the peace of Rehoboam?
    Yes; there was continual war between him and Jeroboam. (He could not unseat his rival, but he kept himself in irritation by continually aiming at it.)

E

How happened it that all this dispeace, and humiliation, and obscuration, fell to the lot of Rehoboam?

Without entering more particularly into the causes thereof, we may say in general that the reason will be found in his wrong choice.

What wrong choice did he make?

He preferred the superstitions of his mother **to the** faith of his father. In other words, **he** preferred **Ammon to** Israel.

How does that appear?

It is expressly said in Chronicles, after a repetition of his Ammonitish maternity, that "he did evil" (or preferred idolatry) "because he prepared not his heart to seek the Lord" (or because he was averse to, and did not choose, the service of the God of Israel.

What renders his conduct in this respect inexcusable?

He had ample opportunities of knowing the true from **the false.**

What striking event occurred when he was about nine **or ten** years old?

The dedication **of the beautiful** and golden Temple built by his father.

What supernatural token was given on that occasion?

The Shechinah-cloud took possession of the most holy place, **and** the youthful prince must have heard of **the** fact.

Had this prince any privilege beside, **as** to early instruction?

Yes; the most **ample.** Solomon, **while** yet unsubdued himself by evil, urged **on** Rehoboam the transcendant importance of heavenly wisdom, saying, "My son, get wisdom, and with all thy getting get understanding." He elsewhere defines the wisdom thus recommended, "The fear of the Lord is the beginning of wisdom."

Had Rehoboam any ancestral reasons for choosing the fear of the Lord?

Certainly: he **could not** be ignorant of the character and writings, and covenant distinctions, of his grandfather, David.

And were there no **national** considerations binding him **to** the same course?

Yes: very many, and very decided. The miraculous history of his nation was something unique and commanding, and it ought to have secured his acceptance in preference to the idle stories of superstition.

How did Rehoboam respond to all these advantages and obligations?

He gave himself to idolatry in the face of them all.

And how did this decision on his part tell on the complexion of his reign?

It necessarily rendered it gloomy and cheerless. **God is the centre of light, and they who turn from Him must walk in darkness.**

Does the fault of his father giving him an Ammonitish mother excuse his fault?

By no means : **he was** bound **to** prefer the **true** to the false when he **had** the means of knowing the one from the other. Many are in far worse circumstances **than** he for making this choice, and yet they are bound **to** make it.

But did the defection of his father in the latter part of his reign not excuse in some measure the conduct of Rehoboam?

Not at all. It should only have made him more circumspect, and more tenacious **of** the David-style of worship and government.

What does this mistaken choice of Rehoboam teach to the young of all subsequent generations?

To reject evil, and "to prepare their hearts to seek the Lord."

What is the character of the obligations resting on the young who live under gospel-testimony in relation to this choice?

Overwhelming on the side of Christian piety; and to disregard them will only be to incur greater condemnation. If the reign of Rehoboam was unsunny because of his wrong choice, the life and fortunes of the unbelieving now must be dark, dark indeed.

But what if maternal influence be on the side of superstition **or** worldliness?

It must be set aside or disregarded. Nothing can excuse us for trifling with the communications and claims of God in Christ.

What was the consequence of Rehoboam's mistaken choice in relation to the typical honour of his house?

It neutralized for him that honour. He could not be a type of the true and the transcendant King of Israel.

What was expected of the successive kings of the house of David?

That each should foreshadow some one or more of the excellencies of the crowning prince **of** that house.

How far Did Rehoboam meet this expectation?
  Not at all. So far from doing so, he was in direct antagonism to the great anti-type of his house.

Mention some particulars in which he differed from the great and coming Son of David.
  In his hauteur, unreason, and violence.

Do subsequent ages ever turn to Rehoboam **to** note the coruscations or **beauties of the** then unrevealed luminary of time?
  No: the light of that luminary is not reflected from him.

What is expected of the followers **of** Messiah now, seeing that by their position in relation **to** His incarnation they cannot typify His excellencies?
  They are to imitate and reproduce these excellencies.

What are the excellencies which Christians must imitate and reproduce **as** suggested by the story of Rehoboam?
  Meekness, ready helpfulness in relation to the burdened, and peacefulness with **all** around, **as far as** may be, and with a due regard to **faithfulness of course.**

What will be the bitter **end of** professors who are found to be unlike the great centre of light at last?
  They must forfeit the honours of the family of God, even as Rehoboam forfeited **the honours of** the family of David.

What in general are the lessons taught by the story of Rehoboam?
  First. That young people **should be** incited **to** make **a** right choice between Truth and **Error.** Both press for attention, and every man must **make a** choice—not **to choose** at all is in effect **to** abide by **the** wrong side.
  Secondly. That professors should remem**ber** the indispensable proprieties of the house and family of God if they would not forfeit the honours and prospects of the same.

IV. ABIJAH.

"And Rehoboam slept with his fathers, and was buried in the city of David; and Abijah his son reigned in his stead." II Chron., xii., 16.

THIS Prince was scarcely seated on his throne when he found himself in critical circumstances. He inherited with his patrimony the enmity of Jeroboam. "There was war between Rehoboam and Jeroboam all their days;" and so soon as Abijah occupied the seat of his father he became a figure in the politics and speculations of Samaria. Jeroboam by this time had become more audacious than when first he gained his throne. His experience had grown, and his ungodliness. He was now prepared for aggressive movements in relation to the house of David. At first, and while Rehoboam lived, **he** was content to resist any attempt on the part of that house to regain the dissenting tribes. Now he **was** prepared to attempt the subjugation of Judah itself, and of its royal house as well. The accession of Abijah furnished, as he thought, a suitable opportunity, and he collected **a** mighty army accordingly. He had much larger resources than Abijah, and fraught with the conviction that victory goes with the "heaviest battalions," he felt confident of success. **But** this **was** just a step too far, and he was doomed to overthrow and disappointment. So long as he kept within his own domain, he was allowed to shape his policy as he thought best; but so soon as he attempted to subjugate the house of David and the tribes that still owned the sway of that house, he found himself checkmated **in a** way which he did not expect.

He reminds us in this respect of Philip II. of Spain. That prince was permitted to work his own cruel and wicked will within his own dominions for years, and bitter were the experiences of many of his subjects in consequence; but when, fancying himself great enough to control nations beyond, he prepared his Invincible Armada, as he was pleased to call it, to put out the light and joy of truth and liberty in Britain, he found unlooked-for reverse. This was, as in the case of Jeroboam, just a step too far.

Abijah in this relation occupied the position of Elizabeth of England. The interests of mankind were wrapped up in the safety of both these rulers—each in his and her own age. Neither the one nor the other was fully aware of the question involved in their respective circumstances, but both were partially enlightened. Both made memorable and recorded speeches when the crisis overtook them; not indeed to the same parties, but both appropriate,—the queen, as we think, the less faulty. Abijah's address was to the enemy; that of Elizabeth was to her own supporters.

And this address of Abijah's we have reason to believe is reliable. It is not the practice of the sacred historians, as with the writers of ordinary history, to manufacture the speeches of the actors in their narrative. No, they report what was actually said; and this makes it safe to draw inferences from their recorded words. It is important to remember this in the present case, as it is chiefly from his address that we are enabled to understand what sort of person Abijah was.

In noticing this reign we shall turn your attention to Abijah's greatness—to his true character, and to his early death.

I. His greatness.

It is said by the sacred historian that he "waxed mighty," and one instance is given of his success in arms. He broke the power of Jeroboam; he scattered the warlike array of that monarch; he took cities from him; and so effectually humbled him that he never recovered strength again in the days of Abijah.

Nor was Jeroboam an insignificant enemy. There is little glory, you know, in conquering the feeble; but Jeroboam was not feeble. He had had long experience in war. For nearly twenty years he had wielded the resources of ten out of the twelve tribes in Israel; and now, when brought into collision with Abijah, he could bring into field nearly a million of men. It was no small matter to contend with such an antagonist. It was no small glory, speaking after the manner of ordinary history, to conquer so redoubtable a chief, and sustained by such a numerous following. No doubt, the men of that time looked with interest and astonishment on this achievement of Abijah. The obscure and unilluminated days of Israel, which had prevailed under Rehoboam, ceased for the time being, and a new era of glory seemed to have dawned for the throne of Jerusalem. The memory of David's victories was revived, and it appeared as if the spirit and power of that illustrious king were again in the ascendant in the son of Rehoboam.

And yet it was not so. This greatness of Abijah's was meteoric and adventitious; it had not the characteristics of true greatness. True greatness grows, and fills the page of history, and becomes the more appreciated and admired the more it is studied. Follow the steps of the truly distinguished, and you will find the excellence that distinguishes them reappearing from time to time, and even in ampler manifestation. Thus with the faith of Abraham, and thus with the wisdom of Joseph, and thus with the prowess of David. The faith of Abraham carried him from his native land, enabled him to hope against hope in relation to the promised seed, and sustained him as he journeyed to Moriah to offer his beloved Isaac on the altar. So of the wisdom of Joseph. It shone in the house of Potiphar; it reappeared in the prison; and it displayed its unusual profundity in the service of Pharoah. And so of the prowess of David. It did not expire with the conquest of Goliah, but marked all his subsequent career. It is ever thus with true greatness; it grows and unfolds itself; and history delights in it, and all following ages study and admire it, and more intimate knowledge only enhances its claims on admiration.

But it is **not** thus with the greatness of Abijah. That **greatness did** not grow, nor re-manifest itself. True, he **had** but brief opportunity to **show** what **he was,** as he **was** early **cut** down. Still, his victory over Jeroboam **was** followed only by **events** which small men are equal **to.** He increased the **number of** his wives, and affected great state and importance. **His** mightiness was not the mightiness of a commanding intellect—swaying his contemporaries for good, and moulding the masses to harmony **or to** excellence; but it **was** the mightiness of Oriental luxury and unworthy pomp. If he seemed to rival David in his achievement against Jeroboam, he forthwith **sunk** into the effeminacy and vain display of Solomon, by **the** increase of his harem and **the** expensive habits of his **court.** Instead of growing in excellence, whether military **or** administrative, **he** rather sunk into **the** magnificence of a self-centred and self-pleasing despot, and his**tory** attaches small importance to his greatness. This one unsustained achievement **is** indeed recorded, but his name is unshrined in the heart of the ages, and his **mem**ory is barely preserved among men. Furthermore, the more fully his one great victory is understood, the more clearly is it manifest that small renown attaches to him because of it. It **was not** because of superior generalship on his **part that** victory declared in his favour. The superiority **in** this particular was wholly on the side of Jeroboam. **The** calculations and arrangements of that prince were perfect, and must have resulted in triumph for his arms had no unseen causes controlled the event. He had brought an overwhelming force into the field, and he made such disposition of his forces as **to take** the troops **of** Abijah before and behind **at** the same time. According to all ordinary calculations, Abijah's case was hopeless. He was in the hands of a superior general, and his resour**ces** were only half of those of his greater antagonist. Only a miracle could save him, and that miracle was indeed wrought. The beleaguered party prevailed, the inferior gained the crown; and the mightier host was scattered and discomfited. And why? Not because of Abijah's goodness, but because God saw meet that it should be so; and some reasons for God's decision in the matter are not far to seek.

First, It was because of the cries of the pious in Abijah's army. Hear the narrative :—

> "And when Judah looked back, behold, the battle was before and behind; and they cried unto the Lord, and the priests sounded with the trumpets. Then the men of Judah gave a shout, and as the men of Judah shouted, it came to pass, that God smote Jeroboam and all Israel before Abijah and Judah. And the children of Israel fled before Judah; and God delivered them into their hand. And Abijah and his people slew them with a great slaughter; so there fell down slain of Israel five hundred thousand chosen men. Thus the children of Israel were brought under at that time, and the children of Judah prevailed, because they relied upon the Lord God of their fathers." (II. Chron. xiii., 14-15.)

You will remember that the great majority of the truly good in Israel at that time were under Abijah, and many of those, no doubt, were in the army. There were not only the pious belonging to the two tribes, but also the pious belonging to the ten tribes. The time-serving in Israel had gathered around Jeroboam and his golden calves; but the pious and enlightened had gathered to the Temple and to the house of David. The two armies represented, speaking in general, the chaff and the wheat in Israel. Jeroboam headed the more numerous, ungodly and self-seeking, while Abijah led the less numerous godly, who sought the honour of God and the preservation of the Temple. In this light you will not wonder that the victory should be found with Abijah—not for his own sake, nor because of any generalship on his part, but for the sake of the pious who crowded or followed his standard. These had forsaken their homes (many of them) to escape the golden calves, and it did not comport with God's purposes that these golden calves should prevail over the territory to which His servants had betaken themselves. As for Abijah himself it is to be noticed, that he boasted of God to Jeroboam before the battle, but it is not said that he cried to the Lord when the crisis arose. It was the men of Judah that cried. Further, it is specially stated that he slew, but others prayed. He is mentioned in connection with the slaughter, but not in connection with the devotions or the divine reliance. (17, 18.)

Secondly, It was for the sake of Jerusalem. God had not forgotten David, nor his loyal services. Solomon, indeed, had been unworthy, and therefore his kingdom was rent and dismembered under Rehoboam, but the Holy One of Israel was not prepared to extinguish, or to allow to be extinguished, the throne of His honoured servant altogether. Had Jeroboam gained this battle, he would probably have marched to Jerusalem forthwith, and set aside the sacred dynasty at once. He had no pious scruples to check him. Policy was everything with him, and Heaven's purposes would have received small consideration at his hands. But God saw meet to secure His own purposes, in the preservation of David's house and David's throne, and therefore the mighty army of Jeroboam was scattered, and all his skilful arrangements nullified. He was driven back to Samaria, and Jerusalem and the Temple, and the sacred house of David, were saved from his inroads, and from his undesirable domination. Then

Thirdly, the interests of unborn generations required this check on Jeroboam as well as the interests of the house and city of David. The truth is, the enlightenment and wellbeing of untold millions in the latter day were bound up in the family of David, and in the history of Jerusalem. The time indeed would come, when the sacred city would be trodden under foot of the Gentiles, but that would be (at least as to its long obscuration) after the family of David had merged in its permanent and heavenly representative. In the mean time, that city must be preserved, and therefore the mighty army of Jeroboam falls and melts away before the arms of the men of Judah.

There were reasons then for Abijah's victory apart altogether from generalship on his part, or even goodness on his part. The Temple of God **was** behind him, the prayers of the pious were on his side, and the purposes of God required his safety. These are reasons weightier far than those which are material or apparent, and yet they are reasons which warriors in general apprehend not. These warriors can count their troops, and compare their cannon with those of the enemy; they can make mathematical calculations concerning the weight of their artillery, or the range of their weapons; but they compute not the force of prayer, nor the interests of God's cause among men—nor yet the bearings of events on distant ages. No doubt Jeroboam was surprised at his discomfiture, and well he might, considering the elements in his favour. But had he seen and understood all, his surprise would have abated, or, at least, have taken a new shape. The truth is, he would have been amazed at his own temerity, in rushing against the thick bosses of the Almighty's buckler. And so with many warriors besides Jeroboam; were their eyes but opened to the true causes of things, they would judge otherwise than they do: they would learn that it is not by chance that battles are decided, nor yet always by the material forces employed, nor yet altogether by the genius of the commanders engaged; but, by the God of battles, and that with a view to interests often wholly invisible at the time, especially to the parties engaged; and they would thus learn to think more humbly of themselves and of their achievements. In the case before us, Abijah no doubt thought himself a great hero, and yet how small a place he occupies in human annals—none in general history—and only a small niche in Jewish story, and that only in consequence of his connection with the house of David. The reasons of his victory were entirely **apart** from himself. But let us notice,—

II. *His true character.*

At first sight, and as reported of in this chapter, he

seems pious; at any rate, he uses the language of piety, **and** professes to cherish the expectations of the pious. **Hear** his ringing speech to Jeroboam and his army before joining battle:—

> "And Abijah stood upon Mount Zemaraim, which is in Mount Ephraim, and said, 'Hear me, thou Jeroboam, and all Israel: Ought ye not to know that the Lord God of Israel gave the kingdom over Israel to David for ever, even to him and to his sons by a covenant of salt? Yet Jeroboam, the son of Nebat, the servant of Solomon the son of David, is risen up, and hath rebelled against his lord. And there are gathered unto him vain men, the children of Belial, and have strengthened themselves against Rehoboam the son of Solomon, when Rehoboam was young and tender-hearted, and could not withstand them. And now ye think to withstand the Kingdom of the Lord in the hand of the sons of David; and ye be a great multitude, and there are with you golden calves, which Jeroboam made you for gods. Have ye not cast out the priests of the Lord, the sons of Aaron, **and the** Levites, and have made you priests after the manner of **the** nations of other lands? So that whosoever cometh to conse**crate** himself **with a** young bullock and seven rams, the same may be a priest **of** them that **are no** gods. But as for us, the Lord is our God, and we have not forsaken Him, and the priests which minister unto the Lord, are the sons of Aaron, and the Levites wait upon their business; and they burn unto the Lord every morning and every evening burnt sacrifices and sweet incense; the shewbread also set they in order upon the pure table; and the candlesticks of gold with the lamps thereof, to burn every evening; for we keep the charge of the Lord our God, but ye have forsaken Him. And, behold, God Himself is with us for our Captain, and His priests with sounding-trumpets to cry alarm against you. O children of Israel, fight ye not against the Lord God of your fathers, for ye shall not prosper.'" (II. Chron. xiii., 4-12.)

Who would expect anything **but** goodness and holy obedience after such talk? And yet it was far otherwise with Abijah. **His** piety is **like** his mightiness, it will not bear examination. Even though we knew no more of him than this speech of **his** reveals, we might well doubt the genuineness of his goodness. Notice particularly:—

First, There is a merging of important facts in the statements **of** this speech. He makes no mention of, or reference to, the conditions attached to the occupancy of the throne by the sons of **David** in the course of it. According to him, it would seem as if fidelity on their part **was a** matter of no consequence. They may do as they will,—they may be consistent or inconsistent, they may be faithful or unfaithful,—and still claim the honours and immunities of the throne of their great ancestor. He takes no notice of the unfaithfulness of his grandfather Solomon, and none of the pride and haughtiness of his father Rehoboam. Had he been truly pious, he would have grieved that his house had given occasion for the disarrangement and dismemberment that had arisen, and his grief and penitence would have withheld him from every thing like presumption and self-assertion, or family assertion. But he had no such regrets. He was a descendant of David,—that was enough, as he thought, to put down all opposition to him. He seems to have felt just as Rehoboam felt when asked to lessen the burdens of the people, viz., that no one had a right to question his rule—that indeed, he had "a right divine to govern wrong." This is not like the sentiment of the truly pious.

You will notice besides, that Abijah takes no notice of the right of Jeroboam to govern the ten tribes—a right conferred by the same authority as that by which the family of David held the two tribes. He treats Jeroboam as a mere usurper, and actually misrepresents the case as between him and Rehoboam. He pretends to say, that Jeroboam took advantage of the youth and tenderness of his father—gaining his royal position in Samaria when there was no one in Jerusalem experienced enough to cope with him. Now, to us it seems strange that he should talk so, when we know that Rehoboam was more than forty years old at the death of Solomon. Rehoboam was in his maturity when the ten tribes gathered around Jeroboam. There was neither youth, nor tenderness, nor humility about Rehoboam to touch the sensibilities of his oppressed people, or to stay the ambition or the determination of his rival. He was, on the contrary, haughty, obstinate, and bent on subjugating the disaffected, if only he had had the power; and that, without listening to their reasonable demands. In one word, the statement of the case, as between Jeroboam and the throne of Jerusalem, implies pride and unfairness on the part of Abijah; and pride and unfairness are incompatible with true piety. But further, concerning this speech, there is,

Secondly, An undue importance attached to external observances of it. He boasts of the Temple at Jerusalem, and the offerings, and the legitimate priests, and the trumpet-blowings, as if these alone constituted religion and secured the presence and favour of God. He seems to have had no misgivings as to the presence among his people of the spirit of true faith and devotion; or rather the truth seems to be, he had little idea of the existence or need of such a spirit at all. The external rites were everything in his eye. These being observed at his capital, and not at the capital of Jeroboam, he felt confident that God would interpose for him and his people, and not for Jeroboam and his people. Now, true piety is not thus; it suspects its own short-comings, and has no confidence in its own performances. It is well pleased to observe the order of divine worship as to externals, but it knows that the heart is not always true even when the forms are unexceptionable. It is not, therefore, ready to boast of its own observances, or to take encouragement from its own fidelity in externals. It rather looks to the grace of God, and commits itself, when any great crisis arises, to the wisdom and determinations of Him who knows how to temper his dispensations to the state and circumstances of His people. Abijah, however, seems to have had no such refined or spiritual ideas. He was familiar with the visible and the literal; and he was content to know that the true priests officiated in Jerusalem, without concerning himself to inquire how far a spirit of enlightenment or obedience prevailed among his people. Nay further, we fear we must charge him, in this vaunting speech of his, with,

Thirdly, Sheer hypocrisy. He talked as if he were a true son of David, and a loyal observer of Heaven's directions, while all the while he was a renegade and an idolater. We have another brief notice of him in the fifteenth of First Kings, and what do we find reported of him there ? Why thus, " That he walked in all the sins of his father, which he had done before him ;" **and we** know that his father, when established in the kingdom, forsook the law of the Lord, and all Israel with him; and we know that Judah under his father's reign provoked the Lord **to** jealousy above all that their fathers had done. Was there not hypocrisy then in this speech **on** the part of Abijah ? He was no devotee of the God **of** Israel, and yet he talked **as** if he were. He walked **in** the unholy and heathenish practices of **the** time, and yet he claimed and expected the protection **of the** God of Israel. He cast scorn on Jeroboam for his false priests and his golden calves, and yet he knew himself to be the adherent of yet more heathenish priests and idols. In one word, he did evil in the sight of the Lord, and used all his royal influence on the side of evil, and yet he talked as if he were faithful to Israel's God, and wholly devoted to the service of Israel's God. (10–12.)

You see then the true character and position of Abijah as exhibited in this speech. He was unfair to Jeroboam, he was overweening in his judgments concerning the house of fathers, he was materialistic in his views of religion, and he **was** hypocritical in relation to God. In one word, he knew the right but did the wrong. He claimed the advantages of the house of David, while he was wholly estranged from the spirit and principles of David. This was truly offensive. It was almost worse **than** the total apostacy of Rehoboam. That prince, when once established in Jerusalem, forsook the God of his fathers, and talked no more in the language of the pious in Israel; but Abijah retained for special occasions the language of piety, while he walked after the manner of the surrounding heathen. That is to say, he would hold God to His covenant, as it were, but regarded himself at liberty to violate that covenant as his convenience might dictate. He would be free to transgress, and yet he would claim the protection of Him whose government he rejected. You can understand how offensive this would be between man and man. Suppose any one of you had adopted a young person—promising to make him your heir, on condition that he should conform himself to your wishes, and devote himself **to** your service. You would **feel** very grieved if you found him, from day to day, disregarding your wishes, lending himself **to** purposes or to parties which were wholly opposed to your honour and your life, and utterly indifferent **to** your feelings and remonstrances; **but,** if grieved **for** this **conduct,** how would your indignation be roused **if** the same party still claimed the fulfilment of your engagement to enrich or to ennoble **him.** With the heart of an enemy, **how** could he claim the privileges of **a son**? And how could he think to hold you to your engagement when he had himself broken the tie that bound his interests with yours? Better that he should break off altogether, and make **no** unreasonable claims, than that he should break **off and yet** claim to possess the forfeited inheritance. **But** this **was** really the conduct **of** Abijah. True, **God** did deliver him from Jeroboam, but that was not for his goodness, nor yet for his vaunting and hypocritical speech: the Holy One **of Israel** had other reasons for His interposition **on** the occasion, as we have **seen.**

And this style of character very much prevails wher**ever** divine knowledge is enjoyed. And **you** ought to **note** it especially as you yourselves **are** in great danger of adopting it—professing, **as** you do, the knowledge of God's gospel. You will observe that Abijah had knowledge, but he was not under the influence of his knowledge. He had seen Solomon, his grandfather, and he heard of David, but he was **not** emancipated from the evil social influences that surrounded him. He did evil because evil was fashionable, and his knowledge was inoperative in practice. He could talk of David, but he fell in harmony with the irreligious portion of his contemporaries. Had his knowledge been so commanding as to tear him from the social ungodliness of his time, and to constrain him to think and feel as David thought and felt, his character would have been single and consistent, but, as things were, his character was hypocritical and inconsistent. He claimed the immunities of a sacred throne while he walked in harmony with the unsacred and idolatrous portion of the community.

And how is it with many professors in our own time? They have knowledge; but does their knowledge mould, regulate, or emancipate them? The Gospel of God's grace shines over them, but a God-forgetting world surrounds them; and where are their sympathies? The gospel they know in a general way; but are they delivered by it from this present evil world? They have heard of the divine David, but does their knowledge of Him so possess them as to enable them to disregard the vain pursuits and mistaken principles of a God-forgetting society? Alas, no! They yield themselves to the evil influences of a self-seeking and self-serving generation. They are the slaves of the visible. They are bound hand and foot by the present, and have no thoughts for the august future, or for the Unseen Divine. They are the servants of the world; and yet, when a crisis in their history arises, they would enjoy the immunities of the divine family. They harmonize with the idolatrous and the world-grasping, and yet they would be saved with the pious and world-renouncing. The restraints and peculiarities of the gospel they have ever disregarded, and yet, when disobedience is no longer possible, they would have all the blessings that are associated with or that arise from these restraints and peculiarities. Is this reasonable? Is it likely that such expectations will be met and realized? O, no! Such conduct but insults God, while it displays ignorance and ingratitude. If any one would enjoy the immunities of the divine family, let him yield himself to the principles and habits of the divine family. If any one would share with the true David, he must be delivered from this present evil world, and yield himself to the commanding influence of heavenly knowledge. If any one would be a partaker with Christ, he must be conformed to Christ. The eye must be single; the heart must be one and undivided. There must be no

F

attempt to serve contrary masters. All things must be accounted loss for the excellency of the knowledge of Jesus Christ—the great Lord and only Saviour!

You should each, look to himself in this respect. The knowledge that leaves a man in bondage to the world is not saving knowledge, **and** will be of no avail in the end. Christ **gave** Himself to deliver us from this present evil world, **and** it is only when **so** delivered that we have evi**dence of** being His. It **is not** enough to be able to talk fluently and piously, we must walk at liberty, keeping God's commandments. Abijah could talk, but Abijah's life **was not** in harmony with **his** talk. We must not only talk piously, we must feel, act, and breathe piously. "We must deny ungodliness and worldly lusts: we must live soberly, and righteously, and godly, in this present world —looking for that blessed hope, and the glorious appearing of the great God and our Saviour Jesus Christ—who gave Himself for us, that he might redeem us from all iniquity, **and** purify unto Himself **a** peculiar people zealous of good works." Then, there, we shall know the sweets of piety, and enjoy the serenities and glorious immunities that attach to it!

But to return to Abijah, we notice concerning him,

*III. The brevity **of his** reign.*

He reigned but three years **in** Jerusalem. This was **but a** brief period **to** enjoy his royalty, his greatness, his victory, and his dreams of aggrandizement. We say not that brevity alone is either dishonour or punishment. We know that some of the best and the fairest have passed speedily away from earth. Manifold considerations and reasons circulate around each individual, and give variety and mystery to the stream of being as developing itself in each. We cannot judge **by** single elements, and as for the whole of the encompassing elements, we cannot comprehend these. God only knows fully the reasons that determine the length of life, or of official distinction, in each man's case. Still, we are not wholly **in** the dark in this matter, and may not unprofitably rest on it for a moment. If a good man may be speedily cut down, or removed from earth, as well as a bad one, we can imagine, or apprehend in some degree, the reason of the diversity. When a good man dies prematurely (that is, prematurely in our view,) it is, either there is evil impending, or because there are felicities more exalted awaiting him. His early death is thus a kindness to him. Were his life prolonged, unlooked-for calamities or untoward combinations might distress him beyond what his heavenly Father sees meet. His connections might dishonour him, or social convulsions might affect him injuriously. Satan might gain advantage against him, and he might himself dishonour his profession. True, his Lord could sustain him, but it may seem better in the eyes of his Omniscient friend to take him away from the evil to come. Besides, heaven is in haste to introduce its loved ones to ulterior honours and heavenly experiences. If, therefore, other considerations require not the prolongation of the earthly life of its loved ones, it will hasten to summon these loved ones to itself. Love is not slow to unveil its treasures or to confer its kindnesses. But for the well-being of the world, therefore, and the upbuilding in godliness of the youthful and immature, we might expect all the good to die young. True, their own meekness requires time for its advancement and completion, but that could be hastened were there no considerations beyond themselves to modify or determine results. There is nothing wonderful then, or inexplicab'e, in the early death of the good. It only indicates their ripeness for glory, and the loving haste of their heavenly friend to introduce them to glory. The truth is, God is not only eager to gather His people to Himself, but He is also in haste to deliver them from this uncongenial and darkened state of things. It is very different with the early removal of the ungodly. They are swept aside because they are offensive. They abuse the divine mercies, and the power of doing so is taken away from them. In many cases, besides, they are removed to make way for the better men. In the case of Abijah before us we may not unsafely pronounce this as one of the causes of his early removal. His son Asa was a better ruler than he, and he was put aside accordingly. **Asa** was, indeed, far from the true standard. His career, instead of growing in brightness, became darkened towards the close. Still, it is said he **did** that which is right, externally at least, and in relation to the public worship **of the** God of Israel, **all** the days **of** his life; and Abijah, who did that which was evil, **was early** superseded by his more dutiful **son.** Thus, brevity of life on earth is a token of displeasure and disapprobation to the ungodly, while it **is a token** of loving regard in the case of the godly.

But this brevity **of** Abijah's reign, considering the family to which he belonged, throws us forward on the stream of history to an illustrious and contrasting reign. If Abijah's removal made way for a better king, the successive deaths of all the merely human occupants of David's throne have made way for a permanent and perfect ruler. There can be no absolute perpetuity without absolute righteousness. David and Solomon reigned long, but neither the one nor the other was fitted for perpetuity. There has, however, arisen in that family **one** whose reign may not **be** measured by years nor yet by centuries. His name shall last as long as the sun and the moon endure. You know to whom I refer. The angel in announcing His birth said of Him, " **He** shall be great, **and** shall be called the Son of the Highest; and the Lord **God shall** give unto Him the throne of His father David, and He shall reign over the house of Jacob for ever; and of His kingdom there shall be no end." The royalty of David terminates and abides on Him. He concentrates in Himself, and intensifies the glory both of David's and Solomon's reigns. Nay, He rises to the spiritual and the divine, and accomplishes that in the universe, and in the spirits of men, which David and Solomon accomplished only locally and typically. Humanity finds its ultimatum **in** Him. No higher development of human nature than that secured in Him is either possible or desirable.

Man's highest glory is to be conformed to Him, and to be ruled by Him. There is absolute safety under His government, as well as absolute excellence under His influence: and there **is** reunion and harmony for the nations under His sceptre. He is not simply King of the Jews, He is King of saints; and these are gathered from all nations, and kindreds, and peoples, and tongues. He is a light to lighten the Gentiles, as well as the glory of God's people Israel, and he cannot be superseded or set aside. Abijah must give place to Asa; and Asa in his turn must yield the throne to Jehoshaphat; **and so** of all the merely human sons of David—but Jesus, **the son** of David, and the divine occupant of David's throne, yields to none! He retains His dignity and authority through all ages. He has neither successor nor rival; and the nations will find rest and hope only as they yield themselves to his rule.

There is pleasure in change, but there is also satisfaction in permanence. **A** succession of rulers has its advantages, so long as these rulers are imperfect and **un**able to meet the wishes or the wants of their subjects; but let **a** ruler arise who is absolutely perfect, and who is fully competent to meet all **the** claims and necessities of his government, then there **is** no longer need for change. There is nothing in that case **to** be gained by change, and only the unwise would wish it. The Perfect is necessarily permanent, even as the Imperfect is necessarily temporary. Hence the removal of Abijah and of all the sons of David until He came whose rule is righteous, and whose administration is faultless. He can not be set aside: and it is not desirable that He should. He must reign until all His enemies are put under His feet. He **can meet** all the necessities of His government and all the wants of His subjects. And these His subjects, enjoying even now all the satisfaction of a permanent and perfect reign, have no need to desire a change with view to governmental improvement. They already possess in their permanent King all that they can wish, or desire, or imagine of good.

He can deliver them from their spiritual adversaries, and sustain them amid their earthly trials. He can defend them absolutely and save them eternally. His government is all that subjects can wish—being loving, tender, competent, and wise. He draws His subjects within the circle of life and peace, presents them to His Father without spot, or wrinkle, or any such thing, and binds them to all that is blissful, and pure, and rejoicing, for ever. There is neither defect, shortcoming, nor forgetfulness in His rule; and His resources are inexhaustible. There are ever permanent and inexhaustible reasons why His subjects should glory in Him, and comfort themselves in the thought of the perpetuity of His throne, and the perfection of His character. The removal of such a ruler, were such a thing possible, would be a calamity for the universe! But He cannot be set aside or superseded. Death hath no more dominion over Him. "Of the increase of His government and peace there shall be no end. Upon the throne of David, and upon his kingdom, to order it, and to establish it with judgment and with justice from henceforth, even for ever. The zeal of the Lord of hosts will perform this!" O, the joy that there is such a King!

And then He confers perpetuity as well as enjoys it. He gives to His subjects eternal life, and makes them joint heirs with Himself. He hath brought life and immortality to light by His gospel, and He fashions those who receive that gospel to a divine similitude. He hath gone to prepare a matchless Paradise for His believing ones, and He undertakes to make them meet for its everlasting enjoyment. They have already entered upon the life that is undying, and by hope they embrace an inheritance that is incorruptible, undefiled, and unfading. O, but His people are a happy people! Happy in their chief, and happy in their prospects under Him! They can not only rejoice in His immutability and perpetuity, but they can rejoice also in the immortality and perpetuity in good which He confers on and secures for them "A perpetuity of bliss," it hath been said, "is bliss." Nay, it **is** bliss upon bliss—it **is** bliss **in fact,** bliss in prospect, and bliss in assured security and continuance! And this bliss the great Son of David gives and guarantees to those who yield to Him as their King. He leads them, and moulds them to perfection, and then change in relation **to** them becomes for **ever** undesirable and unnecessary.

Would you **not** wish to become the subject of this King, if you are not already so? Would you not wish **to** be independent of this fleeting and unsatisfying life? Would you not wish to be heirs of God and of eternal glory? Then, you must seek perfection of nature and fitness for divine fellowship. If you walk in sin, you have neither part nor lot with Him who saves His people from their sins! If you walk in unbrokened worldliness, you have not yet taken the first step to heaven. You **are** not yet delivered from the present evil world, and cannot mount up with wings as eagles toward the Perfect and the Undying. Your only hope is in the divine Son of David. He is the living One, and His life is the Light of men. Because He lives, they who embrace the truth concerning Him shall live also. " God **so** loved the world, that He gave His only begotten Son, that whosoever believeth in Him should **not** perish, but have everlasting life!" He only hath made an end of sin! He only **can** transform the nature! He only hath opened the gates of Paradise for humanity! And He only can secure that perfection of nature which fits for the enjoyments and exercises **of** Paradise! Look to Him: Seek emancipation from sin through Him: Seek under Him to be perfect even as your Father in heaven is perfect; and then you shall find the perpetual and inexhaustible joys of divine love: and early death in that case, should it be so ordered, will be early immortality.

QUESTIONS ON ABIJAH.

What brief expression describes, or characterizes, the reign of the prince?
  He "waxed great," it is said.
What great achievement suggested this statement concerning him?
  His victory over Jeroboam.
What was there remarkable in this victory?
  It was gained by an inferior general, with an inferior force, over a superior general with a vastly superior force.
What was the character of Abijah's greatness notwithstanding?
  Meteoric and adventitious.
How does this appear?
  By his subsequent career, in which we find only what small men are equal to, without any indication of superior power or superior wisdom.
How did he follow up his success?
  Just as the low-minded and self-centred would do: by increasing the number of his wives, and affecting great state and importance.
How then do you account for the victory?
  God had reasons for giving the victory to Abijah apart altogether from Abijah himself.
Mention some of these reasons.
  The prayers of the pious in Israel—most of whom were in Abijah's army: the safety of Jerusalem, which, for David's sake, might not at that time be wholly eclipsed or subjugated: the interests of unborn generations—which were wrapped up in the family of David.
Is it common for warriors to take considerations like these into account when calculating the chances of war?
  Not at all, though these considerations substantially (viz., Prayer and God's covenant purposes) still play a controlling part in human, and even in military, history.
If warriors were more fully enlightened as to the moral and providential government of God, would they attach as much importance to themselves as they often do?
  It is not supposable that they would. Take Abijah as

an example; and see how little he really was while he took on him the airs of a great conqueror. Had he been more enlightened he could not have been so inflated.

But what of Abijah's piety?
We fear it will not bear examination. Like his greatness, it was more apparent than real.

What do you notice in this respect in his speech to Jeroboam?
A want of honesty in relation to God's covenant with David: a want of candour in relation to Jeroboam: a want of spiritual perception in relation to divine worship—and a hypocritical profession entirely at variance with his habits and character.

What was there peculiarly offensive in his pious talk?
It claimed for him as king of the sacred people the protection of God while he was wholly unmindful of the claims of God on him as the occupant of that throne.

How came it that his knowledge and his practice were at variance?
He yielded himself to proximate and fashionable influences, and not to those of Heaven. His knowledge of the divine ought to have controlled him, whereas the idolatrous fashions of his contemporaries did so.

Is this style of character not prevalent in our own day?
Far too much so: many know the Gospel, but yield not themselves to its commanding influence: they sail with the world rather.

And what is the unreasonable expectation of such when some crisis in their history arises?
Like Abijah, they look for the deliverances and consolations of that gospel which they have habitually disregarded in practice.

When is gospel-knowledge saving-knowledge?
When it commands the character, and breaks the habits of worldliness and sin.

What should the young be taught to remember on this point?
That Christ gave Himself for us, not merely to enable us to talk piously but to deliver us from the present evil world: and that we have true participation with Him, only when divine knowledge controls us and not the ungodly fashions of the men among whom we live.

How long did Abijah reign in Jerusalem?
Only three years.

Is early death always dishonour or punishment?
By no means. Many of the best have been early removed.
Do we know any reason why the good should sometimes die early?
Yes; when calamity **is** impending they are in many cases taken away from the coming evil.
Can you mention another reason?
Yes: the divine love toward them. Their heavenly Father is in haste to introduce them to the felicities of His household when important considerations prevent not.
But **how** is it when wicked men are early removed?
They are removed in displeasure, and to make way in some cases for better men—as in the **case** of Abijah and Asa his son.
What great truth **is** suggested by this law of removal and succession in the house of David?
Its perpetual arrest in the case of the crowning Prince **of** that house: He hath neither successor nor rival.
What makes the perpetuity of His throne a blessing?
Its absolute righteousness and competency: The imperfect cannot be permanent, while the absolutely perfect cannot be set aside.
And what distinguishing blessing does this perfect and abiding King of the house of David confer upon His subjects?
He confers perpetuity as well as enjoys it. He gives unto His sheep eternal life—making them joint heirs with Himself.
And what should be the desire and labour of those who have such **a** faith and such a hope?
Entire freedom from sin in all its forms, and ever-increasing meekness for the inheritance that is immortal.
What in general **are** the lessons taught by the story of Abijah?
That there are unseen reasons for the decisions of Providence, which the proud and self-centred never dream of—reasons arising from the house and dynasty of David; in other words, from the cause of God in the earth: that piety is something than mere talk; and that early **death** can be interpreted only in connexion with character, and not always even by that: many social and providential considerations affect the question in each case which we, in the meantime, can not perceive.

V. ASA.

"So Abijah slept with his fathers, and they buried him in the city of David; and Asa, his son, reigned in his stead." II Chron. xiv. 1.

THERE is a wide circumference of unknown agency beyond the horizon of each individual, be he humble or exalted. From this unknown circumference danger or difficulty may spring up at any time. Usually, there is enough to perturb and to exercise every man within his own limited horizon; but though all should be serene and unthreatening within this line, we are not, therefore, to think ourselves secure. The exterior and unseen agencies may be preparing for, or actually executing evolutions, which may threaten or seriously compromise our safety or the safety of our friends, or even our own life, before another year has run its course.

This, King Asa found in the early part of his reign. All within his horizon seemed peaceful—was indeed peaceful. Samaria was not in a condition to annoy him. Abijah, his father, had weakened the military power of that people but a few years before, at the great battle of Zemaraim. Jeroboam, its warlike king, was now broken in spirit, if not actually dead. The other neighbouring peoples were all quiescent. The political sky seemed wholly untroubled and peaceful all around; and yet danger was near. A storm was gathering in the south, not yet visible on the horizon of Jerusalem, but destined ere long to break over the sacred territory. Zerah, an Ethiopian conqueror, had already gathered, or was now gathering, a mighty army for aggressive purposes. **Soon** reports of his approach, with a million **of** soldiers and three hundred chariots reach King Asa. There was alarm **in** Jerusalem then, **no** doubt. Hastily, however, the youthful king collected his forces, and met **the** invader in the valley of Zephathah. The conflict **terminated in** favour of the men of Judah, and the tide of invasion was thrown back. The joyful tidings flew **to** the capital, and great was the rejoicing of the people, **that the storm** had been broken, and their national existence **preserved.**

It **is** often thus **in private** as well as in national life. When all **is** peaceful in the immediate neighbourhood of an individual, there may be germinating, or taking shape in the mind of another individual, far away it may be, some thought or purpose, which may tell seriously and disastrously on the history or the happiness of the party in question. The party himself sees nothing and suspects nothing, **but** the crisis comes on apace, and, when least expected, some great catastrophe occurs, **or** looms with threatening aspect into view. **It is** important to those who live such a life **of** exposure and possible overthrow, to have a mighty Friend—omniscient and powerful—who by his knowledge and skill may be able to turn aside, **or** to neutralize these unexpected dangers. It was because **Asa** betook himself to such a Friend that he escaped subjugation and impoverishment in the case before us. And we all need the watchful care and mighty protection of this all-seeing and all-competent One!

In further noticing this king, we shall remind you: of the excellence **of** the greater part of his reign, of the sad inconsistency **that** marked his closing years, and of his shortcoming as a type of the true King of Israel.

I. The Excellence of the greater part of his Reign.

He was decidedly opposed to idolatry. He not only renounced it for himself, but he used his royal power and authority to put it down in Jerusalem, and throughout his dominions. "He took away the altars of the strange gods, and the high places, and brake down the images, and cut down the groves." "He did that which was good and right in the eyes of his God." He would lend no countenance to the fashionable abominations of the time. His father, Abijah, had yielded to them; his grand-father, Rehoboam, had walked in them; even his great-grandfather, Solomon, had lent his mighty influence to the evil and degrading rites of idolatry. But Asa would not follow in their footsteps. He had a clear and decided perception of the true interests of his kingdom in this matter. He would not have idol shrines in the metropolis of his kingdom. Instead of yielding to the degeneracy and defection of these recent years, he wished rather to bring back the times of David, when no strange god had acknowledged or recognized place in the sacred territory. This you must perceive was good and right. It was good for his people: and it was right in the eyes of the Holy One of Israel. Then,

He sought to improve the peace which God had given him to strengthen his kingdom, and prepare for possible contingencies: "He built fenced cities in Judah: for the land had rest, and he had no war in those years, because the Lord had given him rest. Therefore he said unto Judah, Let us build these cities, and make about them walls and towers, and gates, and bars, while the land is yet before us." He knew the hostility of the house of Jeroboam, and he had not forgotten the eight hundred thousand warriors that had been led against his father Abijah but a few years before. Probably himself had taken part in the engagement on that occasion. He would provide as far as possible against the recurrence of such an invasion, by building fortified places where he thought them likely to be most serviceable, for the protection of his own territory, or for holding his adversaries in check. He would not wait for the tornado; he would provide against it while all was yet serene. Some monarchs would have given themselves to present enjoyment and display—leaving the future to take care of itself, but Asa was wiser: he looked to possibilities, and wished to be provided against them. Not only the ten tribes might again invade his dominion, after **a few** more years had repaired their resources; but there were other enemies to Jerusalem, and to the dynasty of David, not very far away. He knew **not** what might arise, and he did not wish to **be** unprepared. While, therefore, he made an end of idol-edifices and idol-groves, he employed himself further in increasing the fortifications of his kingdom. Nor **was it** long ere the wisdom of this course was made apparent, though the danger came from an unexpected quarter. "Zerah, **the** Ethiopian, (as already noticed) with an host of **a** thousand thousand, and three hundred chariots, came out against him, and came into Mareshah." Now, if any of his fortified places were in **the neighbourhood** of Mareshah (which is scarcely likely), **they** would help to check the invaders, and to shelter the troops of King Asa. And if they were not, still they would **be** useful in holding other enemies in check, **(the ten** tribes for example,) who might have taken advantage of the presence of Zerah's army to commit depredations at some unguarded points. It was wise, then, in Asa to prepare for contingencies, with a view to the safety and preservation of his kingdom. But we **have** other evidence of the excellence of his reign in its earlier years.

He betook himself to God in the day of his danger. **He** did not trust to his own provisions and resources. He had spared no pains **in** making his preparations, but he did not rest in these preparations. He availed himself, no doubt, of everything favourable in making his arrangements for the contest forced upon him, but he looked on high for the victory. "He cried unto the Lord his God, and said: Lord, it is nothing with Thee to help, whether with many, or with them that have no power: Help us, O Lord, our God, for we rest on Thee, and in Thy name we go against this multitude. O Lord, Thou art our God, let not man prevail against Thee." This is very like true piety and very unlike the talk of his father, Abijah, when Jeroboam came up against him with his overwhelming army. On that occasion, Abijah manifested a spirit of boasting and unfairness, but on this occasion **Asa** manifested a spirit of humility and heavenly trust. Abijah cried not to God, but left that to others, while he uttered vaunting and self-laudatory words: but Asa cried himself to the Lord, and withheld himself from everything like boasting or bravado. And there is something very beautiful in this brief prayer of King Asa's. He comforts himself in, while he recognises the omnipotence of the God of Israel: "Is is nothing with Thee," says he, "**to** help, whether with many, or with them that **have no** power." He claims, too that Mighty One as h's own **God** and the God of his people: and he hides himself, **and his** kingdom, if I may speak so, behind the throne **of** the Almighty! O Lord, Thou art our God; let not man prevail *against Thee !*" As if he had said, "The contest is thine, O Lord, and not ours. Our overthrow were thy dishonour, while our victory or protection will be thy glory. Let not man prevail *against Thee.*" No wonder that God should give the victory to such a king! No wonder that God should scatter the hosts which sought the injury of those who thus nestled under the shadow of His almighty wing! But even this is not all:

Asa listened to God by the prophet Azariah, the Son of Oded, and " he gathered together **at** Jerusalem all Judah and Benjamin and the strangers with them, out of Ephraim, and Manasseh, and out of Simeon, and they entered into a covenant, to seek the Lord God of their fathers with all their heart, and with all their soul,"— presenting at the same time oxen and sheep in large numbers at the Temple-altar. He was not unduly elated by his great victory over Zerah, **the** Ethiopian, as his father Abijah had been by his victory over Jeroboam. He sought not to make that victory subservient to his own greatness and luxurious appointments as a self-centred monarch, in the manner of Abijah: he wished rather to influence his subjects for good. Recognizing God **as** the giver of his mercies and distinctions, he would have his people turn more earnestly and more exclusively to the service of Jehovah and to the peculiarities of their national existence. Accordingly, the temple service was re-established on a more ample footing, and all opposing or rival shrines were removed. The court, under Rehoboam and Abijah, had encouraged foreign rites, to the neglect of their own divinely appointed ritual; but now, under **Asa, the** whole influence of **the court** was given to the true interests **of Israel,** and the maintenance of the **ritual of** Moses. One other circumstance marks the thorough nature of Asa's reformation. It is this:

He was impartial in his opposition **to** error **and idolatry.** He **would** not **tolerate the** rites of heathenism, **even** in his grandmother, Maachah. Princes will sometimes allow irregularities in their own connexions, or in the case of some privileged persons, when they will not **allow** them in the general community. Solomon, for example, thought to please his heathen wives by building shrines for their private use, without thereby intending **to** give general license to idolatry: but Asa was more true to principle and to heaven. He would not wink at idolatry, even in the most venerated member of the royal family. Maachah **was** the daughter **of** Absalom, the grand-daughter of David, and she had been the most honoured wife of Rehoboam, as she was the grandmother of Asa himself. One would have thought that she might have been left free to follow her own inclinations in the matter of worship. But no: venerable although she was, and honoured because of her antecedents and connexions, **she too,** must yield to the new order of things; she too, must **have** her private sanctuary broken up, as opposed to the true interests of Israel. What Solomon had permitted, **and** what Rehoboam and Abijah had sanctioned, Asa now sweeps unhesitatingly aside. The fact is thus recorded by the sacred writer: "And also concerning Maachah, the mother of Asa, the king, he removed her from being queen, because she made an idol in a grove: and Asa cut down her idol, and stamped it, and burnt it at the brook Kidron." We can well believe that Maachah was very indignant at being thus interfered with in her latter days, but Asa was true to his purpose, and would make no exception in favour of his aged relative. It is said, indeed, that "the heart of Asa was perfect all his days,"—perfect in the matter of the national worship. He was opposed to idolatry and to all heathenish rites, from the beginning of his reign to the end of it. Nothing could induce him to relax in this matter. The sacred people, as he thought, must abide by Him, who brought them out of Egypt, in preference to all other gods, and they must observe the rites instituted by Moses, as the accredited agent of that Mighty One!

Such was the excellence and steadfastness to principle of this great-grandson of Solomon's. He was opposed to idolatry; he improved his days of peace to prepare for days of danger and trial; he betook himself humbly to God when Zerah, the Ethiopian, invaded his territory with an overwhelming force. He listened to God, by his prophet Azariah, and renewed the covenant with Heaven which his fathers had broken; and he was impartial and persistent in his reforming administration. Here is much to admire, and God looked on approvingly, and God gave him peace round about. With the exception of the invasion of Zerah, which was permitted probably to test the sincerity of his professed adherence to the good and the right, he had no wars for **five** and thirty years of his reign. All that time he was left free **to engage** in the pursuits of peace, to strengthen his kingdom; and to cultivate and extend the knowledge of the holy. It **is** wonderful, when we consider that these ages were the ages of conflict, and when we remember that the elements of conflict were numerous and **active** around him and his people, **it is** wonderful, I say, that he should have enjoyed so long a national repose. But God, the God of Israel, can hold the elements of dispeace and confusion in check when He sees meet, and so long as He sees meet. He secured forty years of peace to Solomon, and He almost repeated the same kindness to Asa. When a man's ways please the Lord, and when a king's policy is in accordance with the mind of the Most High, he can make the very stones of the earth be at peace with the one, and the turbulent nations around **to be** at peace with the other. The distresses of war have a deeper cause than the ambitions of men. God uses these ambitions (without in any **way** approving of them) to punish or to scourge where He sees need for punishment or for stripes. And **so** with peace. Its blessings have **a** deeper cause than the policy or the **power** of nations. God gives it when He would bless, or when he would prepare agencies or improvements for His ulterior purposes. It is well to seek peace, but **it is** also well to remember, that only God can secure it. And it is well to escape from the horrors of war, but it **is also** well to remember, that they have no right to expect such escape whose ways are perverse or disobedient in the presence of the Most High.

So far our notice of Asa has **been** only pleasing, but **that** which follows **is** of **a** different character. There was inconsistency **and serious** faults, **even** with Asa. While we cannot but admire his decision, and the peacefulness of the greater part of his reign, **we** are constrained to wonder **and** grieve **over** his later history. But before noticing this matter, **we** would **remind** you of the lesson which his history thus far furnishes. We too should be true to Heaven. **If** we live in days of unfaithfulness, we should resolutely return to the good old ways. The written word is before us: and therein, **the** Living-Word is **set** forth in all the glory of His divinity, and in all the **fulness** of his grace. He is to us far more than David **was to** Israel. He is the centre of life, and the true Beloved of the upright. If Asa sought to bring back the days of David, **we** ought, in like manner, to fall back on the principles and the purposes of David's son and David's Lord. We are not of the literal family of David, nor are we kings among men; but, if truly believers in Jesus, we belong to the family of God, and to the royalty of heaven. It is meet that we should be faithful and grateful as well. It is meet that we should repudiate all inferior and opposing authorities, and give ourselves wholly and thoroughly to the obedience, and service, and imitation of our true King. It were **as** truly our honour to walk so, as it was the honour of Asa to do that which was good and right in the eyes of the Lord. Society has a perpetual tendency to drift away from the holy and the heavenly, and we should ever be on our guard in relation to this tendency. We should hold fast our profession, and the peculiarities thereof, without wavering, and that, spite of the ridicule, or the contrary fashions of the unbelieving or the worldly. **And** it is thus that **we may** look for long peace and opportunity for heavenly improvement. In yielding to the fashions of the world, and in forgetting the divine and the immortal, we are in the way of dispeace, irritation, and disappointment; but in dwelling habitually by the living Temple, and desiring to see and to be conformed to the beauty of the Lord, we are in the way of peace, and solace, and hope, and ineffable joy. Trials we may have in this way, and in the meantime, but consolations shall not be awanting—consolations appropriate, adequate, and sustaining! What pity that Christians are not more thoroughly Christianised! There cannot be fulness of divine consolation where there is not fulness and entireness of consecration. Be persuaded then, all ye who have caught a glimpse of the Truth, to seek, and to abide by the Lord, with all your heart and with all your soul!

But I come now to notice concerning Asa,

II. *The sad inconsistency that marked his closing years.*

The particulars of this inconsistency are given in the sixteenth chapter.

First, when invaded by Baasha, **he betook** himself to worldly **and** unworthy policy:

"In the six and thirtieth year of the reign of Asa, Baasha, King of Israel, came up against Judah, and built Ramah, to the intent that he might let none go out or come in to Asa, King of Judah. Then Asa brought out silver and gold out of the treasures of the house of the Lord, and of the King's house, and sent to Benhadad, King of Syria, that dwelt at Damascus, saying—'There is a league between me and thee, as there was between my father and thy father: behold, I have sent thee silver and gold; go, break thy league with Baasha, King of Israel, that he may depart from me.' And Ben-hadad hearkened unto King Asa, and sent the captains of his armies against the cities of Israel. And they smote

Ijon, and Dan, and Abel-maim, and all the store cities of Naphtali. And it came to pass, when Baasha heard it, that he left off building of Ramah, and let his work cease. Then Asa the King took all Judah; and they carried away the stones of Ramah, and the timber thereof, wherewith Baasha was building: and he built therewith Geba and Mizpeh."—xvi. 1-6.

Instead, **you see, of calling upon** God when Baasha sought to injure him, as **he did when** Zerah, the Ethiopian, came against him, he betook himself to Ben-hadad, King of Syria, **and** bribed him to invade the territories of Baasha. **The** movement was successful, **and Asa was** relieved **of** his adversary; but what was **the revelation** as to the state of Asa's heart? Why this: that he had forsaken God as his dependence and protector. He might still maintain the forms of the true worship, **but** he had fallen from the life of piety. **He** was **no** longer strong in faith, giving glory to God, but a mere worldly politician. **He** no longer referred himself and his kingdom to God, **but** took **the** burden **of** his safety and of that of his kingdom upon himself. He put his own wisdom **in** the place of divine Providence, and withheld from God **an** opportunity **of** shewing Himself strong **in** the **interests** of his people. This had been very bad and very presumptuous in any case, but it was specially so in the case **of** Asa. Asa had already proved **the** faithfulness and the power of God in the matter of the Ethiopian **invasion**. Why should he adopt a different style of **action** now? God had already shown favour to him, and given him **long years** of peace, why then should he turn his back **upon God** now? Saul, in his extremity, thought himself constrained to apply **to** the witch of Endor, since God would **not** answer him; **but** Asa had no such plea. God **had** answered him before, and God was prepared **to** answer him again: but Asa did not give him the opportunity. Asa preferred the help of a heathen king to that **of** the God of Israel. **It** may **be** said, that Baasha's in**vasion** was not so serious as that of Zerah's, that Asa felt himself competent to deal **with it** without applying for divine help, and that he meant no dishonour to God by adopting appropriate means to checkmate the King of

Samaria. But God himself did not view the matter thus: Hear his prophet on the occasion: "And at that time Hanani, the seer, came to Asa, King of Judah, and said unto him, because thou hast relied on the King of Syria, and not on the Lord thy God, therefore is the host of the King of Syria escaped out of thine hand. Were not the Ethiopians and the Lubims a huge host, with very many chariots and horsemen? Yet, because thou didst rely on the Lord, He delivered them into thine hand. For the eyes of the Lord run to and fro throughout the whole earth, to show himself strong in the behalf of them whose heart is perfect toward Him. Herein thou hast done foolishly: therefore, from henceforth thou shalt have wars." And what was the conduct of Asa under this reproof? It was simply outrageous. Instead of acknowledging his error, and bowing to the reproof of Heaven, he flew into a rage, ordered the prophet to prison, and walked oppressively toward his people.

Here was his second fault; he hardened himself against the reproof of the Holy, declared war in effect against Heaven, and acted the tyrant among his subjects. What a sad spectacle, and how unlike his former self! And how unlike his great progenitor David, when brought up by Nathan with the condemnatory declaration, "Thou art the man!" David bowed to the reproof, and wept for his folly: but Asa stormed and raged under the rebuke, and instead of humbling himself for his folly, just repeated it, nay, doubled and intensified it! What mattered it that he maintained the forms of the true religion in Jerusalem, when he was really insubmissive in spirit? What mattered it that his heart was perfect in opposition to idolatry all the days of his life, when there was lurking hostility in his soul in relation to the God of Israel? Nor can we comfort ourselves in the thought that this rage of his was merely a temporary ebullition of pride and bad feeling, for we hear nothing of repentance on his part—nor yet of liberation of the reproving prophet. He seems rather like a spoiled child. He had been favoured and blessed for so many years, that he thought himself injured or insulted by being called to account: and he had so long fancied that he had laid God under obligation by his firmness in the matter of idolatry, that anything like disapprobation from that quarter seemed to him at once unreasonable and unjust. Nor does further consideration seem to have improved or changed him in this respect; for, between two and three years later, he repeated in relation to his own person the very fault he committed in relation to his kingdom when invaded by Baasha.

Yes: here was his third fault. "In the thirty-ninth year of his reign he was diseased in his feet, until his disease was exceeding great; yet in his disease he sought not to the Lord, but to the physician." Hear it: "he sought not to the Lord, but to the physician." In a subsequent age, Ahaziah, of Samaria, sent in his affliction to Baal-zebub, and thereby incurred the displeasure of God, declared through Elijah. Asa acted in like manner, in his affliction, and the fault was even greater in him. Asa, I say, though still maintaining his consistency, so far as idols were concerned, insulted God as the great and only physician: "He sought not to the Lord." He trusted to the skill of his medical attendants; and thus he died! There is no report of a change in his sentiments. He went down to the grave, so far as appears, with a misplaced trust; and darkness and dubiety rest upon his memory. Nothing could be more promising than his early years, and yet he becomes unpleasing and repulsive as he draws near to the verge of the unseen. True, uncommon honours were paid by his contemporaries to his remains. They made a great burning of odours and spices at his funeral. And it was not unmeet that it should be so. His reign had been long and peaceful on the whole, and in the true interests of Israel: but still, History veils his name so far as his latter years are concerned, and Piety mourns rather than rejoices at his tomb!

We would not willingly place him among the perverse and the rejected; but neither can we confidently number him with the sanctified and the triumphant. If he entered the kingdom of light and immortality (as we desire that all should), his entrance was not an abundant entrance. He left clouds and dubiety behind him, and no subsequent generation can sweep these clouds aside. There they must rest until the light of the judgment day clears up all. His faults, it may **be**, were not greater than David's, but, then, they were uncancelled by penitence and by prayer, so far as we know. David's piety shone bright, as he neared the sepulchre, but Asa's lamp had gone out ere he reached the verge of the shadowy land. He might find his way through the darkness, guided by an unseen and a generous hand, but we cannot say that he did.

Here, then is a question which we would do **well to** ponder. How came it that Asa, so distinguished for piety and for principle in the early years of his reign, became so self-willed and mistaken in the latter years of his reign? We would be disposed to answer, that he sunk in character under the influence of a long-continued peace. He forgot in some measure his dependence while God held back the agencies of annoyance and danger. He lost sight of God as his refuge because there was no enemy threatening him, or pressing upon him. A child, **or** young person, who flees to his parent in danger, will sometimes forget that parent for long hours, or even for days, while all is sunny and unthreatening around him. Thus we fancy it was with Asa. The difficulties of the first years of his reign kept his spirit tender, unpresuming, and willing to avail himself of divine aid. The invasion of Zerah, again was so alarming, that he could not deal with it himself. He must seek the shelter of the Omnipotent Friend of Israel, or be overwhelmed. So long as dangers pressed upon him, he felt his need and acted accordingly; but after twenty years of unbroken peace, he felt altogether otherwise. A great change had imperceptibly crept over him during the quiet and untroubled years of prosperity. He had sunk into the region of ordinary and self-regulating life. He felt no need of God. The forms of piety satisfied him, and the special interpositions of Heaven seemed no longer necessary. He could be his own Providence now, and could secure his own safety by playing one ambitious neighbour against another. He failed to see, that his peace was as much the result of God's combinations, as his deliverance from Zerah had been of God's interposition. He felt as if it were rather the result of his own skilful administration, and thought himself competent, after his long experience as a ruler, to provide for his own safety and that of his kingdom. Hence, instead of seeking to God when Baasha invaded him, he betook himself to diplomacy and bribery.

Prosperity seems to be far more dangerous to a life of faith than persecution; and any one can understand it. When the storm rages and the enemy threatens, the sentinel watches; but when all is peace around, and the enemy is supposed to be far away, the sentinel relaxes his vigilance, or sleeps. So the goodness that gathers strength when threatened, decays and becomes less vigorous when unthreatened and secure. Often you see this in society. When men become prosperous and enjoy long peace, their seriousness evaporates. They may still keep up the forms of religion, and wait on the public services of the sanctuary, but their hearts rest in their comforts, and go not out after God. They have sunk into the ordinary style of thinking and feeling prevalent in the world around them. Not that prosperity is unfavourable to piety, if men were not so prone to self-dependence and creature-satisfaction. Prosperity is calculated to strengthen gratitude and animate piety, if only a sense of dependence can be retained; but the sense of dependence becomes attenuated or overlaid when peace and prosperity abound, and then the mercies that ought to stimulate and nourish piety only minister to self-conceit and self-dependence.

We would do well to take the warning that this subject presents. We have had long peace and external comfort. Have these very great mercies increased our gratitude and devotedness to God? It ought to have been so. It is not by skill of ours, if the social elements have been unperturbed around us. It is not by power of ours, if the earth have brought forth abundantly for man and for beast. God Himself hath been working for us; have we been grateful accordingly? Or have we not rather been—like Asa—unmindful **of our** benefactor, and disposed to take the credit of **our comfort to** ourselves, as well **as** to take the burden of our safety into our own hands? Beware of this mistake. We are all prone to it, and our peaceful, prosperous circumstances, in connexion with our disposition to forget God, have a powerful tendency in that direction. Seek to walk on the high places of faith, and avoid the low-lying intricacies of mere human policy. Refer yourselves to God in sunshine as well as in storm. **If you** call on him in danger, be not less sedulous to praise **Him** in prosperity; and never assume that you **are** competent **to** manage your own affairs without reference to your heavenly Friend. "In all your ways acknowledge Him, and He **will** direct your steps!" In this, Asa failed in the latter years of his life, and by his failure we ought to be warned.

But concerning this king we notice :—

III. His shortcoming as a type of the true King of Israel.

He reversed the order of excellence, and **thereby** failed **as a** type of the excellent. He began well, but he ended unworthily. There was much in his long reign that might fitly foreshadow the Prince divine, but he marred it all by the concluding chapters of his history. Like David, he was a victor in the early part of his reign, and like Solomon, he was a Prince of Peace during the greater part of his administration. By the strength of God he conquered, and by the grace of God he enjoyed peace, but he yielded his hold of the strength of God in his latter years, and forfeited the peace of the divinely-approved. Instead of growing in faith and heavenly dependence, he **sunk** to the arena of ordinary policy and self-dependence, as we have seen. Instead of drawing nearer to God, he fell away from God. Instead of holding on in his upward path, he began toward the end of his reign to descend to the common level of the ungodly and the unbelieving.

And how far he sunk from loyalty and submission in the presence of God appears by his actually imprisoning the Prophet who was commissioned to remonstrate with him for his unwise course. His conscience must have told him that the words of Hanani were the words of God, yet he dared to imprison the messenger of Heaven. Alas for Asa! His history was inconsistent! And what is worse, it ended in darkness! He dishonoured himself, and shrouded his claims to be a type of the Holy. As a member of the royal and consecrated house of David, he ought to have foreshadowed his great descendant; but, like many others of that family, he walked unwisely, and forfeited this honour.

The true Prince of Israel and crowning son of David made no step backward. He held on His way,—his upward way—and was never found sinking to conformity with the unbelieving and disobedient. His path was the path of the just; and the path of the just is as the shining light which shineth more and more unto the perfect day. Of Him his forerunner declared, "He must increase." There is nothing without Himself that can effectually arrest His progress; and there is no weakness or fitfulness in His own nature to turn Him aside, or to draw Him downwards. He is firm to His purpose, and undeclining in his progress. Very unlike in this, not only to His progenitor Asa, but to very many of the sons of men, and very many of the great ones of earth. They begin well, but they end in gloom or despair. They mean to hold an ascending course, but hindrances or temptations arise, and they sink from their former selves. New circumstances present new prospects, and former purposes are forgotten. They are deflected from their course, and they terminate their race of life far away from, or far beneath, their original goal. Adam in Paradise began well, and you know how he ended. King Saul began well, and you know how he ended. And so with myriads besides. It is far otherwise with Messiah, the son of David and son of God. He never goes backward, as I have said, and He never goes downward. He holds on His unhesitating and undeflecting way. See Him in His human history: His first recorded utterance is, "Wist ye not that I must be about my Father's business," and one of His latest **is**, "Father, if thou wilt, let this cup pass from me: nevertheless, not my will but Thine be done!" Though straitened unutterably to meet His baptism, He set His face as a **flint** to go up to Jerusalem where He must experience and fulfil it. Darkness indeed gathered around His closing hours, but it was not the darkness of unfaithfulness or merited dishonour. His fidelity and devotedness only became the more manifest and the more illustrious by reason of the clouds that wrapped His **cross.** He submitted to ignominy and crucifixion, but **His** path was still onward and upward: and so faithful and so unfaltering were His ascending steps that His Father smiled on His progress, set Him at His own right hand, and gave Him to be Head over all things to His Church. And His work is still onward. Enthroned, and honoured beyond thought, and wrapped in the peace of the heavenly and unperturbed Paradise of God, and that for long ages, He still seeks the honour of His Father, the down-putting of rebellion, and the recovery of the lost. Prosperity and peace have not vitiated Him, nor caused Him to forget the consistencies or the proprieties of His position. His excellence, as His glory, is unclouded, and He must reign till all His enemies are put under His feet. Asa ought to have foreshadowed and symbolized this persistent and all-conquering goodness; but he failed to do so; and he thereby darkened his place among the sacred ancestors of the great King. Though a better Prince than either his father, Abijah, or his grandfather,—Rehoboam, he is still of little account in the estimation of the successive generations of the children of God. Had he filled his typical place aright, he would have been honoured and celebrated through long ages; but, because he proved unfaithful and inconsistent, his name is barely remembered, and but little esteemed among the loyal ones of heaven!

Let Christians be reminded by this of an essential

characteristic of true faith. It is meant to be, and ought to be, progressive and ascending. It was so in the Head: it is meant to be so in the members. The righteous holds on his way, and he that hath clean hands grows stronger and stronger. "We are made partakers with Christ, if we hold fast the beginning of our confidence firm unto the end." It will not do to stop half way in the Christian pilgrimage and still expect the crown of fidelity. It will not do to follow the divine Leader half way through the wilderness and then return to Egypt. We cannot in that case expect to reach the Inheritance. We must abide by the tents of the pilgrim-people—we must continue to follow the divine Shepherd of Israel—we must keep on the high ridges of faith and godliness—(not sinking to the low-lying-region of human policy and self-dependence)—if we would enjoy an abundant entrance into the heavenly kingdom—nay, we must not only keep by the footsteps of the flock, we must also add virtue to virtue, as well as grow stronger and stronger in every virtue, if we would prove ourselves the heirs of glory, and the children of God. It is not by indolence, nor yet by inconsistency, that the heavenly prize is to be won. Paul pressed toward the mark for the prize of the high calling of God in Christ Jesus; and he urges diligence and persistency on the disciples; "Be not slothful (says he) but followers of them who through faith and patience inherit the promises." "Let us labour, (he says again) lest, a promise being left us of entering into rest, any of us should even seem to come short of it." We must not only begin well, we must also end well. We must not only begin in the spirit, but we must also walk in the spirit: and we must abide therein to the last. "Onward!" must be our motto continually, if we would not be of them who draw back unto perdition, but of them who believe to the saving of the soul.

And need I remind you that there is that in the divine life which necessitates advancement and development. The labour of the faithful, therefore, will not be in vain. Life is not a stagnant thing in any case: eminently, the divine life is potent and progressive. He who begins **a** good work in any heart will carry it on unto the day of Christ. Without relieving the party from responsibility and diligence, the divine life in the heart **is** essentially a triumphant and controlling thing. It **is** not **to** be permanently quenched or overborne. Restrained—or shrouded it may be for a time, but, when genuine, it will conquer **and** subordinate all to itself at last. Be diligent then, **ye who** have entered on this heavenly life, and weary **not. Your** labour shall not be in vain. You labour **in a** line **with** the operations of divinity. It is God who worketh **in** you both to will and to do of His good pleasure. Only wait on the Lord, whether in peril **or** in peace, and, instead of making the mistake of Asa, you shall renew your strength, and mount up with wings as eagles. You shall run, and **not** be weary. You shall walk, and not faint. Meantime, **wo**rk and watch, and be warned of the danger **to** spirituality in long-continued **peace** and prosperity. If you feel drowsiness creeping over you in relation to divine things, hasten to the throne **of** grace, and seek power **to** shake yourselves free of **the** enchantment: or, if you feel **a** spirit of self dependence stealing over you, pray that the spell may be broken, and that you may not be left to a misplaced **confidence.** Your help is in God, and you must seek it there. In one word, you must seek to grow in grace, and in the knowledge of our Lord and Saviour, Jesus Christ. It is by growth in the heavenly life that the principles of a merely earthly life will be weakened or diminished within you. And **it** is **by** enlarged knowledge of the divine Redeemer **that** faith **will** be strengthened, and a return to mere human policy or creature-dependence will become with you less and less possible. If you can only draw nearer to the central life and glory, and apprehend that life and glory yet more and more fully and truly, you will become less and less disposed to take the burden of your history upon yourself, or to trust to mere human helps. Had Asa not been in a great degree estranged from God, he would never have applied to Benhadad.

Like Asa, then, in the early part of his reign, see that you fall back upon the divine standards, and let your hand be perfect in this respect all the days of your life! But, unlike Asa, let not prosperity beguile you of your faith, or cause you to forget your divine dependence. He fell short as a Type of Messiah. See that you fall not short as disciples of the great and divine Instructor and Chief.

QUESTIONS ON ASA.

What was the character of the greater part of this reign?
Faithfulness and Peace.
How did Asa regard the fashionable idolatry of his time?
With uncompromising hostility.
How did he employ the peace vouchsafed him?
In diligent preparations for possible invasion. Dwelling amid the hostile and the unscrupulous, he knew not how soon he might be summoned to conflict.
Did events speedily justify his preparations?
Yes; Zerah, the Ethiopian, came against him with a host of a thousand thousand and three hundred chariots.
How did Asa conduct himself under this visitation?
He looked to, and trusted in, God alone. Though he had made all attainable preparations for such a contingency, he did not trust to his towers, his fortifications, or his armies.
And how did he conduct himself after the invasion was successfully rolled back?
He listened to the prophet Azariah, and renewed with his people the covenant of the Lord.
And what is it that strikingly shows the thoroughness of his opposition to idolatry?
His conduct in the case of his grandmother; he would not tolerate it, even in her.
How did God manifest His approval of this faithfulness on the part of Asa?
He gave him long peace round about. For five and thirty years he was free to attend to the interests and improvement of his kingdom.
What should this faithfulness on the part of Asa with its happy results impress upon us?

The wisdom of unwavering adherence to Christian **law amid** all the contrary tendencies and influences of **ungodly** society.

What should be our supreme and persistent solicitude?
To be found by the Living Temple, inquiring after, and seeking to behold, the beauty of the Lord.

Were the closing years of Asa's reign in keeping with its early years?
Far from it; though he still maintained the true worship in Jerusalem, his bearing was strikingly changed.

What was his reliance when invaded by Baasha, King of Israel?
His own skilful use of the King of Syria, and not the God of Israel, as in the case of Zerah's invasion.

And how did he treat Hanani, the seer, when remonstrated with for his defection?
He flew into a rage at him, ordered him into confinement, and resented the interference by an oppressive walk toward his subjects.

And how further did he show his insubmissive and God-offending spirit?
By seeking to the physician rather than to God when troubled with disease in his feet.

Did he manifest no return to a proper state of mind before he died?
We hear of no such thing; and charity, which presumes not to penetrate the unseen, and which seeks to interpret what is known as favourably as may be, is constrained to mourn at his tomb, rather than to rejoice.

How came it that Asa, so dutiful in his early years became so perverse in his old age?
We fear that prosperity acted unfavourably on his heart.

Is prosperity less favourable generally than persecution to a life of faith?
It **hath often** been found so.

And why should peace and prosperity be **less** favourable than persecution to the life of faith?
It is only because the heart of man is prone to self-dependence and self-pleasing. Prosperity furnishes opportunity for the development of this tendency, while persecution represses and controls it.

How then should the prosperous and the peace-enjoying **feel** in the midst of their comforts and privileges?
Very jealous over their spirits, lest they be found taking the credit of their prosperity to themselves, and assuming

at the same time the burden and the responsibility of their own safety.

How does Asa stand as a type of the **true** King of Israel?

He reversed the order of excellence, **and** thereby fell short of the honour; he began well, but ended unworthily; whereas true goodness grows better and better.

What is the truth concerning the crowning Son of David in this respect?

His path is that of the just; it shone more and more **unto the** perfect day. His crucifixion but gave occasion for **its** richer and fuller display.

And what is the fact concerning His true disciples and followers, generally speaking?

They go from strength still onward unto strength.

But does the divine life in the heart of the believer not **admit** of retrogression?

Not permanent or final. He who begins this good work will carry it on to the day of Christ.

What **then** ought to be the appropriate desire and aim of every true Christian?

To grow in grace, and in **Christian** knowledge and experience.

And how is it with those who thus grow **in** grace and Christian experience in relation to human policy **or** creature-dependence?

They become more and more estranged from these, **and** more and more fraught with the divine. Instead of descending to the earth with Asa, they ascend to **the heav**enly with the triumphant and the immortal.

What, in few words, **are** the lessons which the reign of **Asa** teaches?

That prosperity is not the **natural ally of** piety.

That continued prosperity **is dangerous to** natures that are **not yet** perfect,—and

That true excellence is necessarily progressive.

IV. JEHOSHAPHAT.

And the Lord was with Jehoshaphat, because he walked in the first ways of his father, David, and sought not unto Baalim: but sought to the Lord God of his father, and walked in His commandments, and not after the doings of Israel. Therefore the Lord established the kingdom in his hand; and all Judah brought to Jehoshaphat presents; and he had riches and honour in abundance. And his heart was lifted up in the ways of the Lord. II. Chronicles, xvii. 3-6.

ASA sets in gloom: Jehoshaphat, his son, rises in splendour. There is no hesitancy or uncertainty in the decisions of the youthful King. He has no affinity with Baalim: he gives himself wholly to the Lord God of his fathers. He walks in the first ways of David, and his heart is lifted up in the ways of the Lord. There is elasticity in his piety, and buoyant gladness. While others grope in wrong ways, or go heavily in right ones, Jehoshaphat soars upward with wings as an eagle, and bears rejoicingly onward toward the faultless and the true. We wonder at the sound of his wings, and at the grace of Heaven bestowed upon him. "The Lord established his kingdom: All Judah brought him presents, he had riches and honour in abundance, and his heart was lifted up in the ways of the Lord."

This was a noble beginning: And O, but it had been well if his circumspection had been equal to his zeal. Had he been as careful to shelter his family from evil influences as he was anxious to have his subjects instructed in the divine law, the fortunes of his house and of his kingdom would have been very different from what they were. He failed, as we shall see, in strict attention to that very law which he was so earnest to have promulgated throughout his dominions, and thus allowed Samaria to conquer Judah in a way that **brought** utter confusion on his family as well as on his realm. What Jeroboam could not do with eight hundred thousand men, that Ahab did with one fascinating daughter!

It is difficult to hit the medium between absolute estrangement from the ungodly and a too great intimacy with them: and here it was that Jehoshaphat's wisdom failed him. Because he had ceased to contend with Samaria in arms, there was no need for his rushing into the closest possible alliance with the idolatrous house that reigned there. He might have maintained unhostile relations with Ahab, without identifying himself with that monarch. This he did not do; and bitter were the results. Had he attended to divine direction it would have been otherwise: but, like Solomon before him, he overlooked or disguarded the express command of God—in the person of his son if not in his own.

How impressively we are taught by such instances the importance of adhering to the divine law. Pity that men will not learn wisdom, nor abide by orders. If such men as Jehoshaphat and Solomon erred by such oversight, what may be expected from less enlightened and less devoted men?

In noticing more particularly the story of Jehoshaphat, we shall call your attention to—his solicitude in peace—his refuge in trouble—and his weakness and want of discrimination in the matter of character and companionship.

I. His solicitude in peace.

That was the enlightenment and piety of his subjects. He did not neglect subordinate matters. He cared for defence, and was active in matters of improvement and larger social accommodations. "He strengthened himself against Israel, and he placed forces in all the fenced cities of Judah, and set garrisons in the land of Judah and in the cities of Ephraim." Besides, "he built in Judah castles, and cities of stone; and he had much business in the cities of Judah." He neglected nothing which a prudent ruler generally attends to, with a view to the safety and well-being of his subjects; but he did not rest in material good. He aimed at something higher at the same time. He wished, along with the safety of his subjects, for their enlightenment: and he sought, together with social improvement, the more general recognition on the part of the people of the laws and claims of God. With this view, he appointed a commission to perambulate the country under his sway, and to teach everywhere the people concerning and out of the law of the Lord:—

> "In the third year of his reign he sent to his princes, even to Ben-hail, and to Obadiah, and to Zechariah, and to Nathaneel, and to Michaiah, to teach in the cities of Judah. And with them he sent Levites, even Shemaiah, and Nathaniah, and Zebadiah, and Asahel, and Shemiramoth, and Jehonathan, and Adonijah, and Tobijah, and Tob-adonijah, Levites: and with them Elisham and Jehoram, priests. And they taught in Judah, and had the book of the Lord with them, and went about throughout all the cities of Judah, and taught the people."—7-9.

Now, this was at once, wise, becoming, and most seasonable at the time.

It was *wise*—even though he sought nothing higher than the unity and coherence of his kingdom. To teach the people the law of the Lord was to teach them at the same time their own miraculous history as a nation. The law was given by Moses, and given to them as the descendants of Abraham. Moses brought their fathers out of Egypt, and to Mount Sinai, that they might receive it. Moses led them through the wilderness besides, and by a pillar of cloud and fire, and prepared the way for Joshua who settled them in Canaan. And Moses had left a promise of another prophet to arise among them like unto himself—only more potent and more glorious—who should give a higher freedom, and conduct to a purer inheritance. Now, what more suited to inspire patriotism and national sentiment than to be reminded of these things? God had not dealt so with any other people. Their history had been peculiar and illustrious, and the knowledge and remembrance of this was fitted to keep them true to their national institutions, and to prevent their mingling themselves up with the less honoured nations around them. The more clearly they saw the peculiarities of their law and their national history, and the more fully they apprehended the claims of Him who had chosen and watched over them, the more likely were they to abide by their national standards. In short, to teach them the law was to bind them to the Temple at Jerusalem; and to bind them to the Temple at Jerusalem was to bind them to the throne of David, now occupied by Jehoshaphat himself. It was wise then in him to teach the people the law. And there was the more need for it, since the ten neighbouring and revolted tribes were now far gone in approximation to heathenism. Already Ahab had brought Jezebel to Samaria, and with her the wickedness of Baal-worship. What more likely than that the errors of the conterminous Israelites might infect the men of Judah? What more likely than that the subjects of Jehoshaphat might intermarry and have intercommunion with the subjects of Ahab, and thus the Temple-services would be forsaken, and the throne of Jehoshaphat proportionally weakened? We know how easy it is for the privileged to forget their privileges, and to yield themselves to the debasements of the ungodly and idolatrous. Nay, we know, that this process is inevitable if there be not watchfulness and earnest adherence to the truth. Was it not wise then, even on the score of policy, that Jehoshaphat should cause his subjects to be instructed in the law of the Lord. This indeed was better far than all material defences. It was his most potent weapon against the inroads of the ten tribes. Had he neglected this, and allowed his people to forget the law of the Lord, the errors of Israel under Ahab would have subdued Judah more effectually than many armies. The possession of the law of the Lord was the grand distinction of his government, and the knowledge of that law by his people, and their enlightened obedience to it, was his best security for their unity, and loyalty, and fidelity. It was wise in Jehoshaphat therefore, to send commissioners through all his territory to teach and to enforce their natural peculiarities. Without neglecting the material defences of his kingdom, its best defence was the general knowledge and reception of the law of the Lord. But, even apart from policy—

It was *becoming* in Jehoshaphat to cause the law of the Lord to be taught to his subjects. His people were a sacred people, and his throne was a sacred throne. His people had been placed in Canaan that they might keep the law of the Lord, and he had been placed on the throne to see that they kept the same law; or, at any rate, to see that they had an opportunity to know and keep it. It was his duty to banish and put down idolatrous shrines from and in his territory: and, when he did so, it was but meet that he should attend to the claims of God's law. It had been but imperfect service to remove the evil without bringing into prominence the good: and it had been to little purpose to do the one without doing the other as well. Without the good, the evil would have re-appeared forthwith in some new shape. When, therefore he took away the high places and the groves (as it is reported he did), it was only carrying out his important undertaking to send commissioners forth to testify concerning the claims of God's law, and to summon the people to the worship of the true God.

Besides, he thus became a true King of the house of David, and a type of the coming Prince in whom the glory of that house was to centre and remain. The divine Son of David, seated on the throne of David, and ruling over the house of Jacob forever, sends forth messengers and commissioners as it were for the enlightenment of the world. From age to age he renews these messengers, and, testifying by them of the grace of God, turns the attention of men anew and continually to the law of the Lord. He would turn men from iniquity: He would disenchant them of error; He would draw them around the true temple of the true God, and He would thus deliver them from the evils of estrangement from heaven, and secure for them the delights and the stabilities of the God-loved and the God-sheltered. And this is just what Jehoshaphat did in his day on the small and typical arena on which he moved. He thus foreshadowed, in so far, the great **Teacher** of **nations,** and the King **of** saints. He, like David and Solomon, **was** thus the type **of** Messiah—David by his victories, Solomon by his temple-building, **and** Jehoshaphat **by** his **labours** for the enlightenment **of the** people! It was becoming then, **on the part of** Jehoshaphat, both **as** a king of the sacred people, and **as a** prince of the typical house **of** David, **to** send **forth,** and throughout his kingdom, commissioners and agents, to teach the people the law of the Lord, and **to** enforce the claims of that law.

But it was *seasonable* **as** well :—Seasonable, **I say,** and **necessary** even, in the light of **the** reigns **that** preceded his. **These** preceding reigns had given great advantage **to error,** and the people had fallen back from the habits **and** usages of the **times of** David and the early years of **Solomon.** To say nothing of **the latter** years of Solomon, **we know that the** reign of **Rehoboam** was almost wholly **in favour of idolatry. So with** that of Abijah : and if **Asa's had** been **of a better** complexion, it was rather negatively good than positively so. He took **away the** Sodomites **out of** the land, and he brought **dedicated** things into the temple, but we hear of no positive **efforts** on his part at public instruction. The Levites, **no doubt,** had fallen from their duties as public **instructors** during **the** reigns of Rehoboam and Abijah, **and we** know not that Asa did anything **to** bring them **up** again to their appropriate service. The probability is, that they had **become** themselves unable to instruct the people in the **law of** the Lord. They had allowed that law to fall into forgetfulness—themselves **had** forgotten it—and Judah was in effect without instructors. It was needful therefore, specially needful, that Jehoshaphat **should** adopt **some** unusual means for the purpose of meeting the circumstances. Had the Levites, scattered through the territory, been competent **for** the **work, the** King would have found it enough **to** issue orders to these parties ; but because they were unable to meet the crisis, Jehoshaphat sent to his princes, or local governors, and ordered them to see to the work ; and having found some few Levites fitted for the undertaking, he sent them to assist in forwarding it. Had Rehoboam and Abijah, and Asa, kept the arrangements of heaven for the enlightenment of the people in working order, Jehoshaphat would not have needed to send forth this special commission ; but in the circumstances in which he found the people, this special commission was wholly seasonable and greatly necessary. Like Asa his father, he might have been content with negative fidelity, but, more zealous and more enlightened than he, he wished to bring his people up again **to an** enlightened and intelligent service.

Thus truly did Jehoshaphat show his estimate and understanding of **his** position, and manifest his zeal for God, and for the good of his people. He adopted the very best antidote against apostacy and idolatry—evils now abounding among the **ten** tribes, and not unknown we fear even in Judah. He exhibited also, wittingly or unwittingly, a new phase **of the** coming Messiah's reign. And further, he took the right method for repairing the evils of the reigns that immediately preceded his own. He wisely considered, not only that the **law** of the Lord was what his kingdom needed, but that also **a** time **of** peace was **the** time to bring the people of Judah to their normal **state as** the depositaries of divine truth. Half-hearted and thoughtless men often defer needed reforms or necessary labours while all is quiet around them—requiring the stimulus of danger to drive them to duty, and then not unfrequently performing that duty imperfectly, or falling from it altogether, because of increasing difficulties. Not so with Jehoshaphat : he set about the needed instruction forthwith, and diligently employed the years of peace afforded him in promoting the enlightenment of his subjects.

Jehoshaphat was right in this, and God gave tokens of His approbation of the course pursued. The peace which he so wisely improved was enlarged and prolonged. His neighbours, instead of invading or distressing him, sent

presents and tokens of good-will; and he grew great and **esteemed. Thus** it is said, immediately after the notice of his arrangements for the enlightenment of his people, "the **fear** of the Lord fell upon all **the** kingdoms of the lands **that** were round about Judah, **so** that they **made** no war **against** Jehoshaphat. Also, some of the Philistines **brought** presents **and** tribute silver. And **the** Arabians **brought** him flocks—seven thousand and seven hundred rams, and seven thousand and **seven** hundred he-goats; and Jehoshaphat waxed great exceedingly." You see that, while seeking the enlightenment of his subjects, he grew in honour and celebrity; and **while wisely** using a time of peace, that peace was extended and made pleasant by tokens of good will **and** friendship from his neighbours.

Then, we have further evidence of his wise devotedness **to the** true interests of **Israel** in a subsequent portion **of his life and reign.** Not content with sending agents **to instruct the people, he** went himself through the land—using his influence as **King** wherever he went in favour of the true worship. **It is** said that "he went through the people **from** Beersheba **to** Mount Ephraim, and brought them **back** unto the Lord God of **their** fathers." No doubt he had reports from the various localities, and was grieved to understand that, **spite** of the mission of instruction, many still **wandered, and** showed preference for the rites of heathenism. **In** these circumstances he determined to use his personal and royal influence **in the matter:** and, by the way, what he **had seen** in the kingdom of Israel while visiting and **acting** with Ahab probably strengthened this determination. He accordingly made a royal progress from South to North; not to dazzle his subjects, nor yet to enjoy the manifestations of their loyalty, but **to** bring them back **to** the true God. There was something admirable in this. **It** was so unlike kings generally: and it manifested so much zeal and becoming devotedness!

But this was not all: Jehoshaphat, knowing that the influence of **a royal** progress might only be temporary, and that the people, however ready to please him during his short visit, might again fall back to foolish customs after his departure, made permanent arrangements for the well-being and enlightenment of the land. He **set** judges in each city, and gave them special injunctions as to their administration, urging upon them **the** claims and the righteousness **of God.** Hear his **words** :—"Take heed" (said he **to them**) "**what** ye do; **for ye** judge not **for** man, but for **the** Lord, who is with you **in** the judgment. Wherefore **now let** the fear of the Lord **be** upon you; take heed and do it: for there is no iniquity with the Lord our **God, nor** respect of persons, nor taking of gifts." "**Moreover,** in Jerusalem did Jehoshaphat set **of** the Levites, and of the priests, and of the chief of **the** fathers of Israel, for **the** judgment of the Lord, and for controversies, when they returned to Jerusalem. And he charged them, saying, Thus shall **ye** do in the fear of the Lord, faithfully, **and** with **a perfect heart.** And what cause soever shall **come to you of your brethren** that dwell in the cities, between **blood and blood,** between law and commandment, statutes **and** judgments, **ye shall** even **warn them** that they trespass not against **the Lord, and so** wrath come upon you, and **upon** your brethren; this do, **and ye** shall not trespass." (xix. 6-10.)

Thus **you** see the solicitudes and doings of Jehoshaphat when at leisure, and unharassed by external pressure or internal dissension. He sought neither *éclat* nor gratification for himself. His supreme solicitude and endeavour was in the interests of piety! And surely we may learn a lesson from this. We are not kings, but still we can have plans and solicitudes, each in his own **narrow** sphere; and no doubt we have. What then **is** the complexion of these plans and solicitudes? **Are** they for God? Are they in the interests of piety and enlightenment? Or, **are** they for our own aggrandizement, or worldly gratification? Let us be warned of mistake in this matter, **and** not sow to the perishing. He that soweth to the flesh shall reap corruption, while they that sow to the spirit shall reap life everlasting. We enjoy peace—we enjoy

ample privileges **as** well: let us improve both. If we cannot make royal progresses **in** the interests of piety, let us attend **to** the means of personal progress therein. Let **us review** and **re-embrace** the historical faith which we profess. **Let us review** and reconsider the ways of God towards **His** ancient people. While the world is eager **after the** remains **of** Grecian art, or amuse themselves **with mere** antiquities, let us earnestly remember the **interpositions** of God on behalf **of** Israel, and learn His **supremacy** and character as thereby displayed. And **let us** give our best thoughts to Immanuel—to His utterances, and promises, and benignant and miraculous works. It **is** by the knowledge of Him that **we are to** find God. Apart from Him, our studies and discoveries will be but refined trifling. We must follow on to know the Lord. **We must** seek to grow in grace, and in the knowledge of **our Lord** and Saviour Jesus Christ. We cannot improve our peace or leisure better. We **cannot** indeed improve our **peace** and **leisure aright** in **any** other way. And in this way **we** will **find good.** God will bless us in and for the sake **of** His Son. Our peace will **be** prolonged and extended. Our days, **too,** will become illuminated from on high. And **we** will thus become more and more fitted for the inevitable alternations of this changing life as well as for the occupations and happy experiences of the better land. It is foolish to neglect the opportunity which peace and health furnish. **It were** foolish to put off heavenly considerations and solicitudes until decay or danger overtakes us. Our disinclination will but increase by postponement; and our facilities for success will lessen in the same proportion. The time of peace is the time to prepare for danger. Besides, we should wish and endeavour to check surrounding and prevailing evil, and also to promote the enlightenment of others. But these ends can be best sought by improving, in the first instance, our personal piety. **A** half-enlightened and half-hearted disciple will have small influence either in checking evil or promoting good. They must themselves be enlightened, and decided, and devoted, who would effectually subserve the interests of heaven among men. Trifle not then with your privileges and opportunities. Betake yourselves to the law of the Lord. Give yourselves **to** the glorious gospel of the blessed God. Employ your quiet and opportunity in perfecting your discipleship. And thus you may enjoy the smile of the Holy, and be instrumental in checking and weakening the evil tendencies of the uninformed around you, and in strengthening the cause of the heavenly kingdom of **your** Lord, and in preparing yourself for the vicissitudes **and** trials **of** life, as well as for the exercises and enjoyments of the world of glory and **of** purity beyond! However humble your sphere, you may still imitate Jehoshaphat in your solicitudes and labours: you may employ your peace **for** Heaven, and not for self or for earth.

But to return to Jehoshaphat; having noticed his solicitude in Peace, we would now remind you of—

II. His refuge in Trouble.

And why should trouble arise to so excellent a prince? Because he had his weaknesses and inconsistencies, which we will notice immediately. In the meantime, think of his refuge, and dependence, and exercise, when evil arose and threatened to overwhelm him. His trouble was, a combination on the part of his enemies, and a hostile demonstration of an alarming character. And the question is, in what direction did he look, or how did he exercise himself in the appalling crisis? Did he collect his people, and **boast** to them of his mighty preparations and resources? Or did he seek to stimulate their patriotism, and **to** inspire them with confidence in his generalship and arrangements? Not **at** all. There **is** no mention on his part of his fenced cities, **nor** yet of the state of efficiency to which he had trained his warriors. What then? Did he hasten ambassadors to Syria, or **to** Samaria, to seek alliances to help him in the impending struggle? One wonders that he did not apply to Samaria at least—seeing that, but the year before, he had helped Ahab in his warlike operations. But there is no hint of any such movement. He trusts neither in his **own** resources nor in the resources of human allies. Neither does he betake himself to false divinities or superstitious rites. He neither offers **his** children to Moloch, nor **asks** aid or influence from **the** priests of Baal. The **truth is, he** looks upward. **He** betakes himself **to the God of** Israel—even to the **God whose** law **he was** so anxious to promulgate while yet in the enjoyment of peace and leisure. He remembers the mighty interpositions of that glorious One on behalf of his fathers, and he earnestly and humbly seeks sympathy and help in that direction. He engages his people to concur in his exercises and entreaties. He **not** only "set himself **to** seek the Lord," but "he proclaimed a fast throughout all **J**udah: and Judah gathered themselves together, **to ask** help of the Lord—even of all the cities of Judah **they** came to seek the Lord." "And Jehoshaphat **stood in the** congregation **of** Judah and Jerusalem, in **the house of the** Lord, **before the new court.**" And **mark how** humble, **how enlightened, and how devout,** his **prayer was.** He said:—

> "O Lord **God of our** fathers, art not Thou God in heaven? and rulest not Thou **over** all the kingdoms of the heathen? and in Thine hand is there not power and might, so that none is able to withstand Thee? Art not Thou our God, who didst drive out the inhabitants of this land before Thy people Israel, and gavest it to the seed of Abraham Thy friend for ever? And they dwelt therein, and have built Thee a sanctuary therein for Thy name, saying, If, when evil cometh upon us, as the sword, judgment, or pestilence, or famine, we stand before this house, and in Thy presence, (for Thy name is in this house,) and cry unto Thee in our affliction, then Thou wilt hear and help. And now, behold, the children of Ammon and Moab and Mount Seir, whom Thou wouldst not let Israel invade, when they came out of the land of Egypt, but they turned from them, and destroyed them not: Behold, I say, how they reward us, to come to cast us out of Thy possession, which Thou hast given us to inherit. O our God, wilt Thou not judge them? For we have no might against this great company that cometh against **us**; neither know we what to do: but our eyes are upon Thee."

Such **was** Jehoshaphat in the exigence that had now arisen—as humble and devout in trouble as he had been active and zealous in peace. He was a true son of

David, and a man of prayer. Nor did he pray in vain. The God of Israel is the hearer and answerer of prayer, and Jehoshaphat was promptly and favourably answered. Upon Jahaziel, the son of Zachariah, came the spirit of the Lord in the midst of the congregation,—

> "And **he** said, Hearken ye, all Judah, and ye inhabitants of Jerusalem, and thou King Jehoshaphat, thus saith the Lord unto you, Be not afraid nor dismayed by reason of this great multitude; for the battle is not your's, but God's. To-morrow go ye down against them: behold, they come up by the cliff of Ziz: and ye shall find them at the end of the brook, before the wilderness of Jaruel. Ye shall not need to fight in this battle: set yourselves, stand ye still, and see the salvation of the Lord with you, O Judah and Jerusalem: fear not, nor be dismayed; tomorrow go out against them; for the Lord will be with you."

And the deliverance occurred accordingly—Jehoshaphat and his people went out against their enemies: they went out in faith, and with the **voice** of song and grateful worship. Weapons they **needed none,** for the advancing enemies became their own executioners. Ammon and Moab turned their swords against each other: and Jehoshaphat and **the** men **of** Judah, instead of sinking before their numerous foes, had only to gather the spoil of their slain enemies. And so great **was** the spoil to be gathered, of jewels and precious things, that it took them three days to gather it. "On the fourth day they assembled themselves in the valley of Berachah: for there they blessed the Lord: therefore the name of the same place was called the valley of Berachah unto this day." "And they came to Jerusalem with psaltery, and harps, **and** trumpets, unto the house of the Lord." They had **called on** God in trouble: God had delivered them: and they now glorified Him!

Here you will observe, **that** Jehoshaphat and his people, in this resort to God, were only acting out the proprieties of their position as Israelites. Only think how Jacob, the father of the tribes, **came** to be called Israel:—It was because of his urgency and success in prayer: "thy name (said the mysterious and divine visitor) shall be called no more Jacob, but Israel: for, as a prince hast thou power with God, and with men, and hast prevailed." And what is implied in the extension of this name to the descendants of Jacob if it be not, that they should all be men of prayer? The tribes of Israel means, the tribes of the prayerful—the tribes of the powerful in prayer—the tribes of God, having their strength and refuge with the Eternal—the tribes to whom God has drawn near, and whose privilege it is, to wrestle with Him in their distresses, and to find the deliverance or the shelter which they need! Thus Jehoshaphat and his subjects, as children of Israel, availed themselves of their privilege, and found the value and comfort of that privilege.

And still more particularly in the case of Jehoshaphat was it becoming in him to draw nigh to God in his trouble. He was a prince of the house of David, and God was specially in covenant with that house. He had undertaken to David, its founder, to have a special regard to its interests, and to reveal His own glory and loving resources in connexion with it. He had constituted Himself the Friend, the Ally, the Helper, and the Refuge, of all the faithful members of that family: "I have made a covenant with My chosen, (said the Holy One of Israel,) I have sworn unto David, my servant,— thy seed will I establish for ever, and build up thy throne to all generations." What then could be more proper or becoming in Jehoshaphat than to betake himself in his distress to the Almighty and Covenant-Friend of his house? It was the duty as well as the privilege of his family. David himself perpetually availed himself of the privilege, and he sung of it as well: "God is our refuge and strength, (said he,) a very present help in trouble!" Solomon again made a beautiful and comprehensive use of the privilege at the dedication of the Temple. Asa, the father of Jehoshaphat, in his turn, used the privilege to purpose. And Hezekiah, in subsequent years, found the privilege still available and undiminished in value. Rehoboam did not avail himself of it when Shishak came up against him, and took away all the treasures of the Temple; and Rehoboam failed to find deliverance. And so with others of the sacred royal family: but they only fell from the privileges and duties of the sacred dynasty, and found overthrow or captivity in consequence. Jehoshaphat, on the other hand, availed himself of the privilege, and enjoyed a signal and memorable deliverance by the grace of the Hearer and Answerer of Prayer.

And need I remind you that it is still thus with the spiritual Israel, and with the royal association of the divine David. *God is their refuge.* God hath drawn nigh to them in the form of humanity, and thus given them an opportunity to wrestle with Him in their hours of darkness and danger, as He did to Jacob of old. He hath come as it were within the sphere of their consciousness and agency. He hath made it possible for them to lay hold of His robe—to detain Him, if I may speak so, until they pour all their plaints into His ear. Had He remained in His own and original sphere of spirituality and Infinitude, they could neither have found Him, nor detained Him, nor refused to let Him go until He blessed them: but, by the incarnation of His Son, He hath condescended to become cognizable, acceptable, detainable, and impressible by urgency and felt need. To the unbelieving, who by the way are not of Israel, He is still hidden, inaccessible, and intangible; but to the believing, who constitute the spiritual Israel, He is ever near and approachable. Holding by His living robe, even by His incarnate Son, they can tell their troubles, or their terrors, and find the sympathy or the deliverance they need: "God is a refuge for them, a very present help in trouble." Their enemies may be mighty, but they have a mightier friend. Their weakness may be great, but they have an adequate support. The floods may descend, and the winds may blow, but their Refuge can neither be invaded nor swept away. More particularly still, they belong to the royal house of the divine David—the Beloved of the Eternal: and God hath made a covenant with their great Representative and **Chief: and** they are included **in** that covenant. That covenant is ordered in all things, and sure: and it is their privilege, **on the** foundation **of** that covenant, to draw nigh **to** God **with** acceptance, to shelter beneath the outstretched wings of Omnipotence, and to rejoice in the unchanging **love of** their Eternal Father. If they are subjected **to alarm or trouble** in the meantime, it is **only to** subserve important ends, **not to** jeopardize their **safety.** They have but to betake themselves to their covenant-God and Father in Christ, **and** their security is assured, aye, and their ultimate **victory as** well. God is their Refuge, the Invisible, the **Invulnerable,** is their defence: the All-possessing and All-condescending is their **portion and joy!**

And prayer is the exercise by which they avail them**selves of their divine** privilege: and daily they give them**selves to it. They** cannot live without it, and their **standing** orders **are in** accordance **w**ith the necessities of their **being.** They are directed **to pray** without ceasing. They are permitted to ask what they **will:** and they are assured that their prayers shall not go unregarded or unanswered: "Ask in my name, (says their divine chief,) and it shall **be done** unto you!" If Jehoshaphat was heard as a son of the covenanted house of David, far more will the believer in Jesus **be** heard as **a** living branch of the True Vine—as **a** loving **and** loved member in **the** mystical body of the Redeemer. And not in trouble **only, but** in all things, these believing ones can **have and enjoy** the sympathy and the grace of the **divine.** God takes pleasure in them that fear Him, in them that hope in His mercy: and He will dwell with them, and walk with them: and they shall be numbered with His people, and He will be their God, and their perpetual delight. O, but they are honoured people who belong to the spiritual Israel, whose life and habit is intercourse with God by prayer! And **O,** but they are a loved people who adhere to the covenant of the divine David, and plead the promises of that covenant continually!

Are you sufficiently aware of your privilege and **duty** herein (I speak to the New Testament members **of the** house of David). You see the happiness of Jehoshaphat **as a** son of the prayerful. You see his happiness too as a member of the sacred, royal, covenanted house of David. God interposes for him. **God** hears his prayer, scatters **his** enemies, fills him with joy, **and** enriches him and his concurring subjects with spoil ! **Are** you, **as the pro**fessed members of the spiritual Israel, and the **followers** and represented ones of the Beloved Mediator, are you using, improving, and enjoying your privilege of access **and** communion **with** the Eternal ? Are you laying hold of His robe daily, and urging your wants upon His attention continually ? You need **to** do **it**. Your spiritual adversaries are mighty and subtle. You cannot yourself conquer them. Nay, you cannot stand before them. Jehoshaphat could not have resisted the combined forces of Ammon, and Moab, and Seir : far **less** will you be able **to** resist the principalities and powers **of** evil—the rulers of the darkness of this world. Without God, you are certain to be overthrown ! Without Christ, you are lost ! Rejoice then that God **is** accessible **in** Christ, and **be** sure that you avail yourselves of His accessibility. **Be** not slow to betake yourselves **to the** divine refuge, **nor** infrequent in your resort to it. Pray without **ceasing** ! You never know what combinations your spiritual adversaries **are** forming against you. You never know when, **or** how keenly, they may assail you. Pray always **then.** And pray that God Himself may undertake for **you,** and stand by **you,** that you may not be greatly moved. The time **will** come **when** the Israel of God shall be able to lay aside **its** solicitude, and give itself to unfearing and untroubled service : but in the meantime it cannot afford to be unwakeful or unprepared. So long as any number of its members **are** in the enemies' territory, so long as they tabernacle where the god of darkness hath power and opportunity against them,—so long they need to be circumspect,—so long they need to watch against temptation,—so long they need to pray with all prayer **and** persistent supplication, that God would stand by **them,** defend them, and deliver them!

But **to return** to Jehoshaphat, we find **in** him warning as well as encouragement and instruction. If we are taught by his solicitude in peace, and incited **by** his refuge in trouble, **we are** also warned **of** our danger by **his** inconsistencies **and mistakes.** This leads me **to** notice,—

III. His weakness and want of discrimination in the matter of character and companionship.

He joined affinity **with Ahab! Only** think of it—Jehoshaphat joined affinity with Ahab! His prosperity **was such as** to make an alliance with his family desirable **in the eyes** of Jezebel and her husband: for **he** had **"riches and honour in** abundance." **And** they had no **scruples to prevent.** Neither **it would** seem had Jehoshaphat, **at** least, **we hear** of **none.** And Athaliah, **the** daughter of idolators, **and** trained herself in idolatry, **was** brought to **Jerusalem** (no doubt with all suitable demonstrations **and** display) **to be** the bosom companion and **counsellor** of **the** son **of** Jehoshaphat, and the heir **to** the sacred throne of David. How outrageous **the** thought! How **it** was brought about does **not** appear. **The** fact however **is** certain. Jehoram married Athaliah. **As a** matter **of course,** after **this union,** Jehoshaphat visited **Ahab at his** capital, and **enjoyed his** hospitality. **The idolatrous character** of the **court of** Samaria, and **the idolatrous rites** associated with its festivities and entertainments, seem **to** have given **him** no uneasiness. He was all smiles and ready compliance in the midst of those who had renounced the God of Israel, and yielded themselves to a hostile and degrading service. It is almost incredible; Jehoshaphat, who had prepared **his** heart to seek the Lord, and who was so zealous for **the** instruction and piety of his people, this same Jehoshaphat mingling **in** the festivities of the court of Ahab and Jezebel without scruple and without protest! But even this is not all. Ahab is involved in **war, and** what does Jehoshaphat do but identify himself and his people with Ahab and his people. When asked to assist in the war, his immediate answer is, "I am as thou art; and my people as thy people; and we will be with thee in the war." Nay, still farther, when Ahab's idolatrous prophets said one thing, and a true prophet said the contrary, Jehoshaphat actually yielded to the false and disregarded the true! Foolish and infatuated Jehoshaphat, we would say!

How are we to explain all this inconsistency? I can see no other explanation of it but either *extreme weakness* or *unworthy policy*. It was not for want of zeal for God, for he was zealous; nor could it be for want of knowledge, for he knew the law. He who was so anxious for the instruction of his people in the law of the Lord, no doubt himself read that law. And he must have known that idolatrous marriages for the sons and daughters of the sacred people, and idolatrous convivialities, and idolatrous alliances, were wholly against the mind and will of God. Why then did he act so? It might be as a matter of policy. He might fancy that thereby he would bring back to his family the ten revolted tribes. He might suppose that the two houses of Samaria and Jerusalem being once united in marriage, the chapter of accidents, or the providence of God, would remove any remaining obstacles to the reunion of the tribes. And the thought was good enough. It was desirable, so far as human views went, that the tribes should be re-united, but how could he think to gain a right end by disobedience, or by improper means? If he did, he was most childish and mistaken in his views. The means must be in harmony with the end, if a good end is to be truly and satisfactorily gained. But we do not think this is the explanation of Jehoshaphat's very foolish and inconsistent conduct. We rather attribute that conduct to weakness, and what the world would call " amiable yielding." We do not suppose that he himself made overtures for Athaliah for his son; but that, pressed by the Prince, or by some of his less scrupulous counsellors, or by circumstances which are not explained, he yielded a reluctant consent. He did not like to say No: at least, not to persist in saying it. And his visit to Samaria, we think, arose from the same weakness. He knew that Ahab's court was idolatrous and heathenish, but being pressed by friendly invitations, he did not like to refuse; at least, not to persist in doing so. Some years elapsed after Jehoram's wedding before Jehoshaphat accepted the invitations of Ahab and Jezebel, (which shows that he was not very cordial in the alliance,) but, once at Samaria, he could not find in his heart to dissent from, or absent himself from, their festal rejoicings—especially when got up for his entertainment. And finally, after all the attention he had received from Ahab and his queen, he could not refuse to help against Syria. At each onward step, he felt that he could not gracefully or politely say, No; and thus he was drawn into full concurrence and apparent identity with the ungodly and idolatrous. He knew the right, but he was drawn step by step into a position which he ought never to have occupied, by influences which he could not, with his facile and friendly disposition, find it in his heart to resist. There was no reason why he should have been unfriendly to Ahab, but there was just as little reason why he should have identified himself with the court and policy of that prince. If he avoided the fault of Rehoboam, who was at war with the ten tribes all the years of his reign, he did not need to have gone to the other extreme, by throwing himself into the arms of Ahab, but he had not courage to resist the human and proximate influences that drew him.

I need scarcely remind you of the consequences of this fatal weakness on the part of Jehoshaphat. In the first instance, he almost lost his life at Ramoth-Gilead, when taken for the crafty and disguised Ahab. Then, he met with divine denunciation: for Jehu, the son of Hanani, met him on his return to Jerusalem, and said, "Shouldest thou help the ungodly, and love them that hate the Lord? Therefore is wrath upon thee from before the Lord!" And then followed the invasion by the Ammonites, the

Moabites, and the men of **Mount Seir.** **His** national peace was broken; and his domestic peace as well, **no** doubt, by the presence and influence of Athaliah in Jerusalem. And then, he was **no** sooner laid in the grave, than his sons were slain by Jehoram, **and** his kingdom conformed to the heathenism of Samaria; and eventually his dynasty was all **but** ruined, by **the** daughter of Jezebel. But for **the** Divine purpose in **the** House of David, indeed, the sacred family had been utterly extinguished! O, if Jehoshaphat could have anticipated the consequences of **his** disobedience and fatal weakness, he would **have** been pained beyond utterance and beyond thought!

And why should **we** not learn wisdom **by** his mistakes? Let us beware how we yield **to** an aggressive and plausible world. Let **us** beware how **we** "help **the ungodly, or** love them that **hate** the **Lord!"** Let us **beware how we** ally ourselves with the idolatrous and unchristian! **We** need not be unfriendly, but we may decline uncongenial alliances with the God-dishonouring. In all ages, such alliances have been in favour of evil and not of good. Let us remember the sanctities of the spiritual Israel, to which we profess to belong, and let us abide in them! Especially let us remember, that the people of the divine David are meant to be prayerful, consecrated and pure; and let us avoid all companionships **and** alliances inimical to such consecration!

QUESTIONS ON JEHOSHAPHAT.

What was the chief solicitude of this Prince while his kingdom enjoyed peace?
  The enlightenment and religious improvement of his people.
What step did he take with this view?
  He appointed a commission to travel through the country, teaching the people in its progress out of and concerning the law of the Lord.
How must this commission be regarded?
  As wise, becoming, and seasonable—*wise*, because such a proceeding was calculated to promote national unity, and

also national purity and preservation—*becoming*, because the very object of the dynasty to which Jehoshaphat belonged was to keep the people true to the law and the worship of God;—and *seasonable*, because during the reigns immediately preceding, the knowledge of Israel's peculiar history and ritual had been allowed, to some considerable extent, to fall out of sight.

Did this commission of Jehoshaphat's foreshadow anything **in** the administration of the Divine Son of David?

Yes, certainly; it foreshadowed on a small scale the gospel commission: "Go: teach all nations, baptising them in the name of the divine."

Did God give any token of approbation of this labour and solicitude **on** the part of Jehoshaphat?

Yes; He confirmed and extended the peace of the kingdom, so that Philistines, Arabians, and all other neighbouring peoples, looked with friendly eyes on his greatness.

What **further step did Jehoshaphat take in the same direction?**

He made, himself, a royal progress through his kingdom, to aid in bringing back the people to the God of their fathers.

And what further did he do with **a view to** give permanence and extension to the work?

He set judges in each city, and gave them special injunctions to act and to decide causes in righteousness and truth.

How may we, as private individuals **imitate** Jehoshaphat in this matter?

By using a time of peace, especially the **season of** untroubled **you**th, in the interests of piety.

And how can we do that effectually?

By giving earnest and persistent attention to the utterances, promises, operations, and mediatorial achievements of Immanuel.

What favouring kindnesses may they expect who give themselves to this course?

Peace, heavenly illumination, and strength for the task of life.

And what social influence **will** they **exert** who walk so, and **are** favoured so?

They will help in some degree to hold evil in check, and they will contribute at the same time somewhat to the enlightenment of others.

JEHOSHAPHAT.

How did Jehoshaphat conduct himself when troubled by the invasion of numerous enemies?

In a manner most exemplary and devout; he trusted not to his own defences, and he sought no human alliances, but turned earnestly to the God of Israel.

Did he make any public appeal to God?

Yes: he proclaimed a fast, gathered his subjects together, and professed in the midst of them, and in their name, his utter helplessness and his earnest hope in God.

Did God take any notice of his prayer, or send him any encouragement?

Yes; Jahaziel assured him that God accepted the battle as His own, and desired His trusting people to dismiss all anxiety in the matter.

How did God then turn their trouble into triumph?

By bringing it about so that their enemies destroyed each other, while Israel had but to gather the spoil.

And how, after three days employed in gathering the spoil, did Jehoshaphat and his people exercise themselves?

In public and united thanksgiving in the valley of Bereshah. This grateful duty discharged, they came to Jerusalem, and to the House of God.

In what manner did they come?

With psaltery, and harps, and trumpets.

What was there appropriate in the men of Judah betaking themselves to God in prayer when their enemies pressed?

They were then acting in character as "the children of Israel." Jacob was called Israel because of his power in prayer, and they on whom the name descended justified in this manner the designation as applied to them.

What special propriety was there in Jehoshaphat's betaking himself to God in trouble?

He was a Prince of the House of David, and God was specially in covenant with that house.

What is the privilege of believers now, in this respect?

God hath placed Himself, if we may speak so, within their reach by the incarnation, and He hath also made a covenant with them in their great Representative, so that they can now find divine refuge, and sympathy in all their perplexities.

And what is that exercise by which they avail themselves of God's condescension and covenant?

Prayer.

What renders prayer a constant necessity for the faithful **in** this life?

The number and vigilance of their spiritual enemies. Like Jehoshaphat, the believing are helpless in themselves: and besides they never know what subtle and dangerous combinations their enemies may be forming against them.

What, in these circumstances, is the direction of the Apostle to his fellow believers?

"Pray without ceasing."

What was the great and ruinous fault of this excellent prince?

He joined affinity with Ahab by marrying his son to Ahab's daughter.

How was this brought about?

It is not said; only the alliance was **made.**

Did Jehoshaphat identify himself in **any** other **way with** Ahab?

Yes; he joined him in war.

Can you suggest any **way** of accounting for **this inconsistency** on the part of Jehoshaphat?

It might be weakness, or it might be policy.

What could policy purpose by it?

The possible re-annexation of the **ten** tribes to the House of David.

But what is the more probable account of the matter?

The inability of Jehoshaphat **to** say No, and to abide by it, when pressed by apparently friendly and persistent influence.

Did God resent this unworthy weakness **on the part of His** servant?

Yes: **a** prophet met him **on** his return to Jerusalem from the war, with this message, "Shouldst thou help the ungodly, and love them that hate the Lord? Therefore **is** wrath upon thee from the Lord!"

What warning does this furnish to us?

We should hold firmly by divine directions, even in the face of an aggressive and plausible world. Better offend the human than incur the anger of the Divine.

What, in few words are the lessons to be learnt from **this** reign?

The right way of improving a time of peace and leisure;

The wisdom of trusting in the Lord alone when trouble overtakes us; and

The folly and danger of allowing ourselves to be turned from the divine directions, either by policy or by persuasion.

VII. JEHORAM.

Now Jehoshaphat slept with his fathers, and was buried with his fathers in the city of David : and Jehoram his son reigned in his stead.—II. Chronicles xxi. 1.

THIS Prince reminds us of Charles I. **of** England. There is **a** remarkable similarity in many points of their history. They both had weak fathers; they both made splendid marriages; they both came into collision with their subjects; they both had undesirable ends; and they both forfeited in effect their thrones, not only for **themselves, but** also for their descendants.

As to the first point of resemblance, **we** would not for one moment put the father of Jehoram **on a** level with the father of Charles, only they **were** both **weak. As** to the second point, the analogy is striking, their respective brides **were** both of royal lineage—both the daughters of kings greater than their bridegrooms—both the daughters of Apostates, (the one from Judaism, the other from Protestantism),—both the disciples and advocates of a perverted religion—**and** both in earnest sympathy with the centre of wealth and power in their respective generations, (the one with Tyre, a proud and idolatrous city, the other with Rome, a not less proud and a scarcely less idolatrous community.) As to the third point, they were both worsted and disappointed in their contests with their subjects. As to the fourth point, their deaths were diverse, but both disastrous. Charles was beheaded by his subjects, who could **not** trust him, while Jehoram died of terrible diseases, and "departed without being desired." And as to the last point, Charles' sons were certainly brought back to the throne, but only to be expelled again with greater ignominy; while Jehoram's were in effect completely extinguished. True, an infant of his family was spared, but that was because of David, and not because of its immediate father. That father had renounced the covenant, and forfeited the throne for himself, and for all his descendants so far as he had the power. If the family of David revived, it was for reasons wholly apart from Jehoram.

Charles, we willingly admit, was a much better man than Jehoram, even as Jehoshaphat was a much better man than James. Still, the fortunes of Charles and those of Jehoram were singularly alike; and the resemblance is the more to be noted, when we perceive that the overthrow of both may be traced in a very great degree to the same cause. To this cause, so far as Jehoram is concerned, we will again advert. In the meantime we will notice, *First,*—The favourable conditions of his youth for a righteous and happy history: *Second,*—His miserable and wicked reign: and then *Third,*—A word on that cause of his ruin of which we have just hinted.

I. The favourable conditions of his youth for a righteous and happy history.

Many men have, what is called, a very unfavourable start in life. They are born under the reign of superstition, or in the midst of ignorance. Their parents are careless, immoral, or incompetent. They are not taught to attach importance to the right, nor warned of the dangers of the wrong. They mingle with unscrupulous society, where false maxims and false principles have currency, and they often learn to hate and to shun, from their very infancy, the persons and things that would be most conducive to their well-being. We cannot wonder if such persons go wrong. We cannot wonder if they continue to pursue a course of evil, terminating in destruction. We may pity them, but we cannot judge them harshly; we must leave them to the judgment of God. He, the Omniscient, the Righteous, the Merciful, will determine rightly their demerits and their fortunes. It is true, they ought, as reason gathers strength within them, and as conscience begins to testify against evil courses—especially if the light of revelation is accessible, they ought, I say, to take heed, **and** to inquire after **the way** of righteousness and safety ; but then, evil principles **and** ruinous prejudices have obtained such **a** hold of their **nature** while they were yet young and unsuspicious, **that we really** cannot wonder **that** they do **not** cease **to do evil and learn to do** well. They are the slaves of **evil** circumstances, in connexion with inherent evil tendencies, and, so far as their fellows are concerned, they are entitled to pity as well as to blame. O, how many of our fellow-men are thus—the evil within them is fostered, and developed, and intensified, by the evil without and around them. There is everything in their companionships and habits to mislead and bewilder them, and nothing to enlighten or guide them. Evil presses—good is unknown or maligned—and they seize or pursue that which only degrades or ruins them. It is thus in all heathen nations ; and it is thus even in professedly Christian nations, where the light of God's word is systematically withheld from the people. Aye, and it is thus in families, even where God's word is accessible, when that word ·is habitually neglected **or set** aside. Alas for the young, whose start in this important life of earth is so shrouded and so inauspicious !

But it was not thus with Jehoram, the son of Jehoshaphat. The circumstances of his early life were not unfavourable **to** his making a right choice and pursuing a wise course. The very contrary was the fact. He had every external inducement and assistance in the direction of the right that any one could wish. He knew the right, and his circumstances were not only favourable for entering upon it, and pursuing it, but were all but irresistible in pressing him unto it.

Notice some of the circumstances :—

First.—His father was a good man. His father not only did that which was right in the eyes of the Lord, but, it is **said,** the Lord was with him, and his heart was lifted up in the ways of the Lord. And he laboured for the enlightenment of his people. He sent commissioners through his territory to teach the law of the Lord. Nay, he went himself from Beersheba to Mount Ephraim, to bring back the people to the God of their fathers. While other kings make royal progresses through their kingdoms to display their grandeur, or for political purposes, Jehoshaphat went through his kingdom as a missionary from Heaven—prepared to use his royal influence in the interests of the God of Israel. And the conduct on the part of the king decided, for the time being, the complexion of society in Judah. Now, Jehoram was a youth then, and what more natural than that he should take impression from the character of his father, and from the fashion of his father's court? Was it anything other than might be expected, if he gave attention to the law of the Lord so earnestly urged upon the attention of the nation? The children of the contemporary court of Ahab and Jezebel gave favourable attention to the rites and practices countenanced by their parents. Why then should not Jehoram give favourable attention to the rites and written laws countenanced by his father? A youth's course or convictions, we know, are not to be overborne by the faith of his parent; but the faith of a parent is entitled to examination because it is the faith of a parent; and if, on examination, it be found in accordance with right and righteousness, it becomes only the more obligatory for being the faith of a parent. The son of Ahab might, with reason, have dissented from the religion of his father had he been better informed; but the son of Jehoshaphat could not rightly dissent from the religion of his father, because no information could make it false. It was amply authenticated, and had been over and over again vindicated against all rival or opposing claims. Jehoram, therefore, was not swayed in the right direction by the faith of his father, and by the fashion of his father's court, but he was also under obligation to adopt a religion so recommended and so vindicated. But—

Secondly.—This Prince belonged to a sacred and favoured nation. The ancestors of his people had been specially cared for, specially delivered,—specially watched over, and specially located. The Mighty One that claimed their allegiance, and that had interposed so effectually on their behalf, had shown and evidenced His divine and supreme excellences over and over again in their history. He had made it evident, that there was no power or authority like to His power and authority—that, in short, He was the true and only living God, who made the heavens and the earth, and who sustained and controlled all things. And this Jehoram knew. The knowledge of the law which he certainly possessed involved the knowledge of God's interpositions on behalf of His people :— for that law was set, as it were, in a historic frame, and could be studied and known only in connexion with the miraculous and gracious history of which it formed a part. Yes, Jehoram knew that there was no God like to the God of Israel, and this knowledge bound him to the service of that God. Obedience is not a matter of fancy or caprice. It is a matter of evidence. Reason must bow to fact and evidence, or, declining subjection, it must take the consequences. Jehoram therefore was bound in reason to accept the authority which had proved itself to be supreme. He was, in effect, constrained to walk in the way of obedience and heavenly wisdom, though the constraint was of such a nature as to admit of resistance if he so determined. His father's character, and the fashion of the times under his father's influence, and the knowledge of the truth which he possessed, left him no choice, but that of wilfulness in opposition to the claims of the true God.

Then, still further to show his obligations :—

Thirdly.—He was a Prince of the house of David, and a special covenant guaranteed perpetuity and glory to that house ; in connexion, of course, with loyalty and subordination on the part of its members. Here then was personal and dynastic inducement added to general and national considerations. How could Jehoram bring himself to disregard the honours of his house, as well as the proprieties of his nation? **We** cannot say, unless it were that, like Abijah, his great-grandfather, he thought to hold God to the covenant made with David, while he himself **took** the liberty of disregarding it. Any way, he was **under** obligation to attend to that covenant; and **this very** obligation, together with **the** covenant from which **it** sprung, furnished further favourable influences **to a** right course in his case.

And there were other considerations and circumstances affecting him—**all** calculated **to** determine him **to** take the right course as **a** rational **being** and **an** accountable and favoured Prince. This for example: He dwelt under the shadow **of the** magnificent Temple **of** Solomon, and he **cannot be** supposed **to** have been ignorant of the **character and** career of that distinguished ruler. **He** must have heard **of** Solomon's glory, and of Solomon's mistakes, and **of** Solomon's dishonour. He must have heard the reason of the dismemberment of Solomon's kingdom. Had **Solomon** only been faithful, and the intervening kings also faithful, Jehoram knew that himself would have reigned over all the twelve tribes of Israel, and not been confined to the government of two. But Solomon was unfaithful, and Rehoboam unwise, **and** therefore the patrimony of the **house of David was curtailed.** Was this not further reason, besides the reasons already mentioned, why Jehoram should have given himself truly to the **service of** God? Further disobedience **might** bring further curtailment; while attention and obedience **would** bring stability to what of good and glory remained, **if not** expansion **of** authority and return to happier fortunes. One would think interest alone, apart from gratitude and worshipful love, would have bound Jehoram to the throne of God, and kept him from the unprofitable service of idols.

Sill further, he had seen the refuge **and** deliverance of his father when invaded by the combined force of Ammon, and Moab, and Mount Seir. He knew how Jehoshaphat set himself to seek the Lord when the danger was reported to him, and how he proclaimed a fast, and how **he** prayed in the midst of the people, and how he was encouraged by Jahaziel; and he knew further, how signal the deliverance that the God of Israel had wrought for **his** house and people on this occasion, when their enemies turned their weapons against each other, and left **to** Jehoshaphat and his subjects only the labour of gathering the spoil. Jehoram was already in the maturity of his powers, if not actually associated with his father in the government, when all this happened; and nothing, **one** would have thought, could have tempted him after this to forsake the mighty deliverer of his nation. He could **not** in reason give himself to any other service, when he **had** ocular and immediate manifestations of the supremacy, **and** goodness, and accessibility of Jehovah.

One other fact may be mentioned—showing how many were the circumstances surrounding him, and constraining him, to determine right, and **to** abide by his determination. No more were needed than those already mentioned, but more were added. Here is the one I specially refer to; he was contemporary with the prophets Elijah and Elisha, and he must have heard tell of them. We may allow that he was uninformed of much that transpired under, or by, the agency of these distinguished men, but he could not by possibility be ignorant of all. He could not, for example, be ignorant of the demonstration by Elijah on Mount Carmel. Nor can we believe that he was ignorant of the translation of that prophet. Now, if he knew of the demonstration on Mount Carmel, and of the national conviction then expressed by the ten tribes that the Lord **was** God, and of **the** slaughter of the priests of Baal, and of the downpouring of the needed and precious rain **at** the intercession of Elijah, how could he but see, that **it was** his interest as well as his duty **to** abide by the Mighty and the True, and to keep aloof from the powerless and the injurious? And Elijah was taken up to heaven! While the bones of the idolatrous priests of Samaria were bleaching on Mount Carmel, Elijah, the representative of the God of Israel, was walking on the high places of **the** universe. How could Jehoram have any hesitation as to the course to be chosen? All things, it is clear, pointed in the same direction:— the character of his father, the history of his people, the peculiarities of his dynasty, the events transpiring under his own observation, and the reports of Prophet-action and Prophet-denunciation in a neighbouring region. All things, I say, pointed out to him the way of safety and honour. Every influence around him was favourable to his making a right decision. Only perverseness and wicked-short-sightedness could enable him to choose wrong. If many men are so placed in infancy and in youth that it is scarcely possible for them to find the right, Jehoram was so situated and encompassed while yet young that one would have thought that it was scarcely possible for him to miss it. He must shut his eyes and close his ears ere he can prefer the wrong. He must put aside what he knew to be true ere he could possibly get hold of the untrue. The right confronted him; the right encompassed him; the right pressed itself upon his attention; the right held out every inducement for its own acceptance, and he must actually break the cordon of right around him ere he could attach himself to the wrong! So favourable were the conditions of his youth for a righteous and happy history! Other men must press through encompassing evil if they would lay hold of good; Jehoram had to press through encompassing good ere he could attach himself to evil.

And Jehoram did burst through all the favourable constraints that were around him. Pity for the infatuated Prince! He tore himself away from the quiet and the desirable, and attached himself, and that with his eyes open, to the degrading and destructive. He renounced the ways of his father. He renounced the peculiarities of his nation. He renounced the law of the Lord—(the precious law which enlightens the eyes and enlarges the heart.) He renounced for himself the covenant made with David, and all the honours and consolations thereof. He renounced the hope of the world and the blessing-bearing seed of Abraham. He renounced all, and became the devotee of idolatry, immorality, and ungodliness. His position, if he could have seen it, was awful. He was without God, without Christ, who is the help of the fallen, and without hope **in this world**. **Nay** further, he **was** the dupe of error, **the** victim **of** demons, and the **heir** of darkness **and** incalculable dishonour!

We may well pity **Jehoram, the son** of Jehoshaphat, while we cannot but condemn him. And we would do well **to** take **warning** by him. Our privileges are **even** greater than his. **If** we **attach** ourselves to evil after **all** the light, and truth, and love, which **have been set** before us, and poured around us, we will incur a manifold and fearful condemnation. "How shall we escape **if we** neglect" all **the** revelations and demonstrations **of New** Testament times?

But we would notice concerning Jehoram,—

II. His miserable and wicked reign.

That is one of the saddest and darkest chapters of history. Its years were not long—only eight—but very much daring crime was pressed into those years, and very much intense annoyance was experienced. Rehoboam's reign was unilluminated and unsunny, but **Jehoram's** may be said to have been wholly in night or deep shadows. The daylight passed from his horizon with the death of his father, and the night settled over him **as** he commenced his independent reign. One of his first acts was **to** slay his royal brethren—six men better than himself,—(2-4.) His mind **was** already filled with dark suspicion, **or he would** not have done this: **and** the doing of it **necessarily** banished all peaceful consciousness from **his subsequent history.** Sleeping or waking, the memory of **this deed** would haunt him. His royal state could not banish it, nor yet **the** unworthy and degrading pleasures of his false religion. It is true that many oriental princes besides Jehoram have slain their kindred on ascending the throne; but these oriental princes had not the privileges **of** Jehoram in their youth. Their natures were not enlightened, nor their consciences armed, by the law of the Lord, as in the case of the son of Jehoshaphat. They stumbled in darkness, and knew not all the enormity of their deed. Even they could not be easy under such a remembrance, but Jehoram must have been agonized. The memory of his father must mingle itself with his consciousness, and this memory, uniting itself with the thoughts of his murdered brethren, must have caused perpetual irritation in his nature. No sweet hour of silent self-communion could he ever enjoy: and no true peace could ever after brood over his being. He might hide it under smiles or fair appearances, but the bitter conviction was ever underneath, and making itself felt all the while.

Then, his subjects revolted, and he could not re-subject them. He attempted it in the case of Edom, but failed. They made good their independence. The truth is, he had weakened himself by slaying his brethren, and the princes whose disapprobation of his idolatrous ways he feared, and thus was unable to maintain his kingdom in its integrity. (8–10.) How grievous this must have been to Jehoram even in the case of the Edomites, but how much so in the case of Libnah! Edom was a foreign acquisition, if I may so describe it, but Libnah was a part of Judah, and only a few miles from his capital. Edom too was a people; and it might not seem very disgraceful for a small kingdom like that of Jehoram's to be unable to reconquer, or to keep in subjection, a neighbouring and numerous nation: but, for a city in his own dominions to defy the power of King Jehoram, that was truly humbling! If Rehoboam was humbled by the loss of ten out of the twelve tribes, what must have been the chagrin of Jehoram to find the cities of his small territory throwing off their allegiance, and maintaining their independence! But he had violated the law of Israel, and it was not to be wondered at if his subjects should renounce their allegiance to him. He had introduced the element of disintegration into Israel, and the men of Libnah followed his example: "They revolted from under his hand, because he had forsaken the Lord God **of** his fathers." And their conduct was more excusable than his. **He** renounced a righteous, and legitimate, and benignant authority, whereas they only renounced a perverted, a tyrannous, and a wicked authority.

Possibly we have the explanation **of** the revolt of Libnah in the next folly reported concerning the king. "Moreover," **says** the sacred historian, " he made high places in the mountains of Judah, and caused the inhabitants of Jerusalem to commit fornication, and compelled Judah thereto." What could be more enormous ? He *compelled* the inhabitants of Judah to observe the degrading and immoral rites of heathenism. It was bad enough, that one so privileged and enlightened as he should forsake the truth, and symbolize with the wicked! It was bad enough, that one so elevated as he should use his influence as king against the God of his nation! But it was worse still, and that by many degrees, that he should *compel* his subjects to sin. He was entrusted with the powers of the nation in the interests of purity and piety, and he used these powers in the interests of impurity and impiety. No wonder if the faithful in Israel should revolt from his government and dictation. Honour **to** the men of Libnah **if** this was the ground of their revolt! It was right and commendable in them to resist the authority that would drag them into disobedience and defilement. They are wise who obey God rather than **man.** Too many are ready to yield to fashionable wrong, **or to** wicked dictation; but the men of Libnah preferred revolt **in** such **a** case **to** obedience or concurrence. Whether, however, this were the cause of **the** revolt or not, they raised the standard of opposition to Jehoram, and thus showed the weakness of his government, and gave acute pain to the haughty spirit of their wicked sovereign. With the memory of his murdered brethren, and the dismemberment of his small kingdom, you may well believe that the consciousness of Jehoram was not a very pleasant one. And the contrasting recollections of his father's glory, in the days when his life was young and comparatively unstained, would **only** add poignancy **or** bitterness to his regrets and his distasteful experiences.

Then came **the** writing from Elijah, the prophet, to add to his **annoyance** and irritation. Here it is:

> "And there came a writing to him from Elijah the prophet, saying, Thus saith the Lord God of David thy father, Because thou hast not walked in the ways of Jehoshaphat thy father, nor in the way of Asa, King of Judah, but hast walked in the way of the Kings of Israel, and hast made Judah and the inhabitants of Jerusalem to go a whoring—like the whoredoms of the house of Ahab, and also hast slain thy brethren of thy father's house, which were better **than** thyself: Behold, with a great plague will **the** Lord smite **thy** people, and thy children, and thy wives, **and** all thy goods; and thou shalt have great sickness **by** disease of thy bowels, until thy bowels fall out by **reason of sickness** day by day." (xxi. 12-15.)

Now, **to say** nothing of **the** difficulties connected with this **writing**,—difficulties **arising** from the fact that, **according to the received chronology**, Elijah had been some twelve or **thirteen** years **dead when** it reached Jehoram, **you may** see both propriety **and** truthfulness in **it**. There was propriety in it, seeing **that** Jehoram had, by marrying Athaliah and adopting **her** religion, become, as it **w**ere, indentified with the house of Ahab; and Elijah's commission was specially in relation to that house. Had Jehoram married into **a** different family, and abode by the temple and the true religion, he would probably **never** have heard from Elijah; but **the fact** of his **marriage to** the daughter of Jezebel being known **to the** prophet **before** his translation, or, at any rate, that **marriage being** about **to** be consummated before that event, and the prophet being aware of the consequences of the alliance, nay, being made fully cognizant of them by divine revelation, what was to prevent his preparing this brief announcement before his departure, and leaving it to be handed to Jehoram after the death of Jehoshaphat:—after the death of Jehoshaphat, mark! It was only after the death **of** Jehoshaphat that the true result of Jehoram's alliance could appear: and before that development the writing had been inappropriate. But, after Jehoshaphat's death, and after Jehoram had shown the extent of his conformity to the house of Ahab, the writing was wholly seasonable and admonitory. And it was as truthful as it was admonitory, as the result made apparent.

And now observe, this writing ought to have led **to** repentance on the part of Jehoram. Even Ahab repented to a certain extent under the denunciations of Elijah: and why not Jehoram? He knew that Elijah's words were not idle words in the case of Ahab, and why should he not lay them to heart in his own case? Why? Just because his heart was fully set in him to do evil. He had yielded himself to certain influences, which we shall notice immediately; and, either he did not wish to resist these influences, or he did **not feel** himself at liberty to resist them,—therefore he treated the message from Elijah with indifference or scorn. Possibly he denied its authenticity in the circumstances, though he knew all the while that it was authentic. Any way, he repudiated it as a warning, and pursued his wicked course in spite of it. But think you that this warning, though disregarded, was therefore without influence? You mistake if you **do**. It increased no doubt the uneasiness of Jehoram, if it did not lead to his amendment. Even general denunciations make men uneasy — much more personal **and direct** denunciations. The very name of Elijah was **no** doubt a terror to him. What then would a message of this character from the hated prophet be? It linked itself, we may well believe, with the other causes of his mental perturbation, viz., his murder of his brethren, and his wicked departure from God and conformity to Ahab; and while it gave renewed vividness to his painful remembrances, it added force and certainty to his fears and forebodings. He would try and shake himself free of the uneasiness, but the image of his brethren, and the threatenings of God by Elijah would still pursue him. His conscience might have become, partially and for a time, deadened concerning his crimes, but the voice of Elijah would **awake** it to renewed activity, and entirely prevent his finding either rest or satisfaction in any thing around him.

Then came the judgments denounced, and the evils, which for a time had been mental only, became real as well.

> "Moreover the Lord stirred up against Jehoram the spirit of the Philistines, and of the Arabians, that were near the Ethiopians: And they came up into Judah, and broke into it, and carried away all the substance that was found in the king's house, and his sons also, and his wives: So that there was never a son left him, save Jehoahaz, the youngest of his sons." (16-17.)

How Athaliah escaped in this confusion does not appear. She may have been on a visit to her mother Jezebel, or otherwise out of the way. However it was, she was either not carried away, or she recovered her freedom, for she reappears on the stage after this, and acts a not inconspicuous part in Jerusalem for a time.

But think of Jehoram: how sad and how desolate his position! With a mind ill at ease—denounced by heaven—rejected by his own subjects—reft of his family and royal possessions—solitary in his palace—and without hope of a happy reverse in his fortunes—is he not an object of pity? Where can he look for solace?—not to the past, that only reproves him:—not to the Unseen, for he hath no friend there:—and not to the future, for that for him is big with terror! All is midnight darkness within him and around him. He complains, but his complaints are unheeded. His very servants shun him.

But his cup of trouble is not yet complete. Disease develops itself in his body. Painfully for two years he labours under it. Mitigations there are none for him. His bodily distemper is only added to his other griefs. He has no comforts to set against his sorrows. His mind is wounded: his domestic affections are blighted: his royal honour is clouded, and trampled in the dust: and now his body, the last refuge of any thing like health or well-being about him, is racked with pain or tossed with restlessness. The weary days flow on, and the weary nights. The weeks grow into months, and the painful months extend over two years, and then the sad consummation comes. His physicians are foiled: his last hopes are gone: his agonies increase: and death lays him low!

Nor is this the end of his dishonour: "He dies without being regretted." The most unworthy have generally some to mourn for them: Jehoram has none. The most unworthy princes have generally a royal burial at last: not so Jehoram. He is not indeed buried beyond the city walls, but he has no place among the kings. Hear the record of his last days:—"So he died of sore diseases: and his people made no burning for him, like the burning of his fathers. Thirty and two years old was he when he began to reign, and he reigned in Jerusalem eight years, and departed without being desired. Howbeit they buried him in the city of David, but not in the sepulchre of the kings." (19-20.)

What an end for a prince, and a prince whose life opened under such favourable auspices:—a son of Jehoshaphat, a prince of the house of David, an heir of divine promises, and privileged with ample means for knowing his distinguished obligations, and for finding the favour of the Eternal, as well as for blessing the people over whom he was set, and for leaving an honoured name behind him! What an end for one so favoured! He dies without being regretted: his people make no burning for him like the burning of his fathers: and his remains are excluded from the sepulchre of the kings! Whence this reverse? How came it that his fortunes were so dark? O, how came it that he lost his way while light was shining all around him? And how came it that he refused warning when dangers and distresses were crowding his steps and destroying his peace? This leads me to notice—

III. *The great cause, or, at least one great cause of his wickedness, his incorrigibility, and his ruin.*

That was his unwise and irreligious marriage. He

married the daughter of Ahab and Jezebel. However such a union could be proposed or thought of by the house of Jehoshaphat we cannot imagine. The law of God was explicit, that no marriage alliances should be entered into by Israel with those who served strange gods. In this way, God assured them, their hearts would be turned from Him, and His anger would be kindled against them. Now, Ahab and Jezebel served strange gods, even the gods of the heathen; and their daughter was trained in this false service. Her influence, supposing her married, could only be hostile to the fidelity of her husband in relation to the God of Israel: and, supposing her a mother, her children would almost certainly be won over to heathenism. This Jehoshaphat and his son Jehoram might have seen even apart from any divine commandment on the subject. They might fancy indeed that she, when married into the royal family of Judah, would conform to the religion of her husband and her new connexions: but such a thought is weakness itself, when the matter lies between the true and the false in religion. The false is ever the more tenacious and unscrupulous: and the true, when brought into collision with the false in domestic arrangements, has to succumb in almost every case: and this, not because the truth is feeble, but because the flesh is weak. Jehoshaphat ought to have known this: and, if Jehoram in his inexperience had urged otherwise, Jehoshaphat should have pointed him to the explicit law of heaven on the subject. Enlightened fidelity in this matter might have prevented the fearful and criminal fortunes of Jehoram, and saved incalculable sorrow to thousands in Judah. But no, policy, or passion, or wilfulness, prevailed over principle in the court of Jehoshaphat. Jehoram led to the altar an idolatrous princess, and she led him to utter and irremediable ruin! Think you, that he would have slain his brethren but for the daughter of Jezebel? Think you, that he would have compelled Judah to sin but for a domestic pressure in that direction? Think you, that he would have incurred the unchecked displeasure of his father's God but **for his** entire subserviency to his impious wife? Not **at all.** Though he had turned aside from God, **or been** less devoted than his father, he could never have gone the length he did, considering his education, if he had not allied himself to an idolatrous and unscrupulous partner. The fact would seem to be, that his wife ruined him. His marriage was the turning point of his history. Up to that time he was at worst but neutral; and he might still have been a respectable if not **a** talented prince and ruler; but from the moment of his marriage **he was a** ruined man. He passed by that alliance from the **camp** of Judah into the camp of heathenism. Instead of drawing his wife, as he might vainly flatter himself beforehand, from the camp of error and destruction to that of truth and safety, he allowed himself, and his kingdom too to a great extent, to be drawn by her from the camp of truth and safety to that of error and destruction. No sooner was his father dead, and himself sole **king in** Jerusalem, than he began to make manifest the new and evil inspiration under which he now existed. The law **of** the Lord was laid aside. The example of **his** father was forgotten. Self swallowed up all righteous considerations, and an idolatrous tyranny took the place **of a** righteous and paternal rule. Infatuation presided in the councils of the king, and unwilling vengeance began forthwith to prepare for the merited dishonour and the certain overthrow incurred!

Such was the fact with Jehoram, the favoured son of Jehoshaphat,—his marriage ruined him! How little he thought of the sad end on which he was advancing when he led to the altar his stately and idolatrous bride!

And this furnishes a lesson to the young in the matter of matrimonial alliances. It speaks with trumpet tongue to those who have been brought up under gospel influences. Such ought never to form alliances with those who yield no subjection to gospel law. The unbelieving will certainly injure the believing. It might be thought rather that the believing would benefit the unbelieving; but this is not found to be the case. The advantage in such unions is almost invariably found to be on the side of the irreligious, as already observed. A distinguished evangelist of the present day writes thus on this question:—" I believe that one of two judgments has almost always fallen on professors of Christianity who have been involved in unequal and uncongenial unions. Either they have lived to regret it through a lifetime of misery, or they have made shipwreck of faith, and gone back to the world. Examples of going back to the world, (he proceeds to say), surround us on every side; and though the examples of the more merciful judgment may not be so outwardly apparent (for many an aching heart alone knoweth its own bitterness), yet no one need seek very far to find examples of these also: but where shall we look to find an example of a professing Christian, male or female, who, having married one who made no such profession, was afterwards made the instrument of his or her conversion?

Argue with a person who is about to contract such an engagement, and they will tell you, what Satan tells them, that this is just what they are going to do, viz: convert their idol after they are married. But do they? Do facts prove that this often happens? I do not say that it never happens. I think it probable that it does; for God is a Sovereign, and converts who and how he pleases. But I do tell you that, after much diligent inquiry, I have never been able to find one case of such conversion. In London, in Edinburgh, in Dublin, and many other large places, I have preached to masses of people in every rank and grade of society, and I have earnestly requested, and that again and again, that any one would write and tell me, if they knew an instance of a professing Christian marrying a man or woman of the world, and being afterwards made the instrument of their conversion. I have at the same time explained my reason for asking this,— that I was anxious to ascertain if it ever was the case; and if it was, what proportion these conversions bore to the number of such marriages. I have received but one answer, **and** that was to tell me, that St. Augustine's mother married her husband before his conversion and afterwards converted him. Surely, if this is the exception, that exception proves the rule."—(*Brownlow North, in Family Treasury.*)

You see, then, that the hope of converting the irreligious after marriage is a slender one indeed, and you see that the advantage of these ill-assorted marriages is ever on the side of irreligion. They injure the parties forming them, **and** they strengthen the cause of evil **among** men. It was so among the Antediluvians. It **was so** through all the history of the Jews, and it is so **still. No** wonder if the Apostle warns against them, saying, **"Be** ye not unequally yoked with unbelievers!" The truth is, marriage requires compromise; and, if the parties be not one in religion, the compromise will ever be found to the detriment of religion, and to the injury of the religious party making the concession. They, therefore who, being themselves religious, care any thing for their own safety, **or** for the interests of the heavenly kingdom, will not enter into alliance with the irreligious. No matter for wealth, or status, **or** brilliant beauty, **or decided** talent, they will prefer fidelity to the kingdom **to** their own personal or temporary gratification. And they will thereby avoid a fate like that of Jehoram's—dark, troubled, miserable, and repulsive!

There is a particular form of this evil which is especially analogous to the cases of Jehoram and Athaliah:—I refer to the union of Protestants with Catholics. The Protestants hold by the Bible and the one Mediator,— the Catholics hold by tradition and the Virgin Mary, with many mediators. The Protestants are, as it were, the men of Jerusalem, while the Catholics occupy the place of Ahab and Jezebel in Samaria. And the union of these parties is found to be all in favour of Samaria, and against Jerusalem, and especially calamitous to the Jerusalem individuals concerned. On this subject **a** writer (in the *Family Treasury*) who resided among **a** people devoted to the Papacy, with a mixture of Protest-

ants in their midst, thus testifies:—" Mixed marriages are a clear gain to the Papacy. The children, in almost every instance I have known, are brought up Papists. In no household is the power of the priest through penance and the confessional so intensely felt. * * * * *
No incident escapes him. He knows every visitor. He is acquainted with the secrets of the chamber, and reigns accordingly. I have seen husbands lapsing into infidelity, living in blasphemy and drink, and dying in despair, because, too intelligent to attend mass, they could not maintain a constant fight with wives and daughters who were the slaves of the priests; and they purchased an inglorious domestic peace by a life of abandonment and a death of perdition!" Here you see Jehoram over again. The same writer further observes:—

"The venom of these marriages is so deadly that, whatever it touches, even though endowed with the strength of natural affection, it poisons,—time, nature, love, suffering, will not cure it—nothing but a miracle of grace! I have seen it alienate daughters from their parents, brother from brother, friend from friend—disrupting the holiest ties, and kindling fires of hate only to be extinguished in the grave. The rancour proceeding from this source is singularly bitter. The malevolent tempers which it evokes are implacable!"

"O, (says he in another place) if I could describe the misery which I have seen in households where the Romish influence began to be felt! I have stood at the deathbeds of men whose wives impelled them in the last moments to apostatize, and have watched, with melting pity, their sun setting in Popery and despair. I have called on servants who were cajoled, bribed, and coerced into the Papacy, by families of rank and influence, who seemed to think that their glory in a future life depended on changing their poor maid into an idolatrous devotee of the Virgin Mary. And I have seen young brides dragged into the Church of Rome from the very altars, where their misery began, by a system of terrorism which it would have required the spirit of a martyr to withstand!"

There is surely something **in this which** claims the especial attention of young people. And I would only say in conclusion, if the young have themselves caught a glimpse of the truth in any degree, let them beware how they ally themselves with those who would put superstition in the place of it, and who would drag them thereby into apostacy and woe! Let them think of Jehoram and Athaliah, and let them prefer single life rather, if need be, to association with the friends and supporters of soul-destroying error!

QUESTIONS ON JEHORAM.

How is it with very many young people in the matter of a start in life?
> They are most unfavourably situated, seeing that they breathe an atmosphere of worldliness and ungodliness from their earliest years.

Can **we** wonder when such individuals go from **bad to** worse?
> Certainly **not**: they are entitled to pity **as well as to** blame.

How was Jehoram situated in this respect?
> Most favourably.

What were the favourable conditions which surrounded Jehoram during his early years?
> His father was a godly man: his people were a sacred people: the dynasty to which he belonged was a covenanted dynasty: the Temple of Solomon overshadowed his youthful consciousness: he had seen the deliverance enjoyed by his father and his people from the combined forces of **Ammon**, Moab, and Seir, and he must have been acquainted **with** the demonstrations of Elijah in the neighbouring territory.

How did these favourable conditions affect his course **of** disobedience?
> They aggravated his criminality, and rendered him utterly inexcusable.

Are the privileges of young people brought up under Christian parents, and in connexion with Christian ordinances and Christian literature greater than those of Jehoram?

Yes: and that by many degrees.

What then must be said of such if, in the face of all their privileges, they choose the service of the world in preference to the service of God?

That their folly and danger are beyond all utterance: "How can they escape who neglect so great a salvation?"

Was Jehoram's reign a happy one?

The very contrary: Scarcely anything can be conceived more distressing.

What bloody deed darkened its commencement?

The murder of his six brethren.

How did this affect his peace as a man?

It rendered calm self-consciousness and pleasing memories impossible for him.

What annoyed him as a King?

The loss of Edom, and the revolt of the men of Libnah—a city almost within sight of his capital.

Had Jehoram any right to complain of the revolt of the men of Libnah?

No, surely, when himself had revolted against the God of Israel.

What possibly explains the revolt of the men of Libnah?

His (the King's) despotic devotion to Idolatry. He was not content to lead the way as an Idolater, but he endeavoured to force Idolatry even on those who wished to avoid it.

Supposing that it were so, how are we to regard the conduct of the men of Libnah?

With approbation certainly: they are wise who obey God rather than men—exalted and powerful though these men may be.

And how must Jehoram have felt under this successful revolt at Libnah?

Most humiliated and grieved.

What next came to perturb him?

The writing from Elijah—denouncing all manner of evil upon him on account of his wickedness.

Why was this writing withheld while Jehoshaphat lived?

Because the full extent of Jehoram's wickedness could not be made manifest until he became sole Sovereign.

Did Jehoram repent on the receipt of the threatenings by Elijah?

Not at all: it made no change in his course, but it must have added to his mental misery. Personal denunciations from such a quarter could not be treated with indifference.

What follows next in the experience of Jehoram?
The wasting away of his substance by the Philistines and Arabians,—and the captivity of his sons and his wives.

Does this complete his misery?
No: bodily disease of the most distressing character is added, and that for two painful years.

And what is his final dishonour so far as this life is concerned?
He died without being regretted.

What was the chief cause of Jehoram's miserable reign and miserable end?
His irreligious and idolatrous marriage with the daughter of Jezebel.

But was there no excuse for his forming such a union?
Not any: God had specially prohibited such alliances, and his father ought to have remembered the prohibition if he did not.

What is the lesson which this furnishes to young people brought up under Christianity?
That they should avoid irreligious alliances: "Be not unequally yoked with unbelievers."

What is the usual result of such marriages?
The defection or the distress of the enlightened party, and the triumph of the erroneous.

Does history furnish any proofs or illustrations to this effect?
Yes: the Antediluvians; and also the Jews through a large number of their generations.

What is that particular form of this evil in these times which ought to be avoided?
The union of Protestants with Roman Catholics.

And why should such unions be avoided?
Because they usually, nay, almost uniformly, bring misery and bondage, if not ruin and despair, on the misallied Protestants.

What in general are we taught by the story of Jehoram?
That misery and dishonour are the certain results of disobedience to God, and that matrimonial alliances ought to be formed in accordance with divine directions, and not merely by human caprice or youthful fancy. It is not meant to limit tastes or preferences further than God limits them; but beyond the limits set by Him no one can venture with impunity. Jehoram did not!

VIII. AHAZIAH.

"So Ahaziah, the son of Jehoram, king of Judah, reigned . . . . He also walked in the ways of the house of Ahab: for his mother was his counsellor to do wickedly. Wherefore he did evil in the sight of the Lord, like the house of Ahab; for they were his counsellors after the death of his father, to his destruction. He walked also after their counsel, and went with Jehoram the son of Ahab, of Israel, to war against Hazael, King of Syria, at Ramoth-Gilead. . . . And the destruction of Ahaziah was of God, by coming to Joram. . . . And when they had slain him, they buried him. Because, said they, he is the son of Jehoshaphat, who sought the Lord with all his heart. So the house of Ahaziah had no power to keep still the kingdom."—2 Chronicles xxii. 1-9.

THERE is often much of mystery when the young are prematurely cut off. It seems as if all the preparations for their life-journey had proved abortive, and as if all the solicitude and love which had been exercised concerning them and lavished upon them had been in vain. Friends cannot but wonder at while they weep, because of their unlooked for departure. All the bright possibilities and great felicities of unfolding life are rendered impossible for them, and their power of ministering to the comfort and well-being of others is forever ended. How sad the thought! And how inexplicable their fate! It is as if a bright morning, instead of growing to a brilliant day, were suddenly turned into darkest night. Many—alas how many—have wept over these unfinished, or rather, scarcely commenced lives! It is one of the mysteries of the broken, disjointed, and disarranged history of fallen humanity that it should be so.

The early and violent death of the Prince now before us had about it all the sadness and abruptness of such events. He had reigned but one year, and he was little more than twenty years old, when he fell under the orders of Jehu. How it would startle his subjects and contemporaries when they heard of it. Possibly they looked for a return of prosperity under the youthful King after all the mal-administrations and misfortunes of Jehoram's reign. Any way, they might reasonably anticipate a long reign in the case of a Sovereign so young. But no: the axe was already laid at the root of the tree ere he left Jerusalem, though he suspected it not, and, forthwith the fatal weapon was put in motion against him—youthful and graceful though he was.

It was a sad and mournful tragedy, but not so **wholly** mysterious as many early deaths are, as we shall see in **our** further remarks concerning **him.** There are three things note-worthy in the brief **record** we have of him, viz:— His counsellors: his choice **as to** his destiny ; **and his** memory.

I. His Counsellors.

These were his connections in and of the house of Ahab. First and pre-eminently Athaliah, his mother, and the daughter of Jezebel, who was ever at his side, and after her, and in entire harmony with her, his cousins and relations at the court of Samaria. To these he listened, and to their influence he yielded himself. Pity that he had been so related and so beset ! His father and grandfather were deeply to blame for this. And pity for himself, as well as for his people, that he broke not away from such advisers ! For they were his counsellors to his destruction, **as we** are informed by the sacred narative. **He** could **not** possibly have worse advisers. They were not only ignorant of the true interests of Judah ; they were bitterly opposed to these interests. They knew not God, and they were the determined upholders of that idolatry which dishonoured God, and brought ruin on those who walked in it. We can well understand the counsel they would tender **to** the youthful Ahaziah. They would advise him to abide by the high places in the mountains **of** Judah made by his father, and to su-

K

persede every officer of the Government who had any sympathy with the days of Jehoshaphat. He would, probably, not think of the Temple and its appropriate services, though he had been born under its shadow; but, if he did, his counsellors would tell him that that was now out of the question. The age, they would say, had outgrown that burdensome and restrictive ceremonial. It might be tolerated among a rude and isolated people, they would admit, but it was wholly unsuited to Israel in their days. They were now in communication with the enlightened nations of the earth, and they ought to conform themselves to the elegancies and the freedoms of more advanced nations. The ten tribes, they would urge, the larger portion of the descendants of Abraham, had thrown off the narrownesses and restrictions of the past, and why should not the remaining fraction of the nation enter upon the same career of liberty and progress? Samaria was now in harmony with Tyre and Sidon, and Tyre and Sidon were now in communication with all the world, and why should Jerusalem be a people by herself—small, despised, unfashionable, and antiquated? Why not put aside her peculiarities, which only made her ridiculous, and become a part of the widespread family of humanity? Jerusalem, they would urge, would thus become more honoured, and more frequented, and her inhabitants would enjoy more freely the pleasures of life. Commerce would grow; riches would increase, and luxurious gratifications would be multiplied. "Look," they would say, "at Tyre—gorged with riches—the emporium of the world's resources—the mistress of beauty and boundless enjoyment! Would you not wish to participate in her riches, and have a share in her enjoyments. Then, do as Samaria has done:—conform to her style of worship; encourage her merchants to settle their agents among you; become part of the commercial and happy world, and forget that narrow system of yours, which would keep you isolated, poor, gloomy and miserable!"

Such, in effect, was the counsel tendered to the youthful monarch Ahaziah, by his mother **and** his **kinsmen. And some** may suppose that he was excusable **for listening to it.** It is difficult, they will remind you, **for a** young man to set himself in opposition to his seniors and his relatives, especially when these seniors and relatives occupy lofty places **in** society. We admit the difficulty, but still we hold that Ahaziah was *inexcusable* for yielding to such advice. It was not with him as it is with many in heathen nations, who are trained in idolatry, and **kept in** ignorance, and who have no means of ascertaining **or** knowing the truth. We dare not judge hardly **of** such, **but** Ahaziah **was** not such. He had known the more **excellent** way. **He** had **seen the** days of Jehoshaphat. He must have **been** about fourteen years old when Jehoshaphat died; and he must have known how earnest his grandfather was to have the people taught the law of the Lord, and to have them abide in the service of God, and in the peculiarities of their national life. He had known too, how great and how prosperous his grandfather had been while walking in the ways of the Lord. And he had seen, **as he grew** into manhood, how different **the** fortunes of his father while devoting himself **to the service of Baal.** Instead of presents **and** friendly **embassies from the east** and from the west, **from** Arabia **and from Philistia, as in** the times of his grandfather, his father had been subjected to invasion, spoliation, and dishonour. The Arabians and the Philistines had come into Judah, and broken into it, and carried away all the substance that was found in his father's palace, and his wives also, and slain all his sons, **save this same** Ahaziah, or Jehoahaz himself. Here was ocular demonstration of the results of the two services;—honour, and riches, and peace, to Jehoshaphat the servant of God; and dishonour, and impoverishment, **and** distress, to Jehoram the servant of Baal! He might **well** have doubted the counsel **of** his mother, when he saw the effects of following it **in** the case of his father. And he might wisely have determined rather to fall back on the faith and fashions of Jehoshaphat than abide by those of Jehoram. Why follow the counsel that had ruined his predecessor?

But supposing that those about him attempted to account for the fortunes of his father in some other way—blaming his subordinates, or his own want of generalship, or his rashness as a statesman—how could Ahaziah listen to them when he had the writing sent by Elijah the prophet to his father? He could scarcely be ignorant of this document—being a Prince in his teens when it was delivered, and causing, as it no doubt did, no little sensation or speculation in the Court circle at the time. And how plainly the document spake! Hear it again,—(we have already quoted it under the reign of Jehoram.)

> "And there came a writing to him from Elijah the prophet, saying: Thus saith the Lord God of David thy father, because thou hast not walked in the ways of Jehoshaphat thy father, nor in the ways of **Asa**, King of Judah, but hast walked in the way of the kings of Israel, and hast made Judah and the inhabitants of Jerusalem to go **a** whoring, like the whoredoms of the house of Ahab, and also hast slain thy brethren of thy father's house which were better than thyself: Behold, with a great **plague will the** Lord smite thy people, and thy children, and thy **wives, and all** thy goods; and thou shalt have great sickness by **disease of** thy bowels, until **thy** bowels fall out by **reason of sickness** day by day."—(xxi. 12-15.)

Now, how could Athaliah explain away this account of her husband's misfortunes? And why should Ahaziah listen to counsel which would involve him in like trouble? Surely he was inexcusable in doing so! Even though urged by his own mother, he ought to have rejected it. The will of Heaven is something higher and more authoritative than even the voice of a mother; and Ahaziah must have known that the will of Heaven was in opposition to the counsel of Athaliah.

But even though kept in ignorance of the writing of Elijah sent to his father, he must have known something of the miraculous history of his nation; and, consequently, he must have heard of the supreme power and supreme claims of Jehovah. A contemporary of Jehoshaphat, and in communication with that Prince, he must

have heard of the law of the Lord ; a Prince of the house
of David, he must have heard accounts of the great and
distinguished founder of his house ; a witness of the
grandeur of Solomon's Temple, he must have heard of
the wisdom and mistakes of that Prince. Nay, a contem
porary of Elijah's, he must have heard of the demonstration on Mount Carmel, and of the utter powerlessness of
the priests of Baal ! Nay, further, a contemporary of
Elisha's, whose influence was felt even in Samaria, and to
whom also the Kings of Syria listened, and whose fidelity
to Israel's God, and opposition to the Baal worship of his
kindred, must have been known to Ahaziah, there can be
no excuse for his listening to the counsel of his mother
and his idolatrous kindred. The inducements and con
siderations which ought to have neutralized with him the
advice of his mother were neither few nor small :—his
early education in the court of Jehoshaphat, his father's
fortunes as an idolatrous king, his knowledge of his nation's history, his interest in the founder of the dynasty
to which he belonged, his knowledge of Elijah's demonstrations, and denunciations, and translation, and his
further knowledge of the character and miracle sustained
authority of Elisha,—all, all ought to have bound him to
the God of his people, and to the services of His temple
in Jerusalem! He could not plead ignorance as an excuse
for his departure from God. He knew the right as well
as the wrong. Admit that the domestic and relational influences were strong, still, the interests at stake were too
momentous to be sacrificed to these influences : and, had it
been a matter unconnected with his own passions and preferences, no doubt he would have judged more wisely ;
but he was himself at heart an idolator. He had no wish
to retain God in his knowledge. He preferred the fashions of Samaria, and the riches of Tyre, to the riches of
Heaven ; and he would rather have the license and the
liberty of idolatry than the restrictions and limitations
of the true worship. He was willing therefore to be misled. He listened to the counsellors that suited his own
wishes—not because he knew them to be right and safe,

but because their views harmonized with his **own**. They counselled him to **a** career of self-pleasing in opposition to the service of the true God; and, because he preferred the **ways of** self-pleasing **to** those of piety, he listened, and shaped his course accordingly. He knew **better, but** was **content to** yield himself to proximate influences **and advice,** because those **influences** and **that** advice **were in** accordance with his own unworthy preferences; **and he was** *inexcusable* **in** yielding himself so. **He** was **to** be pitied as the son of an unworthy mother and counsellor, but he was also to be blamed and condemned for walking **in the** counsel of that unworthy mother, when he had the means of knowing that **her** counsel was wrong and **ruinous!**

Thus with **Ahaziah: but does** Ahaziah stand alone in this respect? **Are there no** Ahaziahs **in our own** time? **Alas,** there are very many, acting just as Ahaziah acted. Their immediate surroundings are all in favour of world**liness and** self-pleasing. Their parents **and** cousins, it **may** be, are all, **as** in the case of the youthful Ahaziah, **for** present enjoyment, present profit, or worldly honour, and they take these **in** effect **as** their guides and counsellors. Any way, they follow them in **their** own self-pleasing ways though they know **that there is a** better course. They have heard of the Bible, **and** they know **somewhat** of its demands. They know too, that there is **a** minority who yield themselves **to** its influence; and **they are** called on to join that minority—even the Church **and** people of God—and to adopt their faith and counsel **if** they would find safety, enlightenment, and immortal hope. But this minority is not fashionable, and the practice of its members seems rigid and forbidden. Besides, the fashionable world ridicules this minority and its habits, and accounts association with it as **low and disreputable.** The glories of Tyre **are not** found there, **nor** is the license of the world admissible there. What is the consequence? Why, that **very** many, unprepared for self-denial, and loving the **ways of** license and self-pleas**ing,** decide, like Ahaziah, **to abide** by the counsels and the guidance of their worldly and fashionable relatives and friends. They cannot renounce the commerce or the companionship of Tyre. They cannot forego the license of self-pleasing. They cannot abide by the obscure and the despised. They decide therefore to go with the stream, to cast in their lot with the majority, and to follow the counsel or the conduct of the irreligious. Ahaziah-like, they prefer the apparent and delusive to the substantial and ennobling, And Ahaziah-like, they will yet find how foolish they have been in their preference !

Be sure, we would say to those who are willing to listen, that you make not this mistake. Be sure that you yield not to proximate or worldly influences unfavourable to Jesus and salvation. No matter for earthly advantages or disadvantages. **Seek** the companionship and the counsels of the believing and the heavenly. Abide by Jerusalem and its peculiarities. In other words, abide by the Church of God, small and despised though it may seem in the eyes of the world! Attach small importance to the glitter of this passing life. Remember, *one thing is needful !* And that one needful thing is, the divine favour and friendship; and know **assuredly**, that the divine favour and friendship are not to be had in the self-pleasing ways of the world. **It is** to be had only in connection with faith and self-denial. **It** is to be had only in and through the crucified and exalted Son of God !

But this will appear more clearly as we attend further to Ahaziah. And we notice :—

II. *His choice as to his destiny.*

That destiny was sufficiently sad, as already noticed in our introductory remark. We cannot but lament for it : and the more so, that he seems to have been an amiable and friendly prince within his earthly and chosen circle. But for his kindness and friendliness indeed, he had not met with so early a death. He had gone to visit his cousin at Jezreel because that cousin was sick, and while there became alarmed for his own safety by reason of the movements of Jehu. He fled to Samaria, and hid himself in that city, supposing, or hoping, that the storm would blow over, or that he would find some way of reaching his own capital in the course of a few days. But he was found in Samaria, carried to Jehu, and ruthlessly slain. The rude conqueror had no pity for his youth, nor hesitated a moment before this Prince of Jerusalem. He crushed out his young life, and hurried on his destructive career. It seems sad, we repeat. **Oh, how** sad, that this young man, the King of Jerusalem, **and** the only remaining grandson of Jehoshaphat, should thus fall in the bright morning of his life! But it was of God that it should **be so**: we can see reason for it, and it is easy to point **that** reason out. It lay with Ahaziah himself, and is to be found in the choice which he made **as to** his destiny. Notice,—

By his parentage he was the heir of two very different fortunes. As the **son of** David, by Jehoram, Jehoshaphat, and Solomon, he was heir to the richest promises; while as **the son** of Ahab by Athaliah, he was heir to the most overwhelming denunciations. Hear the words of God concerning these two houses: first, concerning the house of David:

> "I have made a covenant with my chosen,
> I have sworn unto David my servant,—
> Thy seed will I establish for ever,
> And build up thy throne **to all** generations." * * * *
> "My covenant will I not break,
> Nor alter the thing that is gone out of my lips:—
> Once have I sworn by my holiness, that I will not lie unto
>   David:
> His seed shall endure for ever,
> And his throne as the sun before Me.
> It shall be established for ever as the moon,
> And as a faithful witness **in** heaven." (Ps. lxxxix. 3, 4, and
>   34-37.)

Then, secondly, hear the words of God by Elijah in relation to the house of Ahab:

> "Behold, I will bring evil upon thee, (Ahab,)
> And will take away thy posterity,

> **And** will cast off from Ahab every male,
> And him that is shut up and left in Israel.
> And will make thy house like the house of Jeroboam the
> son of Nabet,
> And like the house of Baasha the son of Ahijah,
> For the provocation wherewith thou hast provoked me to
> anger, and made Israel to sin." (I. Kings xxi. 21, 22.)

See then the position of Ahaziah,—he was both of the seed of David and of the posterity of Ahab. He was heir to the covenant of perpetuity on the one hand, and heir also to the sentence of extermination on the other. Which shall prevail? He cannot inherit both. He must either be preserved with David, or destroyed with Ahab. Which shall it be? Why, that must depend on his own choice and procedure. If he choose the fortunes of David's house, he must keep aloof from the doomed house of Ahab: but if he choose to abide by the house of Ahab, he thereby loses or forfeits his fortunes in David. And you know what his choice was. He had Athaliah and his relatives of Samaria for his counsellors. He in effect renounced David and took the side of Ahab. Having made his election, he was to all intents and purposes a **part** of the doomed posterity of Ahab, and he perished accordingly when that house perished. He was young to die, but he had ventured within the range of the storm that had arisen against the idolatrous and wicked court of Samaria, and he fell beneath its sweep. Nor was he unapprized. He might have known, if he did not, that the storm might arise any day after the death of Ahab. It was only deferred because of the humiliation of that king. It had to arise in the days of Ahab's son, and Ahab's son was now sick in Jezreel: and what more likely than that the agents of vengeance, being human and wakeful, would avail themselves of this sickness for the overthrow of the doomed house? And what was Ahaziah to expect if he threw himself into the arena of the storm? If a man will attach himself to, and identify himself with, a doomed and denounced race, even though not a member of that race, he may expect to share in the destruction when it comes. Still more so, if he **be** really of the denounced race, and if he voluntarily associate himself with the denounced race, what can he expect but **to** share their fate? Ahaziah therefore had **no** right to complain of his early death, nor may we complain concerning it. His fall was certainly swift, and **sad,** and apparently uncalled for at the **time,** but we can**not** object to **it.** We **can only** pity **and lament.** What bright, and happy, and useful days he might have had in Jerusalem had he but chosen to abide by the house of David instead of identifying himself with the house **of Ahab!** Had he but kept at Jerusalem, and not gone to Jezreel, he would have been safe for the time being at **least.** He would not then have **been** in the way of the hurricane that arose against the royal house of Samaria. But his sympathies were with the doomed: his presence **was** determined by his sympathies, and his early death **was** the inevitable consequence. How different had it been, had he only preferred the dynasty of David instead of that of Ahab! **He** was heir, as we have seen, to the fortunes of both. At Samaria, as a sympathizing branch of the idolatrous house, he was certain to incur destruction: but at Jerusalem, as **a** sympathizing branch of the covenanted and the loved, he would have enjoyed security **and honour.** Instead of perishing in his youth, he would have lived, and waxed great like his grandfather, **and** transmitted his crown in due time to a mature and **competent** prince and successor. But he forsook Jerusalem, and hastened to Samaria, just as the thunderbolt **fell** that was to overwhelm all the posterity of Ahab. He **thus** forfeited life and honour, and incurred death and overthrow with the condemned.

While we lament for his infatuation, let us be reminded of our own circumstances. These are strikingly analogous to those of Ahaziah. Like that prince, we are the heirs of two very different styles **of** fortune. Humanity, you know, hath two very different representatives. The one is condemned and death-doomed: the other is accepted, beloved, and empowered to confer eternal life **on** His followers. The one is earthly: the other is heavenly. The one is powerless, though pretentious: the other is able to save unto the uttermost, though shrouded and undazzling to the worldly eye. We are called on to make our election between these two representatives. We grieve for the mistaken decision of Ahaziah, as between David and Ahab: let us beware how **we** repeat the mistake as between **the** first Adam and the second. We are the heirs **of** the first Adam, and also of the second: but we cannot inherit with both. The inheritances are so diverse that we must abide by the one or the other. With the one is condemnation: with **the** other **is** justification and peace. We must make **our** choice. If we abide by the first Adam, and give ourselves to disobedience and worldliness, we must sink beneath the waves of **wrath which** are even now sweeping the unforgiven to perdition, and which will manifest themselves yet more fearfully in the world to come. If, on the other hand, we prefer the second Adam, the Lord from heaven, **we** shall find shelter, acceptance, and love. The matter is as plain to us, as we can now see it was plain to Ahaziah. It was Samaria or Jerusalem with him: it **is the** world **or the** Saviour with us. It was with him, renounce Samaria and its idolatry, and give yourself to the piety and the principles **of** the dynasty of David, and live; or, renounce David and Jerusalem, and die! And it is now with us, the world with **its** unlawful and unsanctified enjoyments, or the Saviour with His immortal purities and pleasures. In other words, it is the world or the Church—the self-pleasing world, or the Christ-filled and Christ-controlled Church! Every man must abide by the one or by the other. No man can inherit with both. Prefer the world, and you will perish with the world: but abide by the Christ-filled Church, and you live with Christ, and become partakers with Him—or, in other words still, abide by the God-forgetting and self-pleasing world, and be swept away by the deluge of wrath that is about to rise against the ungodly; or, enter the ark of heaven and survive the storm! The unhoused and unsheltered world must succumb to the tempest, but the Christ-built ark will ride it out, and all who are within it will be unharmed. The world-bound will die and be disinherited; the ark-sheltered will be reinstated in their inheritance, and be made yet more free and more secure than before!

You must make your choice, ye who hear the gospel. The alternative is before every one of you. **On** the one side is the self-denying Christ of God : **on** the other, the self-pleasing world. Betake yourselves, each of you, **to** the one hand or the other. You must move in one direc-**tion.** To stand still is equivalent to moving wrong :— **to** stand still is to share with the condemned. Pity if, like Ahaziah, you choose Samaria in preference to Jerusalem, and Ahab rather than David! Pity if you prefer **a** covenant that is broken and condemnatory to the covenant that is ratified, and ordered in all things, and sure! Oh, pity if you prefer the brief and cloudy present to the unending and unclouded future!

And **there is** danger that you will make a wrong choice. **You** ought to be warned, and aroused to consideration. Myriads have made the mistake, and so may you. The truth is, proximate and congenial influences are against you. Seniors and friends have in many cases already decided wrong, and you **are** apt, Ahaziah-like, to take them for your counsellors and guides. It needs **effort** and self-sacrifice to prefer the right! But you ought not to hesitate. Make the effort and the sacrifices forthwith. The interests at stake are too important to be trifled with. If the world presses, so does the divine! **If** the world invites, so does the heavenly! If the world seem the more imposing by reason of nearness and visibility, your experience ought to enable you to rectify the illusion. You cannot but know how fleeting and how unsubstantial earthly professions and earthly pleasures are! Then why for the sake of them, deny yourself to the divine and the imperishable? O, be not like Ahaziah, who preferred the brief license and apparent *éclat* of fashionable idolatry, to the permanent lustre and satisfying evolutions of the throne of David as the anointed **one** of God! If, however, you will not be warned, **you** must not complain of the ruin that will overtake you. Your overthrow may not be exactly so swift as that of Ahaziah, but it will not be less overwhelming or terrific.

Nor will it be long deferred even though you are spared to the utmost limit of human life. Seventy earthly years bear a far less proportion to eternity than did the one year's reign of Ahaziah to the forty years' reign of David : so that, if you be disinherited by reason of a wrong choice, it will still be comparatively in your early years. This life is but " the bud of being," and to perish at the end of it, even though one hundred years old, is to lose all the treasures and experiences of immortality. If we lament **for** Ahaziah's early death, as a forfeiture of forty years of royal life among men, oh, how shall we grieve for the forfeiture of those who are cut off from the ineffable and unending delights of the blessed eternity!

But this leads me to notice, concerning Ahaziah,—

III. His memory.

And that is both *unblest* and *unbuoyant*. An early death is not always an unblest memory,—nor yet an unbuoyant one. You must have heard of many who have died young and yet left behind them a memory both fragrant and esteemed. It was not so with Ahaziah. There were few to weep for him, and there were none who could truly bless him. Even his mother Athaliah who had misguided him seems to have been unsoftened by his death, else she could not have acted as she did towards his children. She caused them all to be slain, at least the male portion of them, so far as she knew. Instead of blessing his memory, and guarding lovingly those he had left behind him, she herself became the coadjutor of Jehu in the work of destruction. While Jehu slew, or caused to be slain, at Samaria, she slew, or caused to be slain, at Jerusalem. Instead of mourning for the ruin that had fallen on her son, she herself became the willing instrument of carrying forward and completing that ruin. It would seem as if she wished to supplement the work of the ruthless executioner, and complete the bloody tragedy which he had begun. There was neither tenderness nor benediction in her heart in relation to the unhappy Ahaziah! And if his own mother and counsellor was thus unbenignant and unsoftened toward him, what could we expect from others? His cousins and relatives at Samaria again could not bless his memory, for they perished with him, or rather he perished with them: and, though it had not been so, they might have proved as cruel and unnatural as his mother. Any way, their benedictions, being the benedictions of the ungodly, could have had no benign import in relation to him. His counsellors therefore could not bless him: and the pious in Jerusalem could not bless him. Pity him the pious might, and no doubt did, but for blessings on his memory,—these they could not give. Heaven frowned: how then could the servants of Heaven smile? He had perished under displeasure, and the cloud must rest upon his name. He had forsaken God: and the benedictions of God cannot rest on the rebellious! His name is but a blot on the page of history, and piety can find no comfort in repeating it. Not only heaven, but all on earth in subsequent ages—all at least whose blessing is of any value—regard his memory with displacency. The ungodly care not for it, and though they did, their benedictions would go for nothing: and the godly can only disapprove and reject it. Who of all the struggling and sorrowing sons of men, I should like to know, remembers Ahaziah with esteem? Who finds comfort or incitement to good by recurring to his history? The memory of David hath been a blessing to many, and many have blessed his name as they read his psalms, or thought of his pious disinterestedness; but who hath blessed, or been blessed by, the memory of Ahaziah? The faith of Abraham again hath instructed thousands, and elicited benedictions on his name; but the defection of Ahaziah hath neither blessed nor awakened blessings among his successors on earth. The early death of Abel, too, touches with tenderness the hearts of men even to our own time, and awakens blessings on his memory; but the early death of Ahaziah awakens but a transient, though deep, pity, with no benediction or sympathizing love. The truth is, the **name** of this youthful victim to Jehu's zeal is now nothing among men. It may be **said** to be **a** blank **as** well **as** a blot **on** the page of history, and the world remembers it not. **It** stands as a link in the posterity of David, but without any of the sanctity attaching to it which belongs to that sacred house. It is a name unsacred and a memory unblessed :— that **is, no one** blesses **it,** and no one is blessed **by** it.

And it is **a** memory *unbuoyant* as well. A temporary cloud may **fall upon a** worthy memory, and its claims may for a time **be** forgotten, but time and circumstances sweep aside the cloud, and the memory re-appears with its claims and recommendations undiminished : or, a name may be submerged and dishonoured for a time, and yet come again to the surface, and command the attention and esteem of thousands, or of ages. We could point to names in modern history that have been beclouded and falsified for long years, and yet have now emerged again into daylight, and enjoy the high esteem of the enlightened and the candid. But, alas, for Ahaziah! His name hath no buoyancy. It hath "sunk like lead in the mighty waters," and there is no prospect of its re-appearance at the surface. He detached himself from the buoyant, and he sank without hope of recovery. Had he abode by Jerusalem, and David, and the covenant **of** perpetuity, he would have been borne up and sustained. Had he embraced the hope that cheered the heart of his great ancestor, and foreshadowed by fidelity, and right-eousness, the coming Messiah and King, he too would have become immortal. He would have become buoyant with the buoyancy of the divine! He might have sunk for a time, like David himself, amid the obscurities of death, but he would have reappeared in the retinue of the Triumphant at last, when the pageant of earth shall have passed away. But, by detaching himself from David in favour of Ahab, he detached himself from David's mystic Son, the divine King of Israel, and consequently from the triumphant and buoyant fortunes of that king. Nay more, by attaching himself to the house of Ahab, he attached himself to the sinking and unbuoyant, and he can never reappear in brightness. He may come again at the last day, but not with the forgiven and the faithful. He may be brought again from the depths for a moment, but it will only be to receive his sentence, and to sink again to the undesirable regions of dishonour and rejection with his condemned associates.

Such is the brief and sorrowful story of this youthful Prince. He took for his counsellors, the ungodly and idolatrous; though he had access to the fountains of divine wisdom, he attached himself to the doomed and the denounced, and fell in the tempest that overwhelmed them. And his memory is unblest in the earth and unbuoyant in the universe. We cannot but lament his infatuation and his fate; but we ought not to rest with lamentation. We ought to take warning and endeavour to pursue a wiser course. We ought not to walk in the counsel of the ungodly, but we ought to listen to the words of God! We ought not to abide by the first Adam, but we ought to betake ourselves to the second! And we ought so to walk in the faith of the Son of God, and Son of David, as to leave a blessed and a buoyant memory behind us.

A *blessed* memory, you will remember, is just the echo of a gentle and a loving life. That is, a life of faith upon the Son of God, who loved us, and gave Himself for us. You understand this matter so far as human society is concerned. You know how you feel, and you have an idea how others feel, when any one of your friends or neighbours dies. Supposing the departed to have been gentle, humble, and devout, you think of them with tenderness, and bless, in effect, their memory; and as far as opportunity permits, you express that kindness toward their memory, especially to those they have left behind them. Instead of destroying their children as Athaliah did those of Ahaziah, you would rather benefit, protect, or favour them. On the other hand, if the departed had walked rudely, selfishly, or wickedly, you could only pity; you could not bless. The echo from your nature could be only disapprobation or **regret!** And so of others, so **far** as the life **of the departed hath been** felt. Where **that** life had been unfelt, **of** course, there could be no **echo.** Now, that which takes **place** in the immediate **circle of** the dead takes place also on a larger scale in the universe. Every man's life creates an echo in the material and angelic world, as well as in his own immediate circle. You may not hear **the** response of nature to the character of departed, but **it** sounds in the **ears of** the divine Ruler notwithstanding. You may not understand the sentiments of angels concerning the life and aims of him **over** whose grave you stand, but they have formed their **estimation of** them nevertheless. Nay, more, the life **and** character of each man awakens an echo from the throne of God itself; and that echo is ever faithful and true. It is neither distorted by prejudice **nor by** partial information, **as** is often the case with human **echoes.** It is on the contrary, both just **and** discriminating. **The** result in each man's case after death is, either **a** blessed or an unblessed memory. The ungodly and the unwise are unblest, at best—to say nothing of malediction; but the godly and the pure are blessed and approved—blessed and approved by God—blessed and approved **by** angels—blessed and approved **by** the holy universe. "The memory of the wicked **shall rot, but the** memory of the just shall be blessed." And **I need** only remind you, that a blessed memory, being the **echo** of a blessed life, is also the harbinger of a blessed immortality. In other words a blessed memory is also a buoyant memory.

And a *buoyant memory* is a memory **that** will not die, a memory that cannot be permanently submerged. It may seem to be **so** for a time, but it will reappear spite of every hinderance. It cannot sink to forgetfulness. It

L

cannot be lost. The crowding candidates for attention ever springing up with new generations may seem to sweep it aside, but it will reappear in due time. Death may drag it beneath the waves, and the grave may set its leaden foot upon it at the bottom of the great deep, but it cannot be held there. It will find the surface again. It will shine yet under the smile of Deity.

And you know very well how it is so. He that hath the Son hath life. And he that hath life hath his name written in the Lamb's book of life. And think you that they whose names are written in the Lamb's book of life can be held under permanent obscuration? They are identified with the buoyant; they are one with the triumphant. They are the living members of a living and reigning Head; and will they be left, think, you on the low-lying and dark places of the universe? Their Head hath ascended above all height. He hath broken the spell and the power of the grave. He hath emerged from the dark waves of oblivion, which roll over the tombs of the ages. He hath ascended above the changing and mortal atmosphere of earth. Nay, He hath ascended above the regions of all change and vicissitude. And He hath pledged Himself concerning His believing people. As He lives, they shall live also. As He hath been brought again from the dead, they too shall be raised at the last day. As He hath taken His seat at the right hand of the Majesty on high, they too shall be presented to the Father without spot, or wrinkle, or any such thing. His will is, that where He is there they shall be also,— that they may behold His glory and be made partakers of His divine life. And He hath power to make good His determination in this, as in all other respects. He is not done with our world, though He hath retired from the visible inhabitation of it in the meantime. He is coming again. He is coming in glory. And when He who is the life of His people shall appear, then shall they also appear with Him in glory. Then the buoyancy of their memory and of their being shall be made manifest. Bound to the Triumphant, they too shall be triumphant

Abiding **by** the beloved, they too shall be beloved! And being part and parcel of the retinue of the Illustrious, they too shall be illustrious! **And** their honour shall **be** eternal! And their grateful joy shall be unalloyed **with** any grief! O, how happy to be buoyant in memory through the buoyancy of the divine Messiah! And to be blessed **in** memory with the blessings which fall **upon** Him! **But only they** who live by the faith of Him, **and** in imitation of **Him, can** rightly expect **the** felicity. **If, like** Ahaziah, **you** prefer Ahab **to** David, **you** forfeit **all. You can** then **be** neither blessed nor buoyant **in** memory **when** you die. In other words, if you prefer the world, with its duplicities and delusive prizes, to the loyal, and loving, and self-denying Redeemer, you must make up your minds to dishonour and overthrow! Without Him, you can neither have the blessings of Heaven, nor the buoyancy of immortality!

QUESTIONS ON AHAZIAH.

Who were Ahaziah's counsellors?
  His mother, Athaliah, and his kindred **of Samaria.**
Were these friends his safe counsellors?
  The very contrary. They were the worst advisers he could have listened to.
What may we suppose was the burden of their advice?
  To renounce the peculiarities of his nation, as narrow and antiquated, and to place himself and his Government in sympathy with Tyre and the outlying nations.
Was it excusable in him to listen to such advisers?
  Not at **all.** There **were** weighty reasons **to the** contrary, **and he knew** them.
Mention some **of** these **reasons?**
  1. He had known his grandfather, Jehoshaphat and seen something of the happy fortunes of that king as a servant of Israel's God; and he **had** known the contrary experience of his father as **a devotee** of the idolatry recommended by his relations.
  2. He had heard too of the denunciations **of** Heaven by the writing of Elijah delivered to his father, and seen their fulfilment in his father's history.
  3. And he must have heard in the court of his grandfather much **of the** miraculous history of his nation—as well **as**

of the utterances and demonstrations of Elijah and Elisha.

Why did Ahaziah disregard these considerations?
Because he preferred the present and the fashionable to the unseen and the true. His heart was earthly, and his choice was accordingly unwise and foolish.

Are there not many in our time acting the part of Ahaziah?
Very many. Their chosen companions and counsellors are worldly and their desires are worldly. They have heard indeed of the Book of God and of the Church of God, but these been unfashionable and opposed to the pride of life, they silently evade or openly reject them.

What should young people remember as a protection against this mistake?
That "one thing is needful." What if a man "gain the whole world and lose his own soul."

How long did Ahaziah live and reign?
He lived forty-three years, reigned but one.

Is there not something sad in his early death?
Inexpressibly so:—Early death is ever sad, but more particularly so in the case of the royal and exalted.

Can you account for his early fall?
To a certain extent.

Tell how it was?
He was the heir of good as a descendant of David, but the heir of evil as the descendant of Ahab. His own choice must determine the party with which he must participate. He chose Samaria and therefore perished with the royal family of Samaria.

Having associated himself with Ahab and idolatry, could he reasonably expect to escape the destruction denounced against that party?
By no means: he must share the fortunes of his chosen associates.

Is there any analogy between our circumstances and those of Ahaziah respecting heirship?
Certainly: we too are the heirs of two covenants—the one broken and wrathful—the other established and replete with blessings.

What then is demanded from us in these circumstances?
To choose aright between the first Adam and the second. To refuse the counsel of our Samaria of this world, and to abide by the Christ of God, who is the wonderful counsellor and an infallible guide. To disregard the contumely of the unbelieving and to cast in our lot with the spiritual Israel.

But does this matter belong to us ?
  Yes : to every one who hears the gospel. No one can **be** neutral. To abide by the first Adam is, in effect, to choose wrath; **and** to postpone a right decision **is**, in effect, to make **a** wrong choice.

Is there danger for each of us,—that **we will make a** wrong choice ?
  Yes : proximate and congenial influences are in favour of the wrong, and we are all indisposed to the self-sacrifice which a right choice requires.

What do they forfeit who make a wrong choice ?
  The treasures of heaven and the experience of immortality.

What have you to remark concerning the memory of Ahaziah ?
  That it is unblest and unbuoyant. There was none to bless his memory, and there is no possibility of his name ever again rising to **the** surface.

But his name has survived the lapse of ages ?
  Yes : but not with benedictions. It survives as a link in the posterity of David, but no one blesses it, and none are blessed by it.

What **do you** call a blessed memory ?
  The **echo** of **a** gentle and loving life. And this cannot be when **the** life hath been rude, selfish, and wicked.

Is the echo of a gentle and a loving life confined to earth ?
  No. It is reverberated in blessings from the angelic world and from the divine throne.

And have these blessings **on** the memory any significance as to the future ?
  Yes. They are the harbingers **of a** bright and blessed immortality.

But what do you mean by a buoyant memory ?
  A memory that cannot be permanently submerged.

What is the only security for a buoyant memory ?
  The **same** as for a blessed memory :—even union to the divine. Without this we must sink hopelessly, but with this **a** triumphant reappearance is certain. " When Christ, who is our life, shall appear, then shall we also appear with Him in glory !"

What then is the general lesson taught **us** by the story of Ahaziah ?
  To prefer Jerusalem to Samaria—the second Adam to the first—and the consolations of Christianity to the pleasures of the world.

IX. JOASH.

"Then they brought out the king's son, and put upon him the crown, and gave him the testimony and made him king. And Jehoiada and his sons anointed him and said: God save the king."—II. Chron. xxiii. 11.

IT was sad to see a character like that of Athaliah, trained under evil influences, and determined to abide by the wrong at all hazards. She was brought within the range of happier influences, and but for her pride and prejudices might have attained to the knowledge of the true God, but she scorned and hated when she ought to have inquired and prayed. Nay, she sought in her self-will to disarrange the purposes of Heaven, and she was cast aside a wretched and ruined thing. It is sad, I say, to contemplate such a character and sad history.

But it is almost sadder still to follow the story of Joash; more happily trained than Athaliah, and more favourably situated for attaining to true knowledge and true excellence than she. His end was not better than hers. With greater privileges he must incur yet deeper condemnation. No doubt she had access to the fountain of divine knowledge as well as he, but her nature was pre-occupied with error before she became a queen in Jerusalem: when as his nature was, as it were pre-occupied with good ere he had opportunity to come in contact with evil.—And so much the more criminal was he in his infatuated and inexcusable choice of vanity and idolatry.

But if Joash was worse than Athaliah, the unfaithful members of Christian families are worse still. The light they enjoy or have enjoyed, is greater by far than that enjoyed by Joash. The manifestation of divinity, and of the **way** of safety in Christ Jesus, places all former revelations in shadow; and they who disregard those manifestations, and give themselves to worldliness and self-pleasing in spite of them, incur a criminality beyond all description great. "How shall we escape if **we** neglect so great a salvation?" If it was unsafe **to** despise the servant Moses, what shall be thought of those who reject the Son of God himself? We are ready to condemn Athaliah, and to lift our hands in horror at the infatuation of Joash, but we would do well to look to ourselves, **and** see if we are not more monstrously unwise than even they. That we may be aided, or stimulated, **or warned** aright in this matter, we shall remind you **of** his preservation in infancy, his prime minister and **adviser** and his unworthy and disastrous end.

I. His Preservation in Infancy.

That was very remarkable as you must **at** once perceive. He was completely in the hands **of** his grandmother and her agents. And there were no tendernesses nor scruples about her heart to plead for the helpless infant. She was determined to make a full end of the house of David, not only of those of them who **stood** immediately in her way to the throne, but of those, also, who might arise to question her right to rule. There might be something like revenge in the way, **as** well as ambition. She might think thus **to** cast defiance at the God of Israel, by whose prophets her father's house had been doomed and denounced. While Jehu slew her children at Samaria, she would **give** blow for blow, as she might think, by slaying **all the sacred** family **at** Jerusalem. Jehu had spared none, and she would spare none. She would maintain the contest so bitterly prosecuted by her mother Jezebel against Elijah, and against Elijah's God—even **the** God of the Jewish people. "If (we can conceive her saying, when the news reached her of the bloody tragedy **in** which her mother, and her son, and all her kindred perished)—if the house of Ahab has become extinct,—so shall the house of David. I can issue cruel orders as well as the flustering Jehu, and it shall not be said that my mother Jezebel died unrevenged." Under this firm determination she ordered the immediate destruction of every male member of the royal family; and there were plenty of ready instruments to execute the order. How then could Joash escape? Who could be expected to have courage to attempt his rescue? Still less, who could have power or resources to effect his deliverance in the face of one so powerful, so ruthless, and so unscrupulous? We could not have anticipated for him any human intervention in the circumstances. Yet such was found. His aunt Jehoshabeth, and her husband Jehoiada, both dared and succeeded in the attempt. They withdrew him from the palace, ere the sword had reached him, and secreted him and his nurse in the temple; and they kept him there, and nourished him, and watched over him for six years without any one ever suspecting the fact of his presence in the sacred edifice. Had they hastened him away in the midst of the confusion, and hid him in some distant hamlet or fortress, his safety would have seemed less wonderful; but they kept him in the immediate neighbourhood of the palace of Athaliah. He was never beyond her reach for these six years. She could have slain him at any moment during the progress of these years, if only she had known of his existence. There were neither scruples, nor distance, nor want of power to prevent, Only the screen of the temple wall was between her and her victim; but that slender screen was found sufficient in the providence of God to protect the youthful Joash until the hour of retribution arrived, and then the sword of destruction fell upon the proud and defiant queen, and not on the powerless boy. Nay more, then the defiant queen was swept out of life, and the powerless boy established on the throne of his father David.

This was remarkable—but it becomes still more interesting when we remember how much hung on the life of this child. He was now the only representative of the house of David, and the hope of the world was wrapped up in that house. Destroy that **child's life**, and (miracle apart) the light of prophecy expires, **and the** hope of **the** future is no more; kill Joash and the channel of "the seed of woman" promised in Paradise is cut off, and all the quickening influences to spring from the incarnation will be looked for in **vain**. Only think of it, the forthcoming and invaluable blessing, intended for the nations checked and turned back on their source, and the **subsequent** ages left to the unrestrained action of **the** cruel god of the darkness of this world! What a triumph for Satan, if it could have been achieved! And what **a** misfortune for the world! One wonders **that** the dark enemy of goodness did not find some way of indicating **to** Athaliah, the important secret that **a** Prince of the house of David was still untouched by her **sword. No** doubt he tried **it**; but his subtilty failed **in** the attempt. A higher **and a** benignant power counteracted his machinations, and shielded the precious life. **God** was not to be foiled in **his** gracious purposes! Nor was **the** world **to be left** permanently in the grasp of the usurper. Even **as** Joash supplanted Athaliah, **so** will the Illustrious one on whose account Joash was preserved, supplant in due time the power that prompted her, and used her for its dark purposes. The promises of God must be made good, and therefore Joash lived and triumphed. True, God could still have made good His promises, even though the last of the sons of David had fallen, for He could have raised this same one, or some other member of that house, to life again; but His wisdom and all-embracing providence are more **fully** illustrated and honoured by His preserving the links of His mighty and benignant purpose through the most threatening dangers.

And not on this occasion only has God preserved His cause in the earth when **it** was all but extinct. Think of the Antediluvians, when Noah alone, of all the crowding myriads that then filled the earth, feared God, and testified of His righteousness. How easy then, one would have thought, for Satan to complete his triumphs and forever arrest the progress of good in human history!

A dagger planted in Noah's breast would have finished the strife between light and darkness on earth, and banished heaven from the abodes of men. And there were plenty of unscrupulous agents of evil then available, when violence actually covered the earth. But Noah was preserved spite of all, and in the midst of all. He was as safe amid the sweeping waves of violence, as afterwards amid the sweeping waves of the deluge. Amid the violence, the favour of God compassed him about as a shield: and amid the waves, he was sheltered and borne aloft in safety by the buoyant ark where God had shut him in? Though Satan had conquered all beside, he was foiled, and thrown back in the case of Noah. Satan could neither beguile Noah to disloyalty, nor destroy his life. With innumerable agents at his bidding, he could not prevail against one loyal servant of the Most High.

Nor was it otherwise with David himself, the progenitor of Joash, and the chosen channel of mercy to mankind. He was encompassed with dangers. The powerful sought his life with persistency and determination. King Saul himself attempted with his own javelin more than once to end his career, and to make his reign and his dynasty an impossibility. But it was to no purpose. David survived all, David supplanted the house of his would-be murderer in the throne of Israel, transmitted his crown, and left a precious influence behind him.

And so with the New Testament Church: it has been all but extinct, so far as appearances went, on more occasions than one. Before the appearance of Luther for example, darkness covered the earth, and gross darkness the people. For a thousand years, the progress of evil had been unchecked and the kingdom of worldliness seemed to be completely and universally established. The cruel Church of Rome, Athaliah-like, had destroyed apparently all the seed royal, and there seemed to be none to secrete or care for the smallest member of the heavenly family. All was gloom: the hope of the world seemed to be cut off, and the heavenly kingdom could no

longer put forth blossom or bud. The cruel agents of
darkness ever ready at any point to destroy the faintest
appearance of the heavenly life. There was neither
hope nor prospect of a happy change! Yet from the
midst of this gloom, and contrary to all probabilities, the
truth of God, Joash-like, emerged, and raised again the
standard of heaven upon the earth. The Popes, and
their agents, cried, like the usurping daughter of Jezebel
in Jerusalem "Treason! treason!" But the cry brought
only confusion and overthrow to the Papacy in many
countries. The cause of God is not to be permanently
put down. It survived the usurpation of Athaliah in
Jerusalem, and it will survive the usurpation of the
Mother of Harlots in the earth. And it is well for ourselves that it is so. But for the grace of God, and His
sheltering love in relation to His Church and kingdom
among men, we had been the slaves of superstition today, and the besotted victims of a selfish and unscrupulous priesthood.

And there is comfort here for the true believer as well
as joy for the Church. The humblest saint is not forgotten in the presence of God. If he is not now the
one channel of good to the world, as in the case of Joash,
he is still a part of that precious kingdom which abides
under the shadow of the Almighty, and ministers to
the enlightenment of the world. His adversaries may
be mighty and determined. His great enemy may seek
like a roaring lion to devour him, and myriad agencies of
evil may be ready to lift a hostile hand against him; and
himself may actually aid his enemies by his occasional
unbelief or inconsistency: still, the great divine High
Priest watches over such. He is mightier than Jehoiada:
He will find agents of mercy or guidance as the case
may require: and He will certainly secure the safety and
ultimate triumph of His humble and helpless ones.
They may be as infants in the presence of those who
seek their life, but they shall be protected and saved
notwithstanding. Nothing can separate them from the
love of God which is in Christ Jesus. Not life, nor

death, nor principalities, nor powers, nor things present, nor things to come. Their shielding High Priest is able to save to the uttermost, because He ever liveth to make **intercession for** them. And **as for the power of** their **enemies, He** can effectually curb that. All power in **heaven and in earth** is His. And he cannot fail nor be **discouraged!** Oh the comfort of this for the lowly, and exposed, **and** confiding **ones!** If their shielding Lord and High Priest cannot **be** discouraged, no more ought they. They should strengthen themselves in the grace and might that are **in Him, and** that therefore envelope them! An eloquent **preacher of our own** day when speaking of the preservation of Joash, thus apostrophises the believing :—

"However deeply disguised thou may'st wander, my **brother in the** Lord, however scanty thou may'st seem **to thyself** with respect to spiritual gifts, **let** nothing prevent thee (O thou that feelest thy **poverty,** but hopest **in Jesus), let** nothing prevent thee **from** perceiving in Joash, t**hy** image,—in his history, their own! Continue unknown **to** the world. **Be** even to thy brethren partially disguised. Yet in the gloomy chrysalis state of thy infirmity thou art **a** King's son, who hast found an asylum, though it be in a hidden back room, instead **of** before the altar, yet nevertheless in *His* Temple, **and art** attended to by the hands **of a** great **High** Priest! I **know not** what may have been ordained concerning thee, **but** the hour will at length arrive, though it may be the **last** of thy earthly existence, when the gate **of** thy tear**ful cell** shall open, and thou shalt hear the voice of Him whom thou dost not trust in vain, blissfully exclaiming, 'Come forth!' **and** messengers, **in** dazzling robes of light shall approach to invest thee with the attire and **crown** of that King David whose dominion is infinite. **And the** host of those who have overcome **which no** man can number, shall shout **a** thousand times, 'welcome!' It will then be **Satan's** turn to hold down his head, and a hostile world's to start and be silent with confusion, whilst thou ascendest to the heights of unfading and celestial joy, and with loud and unrestrained accents praises to Him, of whom it is justly written, 'They looked unto Him, and were lightened, and their faces were not ashamed!' And as with thee, so with all thy fellow-believers—even with the whole Church —the 'worm Jacob,' the tossed with tempest, and not comforted." The youthful King **Joash** is a prediction of what awaits her, crown and royal robes lie ready for her, though **at** present, **a** beggar's garment scarcely covers her nakedness. Content thyself until the day of thy investiture with the glory of faith beforehand. The time is at hand when **it** shall be said to thee, " cry out and shout, thou inhabitant of Zion, for great is the Holy one of Israel **in** the midst **of** thee !" In that day shall the Lord defend the inhabitants of Jerusalem. And he that is feeble among them at that day shall be as David ; and the house of David shall be as God, as the angel of the Lord before them."—*Krummacher's Elisha*, 205-6.

See then your security, ye who embrace the truth, and nestle under the wing of the great High Priest, and belong **to** the spiritual household of God. No weapon formed against you then can prosper, and no malignity can **permanently** obscure your heavenly and holy fortunes. **You** are made kings and priests unto God, **and** you shall not only be preserved from those who would destroy you, and usurp your patrimony, but you shall be preserved for manifestation as the sons of God, and for the full and **unclouded** enjoyment of your royal and heavenly inheritance. Joash, alas ! was preserved and established in his kingdom merely as a human link in the chain of Messiah's progenitors, but you shall be preserved as a vital part of the precious mystical body of the living and exalted Redeemer. Joash lived to prove that, he was not in heart of the house of David, as we shall see immediately, nor yet in vital connexion with the great Prince, who was permanently to occupy David's throne, yet his preservation **in** the midst of enemies, and his own successful enthronement in the face of overwhelming difficulties is not the less an instructive illustration of the spiritual preservation and ultimate enthronement of the children of God, spite of all that their determined and disobedient adversaries can do to the contrary.

But this leads me to notice concerning Joash—

II. His Prime Minister and Adviser.

So far the youthful Joash has been passive in the hands of Jehoiada and a watchful providence; but he grew to maturity, and became himself the artificer of his own fortunes to a certain extent. As he grew into manhood, he could choose for himself, and determine the complexion of his government.

And mark how favourable his position was for adopting a right course. He had for his prime-minister and adviser, his preserver and tutor. Jehoiada abode by his throne during a large part of his reign. Though nearly one hundred years old when Joash was born, his life was prolonged far into the life of Joash. His life was continued into its second century, we might almost say, for the sake of the youthful Prince, whom he had so singularly saved. Had Jehoiada died at the usual limit, the training of Joash might have fallen to some time-serving or idolatry-fawning official. His nature would thus have been perverted from the beginning, and he had not been materially better as to opportunity for good, than his immediate predecessor. But Jehoiada was preserved, old though he was, and Joash had the benefit of his counsels and experience until he had ample time to form good habits himself, and to become fixed in good principles. Jehoiada had special claims on his gratitude, and the advice of Jehoiada could not be gracefully rejected. Joash had grown out of a state of pupilage and dependence into a state of enlightment and self-control under the venerable High Priest, and he was thus drawn imperceptibly into the right course. Jehoiada ordered the repairs of the temple, and Joash fell in with the advice. Nay, he seems on one occasion to have outrun Jehoiada himself in his zeal for the work. Jehoiada would undo what Athaliah had so wickedly done in Jerusalem, and Joash was willing that it should be so. Jehoiada led the way in rectitude and piety, and Joash under his guidance did that which was right in the sight of the Lord. The supreme rights of Jehovah were again acknowledged in Jerusalem, and they offered burnt offerings in the house of the Lord continually.

Thus Joash was drawn to the right while his character was being formed, and by the influence of one whom he could not becomingly oppose. And there was no counteracting influence from ungodly relatives. They were all slain, all taken out of the way ere he was yet capable of receiving any evil bias from them. The house of Ahab was extinguished. His own immediate relations, who had been drawn into conformity with that wicked house, were also slain. There was nothing to prevent his adopting the sentiments and policy of his guardian and prime minister. There was everything to aid him, and nothing to draw him aside. One could almost fancy that all his kindred had been slain, not only for their idolatry and wickedness, but also to give the family of David a new start. Even as Noah was preserved at the deluge, to commence a happier order of things, so Joash was preserved amid general massacre as to his kindred, to recommence the dynasty of David on its original footing. That dynasty had been thoroughly corrupted and turned aside, and it was needful that something extraordinary should be done, if it was not to be entirely ruined ; and you see how fitting the arrangements were to bring back the sacred family to its proper and benignant position. All are destroyed but one infant. That infant is placed under pious tuition, and the young king hath preserved to him, almost against the ordinary course of things the faithful High Priest who had saved and educated him, to be his prime minister and adviser in the kingdom. Evil influences are removed ; good influences are furnished early and continued late. Every thing is done that wisdom could dictate, or power secure, to enable the royal family to recover itself. How favoured was Joash ! And what obligations were laid on him to abide by the right into which he had been so marvellously brought ! How different his position from that of his father Abijah. That Prince was two and twenty when he began to reign, and he **did** that which was evil in the sight of the Lord, for **he had** his mother Athaliah as his counsellor **to** do wick**edly.** He walked in the ways of the house **of** Ahab, for they were his counsellors **after the** death of **his** father to his destruction. But Joash was under holier influences. He had **been** placed **in the** hands of **the** faithful, and effectually separated **from all** his corrupted and corrupting connexions. He **ought to** have been faithful surely. Even those whose circumstances are far less favourable **are under** obligation **to** seek **the** Lord; **how** great then the obligation of Joash! He ought to have been consist**ently** devoted **to God!** And he ought to have done that **which is right in** the sight of the Lord, and he ought to have **done so to the end**—only growing more and more devoted as **his** years grew upon him! Never any man had a better op**portunity** for doing well, and **for** leaving **a** name of excel**lence and honour** behind him! Not only **was** a pious **tutor** provided **for** him in his youth, **but** also a faithful prime minister **for** his **ripe** and royal years! But it was all to no purpose. No sooner was Joash left to the **freedom** of his own determinations than he undid all that Jehoiada had done **for** him—aye, and all that **God had** done for him. Instead of bringing again **the days of** David into Jerusalem, he fell back **into the wicked ways of the** house of Ahab! Instead of becoming illustrious **in connexion** with his distinguished prime minister, he **fell** into permanent disgrace. The name of Jehoiada, now for ever illustrious in the annals of Israel, instead of increasing the lustre of Joash's reign, only reminds us of the singular and uncommon turpitude of the later years of that reign. But before noticing the unworthy end of this sovereign, we would remind you of **the** instructive analogy which it suggests.

We are favoured, even as Joash **was,** and in **a** far more glorious manner. I mean **as** to advice and guidance. We **are not** kings among men **as** he was, but we equally need **counsel** and advice, obscure though we are. We have each a royal history to prosecute, and immortal interests interweave themselves with our lowly and passing duties. By nature, too, we are allied to the corrupt, even as Joash was, and if left to the counsel and guidance of our natural relations we will become involved with the evil and disobedient, and be made participators in the judgment which must sooner or later overwhelm them. We need help and effective sympathy. We need to be torn from our erring connections, and to be brought under happier auspices. And what has the great High Priest of New Testament times done in the circumstances? He hath not slain our earthly connexions, and thus freed us from evil counsel and influence, but He hath Himself died for sin, that we might die to it. He hath sought to bind us to Himself by a controlling bond, and thus to separate us from our misleading associations. He hath devoted Himself to our recovery and well-being. He is ready to become the attendant and helper of every one willing to listen to Him, and willing to be guided by His advice.

And need I remind you of his competency. He is the Wonderful Counsellor, the Condescending Friend, the Infallible Guide. Human counsellors, however wise, may mistake or misunderstand circumstances, but there is no mistake with the New Testament High Priest. Only consult Him, and be guided by Him, and you will certainly find safety and peace. True, He hath withdrawn Himself from human cognition, but He hath not therefore lost sight of those who look to Him for counsel. On the contrary, He hath gone into the inner shrine of the temple in the interests of such; and He can hear their cry even there, and He can send thence light and response as His waiting ones require. "Ask what ye will," said He ere he left for heaven, "and it shall be done unto you," ask in my name, and ye shall not ask in vain! Nay more, though at the right hand of the Majesty on high, He is with his disciples, even to the end of the world, and He is the guide and counsellor of each of them as fully and satisfactorily as though there were only one in existence. Let it not be thought that Joash had the advantage in this, that he had Jehoiada solely to himself as counsellor and guide, while the disciples of the New Testament High Priest have each only a fractional share in the regards of their counsellor. O no! the perfections of this New Testament High Priest are such that He can give, as it were, undivided attention and consideration to each. And He is far more fully acquainted with the necessities and interests of His dependent ones than any merely human counsellor can ever possibly be. Then, while ever near in reality, if not apparently, and ever ready to advise and direct, as special cases may arise, He hath also left permanent directions for the guidance of his wards. In the sermon on the mount particularly, as well as in the Holy Scriptures in general, He hath shown us the principles by which we ought to be guided, and pointed out the matters of supreme concernment and pursuit. He hath shown us that humility and not pride is the basis of excellence; that the law of the Lord extends to the thoughts of the heart as well as to the actions of the life; that all religious and other duties should be attended to, as in the presence of God, and not for human approbation; and that candour and magnanimity ought to characterise us socially. And he urges all to enter the strait gate; to seek first the kingdom of God and His righteousness, and to listen to Himself as the only competent and disinterested Teacher! Thus there can be no dubiety on the minds of His wards as to the course they ought to pursue, even while He is shrouded in the inner and heavenly sanctuary; and there need be no undue anxiety concerning His stay behind the veil; for He hath promised to come forth in due time to bless his waiting, trusting, and obedient ones, and to conduct them into the presence of the Father!

Is it not a privilege to have such a counsellor and adviser, and guide? We think Joash favoured in Jehoiada, and so he was; but are we not yet more highly favoured in the New Testament High Priest? Joash had but to avail himself of Jehoiadah's wisdom and piety to secure good! Joash had but to abide by the policy of Jehoiada to leave a name of honour behind him, as well as to bless his generation. In like manner, we have but to avail ourselves of the wisdom and sympathy of our High Priest to secure immortal joy. We have but to abide by the policy and purposes of Jesus, to secure unending honour, and to benefit our contemporaries as well. We are the wards of a divine High Priest, and may enjoy infallible counsel in any exigence of our important history! Incalculable consequences hang on our decisions. It is important that we should have competent and unsinister advice. Jesus is prepared to furnish it, and to lead us safely through this dark territory of sin and mortality, to a fair and unclouded region, where disarrangement hath no longer any place!

Shall we turn from such a counsellor? Shall we listen to those who would seduce us into courses other than those which He approves? There are many such pressing around us, and plausible oftentimes are their representations. Shall we yield to them? In other words, shall we repeat the folly of Joash? Shall we withdraw our attention from the pole star of our safety? Shall we view the grace of God in vain? That grace hath appeared unto all men, "Teaching us to deny ungodliness and to live soberly and and righteously in this present world; looking for the blessed hope and the glorious appearing of the great God, and our Saviour, Jesus Christ:"—Shall we refuse that grace? Shall we put away from us eternal life? Then do not let us blame Joash! Many are disposed to feel indignant at Joash for his stupidity in forsaking the ways of Jehoiada for the empty and degrading rites of idolatry, but they who turn from the New Testament High Priest at the call of worldly interests or pleasures, have no right to cherish such indignation, *unless it be at or against themselves.* They renounce a veritable, a divine, an all-competent adviser, in favour of the delusive and degrading! They re-establish the connexion with the condemned world, and forego for a mess of pottage an immortal inheritance! They give their affections to the things which cannot satisfy, and thereby lose all right of participation with the children of God in the things which cannot disappoint. They lose, O the incalculable loss! they lose their inheritance in that divine love which will prove to those who enjoy it rapture, and sunshine, and safety, to eternal ages! Are you prepared, any of you to make such a mistake? O, no, you exclaim! we would not be the imitators of Joash! Then, you must abide by the divine High Priest, and refuse the seductions of those who would draw you from the Rock, and induce you to build upon unstable sand in preference! But to return to the story of Joash, we notice—

III. His unworthy and disastrous end.

Of *his unworthiness,* we have a note in the 24th chapter, from the 17th to the 22nd verses :—" Now after the death of Jehoiada came the princes of Judah, and made obeisance to the king! Then the king harkened unto them, and they left the house of the Lord God of their fathers, and served groves and idols: and wrath came upon Judah and Jerusalem for this their trespass. Yet he sent prophets to them to bring them again unto the Lord; and they testified against them: but they would not give ear. And the spirit of God came upon Zachariah, the son of Jehoiada, the priest which stood above the people, and said unto them, " Thus saith God, Why transgress ye the commandments of the Lord, that ye cannot prosper? Because ye have forsaken the Lord, he hath also forsaken you." And they conspired against him, and stoned him with stones at the commandment of the king in the court of the house of the Lord. Thus Joash the king remembered not the kindness which Jehoiada his father had done to him, but slew his son. And when he died, he said, " The Lord look upon it, and require it."

And here you will notice three faults—the first bad in any case, but specially bad in the case of Joash—the second worse than the first—and the third a complicated and daring wickedness beyond all description bad.

1st. *He*, in company with his obsequious and unwise princes, "*left the house of the Lord God of his fathers, and served groves and idols.*" Now, to say nothing of the obligations resting on him as a Jew, and nothing of the obligations arising from his position as a Prince of the house of David, was this a meet return for his preservation in his infancy from the votaries of groves and idols? Was it for thus that he had been spared when all his kindred were slain? They perished because of groves and idols, while he had been drawn into a loftier and safer service; where then was his gratitude for being thus favoured? And even apart from God, whose providence had so wonderfully and tenderly sheltered and favoured him, how could he remember Jehoiada, his counsellor and adviser, and yet yield himself to the companionship of idolators? O where the pleasant remembrances of his youth, and where the thoughts of his venerable instructor and guide? Ingratitude, it is said, is the blackest of delinquencies, and Joash was ungrateful,—with a double ingratitude. He was ungrateful to God, and he was ungrateful to Jehoiada, the instrument of God in his preservation and privileges! One excuse there might have been for his departure from the policy of Jehoiada, if that had been possible. If he had discovered that Jehoiada had been misleading him, and that truth and purity were to be found with the devotees of the idolatrous groves, then he might have been excused for the change—but no such discovery was possible. Every thing around him, on the contrary, testified for God, and against idols:—the Temple in which he had been preserved—the books of Moses in which he had been instructed—the history of his forefathers, both of the house of David and of the house of Ahab which he must have known, the character of the idol worship of which he could not be ignorant, and the expectations of the devout in Israel, represented by Jehoiada, with whom he had been so long familiar, all, all testified with trumpet tongue, that in forsaking the Lord God of his fathers for groves and idols—he was forsaking the rightful and the true, and attaching himself to the empty and degrading! Still he persisted, and then

2ndly. *He despised reproof.* "God sent prophets to him (and to his new advisers) to bring them again unto the Lord; and they testified against them, but they would not give ear." This was an aggravation of the first fault. Nay, it was a second and greater fault. It is bad enough to forsake the right, but it is clearly worse to resist and disregard remonstrances and entreaties intended to bring the wandering back to the right. A man may wander from inattention, or from the power of some present inducement, and yet be willing, when his mistake is pointed out to him, to retrace his steps. In that case he is blame-worthy, but not contumacious. It is otherwise when a man has not only gone wrong, but also refuses to be set right. He thus *resists* the authority which before he had only overlooked or forgotten, and declares his determination to abide by the error which he hath committed! And thus Joash treated the Lord God of his fathers, when that august One sent prophets to warn him of his error, and to recall him to the ways of obedience and righteousness. He treated God's agents with scorn, and pursued his mistaken and ungrateful way spite of all their remonstrances! Nor did his folly stop here; but

3rdly. *He commanded to destroy by stoning the prophet of the Lord, Zechariah, who was also the son of Jehoiada, and that in the* house *of the Lord.* What a complication of ingratitude and enormous daring in this one command! Mark, Zechariah was a prophet of the Lord, sent to remonstrate with the people against their unfaithfulness. He was the representative of heaven, and entitled to the respectful regards of the king as such. Instead of this, Joash commanded them to slay him—commanded them to declare war to the death against the Spirit of God that spake by him. Joash was worse than his ancestor, Asa, by many degrees. That prince was angry with Hanani, you will remember, and commanded to cast him into prison, but Joash commanded to stone Zechariah with stones. How daring thus to rush against the thick bosses of the Almighty's buckler! Then, this prophet of the Lord was also the son of Jehoiada; and yet Joash commanded his destruction. How could he? One would have thought that this alone would have been enough to interest Joash in his protection. If Jehoiada had risked the rage of Athaliah, and laboured and watched for years for the safety of Joash, surely Joash should have cared for the safety of the son of Jehoiada! Even though Zechariah had been walking perversely, Joash ought to have done what he could for his preservation—far more so when he **was** walking patriotically and devoutly! How awful the combined impiety and ingratitude that could give such **a** commandment, and against such a person! David would not give consent to the destruction of Saul, though Saul was seeking his life, because Saul was the anointed of the Lord; but Joash commanded the destruction of Zechariah, when Zechariah was only seeking the reformation of Israel, and though that same Zechariah was at once, the prophet of the Lord, and the son of his benefactor! And the very place where the stoning took place **is a** further aggravation of this wicked command. It **was** in the court of the house of the Lord. In the court of that very house where Joash himself had experienced so much care and tenderness from Jehoiada, and the thought of which ought to have reminded him of his venerable friend and adviser! Unworthy Joash! No words can declare the height or the turpitude of thy ingratitude and ungodly daring. Preëminent in privilege, thou art not less preëminent in folly. Special **were** the solicitudes that circled around thy cradle and faithful the hearts that sought to mould thee to piety! But dark and unworthy were thy returns! Thou didst receive the grace both of heaven and of earth in vain!

And now, it were not to be wondered at, if such a prince should find misfortune and sorrow! And what was the fact? We have it briefly recorded in three verses of the twenty-fourth chapter. "And it came to pass at the end of the year, that the hosts of Syria came up against him: and they came to Judah and Jerusalem, and destroyed all the princes of the people from among the people, and sent all the spoil of them unto the King of Damascus. For the army of the Syrians came with a small company of men, and the Lord delivered a very great host into their hands, because they had forsaken the Lord God of their fathers. So they executed judgment against Joash. And when they were departed from him (for they left him in great diseases), his own servants conspired against him for the blood of the sons of Jehoiada, the priest, and slew him in his bed, and he died: and they buried him in the city of David, but they buried him not in the sepulchres of the kings."

Can you conceive anything more disastrous or more lamentable? *He was disappointed in his army!* He trusted in its numbers and in its equipments. When the Syrians came against him he felt no need of divine aid, and sought none. He thought himself competent to deal with any power likely to assail him, and yet, when the hour of trial came, his mighty host was scattered before a comparatively small company of Syrians. He had in effect despised God, and God in his righteous Providence delivered him into the hands of his enemies; and his princes were slain, and all the spoil of these unwise counsellors, who had assured him of safety and conquest by their prowess, was sent to the king of Damascus. Then, *he was diseased in his body*, and that with no common or manageable diseases. When his enemies departed from him, they left him in *great diseases*. Nor did his diseases awaken sympathy on the part of his servants. His helplessness under them rather furnished opportunity which they were not slow to use: for they conspired against him, and slew him on his bed. He died in the flower of his years! He died by assassination too, for the blood of the sons of Jehoiada, his own protector and counsellor for good. His ingratitude returned upon his own head in the conduct of Zabad and Jehozabad. His servants, who ought to have sheltered and served him, arose and slew him! And **he** was buried without honour. He had no place in the sepulchres of the kings. How sad a termination for a royal life, a royal life so singularly preserved, and so highly favoured!

And it is especially admonitory to those who enjoy **a** religious education in youth, and have religious counsel and example in mature life. Let such beware how they depart from the **truth**! Let them beware of all insidious approaches **on** the part of **the** worldly and ungodly who would draw them from the ways of heaven! Let them abide by the great New Testament High Priest! And let them labour to grow in grace, and in **the** knowledge of their Lord, and divine Counsellor and Guide, and thus render defection less and less possible! And let them assure themselves, that the calamities of apostasy, of ingratitude, and of impiety, are not less alarming **or** less awful now than they were in the days of Joash!

QUESTIONS ON JOASH.

What special danger was **this** Prince exposed **to in his** infancy?
   Of being massacred with his brethren and relations by his grandmother Athaliah.
Why should his grandmother seek his destruction?
   In revenge for the death of her friends at Samaria by Jehu. She would not be outdone in cruelty by that warrior. As all her father's house had perished, she determined that a like complete destruction should fall on the house of David.
How was Joash saved when all his kindred perished?
   By the intervention of his aunt Jehoshabeth and her husband, Jehoiada, the High Priest.
What interests hung upon his life?
   The continuation of David's throne, **and** the enlightenment of the world involved in the preservation of that throne.
Has the purpose of God hung on a single thread, as it were, on other occasions, as well as on this?

Yes, when the life of Noah was the only link that bound heaven with earth; and when the life of David seemed **certainly** in the hands of Saul; and also immediately before the Reformation, when darkness seemed to have **gained** universal conquest.

What is the thought which the preservation of Joash suggests **to** the feeble and the helpless?

That God can always help or save, as the interests **of His** people may require, **no** matter for their own weakness.

Where are the faithful secreted in the day of their **enemies'** power?

In the unseen temple of divine love, and under the watchful care of the divine High Priest.

What is the assurance that cheers such?

That they **will be** preserved, and preserved **to** a happy manifestation and enthronement. "They are kept by the power of God through faith unto salvation."

Who had Joash for prime minister and adviser, after he became **king?**

Jehoiada, **the pious** High Priest, who **had** sheltered and educated him. In this you **see** his happy fortune, as compared with **those** of his father Ahaziah, whose counsellors were idolatrous and evil.

Had this favoured prince **no** idolatrous kindred to counteract the influence of Jehoiada on his mind?

No, they had been all slain, and he was free to follow the counsel that was good.

Can you see anything favourable **to Joash in** the entire destruction of his kindred?

Yes; it gave him an opportunity **of** commencing afresh on a right foundation, and **of** recovering the David type of character appropriate **to his** dynasty.

Did he **avail** himself of this opportunity?

Alas, **no! so** soon as Jehoiada was removed, he returned to the wicked and idolatrous ways of the house of Ahab.

Can we, in our humble circles have a High Priest and adviser, amid the difficulties of this our earthly life?

Certainly, we can have the Divine High Priest, who hath passed into the heavens, and who **in** effect invites each of us thus: "Follow me."

Is this High Priest more competent and more exalted than Jehoiada?

Infinitely so. He is the "Wonderful Counsellor, and the mighty God."

And where may we find His advice and directions?

In His "Testament." The principles of safety **and peace** are there fully set forth.

What may be said of those who disregard this advice?

They are unspeakably foolish.

Have they who do so any right to blame Joash?

No, indeed. Themselves are worse than he; *i. e.*, measuring the criminality by the dignity and worth of the counsellor rejected. Joash turned from the human and excellent. They who disregard Immanuel turn from the divine and excellent; they put away from them eternal life.

Repeat in few words the leading faults of Joash, from **the** time of the death of Jehoiada, unto his own death.

He forsook the Lord, and served groves.

He despised reproof.

He commanded to stone Zechariah.

Why should the stoning of Zechariah **be** especially mentioned?

Because it shows at once his daring impiety, and his enormous ingratitude. Zechariah was a prophet of the Lord, which ought to have sheltered him, and he was a son of Jehoiada, which ought, even apart from his sacred office, to have secured his safety in the presence of Joash.

Was it anything like a meet return to Jehoiada for the tender care exercised by him over his infancy to command the stoning of the son of his preserver and benefactor?

The very contrary. It seems one **of the most** outrageous acts that history records.

And what punishments overtook this ungrateful and **infatuated** king?

His army disappointed him; his body was wasted by disease, and his servants, instead of sympathizing with him in his trouble, conspired against him and slew him; his army was his trust and it failed him; his body (and the interests connected with it) were his supreme solicitude, it became the instrument of his misery; his servants, who were meant to minister to his convenience, became the avengers of the murdered son of his benefactor.

But was he not honoured in his burial?

No; he had no place in the sepulchre of the kings.

Is **it** not sad to see a life commenced under such favourable auspices terminate so disastrously?

More sad than any one can tell. His privileges, which ought to have led him to glory, only increased the gloom of his latter end.

Is there not something admonitory in this history for those who have enjoyed religious culture and religious advice when young?

Certainly; such ought to **remember** that **their** privileges **for** improvement will not only render them no service in **the** day **of** calamity, but will actually aggravate their condemnation. It is the unfaithful and privileged that must look for defeat, darkness and woe.

What then ought **to be the** solicitude of the Bible-taught young?

To keep by the counsels, and to walk **in** the influences of the great and saving High Priest therein revealed, seeing that the calamities of apostasy are not less distressing now than they **were** in the days of Joash.

X. AMAZIAH.

> AMAZIAH was twenty and five years old when he began to reign, and he reigned twenty and nine years in Jerusalem. And his mother's name was Jehoaddan of Jerusalem. And he did that which was right in the sight of the Lord, but not with a perfect heart.—II Chron., i, 2.

WE have seen much to grieve over in the ancestors of this Prince,—in Solomon, Rehoboam, Abijah, Asa, and even Jehoshaphat, and especially in the history of Jehoram, Ahaziah, and Joash. And things are not better with Amaziah, the son of Joash. He was in connexion with right, and yet he chose wrong. He listened to Jehoiada in his youth, and yet never discovered the secret of excellence. He began apparently well, and yet ended in dishonour. We should be roused to watchfulness when we see such serious mistakes on the part of those who have gone before us. Things written aforetime were so for our warning, we are compassed with temptation as others, and liable to fall even as others. We would do well to take heed lest we too fall after the same example. In turning your attention on Amaziah we notice :—

I. The character of his right doing.

It was right in him to punish the murderers of his father. It was right in him also to spare their children, according to the direction of Moses. And it was right in him to listen to the prophet—warning him against associating his army with the idolatrous and mercenary soldiers of Ephraim (verses 3-10). Now this was all right enough, but it would seem that he was not animated with a right motive, or actuated by a right spirit, though he did the things that were substantially right. We are not informed particularly in these matters, but we can conceive that he slew the murderers of his father, not from a sense of justice, nor because God had prohibited the taking away of human life, but in a spirit of revenge; or, it may be, because to overlook their crime, was to endanger his own life at the hands of others. He might think it his interest to render regicide a crime from which all would recoil. If it were thus with him, he had manifestly more regard for himself than for God's law; and such a state of the affections vitiates action, however right the action may be in itself. We must not only do that which is right, but we must do it out of regard to God's authority. But this, it would seem, was not the way with Amaziah; "he did that which was right in the sight of the Lord, but not with a perfect heart."

Then, he did right in sparing the children of those who had slain his father. God had so commanded by Moses; but we are led to suppose that he did it from other motives than those of piety. It might be policy, or it might be strong influences brought to bear on him on behalf of the young people, or children, by powerful friends, who might plead the merciful law of Moses in the case,—or it might be from some local or temporary reason of which we are not informed. Any way, it was not from a full and loving regard to God's authority, for it was not with a perfect heart.

And then, as to his dismissing the Ephraimites at the bidding of the prophet, he feared the threat of defeat, rather than cared for the honour of God. Had he had an intelligent appreciation of the state of matters between God and the ten tribes, he would never have hired these men at all. And when he sent them away, it was not from love to God, but from love of self. He had some idea that the words of the prophet might prove true, and he would rather avoid defeat. He obeyed therefore, but not with a perfect heart.

Now, this matter of a perfect heart is something we

ought to study and attend to. We would define a perfect heart to be—a heart fraught with the love of God—a heart that recognizes the righteousness of God's authority—a heart that consents to God's law; that it is good, and that yields loving obedience thereto. There may be much imperfection in connexion with such a heart; but then the foundation of its action is right. The man who has it will grieve for his mistakes or inconsistencies, and strive against them, and will still honour God even in connexion with his very faults. His repentance recognizes the divine claims and the divine excellences. Very different it is with the man whose heart is **not** perfect before God—that is, whose heart is not fraught **with** divine love. He may do that which is right externally, and society may be benefited by his action, but **God** is not honoured. His works are, in the sight of God *dead works*, and he needs to be purged from such dead works. Many inferior motives may induce him to do that which is substantially right, but the grand and vital motive is wanting. Love and heavenly loyalty alone can stamp value and vitality upon action.

And then mark, when the heart is perfect, the history will become so also; or rather, there will be an ever advancing approximation to perfection. Imperfection **will** lessen and disappear from the man. His predominating principle, (ever love to God,) will burst forth and prevail. He will go from strength to strength in the pursuit **of** good, and he will contend mightily against evil. It was so with the apostle Paul. He had, you remember, a law in his members warring against the law of his mind—that is, he had habits and incitements to evil within him warring against a perfect heart—warring against a heart that loved God, and consented to the law of God that **it** was good—and you know his history:—He kept under his body lest he should become a cast-away. He curbed and sought to weaken the law in his members. He laboured to conform himself to the will of God—whose will he approved and loved. He laboured to put off the old man with his deeds, and to put on the new **man**, which,

after God, is renewed in knowledge and in true holiness: and he pressed to the mark for the prize of the high call**ing of** God in Christ Jesus. He yearned after perfect conformity **to** God. He hungered and thirsted after righteousness, and he rested not **in** the conflict until he could **say,**—" I am **now** ready to **be** offered, and the **time of my** departure is at hand. I have fought **a** good fight. **I have** kept the faith. Henceforth there is laid up for **me** a crown of righteousness, which the Lord, **the** righteous Judge, shall give **me at** that day."

Thus with Paul, **and not** with Paul alone. It is **ever** thus when the heart is perfect; that **is,** when the love of God and of His law finds place therein. That love seeks to fill the whole being. It seeks to master every contrary and every unworthy sentiment. It seeks to rule, and **control,** and reduce the whole man **to a** heavenly unity. **And it must** conquer, for **it** is God **in the** heart! Very **different it is** with the man whose **heart** is not perfect. The contest with evil, in his case, **is a** very easy-going **contest, and** it ends certainly, if divine grace prevent not, **in the victory** of evil. While **the** perfect heart, *i. e.,* the loving **heart** expels evil, the heart that **is not** perfect, that is not animated by **love,** retains evil, and allows it **to** grow to the expulsion **of** good. The right doing which springs from inferior motives is readily put aside as occasion arises, and the **law of** self or self-pleasing becomes **more** and more potent. The external good has small power against the perverted heart, and the man yields himself to the pressure, or to the fascinations of congenial **evil,** and he becomes all the while ever less and less disposed to make sacrifices in the interest of that which is right. This, alas! **as** we shall see, was the case with Amaziah. His right doing was speedily put aside in favour of wrong doing. The right which his **heart** had never loved readily yielded place to the wrong, which his heart really embraced, even while externally doing that which was right.

You must often have known such characters in society. You must often have met with people who do that which is substantially right, but not from **a** right motive, that is, not with a perfect heart : and you must know that many such are so restrained by external and providential circumstances, that they continue on through life moderately useful and respectable members of society. Still, they are not in connexion, or communion, with the unseen, and are really dishonouring God by acting ever as if He had no existence, or as if He had no moral sympathies or preferences, or no power to vindicate His **own** laws. It is for the interest of society that men should **be** so restrained, but the **time** will come when their **true** character will be made apparent. Meantime, we see many cases, besides that of Amaziah where the **external restraints are** broken through, and the heart that **is** not perfect, asserts its supreme attachment to evil, and makes manifest its enthralment thereby. You see it weekly in the public prints, which furnish notices of great criminals — murderers — counterfeiters — gamblers, and men-stealers. These for a time, in their early years, might do **that** which was right, but not with a perfect heart — not from love to God, or apprehension of His authority — not from any approbation of the right, or the true, or the divine — but only from secondary or subordinate motives. And what was the consequence? Why temptations **arose** and they yielded. Their regard for right had no true basis, and they easily put it aside for the promising wrong. They had no fear of God before their eyes, and no idea of the lofty and stringent claims of the moral law; and their affections, clinging to evil, and sweeping the uncongenial and obstructive right out of view, hastened them further and further on in the way **of** transgression, until they made shipwreck of all character and of all hope!

We would do well then to be jealous over the state of our heart. It is so far good if we do that which is right externally, but we should not be content with this. We should seek after a perfect heart. We should pray that God would create within us a clean heart, and renew in us a right spirit. If we remain unquickened of God, our external goodness will speedily passaway under the potent influences of evil. If, for example, we wait upon God in His ordinances with a divided heart, we do that which is right externally, but there is no security for the continuance of the habit. Other more congenial occupations will present themselves, and **we** may gradually slacken off from the sanctuary, **or** some personal defect in the office-bearers, or members, may furnish excuse for non-attendance, and we shall gradually sink away from the holy, and become, in the same proportion, absorbed in or conformed to the unthinking and ungodly mass who care for **none of** these things. We may still retain so much of our church-going impressions, as to keep **us** externally decent, but the fire of piety is being lessened or extinguished, and **the** world is taking more and more decidedly the place of God within us! It will not be thus, however, if we truly love God. If we wait on God with a perfect heart, we **will** do **so** persistently. We will not be tempted or driven from **the** sanctuary. We will rather become **more** and more attached to it. We will press forward instead of going backward. We will ever become more earnest in **our** attendance, and more anxious **to** dwell in the house **of** the Lord, to behold the beauty of the Lord, and to inquire in his holy temple! Seek that it may be thus with you, and be warned of the danger **of** a merely external obedience, like that of Amaziah. **Be** reminded of the alternative in every man, in relation **to** the divine, and look **to** yourselves. *Either there is a heart of love to contend with the seductions to evil,* **or** *there is a heart of alienation to resist the inducements to good*: and the **heart in** each **case** conquers: the heart of love resists and scatters in the long run the temptation to evil; while the heart of alienation resists and **sets** aside the inducements to good. As is the **heart,** such will be the history. The heart **of** love will cut itself free of all evil, and become fully conformed to God; while the heart of alienation will cut itself free of all that would draw it **to** heaven, and rush desperately on to the blackness of darkness forever. O, be persuaded and seek that God would take possession of your heart, by the faith of His Son, and by the presence of His condescending spirit, that you may not be left to work out your own ruin and dishonour. You would not wish surely to follow in the same footsteps as Amaziah.

And this leads me to notice:—

II. The progress of his history.

That is not very fully or distinctly marked, as the record is brief, but it is sufficiently so to indicate his rapid progress in evil, and the sad and decided lengths to which he went in the miserable path. One of his first thoughts, after he was established in the kingdom, and had slain the murderers of his father, seems to have been *aggressive warfare.* He proposed to re-subject Edom. And, with this view, he collected the fighting men of his kingdom, organized them, and appointed officers over them. He found himself at the head of an imposing host, no less than three hundred thousand fighting men. Not content with this, and as if to make assurance doubly sure, he hired an additional hundred thousand out of Israel. Now, mark how his heart, which was not perfect, (*i, e.,* which was not fully or truly God's) began to show its preference for evil. He had nothing to do with aggressive warfare. He was king of a nation that had assigned to it a given territory, and the object of whose national life was—to preserve truth, not to invade or conquer their neighbours. Worldly kings may place their glory in conquest, but the kings of Israel had a higher calling. They must keep alive the flame of piety in the earth, and work for a glorious future. As for territory, it was enough if they kept their own free of invasion and oppression, they were not called on to subjugate or harass neighbouring people. It was a characteristic of David's wars that the enemies of Israel forced them upon him. He was ever for peace—while they were for war; and he mourned that he dwelt among the warlike and unpeaceful. He was usually conqueror in the quarrel, but it was not because he delighted in war, or sought it with ambitious views for himself. He only humbled or subjugated those who sought to oppress Israel, or to thwart the purpose of Israel's national existence. Now, Amaziah was not thus challenged to engage in bloody strife. Edom was quiet and unthreatening so far as appears. Amaziah was not called on to invade or oppress that people. Had they invaded or threatened the sacred territory, he might, for the sake of future security have reduced them to subjection or tribute. But he had no such excuse for mustering his armies now. It was only that his heart—not being perfect in the divine service, began to form schemes of ambition and warlike glory. With a heart devoted to God, he would never have thought of such an enterprise. He would only have been too glad if the Edomites left him free to promote the interests of his kingdom. True, Edom had been in subjection to the throne of Jerusalem in the days of his grandfather, Jehoram, but that was fifty years before the time of Amaziah. There was no propriety in his reviving claims, which had been so long ago extinguished—not at least, while Edom was peaceful and untroublesome as a neighbour.

But, supposing that there was excuse for this purposed invasion, in the original announcement of Isaac, that Edom should serve his brother, or even in some unrecorded manifestations of hostility on the part of Edom, we still have evidence of his *imperfect* heart in the fact of his *hiring the men of Israel to aid him*. Had he undertaken the enterprise as a servant of God, he would have been content with his own army, and trusted in God to give him the victory by its agency. The Almighty has no need of assistance at the hands of strangers, and the man who acts in the Almighty's quarrel has only to shelter himself under the wing of his principal. For a King of Jerusalem to hire foreign aid, was to doubt God's power; or rather, it was to trust in an arm of flesh. This was to cast dishonour upon the God of Israel, as if He were unable to defend His own cause, or to confound the opposers of His kingdom! And Amaziah only made matters worse by the character of the aid hired. He hired the fighting men of apostate Israel. He called to his side parties whose arms God would not bless. He thus showed, not only that his trust was in what modern conquerors call " the heaviest battalions," but also, that he had no suitable appreciation of the true state of the ten tribes as the enemies of God, and no difficulty in entering into an alliance, for his own purposes, with the haters of Jerusalem. Had his heart been perfect before God, he would never have taken the apostate Israelites into his pay! And had he had any patriotic or pious regard for the interests of Judah, he would never have brought his own warriors into familiar companionship with the idolatrous and unprincipled soldiers of Ephraim. But the truth is, he neither cared for the honour of God, nor for the purity or religious integrity of his own kingdom. He was simply bent on conquest and personal aggrandizement, and was willing to sacrifice every divine and national interest to his own supposed glory!

Then, he was *cruel in victory.* Ten thousand of Edom were captives, after ten thousand had been slain. These ten thousand captives did the men of Judah, under the guidance or by the permission of Amaziah, take to the top of a rock, and cast them down—so that they were all broken in pieces. How shocking! Had Amaziah feared God, he could scarcely have treated the invaders and oppressors of his country so: then, how very bad to use men who had only defended their own liberty so. It is true that the same style of treating captives taken in war has prevailed among other people—among Greeks, Romans, and Turks; still, we cannot but see in this cruelty of Amaziah further evidence of his departure from God. He might have subjected these unfortunate ones to servitude, if he could not safely send them back to their homes, but his heart was hard and cruel. According to our view, his enterprize against Edom was uncalled for and ambitious—his purposed means objectionable and unworthy—and now the use he makes of his victory is cruel and reprehensible! Every step is just a further departure from that perfect heart which ought to have characterized him, and a further development of the evil which works in the heart that is not perfect, and which enlarges and intensifies itself there.

But if there be any dubiety about these steps in his evil progress, there can **be none** about the next: viz., this, *he became an open and unblushing idolator*. The fact is thus recorded by the sacred writer: "Now it came to pass after Amaziah was come from the slaughter **of** the Edomites, that he brought the gods of the children of Seir, and set them up to be his gods, and bowed down himself before them, and burned incense unto them." Mark it! Folly and infatuation **have now** gained entire ascendancy over Amaziah. Formerly, he served God, but not with a perfect heart—now, he serves Him not at all. Formerly, he rendered an apparent obedience—now, he is decidedly and flagitiously disobedient. **He** is not content merely to forget God, but actually transfers the **w**orship due to Him to other gods. **In** the face of the miraculous history **of** his nation, and in defiance of what himself had **known** of the true God, under the ministrations of the venerable Jehoiada, he set up the idols of Edom in Jerusalem, **and** bowed himself in worship before them. No language can characterize adequately this conduct. It was monstrous and perverse in the highest degree! And we feel this the more when we think of the gratuitousness of this folly. There was not even an excuse **for it.** There was excuse for his grandfather Jehoram, adopting the idolatry of Samaria, though the excuse **was** flimsy and invalid, still, there was a colourable plea; seeing that he adopted the religion of the fashionable majority, and left that of the unfashionable minority. The ten tribes were more numerous than the two tribes, and the ten tribes were in substantial harmony with Tyre and Sidon, and their far spread colonies. Jehoram seemed to join the outlying nations to the neglect of the narrow prejudices of his own small people. But no such plea, flimsy though it is, can be urged in favour of Amaziah's conduct on the present occasion. Edom was neither numerous nor important as a people. To adopt the gods of this people was not joining the fashionable majority. It was rather the voluntary debasement of succumbing to a feeble minority, whose only claim to attention was its very insignificance. A minority we know may be in possession of the **truth**, as with the Christian Church, and this may give importance beyond any majority however great; but it **was** not thus with Edom. Its gods had no conceivable claim on the attention or worship of Amaziah. These gods had not even the semblance of power in the protection or success of their votaries. Amaziah himself had conquered them in conquering their worshippers. And why should he bow down to gods who had not been able to protect their servants from his own hostile inroads and warlike array? Why should he worship those who could not resist himself? Why worship those whom himself had enslaved, and brought as captives to his own capital? Even though he had known nothing of the true God, one would scarcely have expected to find him bowing down to his own prisoners; but when we remember that he knew somewhat of the true God, we really **are at** a loss **to** understand how, if in his senses at all, he could renounce the powerful and the true **in** favour of the powerless and the false. Here is **an** extreme of silliness and perverseness in it that is altogether inexplicable and indescribable! Any way, he was now entirely separated in heart as well as in practice from the God of Israel. And possibly, he felt a brief relief in the fact. He felt free of that ever-present restraint which the ser**vice** of the God of Israel imposed! He now served gods **whom** he could not control, and not a God who asserted unwelcome claims on his obedience! He now bowed before gods who would reprove neither his ambition, **nor** his unholy alliances. He could now carve out his own fortune, and work his unhampered will among the surrounding people! And no doubt he determined to listen no more to the remonstrances or the rebukes of the prophets of Israel! He soon had an opportunity to show his purpose herein: for God's anger being kindled against Amaziah, He sent a prophet to him, who said, "Why hast thou sought after the gods of the people, which could not deliver their own people out of their hand?" And how fared it with this prophet in the presence of the king? Why, his reception was as rough and determined as an unwelcome messenger might expect: "It came to pass, as he talked with him, that the king said unto him, 'Art thou made of the king's counsel? Forbear! Why should'st thou be smitten?'" And this was but a cutting way of saying, "I will have none of your interference: and I will not be slow to punish your insolence if you persist! You know the fate that Zechariah, the son of Jehoiada, met with, when he persumed to interfere with my father. Bear it in remembrance, and begone! And tempt not my displeasure further if you would not incur a similar fate." Here then, at last, we have Amaziah in full-orbed rebellion. He has no longer any hesitation or timid anxieties. Formerly, while yet in but mid-career of his self-glorious and ungodly progress he listened to the prophet of the Lord, and even yielded to his influence: but matters are all changed now. His own divided heart is divided no longer. The evil hath expelled the good: and he scorns the divine messenger, and casts from him the divine reproof. He even threatens the life of the prophet, and rushes thus in effect against the thick bosses of the Almighty's buckler. He is now his own master, and refuses all control: nay, even declares war to the knife with the Lord of Israel, and the King of the Universe! After this, if he repent not, his overthrow may be looked for at any moment. It may be deferred, or it may be partial for a time, but it is inevitable! The potsherds of the earth may contend with the potsherds of the earth, but they can have small success in conflict with Omnipotence! Only confusion and ruin can overtake them then!

Here then we have the sad consummation in the case of Amaziah: and we may well lament over it! He served God with a divided heart, but his divided heart was not of long duration. It speedily yielded its hold of good, and became fully and willingly filled with evil. **Instead of** following in the footsteps of his pious progenitors, Jehoshaphat and David, he gave himself to the wildest folly. Not content with forsaking God, he set up gods for himself! And instead of yielding a grateful **obedience** to the condescending remonstrances of heaven, he resisted and defied the Holy! Is there no warning for us in the manifest absurdity and recklessness **of** his **conduct**? It surely warns against **a** divided heart in **matters** of religion: and too many as already noticed seem to have this divided heart even in our own day. **They** may not in the meantime openly apostatize from God, **or** daringly threaten the life of His messengers; but they occupy the position that leads **to** these enormities. Ere long their ambitions or temptations may drive them to these extreme results. Nothing can prevent it indeed but a complete revolution in their hearts. If evil and self-will have an admitted place within them (even though they do that which is right externally and substantially), that same evil and self-will will **ere long** occupy their whole being, and will issue in time **in the** open renunciation and defiance of the divine! Aye, even though the gulf of darkness were yawning visibly **to** receive them, they will hate and defy to the last! Our only safety is to give our hearts *fully* to God in the faith of His Son, and then we shall go from strength to strength, and from excellence to excellence, and not like Amaziah from folly to folly—or from covert impiety to confirmed rebellion!

But, **we** would now remind you concerning this king, of

III. *The occasion* **of** *his overthrow*.

That was his own excessive and monstrous *pride*. Because he had prevailed against Edom, he thought himself equal to any thing. He therefore challenged Joash, King of Samaria, to a warlike struggle. Joash sought to dissuade him by reminding him of his comparative nothingness, but this only influenced his desire to show off his generalship and to humiliate his neighbours. He forced Joash to the battle; and he received what was to be expected, a thorough beating. He thought to re-enact the conqueror, as in the case of Edom, but found only the humiliations of defeat. "Pride cometh before destruction, and a haughty spirit before a fall." What a disappointment for the impious and unworthy Amaziah! His dreams of ambition and conquest were rudely scattered, and his power for aggression broken. Instead of dictating terms to Joash at Samaria, as he expected, he was carried to his own capital in the train of his conqueror: and instead of enriching himself at the expense of Joash and his people, he had the defences of his throne cast down, and the riches of his kingdom torn away! Amaziah made no further attempts at conquest after this, and that, not because his desire had ceased, but because his means were annihilated. No doubt he had chalked out for himself a splendid career. Having tried his hand on Edom, he thought first to resubject the ten tribes of Israel, and then with his augmented resources, he would carry his arms against Syria, and all surrounding peoples. He would bring back the days of David—not as to piety, but as to conquest. He would lift again his nation to the proud preeminence it occupied in the days of Solomon, by his military genius and warlike successes. He had thrown himself loose of the Temple services, which only cramped his genius, as he thought, and limited his enterprizes: and he had set up for himself gods who would be more accommodating to his wishes, and he now felt himself free to make for himself a name in the earth, and to work his unchecked will in the regions around. He had no fear of any further interruption from the prophets of Jerusalem. He had effectually arrested, as he supposed, any remaining wish on their part to interfere: and he determined to make short work with them if they did!

Such was the dream from which Amaziah was awakened by the result of his campaign against Joash, King of Samaria. You may well believe that his thoughts were bitter when left in his helplessness and humiliation at

Jerusalem. Never again, during the remaining days of the life of his conqueror, did he think of renewing the challenge, or of engaging again in the strife. Often, in history, we find the vanquished renewing the contest, and even snatching the laurel from the brow of their victors: but not **so** Amaziah. He was crushed **once** and for all. Even after the death of Joash, he remained quiescent. He survived his conqueror fifteen years, yet never attempted during all that time to retrieve his fortunes as a military leader. Nor was this because he had grown wise, but because he had been so effectually **disarmed**.

Nor did these long years of forced retirement **and** reflection lead to any improvement in his nature as **a** man. It would seem that he remained proud and offensive still although so far reduced. This is indicated by the manner of his death. His subjects conspired against him, and slew him. This they would scarcely have done had he walked gently and wisely. Subjects will not generally rise against their rulers for small injuries. There must be a succession of wrongs, and these wrongs felt to be grievous, ere the thought of regicide can take deep hold of the mind of the people. No doubt Amaziah had walked haughtily toward his attendants, and roused against himself their deep anger. Probably his temper was soured by his humiliation, and he vented his anger against his broken fortunes on the parties who came within his reach. Any way, there must have been those who had a deep and bitter hatred of his person, else they would not have conspired against his life, nor pursued him to Lachish when he fled from his fate. The truth is he had forsaken God, and God left him in the hands of his enemies. He had renounced the service that might have controlled and comforted him, and he provoked by his querulousness, or by his oppressive administration, the instruments of his downfall and dishonour! How sad the fate of the ungodly! How little the gods of Edom would be able to do for Amaziah in the hour of his extremity!

The proud, my friends, **work out** their own ruin. **In** their haughtiness they **rush** upon the rocks that wreck them. There is no need that God should interpose by **any** direct visitation to punish or to overwhelm those who forsake Him. It is enough to leave them to themselves! They will infallibly awaken sooner or later to the reaction that lays them **low.** Not but that God may overwhelm them when He sees meet by direct judgments, but there is no need for it to secure for them their deserts. Their own agency will bring it about. Amaziah's **is a** striking case to this effect. He **was** unthreatened **in his** capital, and victorious over Edom. There was nothing apparently **to** alarm or to injure him. Had he been but quiet himself, and allowed his neighbours to enjoy the quiet they did not wish disturbed, he might have reigned unhumbled and unimpóverished! But he had incurred the divine displeasure by setting up the gods **of** Edom in Jerusalem. And God, instead of reigning fire upon him from heaven, or dashing his palaces to the ground by a resistless hurricane or whirlwind, **just** left him to his pride and ambition, and he speedily brought upon himself the retribution which he merited. Amaziah, it is said, would not listen to Joash, who sought to arrest him in his warlike way "for, it came of God, that he might deliver (him and his people) into the hand of their enemies, because they sought after the gods of Edom." And so probably, with his death, as we have said, himself provoked the stroke that **slew** him.

And **it** has ever been thus through all the ages. The wicked and the audacious have wrought out their own ruin—directly or indirectly. There was a striking illustration **of** this during the last age in the old world. The greatest captain of that time, or as some would have it, of any other time, had reached the summit of earthly greatness—all Europe was at his feet. No one thought to measure swords with him, or to question his right to reign. He had but to stand still himself—to receive the homage of millions, and **to** retain his glory. But no! He must needs humble **a** mighty northern empire: and for this, he must challenge the rigours of nature. **No** matter! All things he fancied would give way before him. Like Amaziah, he had tasted the cup of success, and he thought to drink of nothing else. On he rushed. Into the midst of the Russian winter he poured his hitherto triumphant legions. He dashed his forces against the frost-king, and recoiled broken and humiliated. His numerous enemies (made his enemies by pride and oppression on his part,) took advantage of the reverse, and, as in the case of Joash and Amaziah, speedily occupied his capital, **and** gave him his first experience **of** retribution and reverse. His own pride, you perceive, brought his **downfall**; but it was of God, that he might deliver him into the hands of his enemies, because he renounced all religious subjection, and acted **as** if himself were omnipotent and unaccountable.

It is, my friends, with the proud and ungodly as with a vessel that has parted from its moorings with none on board to steer it. Such a vessel, if unboarded by the competent, and if unrecovered, *must* drift to ruin. It may seem to sail gaily for **a** time, but it **is** really the sport of the waves, and the certain prey of the yawning deep. It may escape many dangers, and it may drift on **for** many bright and sun-lit days. But it cannot escape. The storms will arise; the winds will blow; the rocks will not remove from its reckless and unguided way. Sooner or **later it** must rush upon its fate. The very velocity of its movements must intensify the shock which shatters it! And so with the proud and ungodly, who have broken from their heavenly moorings, and are unguided by divine piety, they can reasonably expect nothing but destruction.

But very different it is with those who abide by the meek and lowly Teacher and Saviour, and who are guided in their voyage by His word and spirit! They navigate the sea of life in safety. They dash not in pride on the immoveable rocks, but they thread their way by patience and by prayer, into the harbour of divine peace and eternal life. They renounce not, like Amaziah, the covenant made with the house of David, but rejoice in it rather, and wait for its realization. They clothe themselves with humility, and they embrace the righteousness of God which is by faith of Jesus Christ, and wait for his further and fuller manifestation—assured that when He shall appear in glory, they shall be like Him, for they shall see Him as He is. May the wisdom and faith of these lowly and glory-expecting ones be ours. May we be enabled to renounce the pride that ruins and to walk in the meekness of Him who saves!

QUESTIONS ON AMAZIAH.

How did Amaziah conduct himself on ascending the throne?
  He did that which was right in the eyes of the Lord.
Mention some of the right things he did?
  He slew the murderers of his father. He limited his vengeance to the actual murderers,—and left their children unharmed. And he obeyed the prophet who remonstrated against his employment of the Ephraimite warriors.
What draw-back was there on his right doing?
  It was not with a *perfect heart*.
How would you describe a perfect heart?
  A heart fraught with love to God and to his righteous laws. (Wanting this, the conduct of Amaziah, though externally right, was yet essentially defective.)
What is the tendency on the history of a man of a perfect heart, or a non-perfect heart respectively?
  The perfect heart being a heart of love to God, progresses and strengthens itself as the life advances, and issues in heavenly perfection. Whereas the imperfect heart, being without love divine, becomes in its progress less and less careful, even of external right doing, and issues in utter depravity in the world of darkness.
Can you mention an instance of an individual with a perfect heart?
  Yes. The apostle Paul in his Christian life. This servant of the truth loved God, and consented to His law, that it was good, but acknowledged at the same time, that evil was powerful within him.
And what was the result of the contest in his nature?

The entire ascendancy of love. In other words, the entire victory of the perfect heart. Having fought a good fight he finished his course in holy confidence, and with heavenly expectations.

Are there not many in human society even now, who do **that** which is right, and yet not with a perfect heart?

It is to be feared **so**. True, many such are kept by providential restraint, from going all the lengths of wickedness in this world, but then there are even some who break through these restraints, and by their murders or monstrous crimes show the natural tendency of a heart **of** ungodliness.

What should be the prayer of each of us in relation **to** this matter?

That of David, "create a clean heart within me, and renew **a** right spirit."

What is the impressive truth which ought **to** incite us **thus** to pray?

The tendency of love or alienation to intensify or extend each its own existence and dominion. He that hath clean hands will grow stronger, while evil men and seducers grow worse and worse.

What was the character of Amaziah's progress and history?

From bad **to** worse—as might be expected from one whose heart was **not** perfect—i. e., not fraught with divine love.

What was the first step that manifested the true state **of his** heart?

Ambition and aggressive warfare. He proposed **to re-subject** Edom. This **was** not the true spirit of **the David** dynasty.

What was the next manifestation?

His hiring of the men of Israel to aid him. This was insulting God, and associating himself and his people with the idolatrous.

What was the next manifestation?

His cruelty to the conquered Edomites. **He** cast ten thousand of them from the rocks without necessity **or** reason.

Was there any further exhibition of the state of his heart?

Yes. An exhibition at once silly and wicked. He adopted the gods of Edom, and bowed to them in service.

Was there any excuse for this folly?

Not any. Not **even** the shadow of an excuse. To adopt the gods of Tyre, was to adopt the gods of the powerful and rich—to adopt those of Edom, was to adopt the gods of the insignificant and the conquered.

What then may we conceive was his reason for adopting these gods as his?

He wished to be free from restraint, and to have gods that himself could control.

And how did Amaziah conduct himself when reproved for his folly?

In a manner of haughty defiance. His once divided heart was now divided no longer. He was wholly given over to rebellion and self-pleasing.

What must they avoid who would not follow Amaziah to full-blown rebellion?

They must cease from a divided heart. The heart that is **not** wholly God's is in the **way of** becoming wholly Satan's.

What **was** the **occasion of** Amaziah's overthrow?

His inordinate pride. Because he had conquered Edom, he thought **to** conquer Joash of Samaria, and challenged **him** accordingly.

How did he fare in the contest himself provoked?

He was entirely overthrown. Instead of dictating terms of peace in Samaria, he had to submit to every indignity as a conquered king in his **own** capital.

Did he ever recover from this blow?

Never, **so** far **as** aggressive warfare was concerned. He might still dream of conquest, but he was never again in a position for attempting it.

Did he improve under his humiliation?

We have no **reason** to think **so.**

What was the **manner** of his death?

His servants conspired against him and slew him.

What may we infer from this?

That he walked proudly and offensively towards those around him. Had the dagger come from a distance, it might have come from prejudicial and unmerited hatred, but coming from his own attendants it implies an insulting or unjust demeanour on his part. Where a Prince walks wisely in his own palace, his attendants will defend him to the last. It is only the oppressed, or the injured, or those who think themselves oppressed or injured, that lift their hands against the chief on whom they wait.

How does God often deal with the arrogant ungodly?

He leaves them to provoke their own overthrow—as Ama-

AMAZIAH.

ziah did in ancient times, **and** Napoleon the **great** in recent times.

How may we describe the proud and ungodly?

They are **as** vessels parting from their moorings—with none on board to steer them. They must dash on the rocks **sooner** or later.

But how is it with those who **abide by the** meek and lowly Teacher and Saviour, or rather who navigate the sea of life with the Lord as their pilot?

They sail through storms and tempests in safety, and **reach the** harbour of heaven in due time. They renounce, not like Amaziah, the covenant made with the house of David, but rejoice **in it** rather, and wait for its wondrous developments.

XI. UZZIAH.

Then all the people of Judah took Uzziah, who was sixteen years old, and made him King in the room of his father Amaziah.—II Chronicles, xxvi. 1.

NO man, it hath been said, can be declared happy until he has finished his earthly history. And this is true, as far as earthly prosperity is concerned.

There is instability on all human things; and the man who is rich to-day may be poor to-morrow. It is not unusual even for kings to taste the bitterness of reverse. Crœsus, the King of Lydia—as ancient story tells, was rich beyond most of his contemporaries, and fancied himself happy beyond others in consequence. On one occasion he exhibited his treasures and his resources to a Grecian sage, expecting only congratulations and flatteries from the admiring guest, but what his surprise when he found that his grandeur was looked on with distrustful eyes, and that the poor and the virtuous were preferred before him, so far as happiness was concerned. On inquiring the reason, he was reminded that he had not completed his history, and that a few years might change the colour of that history altogether. And so he found it. Cyrus conquered him—Cyrus stripped him of his vast possessions; and he was taught thereby to estimate earthly riches more in accordance with their true value. So with Uzziah before us. He was distinguished for his prosperity, but he did not complete his history in prosperity. He too found the instability of human things, and had opportunity in his latter days to mourn over the departed glories of his early life. And, alas, how many besides Uzziah have finished their life in sadness, **who** fancied in the days of their prosperity that they would die in their nest. The buoyant and the confident would do well to learn, **from** such examples, distrust in relation **to** the glittering things of the earth.

But in turning your thoughts on the things of Uzziah, we shall notice:—

I. The sunny side of his history.

That was long and unclouded. He met with all manner of success in his undertakings, **and** was not thrown back by any striking or unusual reverse. For nearly fifty years he grew in resources, and his name and glory were spread far and wide. He broke the power of the Philistines—the hereditary enemies of Israel. On the west he made his borders secure—nor less so on the east. God helped him, it is said, "against the Philistines, and also against the Arabians that dwelt in Gur-baal, and the Mehunims." As for the Ammonites, so far were they from giving him any disturbance, that they brought him presents. Externally, there was no power to alarm him, and no gathering storm visible in any part of the horizon to cause him uneasiness. And he was not unprepared for exigences, supposing any unlooked for enemy were unexpectedly to appear. Small as his territory was, he **had** as many available fighting men as some of the mightiest of modern kingdoms. France even now, though her army list may be much greater, could not bring into the field, at short notice, after all necessary deductions are made, three hundred thousand fighting men, yet Uzziah could embody more than that number, almost at any moment. Nor was he inattentive to the proper equipment **of** his legions. "He prepared for them, (it is said,) throughout all the host, shields, and spears, and helmets, and habergeons, (or breast-plates,) and bows, and slings to cast stones." Nay more, he encouraged inventors and skilled mechanics; and they made military engines, (long before the time of Archimedes, 500 years) to be on the towers and upon the bulwarks, to shoot arrows and great stones withal. So great indeed, was his military power, and so successful his organization and his administration, that the sacred writer has no terms to express his admiration. "His name (he says,) spreads far abroad, for he was *marvellously* helped till he was strong." If Solomon, in his day, stood at the head of the nations as the Prince of of Peace; Uzziah in his day, stood at the head of all the people in his more immediate neighbourhood, as the Prince, who, though enjoying peace, was most thoroughly prepared for war.

Nor was he inattentive to domestic matters. Some rulers have a genius for war, but, while they shine on their own chosen field, they neglect or treat superficially more important interests, or even exhaust their country as to resources by their injudicious undertakings. But it was not so with Uzziah. He attended at the same time to all necessary matters as to internal economy and arrangement. He fortified his capital. "He built towers in Jerusalem at the corner gate, and at the valley gate, and at the turning of the wall, and fortified them." Nay, more, "he built towers in the desert," for watching and guarding cattle, "and digged many walls." He not only encouraged agriculture, but gave his attention especially to it, as a pastoral farmer, and vine-dresser. It is said that, "*he loved husbandry.*" Like Prince Albert of England, of honoured memory, he set an example in this respect to his subjects. "He had much cattle, it is said, both in the low country, and in the plains; husbandmen also, and vine-dressers in the mountains, and in Carmel." His prosperity therefore, was not a prosperity that dazzles for a moment, and leaves darkness behind it. It was founded in industry, and sustained and fed by the increase of the flock and of the field. He was not merely a warrior that wastes, or that grows rich by rapine, but a worker that accumulates and grows rich in a legitimate way. Of his domestic life we are not informed, but his government and administration were for long years unperturbed, enterprising, sunny, and commendable.

How different it has been with many other occupants

of thrones, to say nothing of private men. They **have** been distressed by revolt among their subjects, or by the lawlessness of turbulent nobles, or by the ambition of aggressive neighbours. Turn **to** any part of history, and you will find perpetual illustrations **of** that which has passed into a saying : "Uneasy lies the head that wears a crown." But while other kings, both in ancient and modern times, have been harassed, invaded, overthrown, or curtailed as to territory, Uzziah dwelt **for many** years in peace, prosperity, glory, and unshrouded **success.**

He had every advantage and privilege in **relation to** the Unseen also. He had permanently the oracles **of** God to enlighten and **to** guide him. While other contemporary kings were wandering and stumbling **in** darkness, under the sway of superstition and ignorance, he dwelt, religiously speaking, in the valley of vision! A light from the higher world was upon his throne and upon his people. Nay, more, there was among his subjects for some years, **a** man who had "understanding in the visions of God." And Uzziah, felt the influence of this man, even as his grandfather Joash felt and yielded in his early years, to the influence of Jehoiada. **Yes,** Uzziah sought God while Zechariah lived, **and** " **so long as** he sought the Lord, God made him to prosper."

In one word, all advantages were his—an undisputed throne—a prosperous and an obedient people—ample resources—success in all his enterprises—wide-spread renown - heavenly oracles—and an accessible prophet who was himself in communication with the Unseen. There was nothing **he** could wish for in reason, that he did not possess. He had heard of troubles in the history of his ancestors, **but** he knew **them** not in his own experience. The dynasty to which he belonged had been seriously **de**flected from its proper course by its connection with the house of Ahab, but it had so far recovered itself, that it only required attention and fidelity on his part to bring back the spirit of David into his house, and to secure for its members the inestimable blessings of the covenant made with that illustrious king.

Now, what was the effect of all this prosperity on the heart of Uzziah? Did he become more grateful and more worshipful because of it? Did he walk more tenderly or more obediently? Was his excellence as a man promoted by his glory and prosperity as a king? Alas, no! He only became more heady and high-minded. He began to feel himself so great that he might disregard laws and arrangements which were binding on other men. This, you know, is usually the way with the exalted in human society. The higher they ascend, the more they fancy themselves at liberty from ordinary rules. Conventionally, and in relation to their fellow-men, their greatness limits them, but morally, and in relation to Heaven's laws, they suppose it liberates them, and enlarges their sphere of enjoyment. They feel as if they moved on a platform above the ordinary range of moral obligations; and they silently assume that the Governor of the universe will not look with such scrutinizing eyes on their transgressions as on those of inferior men. Uzziah seems to have been largely animated with this idea. He thought himself so good that he might set aside the laws of Heaven with impunity. His heart was lifted up to his destruction. Had he been less prosperous, he would have been less presumptuous. Had he had more difficulties to curb and to exercise him, he would have been less disposed to the wanton, uncalled for, and unreasonable violation of the divine arrangements. Is it not a pity to think of it, that the very mercies which ought to have made him humble and circumspect threw him entirely off his guard? Is it not a pity to find that one who had professed to seek the Lord, had sought Him to so little purpose? The truth is, he became inflated and presumptuous in no ordinary degree. The atmosphere of prosperity which had so long surrounded him only ministered to his vanity, and the sunny season which had so long brightened his existence only brought about the greater deterioration of his being. Instead of becoming more excellent under sunshine, he only became less and less so. As his prosperity increased, his worth decreased. As his inflation grew, his stability became less and less assured.

And the true reason of this **was,** that his heart was not right. Like his father Amaziah, while he gave external countenance to the service of the true God, his affections were really centred in self. He did that which was right in the sight of the Lord, but not with a perfect heart. He thought to make his goodness subservient to his glory, when he ought to have made his glory subservient to his goodness. Had his heart been right with God a very different result would have arisen from his prosperity. In that case, his sunny fortunes would have nourished piety within him, and not impiety,—Humility and **not** Pride.

And this shows us, what ought to be our chief solicitude. We should concern ourselves far more about heart rectification than about external prosperity. If the heart be right, all circumstances, whether sunny or cloudy, will minister to its greater excellence. Whereas, if the heart be wrong, all things will but make the wrong the greater. Even mercies will then be misinterpreted and abused. "All things work together for good **to** them that love God," while just as certainly, all things work together for the deterioration and ultimate dishonour of those who do not love Him. Our Lord pointed out the course of wisdom when He said, "Seek first **the** kingdom of God and His righteousness, and all else shall be added **unto** you." The kingdom of God, you will remember, is not meat and drink, but righteousness, and peace, and joy in the Holy Ghost. Seek then, with persevering determination, righteousness, and peace, and joy in the Holy Ghost. Care rather that your nature be renewed, than that your fortunes should be enlarged. With a new heart, your improvement and exaltation are secured, while without it, the amplest fortune will lead ultimately to overthrow,—and the ampler the fortune, the more signal will be the reverse.

Young people are very apt to mistake in this matter. They judge by appearances, and after the sight of their eyes. They take not into consideration all the elements of character and happiness. If a man be rich and prosperous, they are ready to think him happy, and sure to envy him. O, they wish so much for ampler means. They would have no fear of *their* hearts, if only they had riches and wealth in abundance. But they mightily mistake in this. Happiness is not the result of external circumstances—no more is excellence. "A man's life consisteth not in the abundance of the things which he possesseth—not only so ; if the heart be misplaced as to its affections ;—or misdirected as to its aspirations, it only grows worse under sunshine, and departs further and further away from true happiness by reason of prosperous circumstances. The prosperity of a fool, (that is, of one who fears not God,) destroys him." Straitened circumstances check evil. True, the effect of straitened circumstances is not better in the long run than the effect of sunny circumstances if the heart be wrong. Still, they who are straitened have less opportunity to indulge in fantastic and foolish ways, and are more held down to the ordinary and external proprieties of being than they who are more abundant in resources.

True happiness, and true excellence, are to be found in the knowledge and fear of God, and that can be sought and enjoyed as well in lowly circumstances as in lofty. Not only so. Lowly circumstances are more favourable than lofty ones for the acquisition of that knowledge and fear. Nay further, lofty circumstances have a tendency to blind and mislead the feeble mind of humanity, and to render true wisdom and true excellence difficult of attainment. "How hardly," said our Saviour, "shall a rich man enter into the kingdom."

Let us then be reminded, by the story of Uzziah's greatness and pride, of the danger of external prosperity in connection with an unrectified heart. And let us not attach an undue importance to the sunshine that is merely external. The sunshine of divine love and favour (even with external poverty,) is better far than the sunshine or earthly greatness. You will grow excellent under the one, while you will grow inflated and unworthy under the other. But, to return to Uzziah, **we** notice,—

II. *The presumption in which his folly and pride culminated.*

The step which pride takes varies, according to the circumstances or peculiar temperaments which encompass or characterize the parties under its influence. Thus David, in the hour of his elation, ordered the people to be **numbered**. And Solomon, in the day of his glory, **presumed** to build idol shrines for his idolatrous wives **in Jerusalem**. And Amaziah, in the day of his supposed greatness, when at liberty, as he thought, to disregard the laws of his country, set up in his capital the gods of the children of Seir, whose worshippers himself had overthrown. Each, you see, followed the bent of his inclination, but they agreed in this, that they all presumed to set aside the authority of God. They thought themselves so great, that they might exceed the rule of duty without being called to account for it. Other less and distinguished men might not take such liberties, but they, they fancied, could presume with safety. David, who had headed the armies of Israel so successfully, might surely wish to know the number of his fighting men without incurring serious blame, as he thought. And Solomon, who had so recently built the Temple, might surely add a few ornamental structures to his capital—even though their object was not strictly in harmony with the purposes of Israel, without awakening very decided disapprobation on the part of God. And Amaziah, who had conquered the Edomites, and proved himself so signal a leader of the armies of Israel, might surely set up the gods he had conquered without offence. So fancies pride in the human heart. It would take liberties even with God, and it expects exceptional action on the part of the divine government in its own favour. But pride is mistaken. David found it so—Solomon found it so—and Amaziah found it so. A pestilence brought David to his senses, and hurled him from the heights of his pride. A rent kingdom in the case of Solomon taught subsequent ages, if it did not teach Solomon himself, that the wisest and the most honoured will suffer eclipse if they presume to disregard the will and the purposes of God. And overthrow and impoverishment, in the case of Amaziah, taught him the folly of trifling with, or contravening, the commands of God! Pride may transgress, and may fancy itself safe in doing so: but the laws of the universe will not long leave the divine honour and government unvindicated!

But Uzziah—what was the form which his presumption took? Did he number the people—or set up idol-shrines in Jerusalem—or do honour to strange gods there? No. His fault was not so much in setting up rival altars as in taking liberties with God's altar. "He went into the Temple of the Lord, to burn incense upon the altar of incense." He was not a priest: he was not of the family of Aaron: he had not been consecrated to the service of the Temple: he had no authority to act the part he proposed. Nay, he must violate the express orders of God if he enter into the holy place at all, and still more so, if he burn incense on the golden altar. This he ought to have known, and must have known, after so many years of Jerusalem life and Temple intimacy! And the priests reminded him of the fact: for they "withstood the king, and said unto him: It appertaineth not unto thee, Uzziah, to burn incense unto the Lord, but to the priests, the sons of Aaron, that are consecrated to burn incense." But Uzziah was not to be thus deterred. What, he, the King—the successful and all-powerful ruler of Jerusalem, the representative of the house of David too—was he to have his will interfered with by a set of priests! The thing was outrageous. It only roused his ire! Instead of yielding to their remonstrances, he grew angry at their presumption. The presumption, it is true, was all on his side. But pride blinds or distorts the vision, and Uzziah, all unaware, for the time being, of the true state of the case, was ready to burst with indignation at the supposed presumption of these priests. Why should they think to question his royal will! He would teach them who was master in Jerusalem; and he would let them know that he would not be prevented from showing honour to heaven, by their narrow prejudices or official fancies! Honour to heaven, did I say? Yes. It is possible—nay, it is more than possible. It is probable, that Uzziah persuaded himself, that he was about to honour the God of Israel, by burning incense at His altar. He thought himself far above the priests, and he felt as if he would honour the Temple service by himself officiating in the way he proposed. But God asked no such honour at his hands, and God saw meet Himself to interpose in a way which Uzziah could not misunderstand, when the remonstrances of the priests proved vain. The boiling anger at the priest was forthwith transmuted into a loathsome leprosy. His brow, but a moment before flushed with fierce displeasure, became pale with the fearful distemper, even while he stood beside the altar of incense. The priests became immediately aware of the visitation, and so Uzziah himself. They had small need to hasten his exit after that, though it is said they did do so: for the king himself was then in haste to be gone.

No doubt the scales now fell from Uzziah's eyes, and he saw in its true light the folly he had been guilty of. But he ought to have seen it before. Had he been as conversant with the divine oracles as he ought to have been as king of the sacred people, he must have known that the high priest alone was authorized to perform this service. He must have read the appointment over and over again. If he did not, he was guilty of neglecting a most important part of his royal functions. Here is the law: "And thou shalt make an altar to burn incense upon—(said the divine lawgiver to Moses)—of shittim wood shalt thou make it. * * * * And *Aaron* shall burn thereon sweet incense every morning. When he dresseth the lamps he shall burn incense upon it. And when *Aaron* lighteth the lamps at even, he shall burn incense upon it—a perpetual incense before the Lord throughout your generations. Ye shall offer no strange incense thereon. * * * * And *Aaron* shall make an atonement upon the horns of it once in a year with the blood of the sin-offering of atonements. Once in a year shall he make atonement upon it throughout your generations. It is most holy unto the Lord!" Now, why should Uzziah interfere with this sacred appointment! Why should he set his will above the will of God in this matter? Though he were king, he was only thereby the more bound to see that the law of God was fully attended to. Transgression on his part, instead of being admissible, as he fancied, because of his greatness, was only the more offensive and inexcusable for that very reason. Greatness on the part of the disobedient may aggravate the guilt of disobedience, but it cannot excuse it. And it was not in ignorance that Uzziah acted. Even Levites might not interfere with the sacred duty of burning incense. And Uzziah must have known it. He could not be ignorant of the story of the terrible fate of Korah and his company. How then could he presume to act the part he did? Only the infatuation of pride can account for it! He fancied that everything became him, or that any thing would be excused at his hands. He had clearly an overweening idea of his own importance, and a vastly inadequate idea of the divine Majesty, as well as of the sacredness of the divine arrangements. Strange, that he could have lived so long in the neighbourhood of God's Temple, and reigned so long over the people who worshipped at that Temple, and yet could have so faint an idea of the awe and the reverence attaching to the sacred courts, and to the presence of Him who dwelt in the inner shrine!

And how wanton, and how gratuitous, his disobedience! He could propose no benefit to himself, and no advantage to his kingdom, by such conduct. Transgression usually has some plea of pleasure, of profit, but there was neither pleasure nor profit to be had by lawlessness in the case before us. It was the very essence of presumption on the part of Uzziah. It was the very wantonness of self-will. It was disobedience for its own sake. It had not even the excuse of a fancied necessity. To our eyes, it was by many degrees more presumptuous and inexcusable than the conduct of Saul, when, by reason of Samuel's long delay, he forced himself to offer a burnt offering. And yet Saul lost his kingdom for his folly! You remember the address of Samuel when he reached the scene of Saul's mistaken ministration: " And Samuel said to Saul, Thou hast done foolishly. Thou has not kept the commandment of the Lord thy God, which He commandeth thee. * * * And now thy kingdom shall not continue." How offensive then was the conduct of Uzziah! No necessity pressed on him! No feasible reason presented itself to him! Only a capricious and childish fancy possessed him—and for the gratification of that childish fancy, he would break through the fences, and trample upon the sanctities, of the Temple of God. David, in his day, said of the God of Israel—

" The Lord is great, and greatly to be praised,
He is to be feared above all gods.
For all the gods of the nations are idols :
But the Lord made the heavens,
Honour and majesty are before Him—
Strength and beauty are in His sanctuary."

But Uzziah, so far from sympathizing with these reverential sentiments, presumed to take liberties with this august One—intruded himself unbidden into His sacred dwelling place—and had the audacity to become angry with His priests when remonstrated with for his folly!

And how undignified the position into which the vanity and presumption of Uzziah brought him! He must be expelled from the Temple as an intruder. King though he was, and accustomed to the respect and obedience thousands, he must accept the indignity of being turned out of the Holy place. You would not like to be turned out of the house of a neighbour. You would blush to find yourself treated without ceremony, and expelled **as an** unwelcome intruder. And yet Uzziah, the lord of **such** mighty armies, and the proud head of a distinguished community, must be content to accept this indignity. His vanity had sought a capricious and intrusive gratification, and his self-love must now accept the bitter rebuff which such conduct brings. Azariah, the priest, and **fourscore of** his subordinates withstood Uzziah, the King, **and** said unto him: " It appertaineth not unto thee, Uzziah, to burn **incense** unto the Lord. * * * * *Go out of the sanctuary*: (only think of this **as** addressed to **the** king!) for thou hast trespassed: neither shall it be for thine honour from the Lord **God**."

This indignity, you may well believe, **was** bitter to the proud mind of the king. And yet this was but a small **part of** the reproof and sorrow incurred by his presumptuous intrusion. And this leads **me to** notice:—

III. The sad termination of his brilliant *life*.

He was cut off from all his royal splendour, and all his royal employments. By reason of his leprosy, he might no longer mingle in society—**nor** preside, on occasions of festivity and rejoicing, over the grandees of Jerusalem. He had been wont to be the centre of all eyes: **now**, he was **removed** from all observation. He had been wont **to** be admired and praised: now, no words of admiration **or** praise saluted his **ears**. He was conversant only with **his** own loneliness, and his own loathsome disease. How **sad** such a position for any man! How indescribably sad **for** Uzziah! Had he been unused to company, and subject to disease all his life, as many alas are, he could scarcely have felt **it so** keenly. They **who** have **never** known the sunny side **of** life, feel the shadows **of** the shady side less bitterly. But Uzziah had basked in sunshine for many years. His experience of brightness had been more intense than usually falls to the lot of man. He had gone from one sunny eminence to another, until there was scarcely anything loftier to aspire after. When **lo!** from the very loftiest pinnacle of society, and sur_ rounded by admiring thousands, he is precipitated into the very depth of defilement, and lowliness and grief. Even hope fails to light his gloomy chamber; there being usually no recovery for the leprous. Morning after morning he awoke to the most bitter consciousness; his past grandeur was now to him but a dream. His present circumstances, a fearful reality. And he could not escape away from the defilement that oppressed him. Nor was his case the better by remembering the **manner** in which **his** trouble overtook him. It was only the **worse** and the more bitter. It was incurred by wanton and uncalled **for** presumption! By senseless pride and foolish anger! **It** was incurred gratuitously **as** well as wickedly. "O!" he would exclaim, **and** that **many** times **a** day, "had I but withheld **my** foolish **feet** from the sacred temple—had I but been content with my royal honours, and left **the** priests to attend to their sacred duties, I had not been thus immured, dishonoured, and agonized! Trouble incurred in the way of duty is not without **some** solace, **but my** grief is without solace. I had no call to the **service I** undertook. I have no excuse for my temerity! **O, this** regret, this unsoothed and persistent regret!"

And then, he might not mingle with the congregation when they kept holy day. "He was cut off from the house of the Lord." When expelled by **Azariah** and the priests, he was not only expelled for the time being; he was expelled for all time—so far as his earthly life was concerned. It was bad enough to hear the priests exclaiming: "Go out from the sanctuary!" but it was far worse **to** feel that there was for him no return to the sacred **courts.** David himself was driven from the ark by the rebellion **of** Absalom, but he was brought back again to the sacred symbol. Not **so** Uzziah, **he** was thrust from the sacred edifice, never to return; not even to its accessible courts. He thought to **take** liberties in the sacred establishment, and he was not permitted again to visit it! How sad this reverse and exclusion! And how gloomy the life that must be passed in exile from the centre of beauty, and from the fountain of joy!

Surely this story of Uzziah ought not to be allowed to pass without leaving a lesson behind it. And what is the lesson it teaches to us? Why, it illustrates to us *the nature and danger of presumption.* All sin is presumption! All wilful sin is a daring trifling with divine authority! All persistent sin is an attempt, on the part of the sinner, to grasp what God would withhold. And the consequence is rebuff and expulsion!—expulsion, not only from the inner recesses of happiness, but even from the outer and superficial enjoyments already possessed. The incorrigibly presumptuous shall be banished even from the illuminations of earth, and they can never enter the palace of beauty beyond. They are unfit for the companionship of angels, or for the employments of the children of light. Their prospect is outer darkness and endless regrets. Uzziah's exile and leprosy during the remainder of his earthly life, shadow forth the exile and the leprosy of the sinful and impenitent throughout eternity. Only in one thing his earthly reverse fails to set forth all the sadness of the fate of the finally banished. It is this—Though he was cut off from the assembly of God's worshippers, he was not thrown into the society of the reprobate. Now, the finally impenitent will not only lose all elevating converse, but they will also be condemned to the most offensive companionship. They will have to dwell with the devil and his angels; that is with the serpents and the snakes of darkness! O, how sad the prospect! Surely we ought to take warning from the experience of Uzziah, and fear and forsake that sin and self-pleasing which will force on the Holy, if we do not, the necessity of expelling us from all that is fair, and sweeping us into the gulf of degradation and endless woe!

Further, this story of Uzziah teaches us *the danger of neglecting, or attempting to supersede, the New Testament High Priest.* Too many are content to leave Him to His ministrations without seeking to share in their results—and too many are ready in their presumption to arrogate some of His duties, while they decry that which is the foundation of them all—even the atonement which He hath made for sin. And think you that God, who hath made such a wonderful provision for humanity, will smile on those who refuse that provision, and say in effect, that it was altogether unnecessary? O, no! my friends! It is impossible. To neglect, or to attempt to supersede the one Mediator and High Priest, is to insult supreme wisdom, as well as to reject ineffable mercy; and none such, abiding in their impenitence, can rightly expect other than Uzziah's treatment. They shall be driven out of the sanctuary—not only out of the typical sanctuary, but also out of the preparatory sanctuary of earth. They shall never enter the Holy places not made with hands; and they shall never know aught of the felicities of the divine friendship! We would do well therefore to "consider the Apostle and High Priest of our profession." We would do well to commit our cause solely into His hands—trusting in His atonement and intercession—and waiting for His forthcoming from the Unseen, to conduct us into the presence of His divine Father! How happy to be prized by Him—to be presented by Him before the throne supreme, without spot or wrinkle—to be accepted in Him—and to be blessed with Him for evermore! They who neglect Him, and they who will burn incense for themselves independently of His Sacrifice and Priesthood, can have neither part nor lot in His felicity!

We fear there are far too many, even in these enlightened days of ours, whose piety reaches no higher than that of Uzziah, and we would fain have you to examine yourselves in the light of his history. He sought the Lord, but it was not with a perfect heart. He thought to put Heaven off with appearances. His affections were not with God—neither did his desires go out after that glorious One. He could not say, "As the hart panteth for the water brooks, so yearns my soul for the living God." He could not commune with the Holy Supreme, thus:—"Whom have I in Heaven but Thee, and there is none in all the earth that I desire besides Thee?" He could not exclaim with impassioned earnestness, "My heart and my flesh cry out for the living God!" O, no! He had no **such** experiences, and he was content to **want** them! A superficial and unloving service was enough for him. **If** he appeared occasionally at the temple among the worshippers, he felt as if he had discharged all his religious obligations, and was at liberty to forget God—and **to** pursue his own independent ends. He felt no need of special **or** abiding grace! Thus, from **year to** year, and from day to day, until at last **a** fit of more decided devotion seized him, **and** then, instead **of** remembering the atonement made by the High Priest, the blood of which was annually applied to the horns of the altar of incense, **he** seized a censer—passed into the Holy Place—and would have **burnt** incense without respect to sacrifice at all. **In the** first instance, you perceive, he was content with a **nominal and** superficial worship, and then, when roused to something more real, he would rush unsheltered and unhumbled into the divine presence. "Without the shedding of blood there **is no** remission." Uzziah cared **not** for that. **He** would press **to** the altar of incense, where it stood close by the veil of the most Holy Place—without blood—without burnt-offering—and with incense alone! He had not offered, and could not offer, the indispensable preliminary offering **as** the basis of his incense-burning. He was not only presumptuous **in** entering into the Holy Place at all; but he was specially presumptuous in attempting to burn incense without respect to the great annual atonement, which was the foundation of the service he affected, and without regard **to** which even Aaron himself would have found no acceptance for his incense-burning!

See then in Uzziah the image of too many in our own day, and be sure that it is otherwise with you. In the first instance, be **not** content with a merely external service, like that which Uzziah offered for many years, for that **is** of small value in the eyes of Him who searcheth the heart, and who knoweth Himself to be entitled to all love. And in the second place, if desirous of something more, beware how you attempt to worship God without respect had to the great offering and propitiatory sacrifice of Christ. That offering alone lays the foundation of acceptance before God. It matters not how **much incense** you may burn, if **it** have no respect to the atonement of Calvary it is of **no** avail. It is the atonement of Calvary that gives to the worship of the unworthy *fragrance and acceptability.* Without respect to this, we **are** but intruders **in the** sacred temple; but with faith in this—with believing regard to this, we need not fear extrusion **or** displeasure, nor need we doubt of full and loving accept**ance** in the presence of the Holy. The apostle understood this well when he wrote:—" Having therefore brethren, boldness to enter into the holiest *by the blood of Jesus*—And having an High Priest over the house of God. *Let us draw near with a true heart, and in full assurance of faith.*" Yes: In the full assurance of faith. For then the Gracious will receive us, our incense-burning will not be hindered or rejected, and our comforts and heavenly experiences will mightly abound.

QUESTIONS ON UZZIAH.

What was the character of the greater part of this reign?
  Sunny and successful.
How many warriors could he bring into the field?
  300,000.
What was the estimation in which he was held?
  His name spread far abroad, for he was marvellously helped till he was strong.
Were his solicitudes **and** his glory solely military?
  No; he built towers in Jerusalem, and in the desert, and gave his attention to husbandry **as** well.
Was he troubled by invasion **from** without **or** revolt from within?
  No; he enjoyed long and uninterrupted peace.
And were his advantages solely external?
  No indeed. He enjoyed also the revelation of God. And he seemed **even** to seek to improve this privilege, for it

is said, "He sought the Lord so long as Zechariah lived."

What might be looked for from a son of David so happily situated?

Gratitude surely, and progressive excellence.

But what really was the result on his moral nature?

Pride and inflation. He fancied himself so great as to be above all law, and at liberty to do as he liked.

How comes it that such should be the effect of prosperity?

It arises from the deranged state of the affections in relation to God. Let the heart be truly devout, and prosperity will minister to its excellence, but let the heart be misplaced, self-centered, and undevout, and prosperity will only intensify its mistakes.

What then should be the leading desire of young people?

Heart rectification rather than external prosperity. Nay, more, heart rectification as a necessary preliminary to the right use and enjoyment of external prosperity. The mistake among men, both of young people, and of parents in relation to their young people, is, they desire external prosperity *first*, or external prosperity *alone*. In either case they are wrong. They should desire heart rectification first; and external prosperity only so far as it can be made subservient to true moral and religious excellence.

What was the particular shape which the presumption of Uzziah took?

He went into the temple of the Lord to burn incense upon the altar of the Lord.

What did he propose to himself thereby?

We cannot exactly see. It was certainly to please his own fancy in the first instance, but possibly he might persuade himself that he would thereby honour God.

How could he possibly think to honour God in this way?

Why, he thought so much of his royalty and greatness as to fancy that he could confer honour on the temple by burning incense in it.

Did the priests accede to his humour in this, or think the temple honoured by the service on the part of the king?

Not at all. They resisted him, and remonstrated against his purpose, assuring him that it would not be for his honour if he persisted.

How did he receive their remonstrances?

Just as the proud are wont to receive remonstrances—with flaming and indignant anger.

He could not brook that the priests, whom he looked down upon, and even considered as his subjects and servants, should thwart his purpose, or stand in his way.

And how was the contest between them settled?

God interfered, and smote the proud king with leprosy.

Did he then persist in his purpose?

No: he hasted to leave the temple, in conformity with the wishes of the priests.

Was it for his honour that **he** thus dared to interfere **with the** temple service?

The very contrary. **He was** covered with shame as an expelled intruder, **even** apart from the terrific disease which had fallen upon him.

And what **was** the end of his brilliant life?

Seclusion and humiliation—regret and self-reproach.

Was there no solace for his wretched state?

None: so far as this life was concerned. **If** penitent and humble—he might have hope for the unseen, but none on the hither side of time. He mingled no more in human society, and he visited never again the sacred temple, which he had so foolishly invaded.

What is the general lesson which Uzziah's folly teaches us?

The danger of presumption and self-will. No matter how high a man's station may be, he **cannot** safely disregard the divine laws, **or** the divine arrangements concerning worship.

What is the particular lesson we learn from it?

To beware how we neglect, or attempt to supersede **the** New Testament *High Priest*. If it was thus dangerous and offensive to interfere with the duties of the Old Testament High Priest, it must be still more so to interfere with those of the New Testament.

Are **there any in** modern times who may be said to do **so**?

Far **too many.** All do so who attempt to approach God without **His** mediation, or without regard to His propitiatory sacrifice. And there is reason to believe that there are many thus.

But will scientific attainments on the part of worshippers not warrant an approach to God without sacrifice or mediation?

Not any more than the proud prosperity of Uzziah. They who would approach with acceptance must have respect to the constituted and consecrated mediation of the Son of God.

Tell me again, **in** conclusion, the errors to **be** avoided, as suggested by the life of Uzziah?

Mere external service, which furnishes no adequate break**water** against pride or inflation; and worship that is independent of the great Mediator, **and** of His great off**ering** and propitiatory sacrifice.

XII. JOTHAM.

> And he did that which was right in the sight of the Lord, according to all that his father Uzziah did: howbeit he entered not in the temple of the Lord. And the people did yet corruptly.—II. Chron. xxvii. 2.

THERE is something very quiet and unobtrusive in this king's reign. He is neither invaded from without nor agitated from within. No potentate from the banks of the Nile comes against him to despoil him. No Assyrian monarch makes boastful demonstration before his capital. Nor does any Babylonish conqueror carry captive any portion of his subjects. He is allowed quietly to develop his character **as a man** and as a ruler.

And he had much to aid him in choosing his course. To say nothing of the books of Moses, which may have fallen into forgetfulness during his time, he had the history and experiences of the kings of the house of David to warn and to guide him. Especially he had the experiences of his father Uzziah, before his eyes. Then he was a contemporary with Isaiah and with Micah. He might have known the way of wisdom (and that in its plenitude) if **he** had really wished it, by means of these agents of heaven. And he had time to show what his principles really were. His reign, indeed, was short as compared with that of his father, but it was long enough to show what he really was. For sixteen years he had, if I may say so, the fortunes of Israel in his hands, and yet he made no visible improvement of the kingdom all that time. He left it as he found it, and passed away without establishing any claim on remembrance, or leaving any material for eulogy.

But we will notice more particularly:—the style of his goodness, the religious state of his kingdom, and the inadequacy of his administration.

I. The style of his goodness.

That he was a good prince is generally assumed or conceded. Commentators speak of him in a tone of commendation and say that his example was holy. The sacred writer says, that he did that which was right in the sight of the Lord, and assigns as a reason for his might and prosperity, that he prepared his ways before the Lord his God. And one thing seems decidedly to favour this view of his character, viz., there is no glaring inconsistency recorded of him. In very many cases the goodness that is only apparent is seen in its true character in the progress of events. The heart that is unhumbled and unrenewed cannot pass through the trials or seductions of life without showing its pride or self-will. Thus the father and the grandfather of Jotham, though it is said of both of them that they did that which was right in the eyes of the Lord, manifested great presumption and infatuation before they had completed their history—the one in setting up the idols of Seir at Jerusalem, and the other by entering into the temple contrary to the express arrangements of heaven. Time and circumstances brought out, as it were, and made manifest their true character. But no such disclosure is made in the case of Jotham. He continued as he began, and died without any glaring faults attaching to his name. There is little said about him, but that little is more commendatory than condemnatory. His name, too, would seem to favour the idea of his goodness, if we assume its fitness and relation to him who bore it (as many of the Hebrew names are found to be). It means "*the perfection of God,*" or "*God's perfection.*" How happy to bear such a name, especially if descriptive of him who bears it! The signification even of David's name is not loftier or more honourable!

Still, my friends, we have our doubts concerning Jotham's goodness. We fear that it was external rather than spiritual—and negative rather than positive. He certainly does not rank with great sinners, but neither does he rank with great saints. Mark well the report of his right doing. It is not simply said in our text, "that he did that which was right in the sight of the Lord," but it is added, " according to all that his father Uzziah did." And then if we turn back to the account given of Uzziah's right-doing, we find it to be of a rather suspicious character. In the fourth verse of the former chapter, we find it recorded " that Uzziah did that which was right in the sight of the Lord, according to all that his father Amaziah did." And if we turn still further back to the account of Amaziah's goodness, we find it stated (in the second verse of the twenty-fifth chapter,) " that he did that which was right in the sight of the Lord, *but* not with a perfect heart." Here then I fear we have the type of Jotham's goodness. If so, it was not whole hearted. It was not loving. It was not living and potent. He did that which was right externally, but not because he knew and loved God with supreme and absorbing love. He maintained the forms of religion, but felt neither its powers, nor its preëminent importance.

Nor let it be thought that we attach too much importance to this account of his goodness, as of the same type with that of his father and grandfather. The sacred writer is specially careful in this very matter. When he wishes to indicate a loftier piety, he is careful to do so. Thus in the case of Hezekiah it is said, in the twenty-ninth chapter and second verse, " he did that which was right in the sight of the Lord, according to all that David his father had done," and so of Josiah, in the second verse of the thirty-fourth chapter, " he did that which was right in the sight of the Lord, and walked in the ways of David his father, and declined neither to the right hand **nor** to the left." Here, you see, is a different type of **goodness** from that of Amaziah. David was a man after God's own heart—filled with love and true faith, though his history was darkened disgracefully; **but** Amaziah was **a** man **of** *divided mind* and history— having his affections misplaced while his exterior conduct was that **of a** worshipper of the true God—and Jotham's goodness was after the standard **or** type of that of Amaziah—not after the standard **or** type of that of David. Had Jotham's goodness been **of** the true David type, the sacred writers, I have no doubt, would only have been too glad to say so. And even the statement in the sixth **verse of** this chapter may seem **to** favour this view of **Jotham's** goodness. Thus it said, "that he prepared his ways before **the Lord** his God." This style of expression is perfectly consistent with **the** merely external obedience. When a loftier or more searching goodness is spoken of, **it is** the heart that **is** mentioned. Thus concerning Jehoshaphat it **is** said (19-3) by Hanani, the seer, when reproving him for joining Ahab in his wars, "nevertheless there are good things found in thee, in that thou hast taken away the groves out of the land, and hast prepared *thine heart* to seek God." This is something searching and true. The heart is the centre of the being. **If** it is prepared **to** seek the Lord, the ways, **or** the history, will take complexion accordingly, but the converse **is** not necessarily true. The *ways* may be prepared before God, and yet the heart remain estranged from God. That is to say, inferior and earthly considerations may induce **a** man to give external attention to the divine ordinances, while his heart is neither submissive nor rightly directed: and we almost fear concerning Jotham that this was the type of his goodness—we would be glad to believe it was otherwise, but we cannot, with the brief notices before us, be confident that it was so. We think there is room for doubt in the case. We go no further than this:—there is room for doubt as to his goodness in the right and high sense. There is no room for doubt as to his external walk. There is no doubt that he attended to the Temple service, and walked not in the ways of Baalim. There is no doubt, further, that good arose to himself and to his kingdom from this external regard to the proprieties of Israel life. But we think there is doubt as to the spiritual character of his obedience. We cannot positively say that he **was a** true son of David, enlightened, loving, and devoted.

Now, it is desirable that the servants of God should leave a clearer record than this behind them. It is a pity when survivors are left to weigh probabilities, and merely to hope against hope. And too many, you know, die thus. They leave such a record behind them, that, while hope concerning them is not wholly excluded, it is yet not wholly pervading and satisfactory. They were not certainly indifferent to the divine service, but they were not wholly or resolutely devoted to it. Dubiety rests upon their destiny, and only God can determine how far they were the true servants of that which is imperishable, or whether they were the servants of the imperishable at all! How happy when survivors can commit the remains of their esteemed relatives to the dust in *sure* and *certain* hope of a blessed resurrection! How happy when they know and feel that the life of heaven was already begun in the hearts of those that have gone! And when they could as soon doubt of their own existence as doubt concerning the happy fortunes of the departed ones they loved!

And every one of us ought to labour to leave such a conviction behind him. It is not enough to have a name and a place among the loyal externally merely. It is not enough to have **so** much of the semblance of piety as that the judgment of charity must be invoked on our behalf, ere we can be reckoned among the good. We should endeavour to put the matter beyond dispute. We should give ourselves wholly and unreservedly to the Redeemer. We should listen to Him in all things, and keep stedfastly clear of every thing that is inconsistent with His character and purposes. In the words of scripture we should endeavour "to make our calling and election sure." That is, we should make it plain to all who know us, that our loyalty to Him who is "the Truth" is neither half-hearted nor fitful. We should let the friends of the Redeemer have power to say of each of us, "we can calculate upon him—we know his sympathies are wholly with us." And we should let the worldly and the self-pleasing be equally sure that, though they may look for kindness at our hands, they are not to expect from us any unworthy compliances, in favour of questionable or disobedient ways.

Peter, in his second epistle speaks of an "Entrance being ministered abundantly unto the everlasting kingdom of our Lord and Saviour Jesus Christ." And this, we have been in the habit of fancying, relates to the sentiments of survivors on earth, rather than to the action of angels in heaven. It is very pleasant to think of bright and benignant angels attending to, and ministering to, the disembodied believer as he enters into the kingdom that never declines, and this may be, and probably is, the privilege and liberty and the felicity of the true and living disciples of the Lord; but we think the apostle is rather thinking of the ministering saints around the dying couch than the unseen angels around the disembodied spirits. And these, as they close the eyes of a departing brother, rejoice for his victory and emancipation, and congratulate each other, that another has been added to the general assembly and Church of the first-born which are written in heaven. It is not merely a matter of hope with them, that he hath gone to the triumphant side of the universe. It is a matter of certainty. Yes; where the history hath been a history of faith and patience, and consistency, the comfort and the assurance concerning the departed, is great and cheering. Survivors can smile through their tears as they talk of the last struggle, and wish that themselves were as happily shrouded by the luminous though unseen cloud of love—and then as the report of the death goes forth, all who have known the humility and spirituality of the departed, minister in effect by their sentiments and complacency to the abundant entrance of the same into the everlasting kingdom of the Lord. We have had an instance of this very lately in the case of James Hamilton of London, of sainted memory; Ministers and Christians of all denominations wept and rejoiced around his tomb. No doubt crossed the minds of any as to his happy fortunes. His course had been so decided, and so consistent, that all were satisfied as to the result. So unanimous and clear were they that, had that mourning assembly had the keeping of the gate of Paradise, they would have opened it with one consent to **the** spirit of him **around** whose remains they were gathered. And myriads **who** were not present on the occasion, when they heard of the death, sympathized with the sentiments of those who buried him. They had not **seen** him in the flesh, but they had felt the fragrance of his heavenly spirit breathing through his writings, and they too ministered, though more remotely, to his entrance into glory, by their glad consent and approval! And this is **an** illustration of what we regard as an abundant entrance into the **everlasting kingdom.** The party in question lived **in the** Lord, and died in the Lord, and the benedictions **of** Heaven rest upon his memory, while the Church below pronounces over his remains the inspired words **appropriate** to such an occasion. "Blessed are the dead **that die in** the Lord from henceforth. Yea, saith the Spirit, that they may rest from their labours : and their works do follow them." We admit that this is a peculiar case. There are not many men so gifted, **or** so advanced in Christian character and graces, as the party just named, but the same result substantially may be expected in the case of every humble and consistent believer. Every one cannot occupy prominent positions, nor be extensively or universally known **to** the reading Church, but, every faithful one may expect an abundant entrance into glory, according to the extent of the circle in which he moves, and the clearness of the record which he leaves behind him.

And here it is, that Jotham came short. His record is not clear and satisfactory. His goodness is after an inferior type, and he prepared only his ways, not his heart, before the Lord. He followed in the wake of Amaziah, and not in the wake of David. Worldly policy, or earthly influences may account for all the goodness he displayed, and therefore the gates of Paradise cannot be opened to him on the part of survivors, without something like hesitation or uncertainty. Let it not be so with any of you. Let your devotedness be so decided, and your character so consistent, that survivors shall have no doubt concerning you when you are summoned to the unseen. Happily, you have a more glorious leader to follow and to imitate than Jotham had. David was his highest pattern of kingly excellence, but David's Lord is yours. You must not only not rest in any half-way, or Amaziah-like excellence. You must go beyond David himself in consistency and purity. Your guide and example is perfection itself. His excellence is unclouded; his love perfect; his meekness, without a shadow of presumption or self-will, and His purity without stain. Only do that which is right in the sight of the Lord, according to all that your divine Leader did, and then your connexion with him will be apparent. Be faithful, loving, meek, and pure, after His standard, and in the faith of His mediation, and you too shall have administered unto you, at your departure from time, when the destined hour arrives, an abundant entrance into the everlasting kingdom of your Lord and Saviour.

We have now to notice concerning Jotham:—

II. The *religious* state of *his kingdom*.

That was very corrupt and very sad. The truth is told in a single sentence in our text, viz:—"And the people did yet corruptly." They had been walking unworthily in the days of Uzziah, and there was no change for the better on the accession, or during the reign of Jotham. At Jerusalem, the forms of worship were maintained, but the spirit of worship had, to a great extent, died out. And, in outlying and rural places, idolatrous practices were freely and very generally observed. The people, indeed, took their tone **from** Samaria, **and the** standard of Samaria was heathendom.

And we can see how it should be so. During the long reign of Uzziah, prosperity had relaxed the bonds of piety, and given occasion to a spirit of license and worldliness among the people. Filled with good things, and free from alarm, they were content, so far as Heaven was concerned, with a nominal subjection. They lost sight of the peculiarities of their nation, and of the purposes for which they had been called out from among the people. Instead of being witnesses for God, and against all false gods, they were ready to indorse, nay themselves **to** practise, the idolatry of the surrounding people. And the evil was of longer standing than the days of Uzziah, though that reign had greatly fostered it. For one hundred and forty years, even from the days of Jehoshaphat, with the exception of the limited influence of Jehoiada, there had been no positive influence for good exerted from the throne. In the days of Jehoram, Ahaziah, and Athaliah, all was heathenism and folly. And although **a** check was put upon this folly during the minority of Joash, it was but partial and superficial. **And** the evil was ready to burst forth again so soon **as** opportunity was furnished. Accordingly Jehoiada was no sooner removed, than all things in Jerusalem reverted to their former evil condition. Uzziah, as king, had not lent his influence in favour of the evil, but he had done nothing to check it, and the spirit of heathenism had only grown among his subjects during his long reign. Jotham, on his accession, still withheld the countenance of the throne from the false and debasing rites of idolatry, but the people did yet corruptly. The high places were not removed, "the people sacrificed and burnt incense in the high places." And with these practices, we know, immoralities were ever associated, defiling the people and the kingdom. And of this sad state of things, we have the most ample evidence from the testimony of then living witnesses. Isaiah was contemporary with Jotham. In the very year King Uzziah died and Jotham became sole monarch, that prophet saw a vision of the Lord in the temple, and was constrained to cry out, "Woe is me! For I am undone; because I am a man of unclean lips, and I dwell in the midst of *a people of unclean lips,* for mine eyes have seen the King, the Lord of Hosts!" And if this seems but a small ground of condemnation—seeing that all (even Isaiah himself,) are unholy in such a contrast, and under such illumination, we have but to turn to the first chapter of Isaiah's prophecies to see the true state of things in Judah during the reign of Jotham. The first six verses of that chapter run thus:—"The vision of Isaiah's the son of Amoz, which he saw concerning Judah and Jerusalem in the days of Uzziah, Jotham, Ahaz, and Hezekiah, Kings of Judah. Hear, O heavens, and give ear, O earth, for the Lord hath spoken, I have nourished and brought up children, and they have rebelled against me. The ox knoweth his owner, and the ass his master's crib; but Israel doth not know, my people doth not consider. Ah, sinful nation, a people laden with iniquity, a seed of evildoers, children that are corrupters; they have forsaken the Lord, they have provoked the Holy One of Israel unto anger, they are gone away backward. Why should ye be stricken any more? Ye will revolt more and more, the whole head is sick, and the whole heart faint. From the sole of the foot even unto the head there is no soundness in it; but wounds, and bruises, and putrifying sores, they have not been closed, neither mollified with ointment." Another sad testimony to the degenerate state of the Jewish Church and kingdom we find in the fifth chapter, verses 1–7, and Micah testifies in the same strain (or rather the Holy one by Micah,) Micah I. 1–7–9.

Nor do these witnesses confine themselves to general statements or criminations. They tell us of the prevailing faults in detail. Of the women, for example, it is said, that they were "haughty, and walked with stretched out necks, and wanton eyes, walking and mincing as they went, and making a tinkling with their feet." And God, by the prophets, threatens, because of their vanity and immodesty to take away their silly ornaments, and to clothe them in sackcloth and sorrow instead. The catalogue of these ornaments and vanities is given in the third chapter of Isaiah, verses 18-24. You can easily imagine how children would be trained under such mothers and such fashions. Instead of modesty, and humility, and patience, and domestic virtues, and piety among young people there would be vanity, envy, rivalry, extravagance, impiety and crime. Remaining restraints would be swept aside, and universal license and self-will would hold sway.

Then the men were no better than **the women.** They **are** described as avaricious, drunken, impious, and unscrupulous. Hear the woes denounced against them and their crimes: Isaiah, **5th** chapter, "Woe unto them that rise up early **in** the morning that they may follow strong drink, that continue until night, till wine inflame them! And the harp and the viol, the tabret and pipe, and wine are in their feasts; but they regard not the work of the Lord; neither consider the operation of his hands. Woe unto them that draw iniquity with cords of vanity, and sin as it were with a cart rope: that say, Let him make speed and hasten his work, that we may see **it**; and let the counsel of the Holy One of Israel draw nigh and come, that we may know it! Woe unto them that call evil good, and good evil; that put darkness for light, and light for darkness; that put bitter for sweet and sweet for bitter! Woe unto them that are wise in their own eyes, and prudent in their sight! Woe unto them that are mighty to drink wine, and men of strength to mingle strong drink; which justify the wicked for reward and take away the righteousness of the righteous from him!"

And what of the princes or **chief** men? Hear these as described by Micah: They were cruel **as** they were ignorant and ungodly; see Micah iii. 1-3. And the prophets: were they no better? Not at all! Micah iii. 5-6.

And how should such guides lead the wandering people back from their wanderings? If the blind lead the blind, you know what must be the result.

To complete the picture: If **a** true prophet appeared among them, instead of listening and obeying, they hated, rejected, persecuted, or slew him. They had no ears for the words of God, as they had no desire for the knowledge of **the** holy. They were bent on folly, and were ripening, accordingly, for captivity and overthrow.

You see the catalogue: the women were **vain,** the men were selfish and pleasure-loving; the princes, or chief men, were cruel; the prophets had no light, and the true servants of heaven were unacknowledged **or** spurned! How sad that **it** should **be so** with any people! How sad **when** all **the** agencies of **good** become the agencies **of** evil! when the female influence, and the princely influence, and the prophetic influence, are all **on** the side of disarrangement and ungodliness. And if sad in the case of any people, how much more sad when such a state **of** things prevails among a sacred **and** privileged people! And the Jews, **you** know, were **a** sacred and privileged people. They **had** been separated from the nations that they might serve **God,** and testify against evil, and prepare the world for better things. Instead of this, we find them, in the days of Jotham, wholly unconscious of their high duties, and far more ready to imitate the idolatrous than to testify against idolatry. Like an army which forsakes **its own** standards, and joins **the** usurper it was intended to put **down,** the Jewish subjects of Jotham joined the insurgents against **heaven,** and only confirmed the rebellion which they were expected to confront **and** contend against. **We** may well grieve for their insensibility, their unfaithfulness and their folly.

And further, **by** the way, we have reason to grieve that this state of things hath not been confined to Old Testament times. It continues, to **a** great extent, even to the present day, though the privileges of the nations have been mightily extended. The Scriptures **have** been completed, printed, and circulated, and "the people do yet corruptly." The Son **of** God hath been revealed as the Saviour and centre of **the** nations, and the various tribes of humanity remain **yet** scattered and unharmonized.

The darkness is past, and the true light now shineth, and yet it may be said of Christendom, "The ox knoweth his owner, and the ass his master's crib," but the peoples who have been favoured with divine revelation, neither know nor consider. They will not come to the Redeemer, that they may have life; nor will they learn the proprieties of a heavenly discipleship. Women still prefer external display to the meek and quiet spirit which is abiding loveliness. Men still give themselves to worldliness, intoxication and duplicity. **Princes** or chief **men are** still selfish and cruel. Prophets **are** still false and unenlightened, and the true, humble, devoted, truth-telling **servants** of heaven are still overlooked and disregarded, if not spurned or persecuted. No doubt, there are faithful men now, **as** there were faithful **men** in **the** times of Jotham, but **the** state of Christendom, as a whole, is **not** better than **the** state of Judea in the times in question. Look to the state of any nation in Europe **or** America, and you will find but too ample evidence **of** general alienation from God, and general unconsciousness **or** indifference to the great privileges which revelation and Christianity have brought within their reach. We of these times have nothing to boast of over the men of the times of Jotham. This, however, as we have said, only by the way. Having seen the state of Judah under this king, we have now to notice—

III. The inadequacy of his Administration.

See how he employed himself,—"He built the high gate of the house of the Lord, and on the wall of Ophel (a fort on the city wall) he built much. He built cities in the mountains **of** Judah, and in the forests he built castles and towers. He fought also with the king of the Ammonites, and prevailed against him."

And this was all. For sixteen years he occupied himself with building, or war, and made no effort after reformation. "The people did yet corruptly," and he made no attempt to prevent them. Vanity, avarice, drunkenness and profanity prevailed all around him, and he had neither eyes to see it, nor wish to have it otherwise. O, how truly unlike the pious kings of the dynasty to which he belongs! Jehoshaphat, when he found his kingdom wrapped in ignorance and spiritual darkness, laboured to dispel the darkness. He sent commissioners through the land to teach the law, and made a tour himself through his kingdom to bring the people back to God. He did not occupy his attention merely with building. Hezekiah again, after the sad reign of Ahaz, gathered the people together to a special passover, and then sent them forth to break down the images, and cut down the groves, and throw down the high places and the altars through Judah and Benjamin—in Ephraim also and Manasseh. His first and great anxiety was to recall his people to the true God. And so of Josiah: after the apostate days of Manasseh and Amon, he caused to be broken and destroyed all the symbols of idolatry, and bound the people in a covenant to walk after the Lord, and to keep His commandments and His testimonies, and His statutes with with all the heart, and with all the soul. He thought of something other than merely ornamental building. Alas for Jotham! He sent forth no commissioners to teach the law. Though his kingdom was corrupt and far astray, he did nothing to rectify what was wrong. He summoned no special passover. He sent forth no agents to destroy the idolatrous groves or to overturn the idolatrous altars. The people did yet corruptly; but the fact made no practical impression on the mind of Jotham.

It is clear that he had no enlightened view of the position and purposes of his kingdom. He felt not the obligations that rested on himself and on his people to testify for God, and against every thing debasing and erroneous. Holy zeal formed no part of his character. He was content simply to live and to reign. He was content to allow to evil all the advantages it had gained, through years of formality and indifference to divine things. Though in a position to rectify, he put forth no effort in that direction. He just left the moral and religious state of his kingdom to provide for itself, and gave himself to inferior pursuits. True, he entered not into the temple presumptuously after the manner of his father Uzziah, but that was small merit. The consequences of his father's presumption in that particular were too immediate and too manifest to permit of imitation on his part. He had no fancy for the leprosy, and therefore he withheld himself from profane intrusion. But if he left the priests to burn incense, he left also the people to do corruptly. He reigned in Israel indeed, but without any appreciation of the peculiarities of his kingdom, or of the course which the religious state of that kingdom called him to pursue. How then shall we estimate this Prince in relation to the sacred dynasty to which he belonged? Not high by any means. Not indeed among the worst of his house. Not with Jehoram, or Ahaziah, or Joash. But yet not among the truest; not with Jehoshaphat, Hezekiah, and Josiah. He belonged to the house of David, but he was not animated with the lofty zeal of that house. He was not a true representative of the founder of that dynasty, nor an unquestioned type of that great Prince that was yet to carry the honours of that dynasty to its destined and heavenly elevation. His name indeed pointed to the heavenly glory, but not his administration. His name means, as we have said, the *perfection of God*, but he bore that name inadequately, if not unworthily. Had he walked in lofty and devoted loyalty, and given himself to the needed work of reformation and enlightenment, he might have justified (in a human sense) his transcendent name, and shone as a brilliant type of the divinely perfect One; but he left the work of reformation untouched, and lost the opportunity presented to him of attaining undying honours. How differently David himself would have administered the kingdom had he been in the place of Jotham! The piety which in him showed itself in the removal of the ark would have seen to the overthrow of the high places in the times of Jotham. The zeal which prompted to arrange the courses of the priests in the one case, would have prompted attention to the enlightenment of the people in the other. And the energy which was spent in war, in the one time, would have been available for, and would certainly have been employed in, promoting the piety and good order of the sacred people in the other. You cannot believe that the man who prepared to build the temple, and who, when not permitted, prepared and laid aside untold riches for another to do it, would have been content in Jotham's circumstances, when idolatry and corruption so much abounded, simply to build some ornamental gates in the city, and some few towns or castles in the mountains, or in the forests! No, no. David would have yearned after, and given himself to higher service, and more appropriate labours.

If, however, we cannot admire the administration of Jotham in the light of David's zeal, or in relation to the covenant which God had made with his house, we cannot say that he compares unfavourably with many leaders of society in subsequent ages. In other words the would-be wise men of modern times cannot justly condemn Jotham for his inadequate administration. What is it that characterises all the systems of human philosophy, and all the schemes and theories of worldly reformers: What but inadequacy and trifling in relation to those disarrangements of earth which we have already admitted? These reformers but build gates or towers of small beauty, or mansions seen by few in rural or remote places, while the great and weltering sea of human corruption remains untouched or unimproved. They have no adequate idea of the evils to be met, and their small appliances make no visible impression for the better on the world's progress. Their hope is in secular education, or political economy, or in the diffusion of scientific or philosophic discoveries. They see not that these are all superficial and inadequate in relation to the moral and religious state of the world. Nay, in too many cases, their concern is not the improvement of the world at all, further than as that may minister to their own renown. If they can only build some little pavilion to perpetuate their own name, they are not concerned whether the race of humanity is to be thereby improved or not. Like Jotham, too many kings, and philosophers, and leading men, are content to build little things for their own gratification, and to have the great interests of humanity unthought of and unimproved. True, they have not the special obligations resting on them to attend to the moral state of the world which Jotham had to attend to the religious state of Judah, but still, with the book of revelation in their hands, and the trouble of misguided thousands of humanity around them, they are not at liberty to trifle away their time and talents on small ornamental or mere personal gratifications.

Happily, the great son of David, the true Jotham, the prophet of God hath been revealed, and He understands the state of the world, and He is animated with an adequate zeal in relation to it. Happily He is wise in heart, and excellent in working. He has made the necessary arrangements for transforming the world—for banishing Satan from his usurped dominion—and for bringing men back to God. He works, however, on a large scale, and we are not always aware of the extent and beauty of His operations. This we know, at least, that seeing what the exigency required, He hesitated not to descend from His throne, to lay aside His glory, and to offer Himself for the sins of the world. There was earnestness and zeal in this surely! This also we know that He, being now made head over all things, is using and will continue to use, His royal and divine resources, with a view to the enlightenment and rectification of mankind. He will not content Himself with any thing short of a true and wide reformation. He will set justice and judgment in the earth. He hath sent forth His servants to lead the nations to God, and He hath promised to be with them, even to the end of the world. The work may seem to stand still, or to advance slowly, but that is not for want of zeal or competency on His part. That arises from the nature of the contest, and from the resistance of humanity to His purposes, but nothing will be permitted to arrest His work in the long run. He may permit hindrances for wise and suitable ends, but He will not fail to overcome these hindrances in His own time and way. He hath already conquered Satan, the ruler of the darkness of this world, and He will yet fully subvert the kingdom of Satan among men!

Only let His servants be faithful! only let them hold on, and labour on in His name! Only let them trust His wisdom, and His zeal, and His power, and they will yet have to sing of gladsome victory. They will yet have glorious evidence of the competency and the benignity of their King.

Be sure, my friends, that you enlist under His banner. Endeavour to understand the purposes of His kingdom, and be sure that you walk faithfully, and courageously, and hopefully accordingly. He will not, like Jotham, leave things as He finds them. He will not trifle away His resources on things unimportant or unessential. Nor will He fail to grapple with the evil that is in the world, colossal and countless in shape although that is. He will go to the root of the matter: and He will not fail nor be discouraged until He hath righted what is wrong, until He hath set justice and judgment on the earth! He will not cease to contend for the right until His Father's name is honoured in all lands, and until errors are for ever abolished!

See that you are loyal to Him! See that you lend your countenance and energies to His purposes, and rejoice meantime in his power, and in the certainty of His success. He will teach the nations to do that which is right, and that with a *perfect heart*, and the people under His adequate government, will do no more corruptly!

QUESTIONS ON JOTHAM.

What was the character of this Prince?
  It is thought to have been good. He did that which was right in the sight of the Lord.
Is there no dubiety resting on his character?
  We think there is. The standard of his right doing was not first-class. Besides it is said, he prepared his *way* before the Lord—not his *heart*.
What was the true standard for the kings of the house of David?
  David certainly. His piety was neither half-hearted nor doubtful. But Jotham's goodness was not after this standard—it was only according to the goodness of his father and grandfather.
What was the difference between the goodness of his father, and grandfather, and that of David?
  That of his father and grandfather, seems to have been merely external, while that of David was heartfelt and spiritual.
What then is the perplexity in attempting to classify this Prince?
  We are unwilling to reckon him amongst the bad, and we cannot heartily place him among the good.
Is it not too often thus even in our time?
  Alas! Yes; friends hope concerning the departed often, but their confidence is not certain. How can it be, when those they deplore were thought not wholly estranged from the ways of God, yet not wholly devoted to them. They did that which was right according to the standard of their fathers, but not according to the standard of the divine standard.
What is their duty in this respect urged by the apostle Peter?
  That Christians should make their "calling and election sure." That is, that they should give themselves decidedly to the truth, while yet in health, that their friends when gathered around their mortal remains, may be enabled to cherish the most assured confidence as to their happy state.
Is it not cruel to survivors to leave them in uncertainty and suspense in this respect?
  Certainly; the loss of friends is distressing enough, with-

What **case of happy** certainty is mentioned in this notice of Jotham?

That of James Hamilton of London, whose remains **were** accompanied to the tomb by Christians of every **denomination**, and that with a holy confidence and hope.

The standard for Jotham was David, what is the higher standard for Christians now?

The divine David, the incarnate Redeemer. He hath set us an example that **we** should follow his steps: and that example **is** perfect.

What was the state of the kingdom of Judah under Jotham?

Very sad. It is said by the sacred historian that, "the people did yet corruptly."

Have we **any** witnesses to this corrupt state **of Judah under** Jotham?

Yes: **Isaiah and Micah.**

What does Isaiah say about it?

That "the whole head was **sick**, and the whole heart faint, **and** the **whole** body full of putrifying sores."

What is the testimony of Micah?

That the wounds of Jacob were incurable or desperate, seeing that corruption had come into Judah, as to Samaria.

What particular evils do these prophets deplore?

Vanity among females, drunkenness among men, and cruelty and unbelief among Princes. Now this had been sad among any people, it was especially **so** among a favoured and consecrated people.

Are the favoured and consecrated of **New Testament** times free from these faults?

Alas! No: vanity in the one-half of society, and inebriety in **the other,** together with infatuation among professing Christian **Princes, are** rather the rule than the exception.

Is the new world **no** more free from these faults than the old?

We dare not say so, there **is** much goodness in America, but there is also much pride, intoxication, and cruelty **as** well; and this is the more inexcusable seeing that the enlightment and privileges of America are so great.

How did Jotham employ himself in the midst of his degenerate subjects?

Chiefly in building.

Did he make no efforts **at** reformation?

None, so far as appears. He was content simply to reign, and took no care about the moral or religious state of his kingdom—very unlike in this **to** Jehoshaphat, Hezekiah, and Isaiah.

Is there not too much of this inadequacy, **and** culpable indifference in relation to divine purposes in modern times?

Yes, men occupy themselves in building, **or** other unimportant matters, while the world needs rectification, and too many indulge themselves in inadequate theories of improvement, to the neglect of Heaven's remedy for human sorrows.

What in these circumstances is the comfort of the enlightened?

That the true Son of David hath been revealed—that He understands and is animated with an adequate zeal in relation to it.

What is the purpose of His reign to effect?

The full rectification of the nations. He will set justice and judgment in the earth.

Does the work advance as rapidly **as we** would desire?

No; the work is of such a nature as to require time; but it certainly will be triumphant in the long run.

Has He achieved any preliminary victory by which to give assurance of ultimate victory?

Yes; **in** His personal contest with evil **and death.**

What ought each of us to do forthwith **in** relation **to** this Prince, if we have not already done so?

To enlist under His banner, and to promote in every way His benignant and wonderful purposes in the earth. For the world's sake we ought, as well as for our own.

XIII. AHAZ.

"Ahaz was twenty years old when he began to reign, and he reigned sixteen years in Jerusalem, but he did not that which was right in the sight of the Lord, like David his father."—II. Chron. xxviii. 1.; Isaiah vii. 1-14.

AHAZ has small claims on attention, and none on esteem. He did nothing entitling him to respect or remembrance. He was no blessing to his own time, and he awakened no influence of good for future generations. He contributed nothing to human progress or to human weal; but the contrary. He might, therefore, be safely passed over or forgotten, so far as himself is concerned. But he was of the dynasty of David, that is something important; he was king too, for a time, of the sacred people, and he was the occasion besides of divine utterance. On these grounds, if on no others, it were proper to give his history our attention in our progress through the brief notices of the Kings of Judah. But there is a further reason for this attention. Ahaz shows us what a man may become when decidedly alienated from God. Ahaz was unamiable, unfortunate, and unblest, by reason of his impiety. We ought to be warned accordingly to avoid impiety, and on the contrary to yield ourselves willingly and unreservedly to the influence of Heaven.

In remarking on his history, we shall notice his wickedness, his incorrigibility, and the sign that illuminated his reign.

His wickedness.

That was unusual and great. He seems to have been worse than Jehoram himself. We can scarcely wonder at the course of the son of Jehoshaphat, after he married into the house of Ahab and Jezebel, but we may well wonder at the conduct of Ahaz. The leaven of Samaria ought to have been banished from the court of Jerusalem, now that several generations had passed since its introduction, and after the wicked and cruel usurpation of Athaliah. But no; Ahaz had learnt nothing by the experience of his ancestors, and cared not even to save appearances, by continuing the state of things as left by his father Jotham. He gave himself at once and unblushingly to the ways of the kings of Samaria. Isaiah was then prophesying—mourning over the deadness and ingratitude of the sacred people—denouncing the judgments of God against all pride and ungodliness, and unfolding the visions of the holy: but it mattered not to Ahaz. He had no sympathy with Isaiah, nor yet, with Isaiah's God. He turned from the prophet as he turned from the temple, and gave himself to the service and to the degradations of idolatry more particularly.

First—*He renounced and disclaimed all the proprieties and expectations of his house.* He was a son of David, but as unlike David as it was possible for him to be. "He did not that which was right in the sight of the Lord, like David his father." David sought to intensify and advance the piety of his people, by bringing the ark to Jerusalem, and leading the way in the exercises of devotion, but Ahaz sought to turn his people away from God, and himself led the way to the shrines of idols. David thought to build a temple for God's worship, but Ahaz treated the temple with scorn and indifference, now that it was actually built. God entered into covenant with David, promising to give perpetuity to his throne, and expecting obedience on the part of the favoured family, but Ahaz cared nothing for the counsel, nor for the mighty and mystic Prince that was to arise among his descendants to rule over the house of Jacob for ever. He cared rather for the momentary and delusive gratifications of disobedience and foreign fashions. Alas, for Ahaz! He belonged indeed to the family from which Messiah was to spring, and he might himself have been a type of some of the innumerable excellences that characterize the Heavenly beloved; but he willingly forfeited all the honours of his paternity, and all the delightful anticipations of a wondrous future. He was a link in the human descent of the second Adam, the Lord from heaven, but he hath neither part nor lot in the immortal kingdom and inalienable paradise of that Divine representative. Though a prince of the house of David, and king of God's chosen people, he cared no more for the peculiarities of Israel than he would have done had he been born in the darkest heathenism!

But this is only one half of the charge against Ahaz. He not only renounced the covenant made with David, he actually outdid the wicked in their wickedness. Not content with following in the ways of Ahab, of Samaria, he sunk to a yet lower level—he did, it is said, after the abomination of the heathen whom the Lord had cast out before the children of Israel! There were three stages of disobedience and vileness marked in the history of the Kings of Israel and Judah, and Ahaz sunk to the lowest. The three were—1st, the sins of Jeroboam, 2nd, the gods of Jezebel, as introduced by Ahab, and 3rd, the wicked practices of the disinherited Canaanites. Ahab, you remember, not content with the calves of Bethel, threw himself into the service of Sidonian Baal. And Ahaz, yet more perverse than Ahab himself, devoted himself to the service and abominations of Moloch. Of Ahab it is said, "That he did evil in the sight of the Lord above all that were before him, and it came to pass, as if it had been a light thing for him to walk in the sins of Jeroboam, the son of Nebat, that he took to wife Jezebel, the daughter of Ethbaal, King of the Zidonians, and went and served Baal and worshipped him. And he reared up an altar for Baal in the house of Baal, which he had built in Samaria. And Ahab made a grove—and Ahab did more to provoke the Lord God of Israel to anger than all the kings of Israel that were before him."

Observe the bad preëminence of Ahab up to his time! And notice the account given of Ahaz, a son of David, in comparison. "He walked," it is said, "in the ways of the Kings of Israel, and made *also* molten images for Baalim. Moreover (that is, over and beyond his conformity to the Kings of Israel,) he burnt incense in the valley of the son of Hinnom, and burnt his children in the fire, after the abomination of the heathen whom the Lord had cast out before the children of Israel!"

How awful and cruel was this to burn his children in the fire! How could a parent ever think to do such a deed? If the heathen, who knew not the mercy of God, and who yearned for some adequate propitiation, thought to give the fruit of their body for the sin of their soul, how could an Israelite sink so low as to adopt this practice? He must trample out the instincts of his nature before he could treat his children so, and he must utterly ignore the revelations of God, and the character of the merciful, ere he could entertain the thought. It was wholly alien to the mind of God, and God condescends to assure us over and over again, that it never came into His mind to make such a requirement.

Nay, we are well assured that nothing rouses the anger and the indignation of the Gracious more than this cruel and unnatural abomination. Here is the manner of it, and you can judge for yourselves. "The rabbins tell us that the image of Moloch was made of brass, and placed on a brazen throne, and that the head was that of a calf with a crown upon it. The throne and image were made hollow, and a furious fire was kindled within it. The flames penetrated into the body and limbs of the idol, and when the arms were red hot the victim was thrown into them, and was almost immediately burned to death. Its cries were drowned by drums and other noisy instruments." Now, judge of Ahaz by this, and you will see the heartlessness, and the cruelty, and the degradation of his character. And remember, he had the revelation of God within reach, and the Temple of God before his eyes, and the animal sacrifices to offer which God's worship demanded, in token of penitence, and in hope of brighter and more available things,—remember these things, and you will understand the perverseness and exceeding wickedness of this man. He was wicked with abominable wickedness, and spite of mighty restraints to the contrary. He must violate, at once, the requirements of God, which were before him, and the instincts of his nature, which were within him, and the dictates of common humanity, which are permanent as our nature, he must violate all ere he could act as he did, and he did violate all. Instead of sustaining the cause of truth, and righteousness, and mercy, against the perversions and cruelties of heathenism (which he was bound to do), he yielded himself to the abominations of heathenism, even to the abominations of those expelled and vile Canaanites who had preceded the Israelites in the occupation of the land! Add to this—

He used his influence for evil as widely as he possibly could. It was not enough to desecrate his capital, and to worship cruel idols in the valley of Hinnom, he must needs extend his royal wickedness into every part of his territory. "He sacrificed," it is said, "and burnt incense in the high places, and on the hills, and under every green tree." Wherever a suitable site, or elevation, was found, there he performed, or caused to be performed, the rites of his idolatrous worship. He was a zealot for evil. He was not simply its captain, he was its eager supporter and apostle. No one in all his dominions was left in doubt concerning his creed or his preferences. The tokens and the agents of his apostacy were every where. The land groaned under the defilement, and Heaven looked on in sacred indignation!

What was to be expected under such a king, and in such circumstances? What but judgment, reverse, and trouble! The blessings and cursings pronounced at Ebal and Gerizim in the days of Joshua were still valid and in force. According to these, obedience was to bring all good, while disobedience was to bring all evil. Ahaz was not under the reign of benediction, then. He had placed himself in the way of malediction and wrath rather, and accordingly we find that his days were passed amid the mutterings and reverberations of Heaven's righteous displeasure. Enemies assailed him, first from one side, and then from another. All around him were hostile. If a man's ways please the Lord, He maketh the very stones of the field to be at peace with him. But Ahaz's ways did not please the Lord, and enmity was allowed scope against him. The Syrians assailed him; and Samaria assailed him; and Edom assailed him; and the Philistines assailed him; and all with success. He **was** uniformly worsted or defeated. No gleam of victory cheered him, and no power effectually helped him. Syria smote him, and carried away a great multitude of his subjects captives, and brought them to Damascus. Pekah, the son of Remaliah, slew of his warriors one hundred and twenty thousand in one day. And his own son was slain on the occasion, and the governor of his palace, and Elkanah, his own particular friend and attendant. And, besides the slain, Israel carried away captive two hundred thousand men, women, and children, and they took much spoil **as** well, and brought it to Samaria. Then the Edomites came, and smote Judah, and carried away captives. And the Philistines also invaded the cities of the low countries, and of the south—possessed themselves of the same and dwelt there. Thus from every direction, from the north and south, and east and west, his enemies made successful inroads upon his dominion—and further, when he was brought low by his immediate neighbours, he looked beyond, and sought aid from Assyria: but he sought it in vain. Though he robbed the temple to buy the assistance of Tiglath-Pileser, that monarch but distressed him, and helped him not.

O, how sad were the experiences of this wicked **king.** Every post, as it were, brought him news of some **disaster,** and every new disaster reduced his resources the more, rendering it still less and less likely that he should be able to recover himself. True, God for His own gracious purposes checked and overthrew some of Ahaz's adversaries, but not before Ahaz himself had been brought low. God would not have Judah wholly extinguished, but He still allowed His desolating judgments to fall on the apostate land. Ahaz had thought to place himself in harmony with the outlying nations, and to free himself from the restrictions of the sacred Temple, but he found only disappointment and overthrow. He found the world to be at once an uncertain friend, and a powerless ally against the retributions of Heaven. He meant to be great, and he became small. He meant to be free, and he became fettered by misfortune. He meant to be happy, in a way of self-will and disobedience, and he found only misery and dishonour! Alas, for Ahaz! How admonitory against a career of self-pleasing.

But this leads me **to notice—**

His incorrigibility.

It is difficult to set forth all his stubbornness and desperation. Nothing seemed to move him. Reverse followed reverse, and trouble followed trouble, as we have just seen, yet still he held on his disobedient way. To take the mildest view of his conduct—

He was unhumbled **under** *discipline.* Though overwhelmed by defeat, he gave no sign of penitence. Though his own son was slain in his contest with Samaria, he remained insensible to the correction. Though his captive people were sent back to Jericho, under the remonstrances of a prophet, his heart was not touched. Though the Philistines dwelt in his cities, he made no movement toward a return to God. Though Tiglath-Pileser (his last earthly hope,) disappointed and distressed him, he remained incorrigible still. He seems, indeed, to have been more hardened than the wicked Ahab even, and that by many degrees. The mere announcement of the divine judgments to Ahab of Samaria, caused him to put on sackcloth and to go sorrowfully; but the experience of the divine judgment made no impression on Ahaz. God sought to rouse him to a sense of his folly, but he would not be roused. God sought to soften and subdue him, but he would not be softened and subdued. Like a stubborn boy, whom no chastisement can make submissive, Ahaz retained his spirit of insubordination and self-will under all and in spite of all. Nay

He grew worse under discipline. Hear the testimony concerning him: "In the time of his distress did he trespass yet more against the Lord." Instead of accepting the chastisements of Heaven, and seeking to improve them, he only became more determined in his ungodly ways. Instead of appearing before the temple as a suppliant and penitent, "he gathered together the vessels of the house of God, and cut in pieces the vessels of the house of God, and shut up the doors of the house of the Lord, and he made him altars in every corner of Jerusalem. And in every several city of Judah he made high places to burn incense unto other gods, and provoked to anger the Lord God of his fathers." You see, he was not simply indifferent to God, he was positively and actively hostile to Him. He was not simply swept away by the currents of evil, he was a determined and bitter opponent of good. As his reverses increased, his spite against the temple increased, as his resources became less, his hostile demonstrations became more decided. At first, he had left the temple open to the few in Jerusalem who cared for its services. For a time he thought it in dignity enough to neglect its services, and to speak slightingly of its ritual, but now, as his misfortunes grew, he would revenge himself for these misfortunes on the temple of his nation, and he destroyed its furniture closed its doors, and made an end of its services. Instinctively he felt that his misfortunes were from God, and, instead of humbling himself, and acknowledging, and renouncing his error, he determined to injure the temple and the cause of God to the fullest extent of his power. If you translate his conduct into words, it would be something like this, "Well, if the God of Israel will not allow me to worship whom I like, but must needs frown on my arms and enterprizes because I will not yield to His service, I, on my part, will not permit the continuance of His service in Jerusalem, but will patronize and multiply the rival shrines of other gods in all my capital and in all my remaining territory." Is this not fearful? **He** actually declared war against the God of his fathers, spite of all the demonstrations that God had given of His supremacy and might. But this is not all—

He refused even the condescending advances of the Most High. God, pitying his infatuation, and determined to save Jerusalem for David's sake, sent Isaiah to him, when " his heart was moved with fear, and the heart of his people, as the trees of the wood are moved with the wind." Here was the state of things: Rezin, the king of Syria, and Pekah, the son of Remaliah, had determined to subvert his throne and dynasty, and he had no power to resist them; but God, by Isaiah, assured him that these confederates should be overthrown in a few brief years, and offered to give him a sign to that effect. "Moreover the Lord spake against Ahaz, saying, "Ask thee a sign of the Lord thy God: Ask it either in the depths or in the height above!" One would think this would have softened him. One would expect that, after thus being reminded of his true defence, and of the care of God over him, and of God's willingness to be described still as his God, he would have changed his course, renouncing his idols, and yielding himself again to the service of the divine sovereign of Israel! Not at all, Ahaz had no such relentings, and no such thoughts. Hear his answer to the condescending One, " I will not ask a sign, neither will I tempt the Lord." What obstinacy! And what a flimsy covering for his obstinacy! He would not ask a sign, because he would thereby confess his belief in God and commit himself to further obedience. And his declaration that he would not *tempt the Lord*, just means that he did not wish to recognise the authority of God in any degree. He wanted nothing to do with Isaiah, or with Isaiah's

God. Though he feared his enemies, he did not wish a deliverance that would require penitence or submission on his part. Not content with shutting up God's temple, he rejected all overtures at the hands of God's prophet. It mattered not that his enemies encircled him, he would have nothing to do with the only power that could really help him. And further, *he crowned his folly by one of the most perverse and insulting declarations on record* : "Because (said he,) the gods of the kings of Syria help them, therefore will I sacrifice to them, **that** they may help me." How wicked and uncandid this declaration! And how gratuitous and unblushing **the** wickedness! He would have us believe, that, though he had been serving the God of Israel, the God of Israel had been unable to defend him against the gods of Syria. He would throw the blame of the misfortunes on the God of his nation, and not upon his own disobedience. He takes **no** blame **to** himself, but wantonly throws all the blame on the pretended powerlessness of his defender. He knew well that this was slanderous and untrue. He had ample means of knowing the supremacy of the God of Israel, and the powerlessness of the gods of Syria. He could not be ignorant of the frequent defeats of Syria under Benhadad and others, by the armies of Israel and that against all odds, and against all human probabilities. He knew too that God was, even in his own time, prepared to control Syria, and Samaria also ; if only he would have renounced his disobedience. He knew full well that it was his own wickedness, and not the power **of** the gods of Syria, that brought defeat on his arms. And he knew further that, because God would not have Jerusalem entirely overthrown at that time, the revolutionary purposes **of** Syria and Samaria would be checked, even in spite of his own perverseness. And yet, in the face of all this knowledge, he would have us believe that his idolatry was the result of enlightened conviction, and **not** the dogged determination of incorrigible obstinacy! He talks as if the God of Israel must be regarded as powerless, because He would not protect the perverse and the disobedient, and, as if the gods of Damascus were to be esteemed powerful because their votaries had been used to punish refractoriness and obstinate disobedience! How transparent his folly! And how ungrateful and audacious his conduct! O, but he was determined in his evil way!

You will not wonder that a special stigma should attach to the name of this king. Other kings had shown themselves to be unworthy, but Ahaz exceeded them all. And God points him out with emphasis to the special attention of posterity. In the twenty-second verse it is said: "In the time of his distress, did he trespass more and more. This is that king Ahaz!" This is the king distinguished above all others for obstinacy and wilful, persistent disobedience! It is as though God intended to point him out to the whole world as a prodigy of folly and wickedness; as if the Holy one had said, "This is that *infatuated* man, who presumed to strive with his maker, like the clay quarreling with the potter; or, like briars and thorns setting themselves in battle array against the devouring fire. This is that *ungrateful* man who, when I chastened him with parental tenderness, in order to prevent the necessity of executing my everlasting judgments upon him, only multiplied his transgressions against Me—breaking through every hedge which I made to restrain him, and throwing down every wall which I erected to impede his course. This is that *impious* man, who, in the madness of his heart, determined to banish me from the world, and to blot out the remembrance of my name from the earth."

Such is the bad pre-eminence of Ahaz; and thus he became the type or foreshadowment of the great Apostasy of the latter days. He ought, as a son of David, and an occupant of the throne of Israel, to have been a type or foreshowing of his illustrious descendant. Instead of this, he is a type of Antichrist. You know there are no relentings with the false church. Plagues and punishments go for nothing in her history. Instead of renouncing her errors in the day of chastisement, she only increases her devotion to them. She multiplies her mistaken rites and practices to ward off calamity, and only increases thereby her criminality. True penitence is no part of her religion, and true reformation enters not **into** her policy. We have a glimpse of her obstinacy in the account of the sounding of the sixth angel. Then, you remember, the four angels bound in the River Euphrates **were** loosed, and the number of the array of the horsemen **were** two hundred thousand thousand, and by them was the third part of men killed, by the fire and by the smoke and by the brimstone which issued out of their mouths. And mark the testimony of prophecy concerning **the** survivors of these judgments: "The rest of the men which were not killed by these plagues, yet *repented not* of the work **of** their hands, that they should not worship devils, and idols of gold, and silver, and brass, and stone, and of wood—which neither see, nor hear, nor walk,—*neither repented they* of their murders, nor of their sorceries, nor of their fornication, nor of their thefts." They are on **a** large scale what Ahaz was on a small scale. Like him they are obstinate and irreclaimable. It matters not what judgments and plagues overtake them, they abide in their disobedience, and only become more and more devoted to their wicked ways. God would hedge up their path against destruction, but they will not have it so. They disregard His fences, and plunge on to their ruin. And Ahaz preceded them in their infatuated course. Instead of shining in the light of the perfect, he carried the standard of the apostasy. Instead of heralding the sun from the world of brightness (which he ought to have done) he foreshadowed the obstinate and the proud, who should yet arise, shroud the sun in clouds, and immerse mankind in gloom!

O, but we should beware how **we** walk in his steps! We should humble ourselves under the mighty hand of God—especially so in the day of reverse and darkness. God is then seeking our good, and we should lend our willing attention and concurrence. We should neither be indifferent nor dissatisfied under His chastisements! On the contrary we should accept these chastisements in penitence, and endeavour to improve them. We can gain nothing by obstinacy and incorrigibility. Especially let us attend to God's forthcoming and announcements, and if he condescend to give us a sign, as he did to Ahaz, let us not decline it, as that wicked king did, but let us carefully and persistently give to it our best attention! This leads me to notice concerning Ahaz:—

The sign that illuminated his reign.

This we find in Isaiah vii. 10-14. There is a difficulty connected with this sign, as applied to the times of Ahaz. It seems to stand out from the then course of events and to be greater than the occasion demanded. The explanation is to be found in the ordinary style of the prophet Isaiah. He announces and takes cognizance of events connected with Jewish history, but his mind is so replete with a loftier order of things, and the analogies between the Jewish history and that loftier order of things are so striking, that he cannot help speaking, as it were, of the two things in the same breath. Now the two things before his mind are, First, speedy deliverance from the machinations of Rezin, king of Syria, and Pekah, son of Remaliah, who meant to subvert the throne of David, and secondly the emancipation of the true Israel of God, from the machinations of the powers of darkness, who meant to subvert, or to render impossible the reign of righteousness upon the earth. These two things are both before his mind, and the larger subject, of course, predominates in his language. It is the grand sign of the incarnation in the interests of the Israel of God that shapes his expression, but he means to say, at the same time, in relation to then existing things, that by the time an unmarried female can have a son capable of distinguishing between the pleasant and the unpleasant, that is, within three or four years, the conspiracy of Rezin and Pekah shall be utterly broken. And such indeed was the fact: for the King of Assyria slew Rezin of Damascus, and Hoshea, the son of Elah, slew Pekah, the son of Remaliah. These parties meant to put another king on the throne of Jerusalem, but God meant to preserve the family and the dynasty of David, **and that spite of the** wickedness of Ahaz!

And there was special propriety in giving this sign **at the** time. The few hidden and faithful ones **of** God needed encouragement. Matters with them were all but desperate. The conduct of the king was so outrageous, and the subserviency of the court and **the** country was **so** complete, that to the eye of sense, limited to the passing years, it seemed as if the cause of heaven **was about** to be entirely subverted. The adversaries of Israel were strong, and Ahaz was powerless against them; nay, Ahaz himself was so corrupted and unfaithful, that only overwhelming judgments could be looked for, as the consequence of his conduct. There was nothing but ruin before them, so far as men could see, or do anything to prevent. Only a word from heaven could reassure them. And that word Isaiah was commissioned to pronounce. It was not for the sake of Ahaz, who had declined all intercourse with heaven, and insulted the Most High, but for God's true and exercised people that this sign was given. We know not the names of these faithful ones, but doubtless there were some few of them in Jerusalem. Isaiah would not **be** alone loyal in these degenerate times. There might be seven thousand scattered throughout Judea, as in the days of Elijah, for anything **we** can tell **to** the contrary. True, Isaiah himself mourned the general unbelief, crying, "Who hath believed our report, and to whom is the arm **of** the Lord revealed?" But no doubt there were some **who** had not bowed the knee to Baal; and for their sakes the assurance was given that the throne of David should not be utterly subverted, notwithstanding the wickedness of the present incumbent.

But we need not rest on the Jewish analogue, seeing that the higher order of things hath now been unveiled. The sign in all its plenitude hath been made manifest, and manifest for the world. "Behold, a virgin hath borne a son, and his name is *Immanuel!*" And His name but indicates the great, glorious, wonderful truth concerning Him. He is that Eternal Word, who was with God, and who was God; that Eternal Word which was made flesh and dwelt for **a time** among men, permitting them to catch glimpses of his glory, the glory as of the only begotten of the Father, full of grace and truth. And the virgin who bore Him was of the house and lineage of David, so **that** he was the son of David, as well as the **Son of** God.

And this, my friends, **is a** sign **for all** nations, and **for** all parties in all nations, and for all indeed, engaged in or interested in the moral contest going on in the **world**. For example—

It is **a** sign **to the** powers **of** darkness—the great enemies of goodness and righteousness. It **is** a sign that they will not be permitted to rule unchecked **over** the deluded tribes of men. They are too subtle for unaided humanity. And they have mighty advantages in their **own** invisibility, and in the moral **weakness** of their dupes **and** victims. So long as they had only men to deal with, or so long as the help sent was confined to angels, the dark and cruel demons expected nothing but success, aye, and they had a long career of success during **the** ages preparatory to the incarnation. But the incarnation—the advent of Immanuel put **a** new face on the contest. Then, myriads were enabled to break away from the dark tyranny; and then Satan saw that Heaven was in earnest, and that his reign **among** men must come to an end. He might still have long ages **of** partial dominion, but **he** could not mistake the sign. God with humanity was **an** element in the contest which he was **not** prepared to overcome. He might still show his bitterness and his spite: nay, **he** might still ruin many by flatteries and by false pleasures, and especially by delusive stimulants, but his permanent and final success became impossible. Once God had shown himself unmistakeably on the side of humanity by the advent of *Immanuel*, the result was clear and certain. God must conquer, and they on whose side **he** stands must have the victory. Men might fail to see it, but the dark enemies of humanity knew it well. They acknowledged the divine origin, and the holiness of Jesus, when he confronted them. They begged his forbearance, and they obeyed His behests, though reluctantly, when ordered by Him to come out from the possessed. The truth is, they were not slow to read the sign, or to calculate the effects of the miraculous appearance of *Immanuel*. It was a sign to them of ultimate and certain defeat.

But further, this virgin-born one

Was a sign to the hosts of light as well.

The angels of heaven were not less alive **to the** great event than the powers of darkness; nor **were** they less prompt to perceive or to calculate the effect of it on the history of our fallen world. They were familiar with the mighty processes of the Almighty One. And they knew so well that so unusual a step on the part of the Omnipotent, as that before us, could have only the most profound significance. Here, they saw at once, was the hiding of the Divine power, and the forthbudding at the same time of unthought of manifestations of Divine wisdom and mercy. It was to them the sign of glorious evolutions and glorious results. They desired to look into it, and they eagerly and reverently watched the sufferings of Immanuel, and anticipated the glory that must follow! It is interesting to know, is it not, that the powers of light were not less wakeful in this matter than were the powers of darkness. But it is of more consequence to us to notice, that the advent of Immanuel was, and is—

A sign to the sons of men.

It **is a** sign to the sons of men of eternal counsels on their behalf. The incarnation was not the result of impulse. It was not an unannounced wonder. It had been determined on in the counsels of eternity, even before the foundation of the world. It was the expression of a long-hidden and cherished love to humanity on the part of God. How precious such a sign, and it is a sign of ulterior achievements **as** well. It cannot be that such an identification of interests as that made in Immanuel will

be fruitless. God cannot take injury by allying Himself
with men, but men must derive good from being brought
into alliance with God. It was strange if God could ally
himself with humanity, and yet humanity remain unblest!
It was impossible. The contrary must be true. By this
alliance all the nations of the earth must be blessed. Even
apart from promise, we might assure ourselves of it.
There may be many unreclaimable ones like Ahaz; but
there must be many also who will not receive this grace
of God in vain. Besides, the very fact of God's allying
himself with humanity in the person of His Son, (apart
from the special application of it), gives a sunny light to
human history. Hope springs anew in human hearts in
consequence. The tide of evil is now seen to be under
control. The voice of mercy is now heard echoing among
human habitations; and the most desponding know that
there is a hope for the fallen, even though themselves
have not yet attained to its realization. This itself is a
mercy. It beats down despair, and lends preliminary
encouragements to those who seek escape from delusion,
remorse, and fear! But more particularly and emphatically, this advent of Immanuel—

Is a sign to the faithful and loving ones of our own day.
It is a sign indeed to us, (individually and collectively,)
if we be indeed true disciples. True believers have much
to try them in this ungodly and reckless age. They have
to grieve not only for the darkness and ignorance of the
outlying world, but also for the inconsistency and unfaithfulness of many who belong externally to the sacred
people. As in the days of Ahaz, Isaiah, and the faithful few, who sympathized with him, had to grieve, not
only for the idolatries of the heathen nations, but also for
the infatuation of the Kings of Judah, and of the time
serving who sustained or imitated him in his folly: so
now, the faithful among the spiritual tribes, have to
deplore the state of the Church as well as the state of
the world. Everywhere division and worldliness prevail. The true principles of the gospel are merged or

forgotten, and subordinate considerations mould the history of whole communities as well as that of individuals. With much profession and activity among disciples, there is yet much of worldliness mingled. The case is not so desperate as in the days of Ahaz, but still it is discouraging in the light of the interests at stake. Millions remain under the **power** of darkness; thousands are misled by plausible errors; thousands perish by intoxication; thousands more are left untaught in heavenly truths by their parents; theatres and balls and extravagances abound; while the ways of Zion do mourn. Morally and spiritually-speaking, there is confusion every where, and **no** power in human society to rectify it. Nay, mighty and ever-uprising elements increase it. There is therefore much to grieve and little to encourage the faithful, who long for the triumph of truth and the reign of righteousness! What is to be done? And whither shall these loyal ones look for a ray of light amid **the** darkness? Whither, my friends, but to the great sign of Heaven—*the virgin-born Immanuel?* His advent is an abiding pledge and earnest to the faithful few. He **is** *with them*, and He will yet ride forth conquering and to conquer. His apparent progress may not be so rapid as they could wish, but He hath His own **ways** of action, and His own reasons for the rate of **His** progress! Enough that He is *with them*, with them even to the end of the world! With them, to secure their safety and ultimate victory. Let them comfort themselves and be patient! The darker the hour passing over them, the more need to look to the great sign and pledge of heaven. I repeat, things are not so dark now for the faithful few as they were in the days of Ahaz: and if Isaiah could find comfort in the virgin-born Immanuel (the only promised,) much more may the faithful of our own time find comfort in the virgin-born Immanuel after His actual coming. And other signs have been added to the great sign of the Incarnation. There is the sign of the prophet Jonas, which is an index of the power **of** the Incarnate One, **as** well as evidence of His truthfulness; and there is the sign of Pentecost, which is a pledge of a new order of things; and there is the sign of the ingathering of the first fruits, which is an earnest of the coming harvest! With these great and unequivocal signs, there can **be no** doubt as to results! Only let the faithful abide in their fidelity, and all **will be,** all must be, well. Behold, He **comes** quickly, He, the virgin-born Immanuel, comes to complete His works, and the saints shall reign; and the dead shall rise; and the halls of immortality shall open **to** the rejoicing redeemed, who have waited for their King! Comfort yourselves mourning believers with these words. And let those who would share with the redeemed and hope fraught, **join** them in the discipleship of Immanuel now. Let them renounce all sympathy with every incorrigible Ahaz **of our** time, and seek the companionship of the heavenly-minded Israelites.

QUESTIONS ON AHAZ.

What was the character of this Prince?
 Very wicked.
Was his wickedness of an ordinary type?
 No, it was unusual and great.
What distinguished prophet exercised his prophetical office during this reign?
 Isaiah.
Did Ahaz listen to Isaiah?
 No indeed. He renounced both Isaiah, and Isaiah's God.
Mention some of the evidences of his great wickedness?
  His disregard of all the proprieties and expectations of his house, he gave himself to the worst abomination of heathenism, and he used his royal influence as widely as he possibly could in support of idolatry.
What are the three stages of idolatrous folly noticed of these **times?**
  The sin of Jeroboam, the abomination of Zidonia-Baal introduced by Ahab, and the awful cruelties and pollution of the Canaanites who were thrust out before Israel.
Did Ahaz rest with the first or second of these?
 No; he gave himself to the worst practices of the third.
What particular crime is specified as perpetrated by him under this corrupt superstition?

He burnt his children in the fire.
Tell the manner of this cruelty?
The image of Moloch was of brass and hollow, a raging fire was kindled inside of it, and when the arms of the image were red hot, the children were thrown into them.
What was to be expected under so impious and cruel a **king**?
Only misfortune and Divine judgment.
And what was the actual experience of himself and people?
They were assailed by invasion from all sides, and beaten by all their enemies. Even the king whom Ahaz bribed to help him, helped him not.
How did the experience of Ahab differ from his expectation?
He meant to be great, and found himself small, he meant to be free, and found himself entangled and fettered **by** misfortune.
Is there any lesson for us in his disappointment?
Certainly, we ought to beware of the illusion which associates prosperity with disobedience.
Was there no yielding or softening **of heart in Ahaz under his** misfortunes?
None at all, he remained wholly unmoved.
Mention some particulars of his conduct and chastisement?
He not only remained unhumbled under discipline, but he grew worse and worse. "In the time of his distress, he trespassed yet more against the Lord!" He refused the condescending advances of the Most High, he crowned his folly by one of the most perverse and insulting declarations on record. "Because," said he, "the gods of the kings of Syria helped them, therefore will I sacrifice to them that they may help me.
How did he show his increasing spite at God?
Instead of mere neglect he commenced actual hostilities against God's house and worship. He cut the vessels of the house of the Lord—he closed the doors of the temple, and he made opposing altars **in every** corner of Jerusalem.
Had he any right **to** insinuate, or reason for insinuating that God had been indifferent or powerless in relation to His worshippers?
None at all; himself alone was to blame if God left him in the hands of his enemies.
Was any special stigma attached to the name of this wicked Prince?
Yes; he is spoken of as "that king Ahaz."
Of whom was he, in his incorrigibility a type?

Of antichrist surely. He ought to have been a type of the illustrious king of the house of David, instead of which he was a type of the great enemy of that house.

How should **we** conduct ourselves under reverse or chastisement?

Not like Ahaz, in impenitence, but like David in penitence **and** humiliation.

What was the sign given to him **by** God spite **of** his refusing one?

The birth of **a** child of **a** virgin, whose name was to be Immanuel.

Where arises the difficulty concerning this announcement?

From the union in the prophet's mind of two deliverances, the latter and greater of which gives shape to his language, while the proximate and smaller, is that which obtrudes itself upon the attention.

Was there any special propriety **in** giving this sign **at the time**?

Yes; for the encouragement of the faithful few.

And was this sign **for** the times of Ahaz merely?

No; in its greatest and ultimate sense, it was a sign for all subsequent ages, and for many parties.

Mention some of these parties?

It, the virgin-birth of Immanuel, was a sign to the powers of darkness that their reign must cease—it was a sign to the hosts of light that glorious revelations were yet to be made—it was a sign to the sons of men that happier and purer days would arise—it is a sign to the faithful and loving **in our** own day, that the rule of evil will not be eternal.

Is there any special need for this sign now?

Yes, very special need for it—for evil is rampant, and that in many shapes.

Have other signs been added to this sign of the Incarnation?

Yes, the Resurrection of Jesus, Pentecost, and the ingathering of the first fruits.

And what is now required of the adherents of the true house David?

Only to be faithful **and** confiding, and they shall have the victory in due time.

What in general is the lesson taught by this reign?

That impiety is only offensive when developed and unforsaken, and that the signs and purposes of God in and by Immanuel will be accomplished spite of the unbelief of the unbelieving, or the opposition of the wicked.

XIV. HEZEKIAH.

"Hezekiah began to reign when he was five and twenty years old, and he reigned nine and twenty years in Jerusalem. And his mother's name was Abijah, the daughter of Zechariah, And he did that which was right in the sight of the Lord, according to all that David his father had done.—II. Chron."

HEZEKIAH was a good prince—one of the very best indeed in the line and lineage of David. This is wonderful, considering his immediate paternity. His father, Ahaz, was perhaps the most wicked of all the princes of the house of David. Only the sovereignty of God can account for this phenomenon—that such a son should spring from such a father.

But sovereignty works by means (though not always traceable by us), and here we fancy we can see the means employed in the enlightenment and piety of Hezekiah. His mother, it is said, was the daughter of Zechariah. Now in the days of Uzziah, nearly one hundred years before the time of Hezekiah, there was one of this name of whom it is said, that he had understanding in the visions of God. Abijah, the mother of Hezekiah, was probably the granddaughter or descendant of this good man, and she is described as his daughter, not merely because of her descent from him, but rather because she was of like character with him.

Under her pious influence, Hezekiah acquired very different views from those of his father, and was enabled to prefer the service of God to the follies of idolatry. Great is the contrast presented by the father and son.

In turning your attention on this son of David, we

shall notice him as a Prince in authority; as a Mirror of the great Unseen; and as a Man under discipline.

I. **As a** *Prince in authority.*

As such, he used his influence in the interests of the true religion, and he was unhesitating and prompt in taking his side. He was no sooner seated on the throne than he began the work of reformation. He found matters in a sad state;—the temple clouded, idolatry rampant, every kind of immorality unblushingly practised. Religiously speaking, the people had wandered from their rest, and all manner of confusion and distress was the result. Wrath was upon Judah and Jerusalem; but happily Hezekiah knew the cause and understood the case. He hastened to bring back the people to the worship of the true God. With this view he had the temple re-opened. His father Ahaz had closed it, and left it to dilapidation and decay. That wicked prince was not content to forsake the temple himself, but he made an end of its services even for the small minority in Jerusalem who still wished to wait before it. Hezekiah was one of that minority, but he dared not interfere. If he did remonstrate at all, his remonstrances were vain. So long as Ahaz lived there was no relaxation in favour of the faithful and the pious; but he was no sooner laid in the dust than Hezekiah commenced a new order of things. "He, in the first year of his reign and in the first month, opened the doors of the house of the Lord, and repaired them."

Next, he summoned the priests and Levites (whom his father had scattered and overlooked), with a view to the purgation of the sacred edifice, and the re-establishment of the Mosaic ordinances. Hear his address to the assembled temple officials. It is brief, clear, and decided (v. 5–11).

The priests and the Levites set to work forthwith, and in the course of eight days had everything in order for the resumption of the temple services. The king was informed of the fact, and he was not slow to act upon it.

He ordered an immediate commencement of the sacred rites, and attended himself, and took part in the worship. He did not open the proceedings by commission; nor did he worship by proxy; nor did he manifest either coldness, or indifference, or formality, in the service. On the contrary, he manifested all promptitude, all ardour, and all devotion. He rose early in the morning, like a man thoroughly in earnest, and gathered the rulers of the city, and went up to the house of the Lord. When there, he was as reverential as the humblest, and far more decided than many that took part on the occasion. When the offerings were completed, "the king, and all that were present with him, bowed their heads and worshipped. Moreover, Hezekiah the king and the princes commanded the Levites to sing praises unto the Lord, with the words of David and Asaph the seer: And they sang praises with gladness, and they bowed their heads and worshipped." This was beautiful and becoming, and was something very different from the state of things which prevailed under Ahaz but a few weeks before.

There are one or two things in this inaugural service at the temple worthy of notice, as showing still further the decision and devotion of this distinguished prince. Mark, for example, the number of bullocks, rams, lambs, and he goats offered for a sin offering. (21–24.) For the sin of a priest or of the whole congregation, one bullock only was prescribed, in Leviticus, to be offered, but here there are seven, you perceive. And why this sevenfold offering? Why, my friends, the impieties of the nation under Ahaz had been excessive, and of long continuance, and Hezekiah would mark his sense of the fact by the number of bullocks offered. He did not alter the Divine appointment in this, he only gave sevenfold expression to his penitence and worship. He had seen and deplored the enormities of the late reign, and he felt constrained thus to show his sense of them and his sorrow for them. His grief and humiliation were something unusual, and his offering expressed the fact. Then, mark his emphatic desire that the burnt offering should be for *all Israel.* **He was** not content to make atonement for his own immediate subjects. His heart embraced the ten apostate tribes as well. True, they were still alienated from **the** temple of God, and had expressed no desire to **return,** but they were, notwithstanding, **in** his patriotic heart, **a** part of the sacred people. He could not **wipe** out their **sin** by any atonement he could make **for them,** while they themselves continued impenitent, but he could show his sense of their **needs,** as well as his desire for their recovery and reconciliation. And mark once more, his scrupulous **attention** to all the parts of the prescribed worship. **He had not** forgotten nor neglected the arrangement concerning praise any more than those concerning sacrifice. "He set the Levites in the **house** of the Lord with cymbals, with psalteries, and with harps, according **to** the commandment of David, and of Gad the king's seer, and Nathan the prophet. * * * And when the burnt offering began, **the** song of the **Lord** began also, with the trumpets, and with the instruments ordained **by** David, King of Israel. **And** all the congregation worshipped, and the singers sang, and the trumpets sounded: and all this continued until the burnt offering was finished." And then the people, by the direction of the king, came near with their thank offerings in great abundance. And Hezekiah rejoiced, and all the people. We wonder not at their joy after such a change and in connexion with such **a** demonstration.

By the way, **it** may **seem** as if **the change effected was** easy, and that it required **no** great courage on the **part of** Hezekiah to bring it about; but this is a mistake. **It was** easy only because of the determination of the king, in connexion with the grace of God. No doubt the majority of the people were still idolaters at heart; and these would have been well pleased if left free to worship their idols, but they cared not to contend with so resolute **a** reformer as Hezekiah showed himself to be. Besides, the very excesses of Ahaz may have created a salutary reaction among the less fanatical devotees of Baal, and they might feel disposed to yield to the extreme course of

Hezekiah (as they viewed it) on the one side rather than continue to countenance the ultra-idolaters on the other. Any way, it required courage and determination on the part of Hezekiah, and we cannot but admire his decided and unhesitating course. Many men in his circumstances would have temporized or trifled, even though not themselves animated by idolatrous preferences. From indifference, or from indolence, or from timidity, they would have allowed matters to remain in very much the state in which the former sovereign left them. Preferring popularity to principle, they would have allowed the priests of Baal, or of Moloch, to retain their place and their influence in society, and if pressed by petitions from the faithful minority, they would have put them off with promises, if they did not put them aside with insults. But Hezekiah pursued the independent and faithful course. He braved the displeasure of the idolatrous, and more numerous and more influential party. He was willing to take the unpopularity connected with a return to what was sneeringly described as the antiquated rites of the past. He did not ask even whether it would be safe to revolutionize the worship of the kingdom so suddenly. He was determined to use his authority for the God of Israel, even though a political revolution should be the consequence. He went straight to his object. And his very boldness overawed his opponents. The faithful rejoiced: the moderates concurred: and the resolute idolaters withheld opposition—only denouncing in secret, or with bated breath, the zeal of the king, and the re-opening of the temple. So faithful and determined was Hezekiah!

And this was not all. Not content with re-opening the temple in Jerusalem, and re-establishing the ancient worship in the midst of Judah alone, the prince formed the daring purpose of inviting all the tribes from Dan even to Beersheba, to a Passover celebration at his capital. It was much to reform the religion of his own subjects, but it was far more to seek the re-union of all the tribes in worship. No such attempt had been made for more than two hundred years. From the times of Jeroboam, the ten tribes had been wholly cut off from the feasts at Jerusalem. Thoughts of recovering dominion over them, by conquest, or by intermarriage with their rulers, had indeed occupied the minds of the Kings of Judah; but the thought of leaving them free politically, and yet seeking their religious unity, had not before entered into the counsels of the court of Jerusalem. It was Hezekiah that conceived the patriotic and pious purpose, and his zeal was adequate to the out-carrying of that purpose. He sent messengers in every direction, inviting all the tribes to the solemnity. He sent also encouraging words with the invitation, and said nothing of past differences or heart-burnings, said nothing that might annoy the men of Israel, or hinder their return.

And he acted with wonderful promptitude in this matter. He would have no delay, though he might very plausibly have put off this invitation and solemnity for some months. The time of the year at his accession was such that he could not have all the preliminary purgations, as to the temple and the priests, and yet hold the Passover in the first month, according to appointment. He might therefore have postponed the invitation to the tribes until the next Passover. But this did not suit the ardour of Hezekiah. He wished immediate attention to what seemed to him a desirable project. And true zeal will not easily be disconcerted. He discovered that there was a latitude as to the observance of the Passover. Though appointed for the first month, it might, in the case of those who were involuntarily disqualified for its observance, be observed on the second month. He determined to avail himself of this permission, and issued his invitation accordingly. Happily, Hoshea, the king of the ten tribes, did not object, and, though many scoffed and sneered at the proposal, there were not a few who availed themselves of the invitation—repairing to Jerusalem, and reuniting with their brethren of Judah, in the solemnities of the divine worship! You see then how worthily and **how** wisely Hezekiah **used** his kingly authority. He was at once patriotic and liberal. He made no attempt at subjugating **the ten** tribes by force, like Rehoboam: nor did he attempt to recover authority over them by marrying into their royal house, like Jehoram, the son of Jehoshaphat. He was content to leave them at liberty politically, if only he could bring them back religiously. It was not for the sake of the tribute that he invited them to Jerusalem. It was not for his own aggrandizement that he sought their fellowship. It was solely for the honour of God and the well-being of the invited themselves.

How few kings are there who use their authority **thus**! Too many **are** anxious for **the** extension of their territory, without much regard to moral considerations. Still less are they swayed by religious considerations. They use their authority far more for their own honour than for the honour of God. Look through history, and you will find that the royal authority hath been far oftener perverted and abused than used conscientiously, and for the advancement of true religion! Even in the family **of** David you will find few men like Hezekiah. Some **of** that family are outrageously wicked. Some are indifferent or unenthusiastic for good. Only Jehosaphat and Josiah approach the standard of David and Hezekiah. And Hezekiah is therefore specially to be remembered and specially honoured. He used his authority temperately and without tyranny, and yet resolutely and without faltering. **We** usually honour the man who uses *wealth* for worthy **and** disinterested ends. We should not be less disposed **to** esteem the king who uses his authority for worthy and disinterested ends. And when **we** know how much evil arises to mankind by the abuse of authority on the part of the ruling, we should be ready to hail the faithful and the true in this respect with unmeasured approbation.

But we ought to do more than admire. We ought to imitate. We are not kings, like Hezekiah; but every head of **a** family is in authority **as** well as Hezekiah.

(Hear it, ye fathers and mothers.) Our authority, indeed, is limited, as compared with his, but it can be abused or rightly used as truly as his. Many parents like the father of Hezekiah close, in effect, the temple of truth and piety to their children, by the education they give them, and the example they set before them, and actually, though not intentionally, sacrifice them to Moloch. Others, again, are indifferent in matters of truth and error, if only external things are prosperous, and they leave the highest interests of their children to take what shape a self-pleasing and ungodly world may give them. While a few, Hezekiah like, make it their first care to lead their little ones to the temple and to the knowledge of God. And the question for each of us being at the head of a family, to answer is, to which of these classes do I belong? And I using my authority, and my parental influence, for God, or for the idol-serving and self-pleasing world? Am I true to the divine, or am I devoted rather to the material? Am I careful concerning my responsibilities as a parent, or am I unmindful that any responsibilities rest upon me as such? Oh bethink you, my friends—authority is no unimportant talent! And it is only rightly used when used in the interests of true religion! Happy, if like Abraham, you are faithful in that matter, and enjoy like him the testimony of heaven,—you remember that testimony: "And the Lord said, shall I hide from Abraham that thing which I do. For I know him, that he will *command his children* and his household after him, and they shall keep the way of the Lord to do justice and judgment: that the Lord may bring upon Abraham that which He hath spoken of him!" Happy, again, if like Joshua, we can say, each of us, without hesitation or misgiving, "As for me and my house, we will serve the Lord!" And happy further, if, like Hezekiah, our first and permanent concern shall be to gather together our household, to go up with them to the temple of God, and to bow there believingly, reverentially, lovingly, and worshipfully! Only the family that is trained for God hath any true aim in existence! And only the authority that is used in the service of God can awaken an echo of cheer or approbation in the spirit Universe!

But to return to Hezekiah. **We** regard him

II. As a Mirror of the Great Unseen.

By the Great Unseen we mean, on the present occasion, that illustrious Prince of the House of David in whom **the** glories of that dynasty were to culminate and so abide. This prince, you know, was to be the Son of David and the Son of God; and His manifold and matchless excellences were meant to be foreshadowed in **the** lives and reigns of his royal and sacred ancestors. Many **of** these ancestors failed to apprehend their true position, while some of them set themselves in direct opposition to the covenant under which they reigned. Not so Hezekiah. He walked in the ways of David, and gave himself truly and heartily to the duties of his house. We find, in consequence, important traces or foreshadowments of the reign of Messiah in his administration. Even as we find such in the reigns **of** David, Solomon and Jehoshaphat. In David, for example, we find a vivid glimpse of the Beloved and the conquering. In Solomon again, we catch an imperfect and blurred image of the Prince of Peace—the fountain of wisdom and the builder of the spiritual temple **of** God. Then Jehoshaphat in his day foreshadowed the great Teacher of the World—sending forth a commission of instruction to every part of his dominions: and Hezekiah was not behind any of these as a Mirror of the great Unseen, then yet to come. The representation was, in his case of course, small and feeble, but it was true and striking so far **as** it **went.** The merely human can act only on a limited scale, and **in** a limited sphere, yet it may represent, in miniature, the boundless and the divine. Thus we find three things in the administration of Hezekiah specially significant of the work of the great Mediator. We might not have apprehended them so clearly before the Incarnation, but now, in the light of that great event, **we** cannot but recognize and admire. The three things we mean are : 1, the re-opening of the temple ; 2, the untrammelled invitation to all Israel to observe the Passover ; and 3. the successful intercession of the king for the humble but ceremonially unsanctified. Of the first and second of these we have already spoken, and the third is recorded in the 30th chapter, 18, 19, 20 verses, thus :—"A multitude of the people, even many of Ephraim, and Manassah, and Issachar, and Zebulun, had not cleansed themselves, yet did they eat the Passover otherwise than it was written. But Hezekiah prayed for them, saying, The good Lord pardon every one that prepareth his heart to seek God, the Lord God of his fathers, though he be not cleansed according to the purification of the sanctuary. And the Lord hearkened to Hezekiah, and healed the people." Now, who does not see in these things a true type, though small and imperfect, of the great work of the Redeemer—the divine son of David?

First, the divine son of David hath re-opened the Temple of God to humanity. He is like Hezekiah in this, though on a more magnificent scale. You need not be told how entirely humanity had turned its back on truth and purity when Messiah appeared. The nations had, as it were, closed the Temple of God. They had left it, so far as they were concerned, to desolation and decay. They had turned every one to his own way—each differing from the others, but all equally estranged from God. Even the Jews, the chosen people, who ought to have kept the temple open, had sunk into superstition, pride and estrangement : and as for the Gentiles, they were wholly lost in the mazes of vain speculation, or the degradations of vile affections. But the great reformer appeared—the divine Hezekiah—the strength of Jehovah appeared, appeared full of zeal, and single-eyed loyalty to the true God. He was not to be deterred by the threatening attitude or menacing looks of the myriad supporters of established Error. He meant a thorough reformation—he meant to lead the nations back to God ; not the Jews alone, but also the Gentiles. And he re-opened the temple of divine truth to humanity with fearless and unhesitating hand. He did so **at the** risk of his life. Nay, he sacrificed his life in doing so. Still, he re-opened the temple and re-established the true worship of the true God in human society. And this work He hath prosecuted through centuries, and he is prosecuting it still. He means to subvert every form of false worship, and to make the name of his Father great among the Gentiles—even from the rising to the setting sun. Many of his servants, in the prosecution of this work, have fallen by the hands **of** Idolaters and opposers, but still the work goes on. Ahaz-like, Satan hath everywhere established false **shrines** and polluted groves, but Hezekiah, like Messiah, will **overthrow**, or cause to be overthrown, these shrines, and cut down or cause to be cut down, these groves. The earth is **the** Lord's, and his divine son, of the House of David, **will** not leave any part of it under the dominion of the enemy. The completeness of Hezekiah's reformation of Judea is a clear foreshadowment of the completeness of Messiah's reformation in the world. "The earth shall be filled with the knowledge of the Lord as the waters cover the sea." Is there not gladness in the thought, as well as great encouragement? The estrangement of the world, you know is awful: the power of evil is apparently beyond rectification or eradication. But the Divine Prince of the House of David is adequate to the work; and he will be not less successful in relation to the world than **was** Hezekiah in relation to Judah and Jerusalem. Meantime, mark the second suggestion.

I mean, *that founded on the Universal Invitation of Hezekiah to all the tribes, including the apostate ten, to come to Jerusalem to the Passover*—6-9. Who does not see a foreshadowment of the gospel invitation and message here? "Go" (said Jesus, after He had by His death opened the temple and mercy seat of God for all the world)—"Go, preach the gospel to every creature; go, teach and disciple all nations!" Go tell mankind all the world over that the Temple of God is re-opened. Assure them, too, that Passover has been prepared under the auspices of an adequate prince for all sinful and exposed ones. Invite them to come **and** find shelter from wrath—from the sword of the destroying angel. Tell them that reconciliation hath been made! Tell them that God is accessible to the unworthy, and tell **them** that the way to immortality **and** glory hath been thrown open to all. Oh, tell them that God is gracious and merciful, and that he will not turn away from them, **if** they but listen to this invitation and return to Him!"

Such, in effect, **was the** commission **of** Jesus, **the re-**opener of the temple of heaven: and great hath been the company of them that have published it. Hundreds and thousands are even now entreating the nations, each in its own language, to come to the great Passover. Many, as in the case of Hezekiah's messengers, scoff and deride, but many also, as in the typical case, listen and come—churches **are** being formed or built up on every continent and also on many islands. The message hath not been wholly in vain up to the present time, and we have reason **to** expect, that it **will** yet be more generally regarded and responded to in time to come. The mountain of the Lord's house, **and the** re-opened temple, have already been exalted above **the** top of the mountains, and we are assured that all nations will yet flow to it, and you are invited to come to this passover, my friends, if you have not already come. **O,** that you may apprehend and obey the summons. If Hezekiah rejoiced for **the** partial re-union of the tribes around the temple of Jerusalem: far more shall the Shiloh centre of humanity, and all His en-lightened people, rejoice for **the** recovered unity of **the** nations around the gospel temple of love! The unholy diversities of mankind shall then be ended. The days of division and hate shall then cease. There shall be one fold and one shepherd, and all the bright things of prophecy concerning the peace and unity of mankind around the one divine centre and king, shall yet be fully realized! How happy **to** know amid the conflicting claims of human religions, that there is one religion di-vine, and that that one divine religion is fitted and des-tined **to** set aside **all that** is false **and** delusive, and to fill the world with light, and with **love,** and with social purity and social harmony!

But there is a third noticeable fact in the reformation of Hezekiah, which I mention, viz:—

His successful intercession for **the** *humble ones who listened to his invitation, but who were ceremonially unsanctified.* Have we not in this **a** striking type of the intercession of the great and divine King of Israel? You know He **is at** once the passover and the intercession for sinful humanity. Yes, he **who** died **to** shelter us hath gone **to** heaven to plead for us. **He who** hath been set **at** the right hand of the Majesty on high is a Priest upon His throne, and makes continual intercession for us. Nor does He plead merely for the ceremonially unclean. He pleads for all, even for the vilest, who come to God by Him. Nor does he plead in vain. "His blood cleanseth from all sin, and His voice **of** intercession **is** never disregarded. Him the Father heareth always"! "**If** any man sin, we have **an** advocate with the Father—an advocate far more influential than Hezekiah—even Jesus Christ, the righteous—who is the propitiation for our sins, and not for ours only, but also for the sins of the whole world." Hear it —"for the sins of the whole world." No nationality is **excluded,** and no hindrance lies before any awakened one. If there be an individual present conscious of guilt, let him make known his case and his fears to the great advocate, and he need not doubt the result. Jesus will plead for him, and God will heal him. He who listened to the prayer of Hezekiah will not disregard the pleadings of His **son!** He who listened to the intercession presented on the foundation of **a** typical sacrifice and passover, will most assuredly accept the intercession which is founded on the great propitiation for the world, and offered by the great Propitiator Himself? O, there is everything to encourage those who would draw nigh to God! His temple hath been re-opened for the world—an adequate passover hath been prepared—all nations are invited to come and keep that passover. And He who is Himself the passover and the propitiation is ready **to** intercede, and that with success, for all who desire to enter the re-opened temple, **and** to behold the beauty of the Lord! Be persuaded, my friends, every one of you, to avail yourselves of the invitation **and** the arrangements, if you have not already **done so.** Renounce your false confidence, and your disobedient ways. Hasten **to** the Jerusalem passover—and employ and trust to the intercession of the New Testament High Priest. Though king in Jerusalem, He is also Priest of the Most High God ; **and** he is able to save to the uttermost all them that come unto God by Him—seeing He ever liveth to make intercession for them. He hath not only opened **the** temple ; **he** hath also furnished the sacrifice, and He is Himself the High **Priest that** presents the blood **of** that sacrifice before the mercy seat, and secures, by means of it, forgiveness and grace for all penitent and believing ones who follow Him. In **one** word, His obedient and trusting people are complete in Him—seeing that in Him dwelleth all fulness— even all **the** fulness of **the** Godhead bodily ! Why then should any remain estranged from Him? Why should any be so untrue to themselves as to stand aloof from Him ? They were wise who listened to the invitation of Hezekiah, and who availed themselves of his prayer, but unspeakably wise they who listen to the invitation of Messiah, and avail themselves of His intercession ! Be sure that their wisdom is yours.

Having thus seen Hezekiah as a prince in authority, and also as a mirror of the great Unseen, we have now to notice him

III. *As a* man under discipline.

It is not **to be** supposed, that a man so devoted and **so** energetic for good as Hezekiah was, would go untried. He who tried Abraham, by asking of him the sacrifice of his son, even after that patriarch had shown his faith **by** leaving his native country at the divine command, may well seek a further proof of Hezekiah's devotedness, even after the reformation **he** had wrought. A man who **is** strong in one direction **may** be weak in another : and **it** is seen proper by God to test the character of his servants at various points. Hezekiah was clearly able to face the opposition and the scorn of idolaters, and to take the odium of a return to the ordinances of Moses, but would he be able to trust in God in the face of an overwhelming demonstration of hostile power? That is now to be tested. The King of Assyria turns, under the permission of God, his all-conquering armies against the Reformer of Jerusalem. Already the proud and boastful lieutenant of the advancing Sennacherib is before the walls of the city. Hezekiah is hemmed in. He has no power to contend with the swarming and warlike Assyrians. He hath no allies, and he is not at liberty to seek them. The position of his capital alone, with its strong walls, furnishes him a temporary respite, by arresting the success of the invaders. What is to be done? Why, speaking after the dictates of sight, without entering on the domain of faith, there are only two courses open to him: and, if his zeal for God be either superficial or merely political, he will feel himself constrained to adopt the one of these two courses, according to his temperament. Either he will fight to the last, against all odds, and die in desperation, or he will submit to the conqueror, and yield his neck to bondage. History furnishes illustrations of both courses. Leonidas, for example, with his three hundred Spartans at Thermopylæ, disdained to yield to the Persian invaders, and died in the unequal strife; while many cities have opened their gates and accepted bondage or tribute when they found that there was no hope of successful resistance. But Hezekiah adopted neither the one course nor the other. Neither desperation nor submission. His devotedness to God was not a matter of policy, nor yet the result of impulse. It was a settled principle in his nature, and it dictated a course of its own. He betook himself to the God for whose honour he had contended in the reformation he effected. He sent to Isaiah, the prophet of God, imploring his prayers. Himself took the boastful letter sent to Him by the invaders, and spread it before God in the temple: and then he acknowledged the power of Sennacherib over the people whose gods were no gods, and begged that the God of Israel, who was the true God, would show His might and supremacy, in the defence or deliverance of His helpless servant. And his prayers were not in vain. The arm of God was made bare in his behalf—a breath from the desert, or an angel of vengeance swept over the hosts of Sennacherib, and the strength and the flower of his army withered in death. Sennacherib was disconcerted and made powerless, and Hezekiah and Jerusalem were saved.

Nor was Hezekiah only saved. His integrity and his faith were vindicated. He came out of the trial strengthened and filled with grateful praise. As Abraham returned from Mount Moriah after the trial of his faith, with an overflowing heart, so Hezekiah saw the remains of the threatening hosts of Assyria file away from the heights of Zion, with profound and worshipful emotion. The trial had been severe, but it both vindicated and strengthened the loyalty and the faith of this reforming king.

But one trial was not enough. Hezekiah must be further tested. The next trial was in his person. His health gave way, and an early death seemed imminent. This trial, by the way, served a double purpose. It both checked a tendency to elation, arising from his great deliverance, and furnished another test of the depth and character of his faith. And how did he stand the test? Did he yield under it either to unbelief or to impenitence? Not at all. He bowed to God and committed himself to the disposal of the Supreme arbiter, with many penitential tears. He grieved to think that his days should be cut off ere half of his work for God was accomplished, and only asked to be remembered graciously by his divine Friend. And God did remember him, and God added fifteen years to his life, and God caused the shadow of the degrees to return ten degrees on the dial of Ahaz in token of his purpose. Hezekiah recovered from his sickness in consequence by the prescription of Isaiah, and beautiful and touching was the song he sung on his recovery! **Again, he came out of** the trial, vindicated and improved.

But a third trial awaited **him**, and from that he **took** damage; or rather, in that he showed his weakness. **The** ruler of Babylon, Merodach-baladan, sent an embassage **to** his court with a present and with flattering words. Hezekiah **drank** in the seductive poison. He forgot, for the **moment,** his dependence **on** God. He took to himself the **credit of** his prosperity, and showed all his riches and his treasures, just as a man who knew not God, would show his. He **was** flattered by the friendship **of a** Babylonian potentate, **and he** wished to show his new ally that he **was** not unworthy of his regards. He forgot, or **merged** his position **as** the head of a God-cared people, **and** acted as **if** he were the brother and the equal of oppressors **and** ungodly tyrants. He thus lost an opportunity for honouring God and testifying for righteousness in **the** presence of the aggressive and self-seeking. **God** disapproved of his conduct of course, and sent Isaiah to inform him of His disapprobation. Nay, God saw meet, in the circumstances to lift the veil **of** the future for **a** moment, causing His unworthy servant to know that **all** his vaunted treasures would be reft away by the very power which had flattered and beguiled him, and that his own sons should yet **be** captives and eunuchs in the palaces **of** Babylon. **How** bitter the thought, and how undesirable **the** knowledge this vouchsafed him! His piety, however, did not forsake him. Though his weakness had been made manifest, he was still in heart loyal to God. He bowed to the divine announcement in all humility, saying, "Good **is** the word of the Lord." He could not but mourn the prospect, but **he** had **no** right, as he felt, **to** complain of it. He was thankful for the respite granted for his own day, and no doubt laid earnest supplications before the throne of God for the mitigation or reversal of the sad prospect in relation to his descendants.

Thus, the discipline by which Hezekiah was exercised **and** tried promoted **at** once his faith, his humility, and his devotional habits. Had his piety been superficial, such trials would have wiped it out, but being real and heart-entrenched, these trials only deepened its hold on his being. He learnt more fully and impressively by personal experience the faithfulness of God, and the weakness of his own heart; and such knowledge necessarily increased his admiration of God, and his distrust of himself. Besides, the painful knowledge of the future, given to him in judgment, actually proved a mercy in connexion with his gracious habits. It was like Paul's thorn in the flesh. That was a messenger of Satan to buffet the Apostle, and yet it was useful to balance the Apostle's nature after his heavenly visions and experiences. But for this Paul might have become inflated and darkened in mind and history; whereas by this he was kept humbled and dependent. So of Hezekiah's undesirable knowledge of the future. Without it, he might, with unwonted honour and experience in the matter of Sennacherib, and also in that of his miraculous recovery from sickness, have become vain and unstable; but with it, he was kept humble and prayerful! Thus we see the wisdom and the goodness of God to His faithful ones in the very judgments which He executes. He is even in advance of the subtle enemies of His servants, and far beyond them—so that He can always check, or overrule, or render subservient to good, the evil which they seek to bring about. Their machinations are not only frustrated, they are made the means of higher refinement and more exalted fortunes for the lovers of the true and the divine. Thus the weakness of the faithful may be made apparent, but the discovery or the manifestation of these weaknesses only quickens and gives ardour to their approaches to God. Their sorrows may, for the moment, abound, but those sorrows only tend to soften their hearts—to darken to them things that might beguile and to mature them for the higher life.

Oh, my friends, be sure that you love God as manifested in Christ Jesus, and then your mercies will be sweet indeed, and your very trials, like those of Hezekiah, will prove blessings in disguise. They will deepen your love, and intensify your humility, and furnish you with occasion for penitential supplications and for divine fellowship. Every character must be tested, sometimes by flatteries and sometimes by fears, but happily the result will ever be in the experience of the genuine children of God. Their graces will, by means of these trials, shine the brighter—their safeguards will by **the** same means be increased—and their wings will by the same means grow **for** that heavenly flight, which is to land them in the world where trial and discipline, and sorrow and **tears** are **for** ever unnecessary and unknown.

O, that **God** by His **Son** Jesus may take possession of your hearts, and make you all by His indwelling spirit His children indeed! And, O, that being His children, you may be able to use, Hezekiah-like, such authority as you are intrusted with for the advancement of His honour. May you be able besides to keep the Christian Passover with joy—not for seven days only, nor for twice seven days even, but all your lives long! And may you grow only more excellent and more humble by means of the trials through which you may be made to pass!

QUESTIONS ON HEZEKIAH.

How did this prince use his authority?
   Promptly and decidedly for Heaven.
What steps did he take on his accession to the throne?
   He had the temple, which his father closed, immediately re-opened. He summoned the Priests and the Levites to the work of purgation and preparation with a view to the recommencement of the temple worship, and he joined devoutly in the worship so soon as the necessary arrangements had been made.
Mention some things that in this inaugural seemed worthy of notice?

He offered a seven-fold sin-offering, expressive of his deep sense of the evil of the national apostacy. He earnestly desired that the offering should be for all Israel—for the ten tribes as well as for the **two.** And he made all necessary arrangements for triumphal praise as well as for deep and penitential sacrifice.

How do you explain the apparent ease with which he carried his reformation?
The decidedly opposed were overawed by his determination. Had he been less decided, his course would have been less easy. Besides, we may suppose a disgust had been created in the mind of the unconcerned by the excess of idolatry, practised under Ahaz, which made them more tolerant of the change than they would otherwise have been.

What daring purpose did Hezekiah, in his zeal next form?
He proposed to invite all of the ten tribes who might be willing to attend to a great passover, while leaving them all free politically, he wished to see them all united religiously. This was something new in Israel.

And did he carry his purpose into immediate effect?
Yes, and that though the time was scarcely suitable;—seeing that the preparations could not all be made, and yet hold the passover in the month appointed for that ordinance.

How then, did he avoid this difficulty?
He availed himself of a latitude allowed in the divine law on the subject—allowing the observance to those who were unintentionally disqualified, to observe it on the second month.

Is it usual for kings to be prompt and decided in using their authority for God?
Alas, no! The divine honour is too often the last thing thought of by those in authority; and Hezekiah is entitled to esteem accordingly.

Who ought especially to imitate Hezekiah in this matter of authority?
Parents certainly. The parental authority is less extensive than the royal, but still it ought to be used promptly and decidedly for God.

Is it common for parents to use it **so**?
We fear not. Too many **are** content to leave the things of God uncared for. Their chief anxiety in relation to their children is their worldly prosperity or advancement.

Should christian parents be content **with this inadequate use** of parental authority?

No indeed. We ought, Hezekiah like, to use our authority as well as all our influence, to keep these young people within the heaven assigned limits of safety and peace.

May Hezekiah be accounted as a type of the divine prince of the house of David in any special sense?

We think so. There **are** three things in which he seems to foreshadow that illustrious one.

Mention the first of these three things?

His re-opening the temple of God after its having been closed by his father. This the great and divine son of the house of David hath done spiritually.

What was the second suggestive act of Hezekiah?

His untrammelled invitation to all Israel to come to a great passover at Jerusalem. This seems to foreshadow the commission of the apostles to all nations to come to the gospel passover.

And what was the third?

His successful intercession **for** the unsanctified. This clearly suggests the availing intercession of Jesus for his believing people, who are all in themselves unsanctified and unfit for divine intercession and fellowship.

Repeat the three great truths foreshadowed by the conduct of Hezekiah?

The temple of **God** is **now** open for **the** world—all, of any nation are invited to come to the great and available passover, and the divine prince of the house of David, who is Himself the passover, is prepared to intercede for all who truly and humbly come: so that none need fear rejection or disappointment.

Have these truths any bearing upon our views or interests?

Most assuredly. They furnish opportunity and encouragement for all **who** wish **to** enjoy the divine forgiveness and the divine favour.

What then should be our unhesitating course?

To renounce all other dependence, to hasten to the passover, and to trust in the intercession of the New Testament High Priest.

Was this zealous prince, Hezekiah, subject to any particular trials?

Certainly. It is the manner of God to test and discipline his people.

What was the first great trial to which he was subject?

The invasion of Sennacherib.

How did he come out of this trial?
 Uninjured and rejoicing.
What was his next trial?
 Prostration **as** to his body, and threatened death.
What **was** the result in this case?
 Deliverance and gratitude.
What **was** the third?
 Flattery from **Babylon.**
Did **he** take any injury **from** this?
 Yes, he forgot his dependence **and** his glory—and acted in a vain-glorious and self-reliant spirit.
And did God express any disapprobation for this?
 Yes: and announced judgments in consequence.
What was the effect upon him of God's displeasure?
 It humbled him, and kept him humble for the rest of his life.
Was this not bringing good out **of evil?**
 Certainly, and this is the **manner of God** with His true people. Hezekiah might have been unduly elated by his miraculous deliverance and by his miraculous recovery from sickness—this threatening on the part of God held his vanity in check—It was to him what Paul's **thorn** in the flesh was to Paul.
What is it that transmutes every dispensation into blessing?
 The loving God in the heart; all things work together for good to the loving and confiding.
Repeat the great lesson to be learnt from the life of Hezekiah?
 To use promptly authority for God. To hasten to, and to keep the christian passover, and to exercise ourselves in humility **and** trust amid the discipline and trial of this our preparatory life.

XV. MANASSEH.

And the Lord spake to Manasseh, and his people; but they would not hearken.—II Chron. xxxiii. 10.

WE turned your attention recently to the story of Hezekiah. He was a striking type of his great descendant, as to zeal, enlightened desire for the unity of Israel, and intercessory influence. No such typical intimations are seen in the story of Manasseh, his son; and yet the story of Manasseh is worthy of attention. It brings out very vividly a transcendent and precious excellence of the divine character. In noticing this story we shall remind you of his early and excessive wickedness, his wonderful recovery, and the suggestive character of the story of Manasseh—still further illustrating the divine mercy.

1. *His early and excessive wickedness.*

This was something to be wondered at—considering his parentage, his knowledge, and his circumstances. There have been monsters of wickedness in other nations, and on other thrones, but they have not had the advantages which Manasseh had, nor yet the inducements to piety and obedience which were set before him. Many of the Roman emperors, for example, were vile, and cruel, and wicked beyond expression, but they had not been trained under the influence of such men as Hezekiah and Isaiah, neither had they enjoyed such a demonstration of God's supremacy, and care for his own, as that which the father of Manasseh had enjoyed, and with which Manasseh must have been thoroughly acquainted. I refer to the overthrow of Sennacherib's army before Jerusalem. The truth is, Manasseh preferred darkness to light, and the service of Satan to the service of God—not ignorantly, as **too many have** done, **but** with his eyes open. And he ex**ceeded in** wickedness, if that were possible, even **his** grandfather **Ahaz; and** that is saying much.

It may be said **in** extenuation, that he came early **to** the throne—being only twelve years old when Hezekiah died, and much of the blame attaching to his early administration may be put therefore to the credit of his advisers. But how came he to have such advisers? His father would not leave him in the hands of idolatrous and wicked counsellors. Nor would his father leave him unadvised concerning the course he ought to pursue. Hezekiah would not be less solicitous than David, concerning his successors, and we know how earnestly David urged fidelity and piety upon Solomon. "Keep," said he, when about to **die,** "keep the charge of the Lord thy God, to walk **in His** ways, to keep His statutes, and His commandments, and His judgments, and His testimonies, as it is written in the law of Moses—that thou mayest prosper in all that thou doest, and whithersoever thou turnest thyself." Thus David; and think you that Hezekiah would leave Manasseh uncounselled? We cannot suppose so; and we fear that Manasseh must have dismissed the **good** counsellors appointed by his father, as well as disregarded the advice of his father, in choosing for himself counsellors more suited **to** his evil dispositions and evil desires. No doubt, unworthy men gained his ear, and his confidence, but this had not been, if he had not been willing **to** be misled—if he had not wished to be free of the restraints of righteousness, and eager to pursue a course of self-pleasing and unworthy gratification. His course may be indicated thus:

First, *He undid the work of his father—the good Hezekiah.* He reared again what his father had pulled down, and pulled down what his father had built up. He renewed the high places and the groves of Baal, and scattered on the other hand the priests of God's temple. The faithful had to hide away, while the men of ill-omen, and ill-preference enjoyed the smiles and the favours of his court. Oh, but there was sorrow in Jerusalem and Judah, on the part of the few enlightened, when this undesirable change was established, and then was seen the truth of that saying of David, "The wicked walk on every side when vile men are exalted!" And this change was presumptuous on the part of Manasseh in no common degree! Why should he, a youth in his minority, presume to undo the work of his father? Had his father departed from the sacred writings of his country, or set aside the covenant on which the throne of David was founded, we could not have found fault with him for hastening to retrace his steps, and to place himself and his people in harmony again with the sanctities and antecedents of his nation, but his father had but done what every true-hearted Israelite was bound to do in the circumstances, and why should this stripling king subvert the work so wisely done and seek to set aside the peculiarities of his dynasty? He might have taken time to consider what he was about to do, and to investigate the claims of his father's God. He might have yielded himself to the guidance of the counsellors appointed by his father, until, at least, he had attained to his majority. But no. He seems to have been impatient to break away from the salutary restraints of Heaven, and to free himself from all the moral proprieties of his position. Then

Secondly, *He gave himself to the very worst forms of idolatry.* He **not** only worshipped the sun and the moon, and the heavenly luminaries, but he gave himself also to the vile, and cruel and debasing practices of the Canaanites, whom God had cast out of the land for their wickedness. He actually, like Ahaz, burnt his children in the fire to propitiate the cruel Moloch. The image of this monster god, you will remember, was made of metal, and heated red hot, and, while in this state, the little ones were thrown into its fearful arms. Who would not be indignant at a parent for using his helpless children so? And who endorses not the indignation of the Holy Jehovah against such practices? It had been bad enough to have forsaken the true God for the false, even though the false had been refined and gentle; but how abominable to forsake the worship of the mighty and the merciful for that of the powerless and the cruel. Surely Manasseh must have rated the service of the Holy at a low rate indeed when he could prefer to it the admonitions and the cruelties of heathendom! But no. This is not the way to view his conduct. It was not a preference of what he deemed best that guided him, but a preference of that most congenial to his own depraved heart and nature.

Thirdly, *He added to his idolatry the insult to heaven of the practising of witchcraft*—that is to say, he would penetrate the secrets of the unseen, spite of all hindrance. He would intrude upon God in His own reserved domain. Not content to renounce and forsake God as the God of his nation, whose temple rose within sight of his palace, he must needs break the barriers of the Invisible, and, by the help of the designing or the devilish, find out for himself the hidden and the future. This was, in effect, joining the rebels of darkness, defying God, discrediting His revelation, and seeking to subvert His throne. The attempt, of course, was vain: he could neither penetrate the unseen nor formally transact with the spirits of darkness, but it showed his desire. Rather than listen to the divine and the competent, he would consort with witches and necromancers, to find out, by underhand and disobedient ways, the things that God had hidden from human view. He preferred the dark cave, and the senseless jargon of the ungodly or immoral wizard, to the living and holy oracles of God—written in His word, or uttered in his beautiful temple by Urim and Thummim. Was this not insulting to the most High? Why, to say nothing of the criminality of it, what could be more ungraceful or disparaging in relation to God? It was condescension unspeakable on the part of God to utter His oracles in the ears of men. What then could be more ungrateful on their part than to disregard His condescension? And what more disparaging to God than to have his doctrines set aside in favour of those ignorant and demon-blinded men? It were a sign of folly and debasement surely, and not of wisdom, for an individual to prefer the incoherent utterances of a drunken man as a guide in any matter of importance, to the clear and truth-dictated utterances of a heaven-sent angel! Reason and common sense would cry out against such a preference! And yet even worse than this was the folly of Manasseh in preferring the words of the necromancers to the words and the oracles of God, which are as silver seven times purified. But even this is not all.

Fourthly, *Manasseh insulted God in His very temple.* He was not content to forsake the House of God, and to go and build for himself idolatrous shrines elsewhere: he must needs defy God, as it were, to His very face. He actually built altars to Baalim in the courts of the temple, and introduced a carved image into the sacred edifice itself. He carried his presumption and his daring into the very presence of the most High. Sinners often seek to hide away from God, and are willing to leave his courts undefiled if only they may be permitted to practise their follies in secret and away from the divine restraint; but this would not satisfy the insensate spirit of Manasseh. He was not content to worship his strange gods in some secluded, or remote, or at least, separate locality. O no, he must practise his abominations in the very temple itself. It is as if a neighbour, determined to annoy and distress you, should come into your very house for the purpose. Ordinary enmity would content itself with calumniating or injuring you at a distance, and extraordinary and ruthless must that enmity be, which would seek your very presence, and that in your own dwelling place, that it might show its spite, its opposition, or its contempt. But such was the conduct of Manasseh in relation to the God of Israel. He not only gave himself to other gods, but he also, so far as he could, dethroned the true God, dispossessed Him of His temple, and installed another divinity or other divinities there. One would have expected that this at least would have aroused the divine indignation, and that a thunderbolt from the hand of the Almighty would have shattered the intruded image, and laid the intrusive and daring Manasseh low! But it was not so. God withheld His hand. Nay, more, God sent remonstrances by His prophets, if haply he might turn the foolish being from his folly. But here again the hostility and disobedience of Manasseh appeared. For, fifthly. *He refused their admonition and remonstrances.* Nay, he turned upon the messengers and slew them. He who dared to defile the temple, was not slow to remove the prophet reprovers. If God was patient and forbearing with him, he was far from acting so in relation to God's messengers: he overwhelmed them, so far as his power went, with swift destruction. Even Isaiah, now venerable with years, and yet far more venerable by his converse with the vision of God—even Isaiah must be punished for daring to remonstrate. And how punished? Listen; tradition says he was, by the order of Manasseh, sawn asunder. How enormous the wickedness and the cruelty of such an order! How we wonder, when we read the beautiful utterances of the evangelical prophet, at the audacity and the heartlessness of the man who could order his execution, and calmly see such a life extinguished, and in such a manner. We cannot forget that Isaiah had been the friend and the comforter of Hezekiah, Manasseh's father, as well as the honoured exponent of the divine will and the divine counsels, and we wonder with great astonishment how Manasseh could treat him so. But it is only a tradition, and may not be true. Admitted, still the tradition implies the estimate of posterity as to his character. Such a tradition could never attach itself to the name of Jehoshaphat or Josiah. The very acceptance of such a tradition implies the conviction of those who receive or transmit it, that Manasseh was capable of the deed—and that, indeed, it was in keeping with his character.

It is not needful to go further. You have now before you enough to enable you to estimate this prince. He reversed the reforming arrangements of his father—he openly established and practised idolatry, and that in its vilest forms—he practised witchcraft besides, and consorted with diviners. He insulted God in His very temple; and further, instead of listening to the Prophet-messengers of Heaven, seeking to turn him from his folly, he rejected and slew them. The truth is, he exceeded all bounds in his wickedness and presumption. The ordinary crowd of wicked and reckless men he left far behind, and fiercely rushed in relation to the divine, where even the abandoned fear to tread. So bad, indeed is he esteemed to have been, during his early administration, that a very sober and sedate writer on his character says, "*that he was, perhaps, the most wicked man of all the human race.*" Mark his terrific pre-eminence. *Perhaps the most wicked man of all the human race!* There have been crowds of daring, wicked, tyrannical, and cruel men in every generation. We shudder to hear or to read of their infatuation, and their doings! And can it be that the son of Hezekiah should exceed them all in wickedness? But suppose that this is a mistaken judgment: he was clearly and confessedly among the worst. If not wicked above them all, he was at least among the first three, or, at any rate, among the next thirty. His temerity and impiety were enormous, and with scarcely any palliating circumstances. We can only stand amazed and horror-stricken while we think of his early history.

What then was his subsequent history? Did he, like most reckless and wicked men, go from bad to worse? Did he madly rush upon his fate and bring upon himself swift destruction? Did he fall, like his son after him, and like some of his ancestors before him by assassination? Or did he die of fearful diseases, like Jehoram, the son of Jehoshaphat? Did the lightning of Heaven scathe or blast him and leave him rent and ruined, and a beacon-monument for all subsequent generations? This, we certainly would have expected: but it was not so. This vilest of men actually found mercy at the hands of God, and this leads me to notice:—

II. His wonderful recovery.

The first step toward this was penal, and might not have resulted favourably. He was dashed from the throne which he had so dishonoured—taken alive, carried to Babylon, which his conqueror, Esarhaddon of Assyria, had then recently conquered, and placed in confinement there. It was thus, stripped of all his power, and separated from all his corrupt courtiers, and tools, unsustained and unimpelled by their presence and promptings, he had opportunity for reviewing his career, and he could not hide from himself its real character. The mental process which now commenced within him is not recorded, only the result; but we can imagine its outline. At first he could only execrate his own folly. As he paced his apartment in prison, and realized his captive, and dishonoured, and forlorn condition, no doubt he often burst out with denunciations against himself and his chief advisers. "O, my stupidity," he would cry, "my inexcusable stupidity, to listen to such and such counsellors, and to pursue such and such a course! I deserve to be trampled for ever in the mire, and to have my name execrated in all coming time! That I, a son of the saintly Hezekiah, and a descendant of David, should have torn down from the battlements of Jerusalem the banner of Heaven! That I, so privileged, and so favoured, should have defied and insulted Jehovah, who had proved so irrefragably His power and supremacy in the history of my nation! And that I should have burnt my own children, and slain the people and prophets of the Lord as well! Oh, it is agony. O, it was madness, unutterable madness! Where shall I hide my unworthy, my execrable head? O, that I had died among the briars, on the day of my capture, rather than be reserved to such remembrances and such regrets!" He was now, you understand, fully alive to the folly of his career.

And he could not but remember the character and the counsels of his father, so different from the course he had pursued; but the remembrance only agonized him the more. He had as yet no thought of mercy! It did not seem possible that mercy could reach him. He had sinned, as he thought, beyond recovery or forgiveness; and his thoughts and reflections, and anticipations, were only remorseful and painful. He had precipitated himself into a gulf, as he felt, from which there was no escape. He had fallen so deep and so low that he never could recover the heights of holiness and of hope where his father walked in his early recollections, with him, as a boy, by his side. No wonder if despair—black and dread despair, settled down upon his spirit. How long it settled there, we cannot tell; but we know that it was not forever (as it often is in the case of wicked men when brought face to face with their own outrageous impiety); I say it was not forever. In the progress of days or months of self-reproach, and dread expectation, a faint ray of light began to steal over his nature—a very faint at first, but gradually becoming more and more decided. His rage became penitence: his execrations and self-reproaches became sorrow: his rebellion became submission: his submission became prayer: and his prayer rose to ardent and strong crying and supplication. The superincumbent mass of folly and delusion, accumulated during years of disobedience and rebellion, being swept aside by his adversity, the small seed of truth deposited by his father in his youthful heart, began to develop itself. Faith grew as the truth gained power within him. His spirit became calmer, but not less intense in its exercises. Prayer and self-humiliation now formed his daily occupation. The mercy of God unveiled itself to his wondering eyes. The forbearance of God toward him, in that he was not slain outright, encouraged him. Hope budded, though feebly and blushingly at first, under the shadow of his faith. He was enabled to hold on and to press forward. And, wonderful to be told, even Manasseh, the daring, the impious, the cruel Manasseh, was enabled in some measure to apprehend to lay hold of **and to** trust on the mercy of God!

Are you not amazed? Why, **the** fact almost staggers **for** the moment **our** convictions **of the** righteousness **or the** vigour of the divine administration! If any man ever sinned away his day of grace, and rendered mercy in relation to him impossible and unadvisable, **it** was, as we would have supposed, Manasseh. But, happily, God's thoughts are not as **our** thoughts—nor His ways as our ways. At a human bar, Manasseh might have cried for mercy **in** vain! But at the throne of grace, he found forgiveness and **peace**!

It **is** interesting **to** think while ruminating on this wonderful change in Manasseh, of the probable intermediary causes of it. It must be referred ultimately, of course, **to** the sovereign grace of God; but then God acts mediately and **by** second and subordinate agencies and influence. What **then** were the **second** and subordinate agencies and influences of this happy repentance of Manasseh? We are greatly disposed to think that these are to be found in the prayers and piety **of** his father, Hezekiah. To that monarch it was revealed, because of his vanity, as you know, that some of his descendants should be prisoners and eunuchs in Babylon. Hezekiah bowed to the threatened calamity saying, "Good is the word of the Lord!" But think you that His affectionate and parental heart would **rest** there? O **no**! He would plead with all earnestness, **we have no** doubt, for the expatriated Princes. **He** would pray that their reverses might be shortened and sanctified to them, and that God would bring good out of the undesirable evil. At the same time, while secretly pleading with God, his pious solicitude would make him earnest in talking with his youthful son, Manasseh. May we not suppose that he told him of the coming captivity, and urged him if the calamity should come in his day to humble himself before God in the hour of his humiliation—seeking deliverance from Him who alone could secure it. And may not the words of Hezekiah have come forcibly to the mind of his captive and humbled son when reproaching himself for his folly? **We** think it probable: but anyway the prayers of Hezekiah were still before the throne of God, and his character and example were brought **anew to the** remembrance **of** Manasseh in the day of his sorrow. And the prayers were answered by the softening influence of the remembered example. If so, **it was** through his pious father that the grace **of God reached** Manasseh, and pious parents should take encouragement from the probable fact. Let them **not** cease **to** pray for their young people, while they have **life** and opportunity. Their prayers may be answered when they themselves **have** gone to **the** unseen. They may have no intimation **of** coming reverse for their children, as Hezekiah had, they may not be impelled to pray as he was, by conscious delinquency in connection with the sad fortunes of their children; but they may well assure themselves that difficulties and trials will meet or overtake every one of their loved ones; their characters will be tested; their hearts will probably be wrung with grief; and they will need the sympathy, and the grace, and the support of God! Let the pious parent think of this, and plead for support and deliverance for his children when these children have only God **to** look to.

It is also interesting to notice, in relation to penitent Manasseh, how speedily remedial influences came into play, after his repentance and reconciliation with God, with a view to his restoration to his throne. What these were, we are not informed, but it has been supposed that political considerations moved the heart of his captor, if generous sentiments did not. Esarhaddon cared nothing for the humiliation of Manasseh but he fancied that he might attach the Jewish monarch to his interests by dealing generously with him. Manasseh might be a sort **of** royal lieutenant on the confines of his empire towards Egypt—the only power from whom Assyria expected any annoyance. He might be mistaken in this, and Manasseh might be able to lend him but small assistance in the day of his extremity. Still the thought prompted him to set the captive free, and even to restore him to his capital,

U

with a somewhat enlarged territory—for Samaria seems then to have been added to his original domain. Thus Esarhaddon, all unconsciously, and moved only by political and selfish considerations, reversed on the repentance of Manasseh, the judgment which himself (with like unconsciousness) had executed against the same Prince, while yet in his impurity. We are reminded by this how wonderfully God overrules the policy of nations and Emperors for the accomplishment of His gracious purposes concerning His people. The world suspects not how completely its movements are made contributary to the exercise, or to the improvement, or the deliverance of the penitent, the believing, and the God-revering. The hearts of kings are in the hands of God, and He turneth them, like the rivers of waters, withersoever He will. And you may rest assured that He will not turn them to the detriment of His own, but rather make them subservient to the best interests of them He loves. It was clearly so in the case of Esarhaddon and Manasseh. Further,

We are pleased to find that the restored king set himself about the work of ratification and reformation on his return, but he acted at great disadvantage in the work. His former folly could not be forgotten either by himself or his people. His sad and painful remembrances weakened his power for action. He could not go about the work of reform with the same buoyancy, and freedom, and power, with which Hezekiah went about it.

And then, he found that it is easier to mislead a people than to recall them when misled. The corrupt will willingly follow the lead of those who renounce Heaven, but they prove little tractable when it is sought to lead them back to the Holy. So Manasseh discovered. His influence, which had been all controlling in the days of his Idolatory, he found to be but partial and limited in the days of his reformation and piety, still, he laboured on in the good cause; and though he made no brilliant change in the aspect of Judah and Jerusalem, he yet proved the sincerity of his repentance, and arrested for a time, the downward progress of his kingdom. His later years we fancy, were but sad and regretful. His **memories** were not cheering or invigourating—his small success in the matter of reform would keep him humble—and possibly the manifest irreligion of his son, Amon, would depress and grieve his heart : And the more so when he remembered that himself had deposited the seeds of impiety in that youthful heart. Even as Hezekiah had prepared the way for his repentance, so he had prepared the way for his son's overthrow. Amon was a reproduction of his former self ; but his happy change did not bring **a** like change to his son. He saw him ready on his own demise to head the idolatrous and influential portion of the community against the God of Israel, as himself had done after the death of Hezekiah. Altogether, his latter days were shaded and unbrilliant, and he is remembered now, not as a distinguished, or loyal, or successful Reformer ; but as *a monument of the divine mercy !*

And this my friends is the grand lesson of his history —viz., *the extent and greatness of the divine mercy.* Who could have imagined that even Manasseh, the idolater, the necromancer—the defiler of the Temple—the destroyer of his own children, and the executioner of the Prophets of the Lord; who, I say, could have imagined that he would have found mercy ? His daring and impiety **were** unusual, and he had not the excuse of ignorance **or** impious upbringing, and yet God pitied him—gave him softening grace—and actually received him, when penitent, again into favour! There must be a depth and a boundlessness of compassion with God, of which we have no conception ! It is so with His wisdom, it is so with His righteousness, it **is** so with his faithfulness, and so with His mercy ! The truth is, all God's attributes are infinite, and His mercy not less so than **the** rest. And there is ineffable encouragement in the fact to every penitent one. It is impenitence on the part of men—not implacability **on** the part of God that stands in the way of forgiveness. It is not the greatness of the sin that bars reconciliation. It is the hardness of the heart of the sinner. Accordingly the sinful penitent need never despair. The mercy of God is infinitely **beyond** his demerits, great although these are. Let him pray **and** hope; let him mourn and entreat. The dawn of love, and the forthshining thereof will aston**ish and** cheer him **in due** time. His very penitence **itself** is an earnest of his acceptance—not the **cause** of it, **but an earnest** of it. Impenitence **alone raises** an impas**sable barrier between the** sinner and **the** throne of love! Only think of it: "There is no limit to the mercy of God. No mountains of transgression rise so high that this flood cannot cover them. Sinners, the chief, are **wel**come to complete forgiveness. Although the Prodigal son has wasted all **in** riotous living, **let** him but arise and **go to** his Father, **and** he will be received without upbraid**ings.** In gospel times this blessed truth has been much more **fully** made known. The blood **of Jesus Christ, God's son,** cleanseth **from all sin.** Whosoever will let him come, **the same** blood of the **Lamb that is** needed **to** wash away **the sin of a** little child is **sufficient to** free **the** hoariest sinner on earth **from every spot** and wrinkle. **No** human being **of** any age or any character needs **to** hesitate and hold back, from a fear lest his sins should **prove** too great, or too deeply engrained by time; Christ saves to the uttermost. Not one of all the human **race,** through all the generations of time, who come to the mercy seat with his sins, will be sent away with the burden on his back be**cause** that burden **was too** great **to** be **removed.** If through the window **of** Scripture, **we** could **see** only such holy men as Samuel, and Daniel, **and John** going in **at** the **gate** of heaven, we would be cast down—we would not dare **to** hope **that** such as we are could be admitted there. If only great saints got it, we who are great sinners would lose hope. But when we see Manasseh and men like **him** going in and getting welcome, there is hope for us. **If,** we follow their steps in repentance, we shall be **per**mitted to join their company in rest. **If,** like **them,** we arise and go **to** the Father, like **them we** shall be permitted to lean on His bosom, and dwell in His house!" We now notice:—

III. The suggestive character of the story of Manasseh still further illustrating the divine mercy.

He ought to have been a type of the great prince in whom the glory of his house and dynasty was to culminate. As an ancestor of Messiah, he ought to have foreshadowed some one of the many excellences or characteristics of that great personage; and had he walked obediently no doubt he would have done so. To say nothing of David and Jehoshaphat, his own father Hezekiah had, as we have already noticed, foreshadowed the burning zeal and successful intercession of the prince of peace; and Manasseh, according to his temperament and circumstances, ought to have continued the anticipative representation. But this he did not do. On the contrary he placed himself entirely out of the line of the coming glory. He threw himself into the ways of disobedience, and thereby forfeited the honour of foreshadowment during his early years, and unfitted himself for regaining it, even in the days of his repentance and reformation during his later years.

If, however, he failed as a type of Messiah, he may be regarded as an embodiment of the people over whom he ruled so long. His history suggests their history. His impiety, as an individual, was their impiety as a nation. As he forsook God, so did they. As he went from bad to worse, so did they. As he insulted God, so did they. As he refused remonstrance and entreaty on the part of the prophets, so did they. As he incurred dethronement and captivity because of his hardened and irreligious ways, so they incurred disinheritance and captivity for the same reason. With some brief arrests under good kings, they, as a nation, went from bad to worse, all the way, from the days of David to those of Zedekiah. Every means was taken to keep them true to God, and separate from idolatry, and yet to idols they would go. Witchcraft was denounced as rebellious, and yet to witches they would seek. Wine and wickedness of every form were prohibited, yet to wine and wickedness they would give themselves. All that ingenuous and powerful love could do to keep them faithful to heaven and to righteousness God did, and yet they gave themselves to unrighteousness and ungodliness. Through long centuries the Holy One laboured to reclaim and to enlighten them, but they would neither be reclaimed nor enlightened; and He was constrained at last to give power to Nebuchadnezzar to burn their city, to overthrow their temple, and to carry them away into captivity and exile! It fared at best with them just as it fared with Manasseh!

And this, one would have thought, would have been the end of so perverse and ungrateful a people. They had exhausted apparently the patience and the mercy of Him who sought their good. They must be content, now and henceforth, as we would have supposed, to wear the chains of servitude and to weep for the good they had for ever forfeited. And yet what was the fact? Why, just as in the case of Manasseh, their captivity led many to penitence and juster views, and the mercy that restored that once impious, but subsequently penitent, monarch, reappeared and reasserted its power in the case of the captive people. God in His ineffable, inexhaustible grace, raised up for them a deliverer. Cyrus did for the nation what Esar had done for Manasseh, and Cyrus was but the agent of the divine mercy. God led that conqueror to victory and dominion with a view to this service, and so arranged matters, by the prophecies of Isaiah, and by the presence of Daniel at court, as to dispose the heart of the conqueror to liberate the humbled and penitent people. After seventy years of bitter and captive experiences on the part of the expatriated Jews, the freedom-giving edict went forth, and the long-estranged people returned to their sacred city—the wondering witnesses and the wonderful illustrations of transcendent and divine mercy. O they might well take up the song of their nation on that great occasion concerning their God:—saying "He is indeed good, and *His mercy endureth for ever!*" Nor is His mercy only enduring. It is profound and illimitable as well. It has a length, a breadth, a height and **a** depth which passeth knowledge. It extends to nations as well as to individuals. It turns not away from the most flagitious, when once penitence sways the being. Nor will it turn away from an entire people though that people have carried their ingratitude and their insults to the highest possible point, if only that people can be brought to a proper state of mind. Behold its extent in the accept**ance** and restoration of Manasseh! And behold its amplitude and infinitude in the restoration of the captive Jews! Had God's ways been as ours, no such facts as these would ever have marked the annals of time **after** all the wilfulness and ingratitude of the parties in question.

And a further illustration of this inexhaustible mercy **in** the history of the Jewish people awaits, we believe, the coming ages of humanity. That people are even now enduring a second and yet longer expatriation than that of Babylon from the sacred territory. Though restored **to** their homes by Cyrus, they turned again to wickedness as you know—not exactly **in** the old form, but in the old spirit, and so insensate were they, that, when God sent His Son to them they rejected and **slew** Him. Not content with killing the prophets, they **slew** the heavenly heir Himself, and threw from them the grace of God. For this they were again cast from their inheritance, and given up to all indignity and grief. And now, **one** would suppose they would be left to the consequences of this own persistent rebellion and folly. Not so. God's mercy in relation to them is not exhausted yet. They will in coming years be led to discern their error. They **will** mourn for Him whom they have pierced: and the world will be startled by their second return, after centuries of exile to their own God-given land. Mercy, in relation to them, is, in the meantime, in abeyance, but it is neither dead nor exhausted. It will yet burst from its obscurity and shine in the eyes of all nations by the return of the long-estranged children of Abraham to their pleasant and long-forfeited home!

Nor only in the **case of the** Jews is God's mercy made manifest. It **is so in the case of** all the Gentile nations. Though these nations have renounced Him, and insulted Him, and trampled, Manasseh-like, on every one of His **laws,** still mercy **is not clean** taken away from them. **The voice** of the Gospel-messengers is even now heard in **all** lands. The vilest is invited to return. God Himself hath furnished the means of forgiveness and acceptance. The offered amnesty is universal: "Whosoever will, let him take of the **water of** life freely!" "**Ho!** every **one** that thirsteth, come to the waters! Come, buy wine **and** milk without money and without price!" "Let the labouring and heavy-laden but **come, and** they shall find **rest to** their souls!" Such is the voice and spirit of the **divine!** And this **in** the face of every indignity and every disobedience. God's compassion is not a compassion that has only the sorrow to stimulate it. It is a compassion that must be exercised in the face of unmerited enmity and insult! O, how innumerable are the rebels! and how infinite **the** offences! and how bitter the hate! And how persistent and renewed, and long-continued the disobedience! And yet mercy still pleads and warns, and offers full and everlasting forgiveness! What a spectacle to angels! **A** world **in** rebellion—vengeance withheld for ages—and mercy **with** her angel wings and fragrant presence, flying **in every** direction, seeking **to** induce the rebels to accept **of** pardon and shelter, **ere the** irresistible retribution descends!

O, hasten, every one **of** you, to accept of this mercy **and** salvation while yet there **is** opportunity. If you disregard the voice of love, you must perish at last with the incorrigible! But if you accept of the amnesty offered in Christ Jesus, you will, like the penitent Manasseh, in relation to His crown, and **like** the chastened captives of Israel, in relation to Palestine, be restored to your original inheritance in the favour of God, and be fitted for participation with His children in light for evermore. Better this, infinitely better than all the wealth of earth! Be persuaded of the error and wickedness of your ways while estranged from God, and **seek** His face with unslumbering earnestness; you will **not** seek in vain. " Let the wicked forsake his way and **the** unrighteous man his thought, and let him return to **the** Lord, *who will* have mercy on him, and to our God, *who will* abundantly pardon! All things are ready in the great Mediation!

And let the returned take up the **song of the ancient** church, accommodating it if they will, **to** their own more advanced circumstances (Psalm cxxxvi.)

QUESTIONS ON MANASSEH.

What was the character of Manasseh's early reign?
  Excessive wickedness.
What is it that makes this remarkable?
  His parentage and advantages.
He was but twelve years old when his father died. Is it to be supposed that so good a man as Hezekiah would leave the youthful king in the hands of evil counsellors?
  No surely. We may reasonably believe that some of the best men about the court were appointed to aid him.
How then had he got into such wicked ways?
  Some of the designing and idolatrous must have had access to him and he, by reason of corrupt inclinations, must have preferred their advice to that of the honourable and the pious.
Mention some particulars of his administration and folly?
  1st. He undid the work of his father by renewing the high places, &c.
  2nd. He gave himself to the very worst forms of idolatry.
  3rd. He practised and encouraged witchcraft.
  4th. He insulted God in His very temple.
  5th. He refused admonition and remonstrance.
Why, by the way, should witchcraft be reckoned a crime?
  It is an attempt to discover, by underhand means, what God has reserved, and a disparagement of His revelations —as if they were insufficient or unnecessarily restricted.

What does tradition say about the venerable Isaiah in connexion with Manasseh?

That he was sawn asunder by order of that prince. This, if true, was a crowning enormity in the history of Manasseh; and even if not true, it shows what his successor thought him capable of.

What has been said **of** this **Manasseh by a** sober and sedate writer?

That he was probably "the most wicked man of all the **human** race."

And what is the wonderful fact concerning this most wicked of men?

That he actually found mercy. We would have thought this impossible apart from the fact.

What was the first step towards this result?

The judgment which his crimes brought upon him. He was dashed from his throne and carried away to Babylon **as a** captive.

How did this promote his recovery?

It separated him from his corrupt advisers, and forced reflection on his past history.

What was the first effect of this reflection?

Despair, we presume. He must have felt himself utterly beyond the range of hope.

Did not faith and hope ultimately find a place **in** his heart notwithstanding?

Yes: He became **a** true penitent.

What does this result emphatically teach us?

That God's thoughts are not as ours, and especially **that** God's mercy is unbounded. The prime cause of this result was of course God's sovereign grace.

What may we suppose were **the** secondary and subordinate causes of it?

The prayers and example **of** Hezekiah.

How could this tell upon the mind of Manasseh?

Through early memories and heavenly associations—memories and **associations** made potent by special divine influence.

But why should special and divine influence make the memories and associations of Manasseh potent for his re-creation?

We cannot explain it; Only this we have reason to believe, that God hath attached such influence to believing and earnest prayer, and Hezekiah's prayers were not forgotten before God. Himself was long since dead, yet the influence which his prayers had evoked was forthcoming and effectual.

Is there no encouragement in this for pious and **prayerful** parents ?

Certainly : Their prayers, though unanswered now, may become influential long after themselves have gone to the unseen.

But had not Hezekiah special reason to pray for his children ?

Yes : Their coming reverses had been announced to him, and this must have stimulated his sympathies (parental) **and** his devotions.

Have parents no reason to fear and to pray in relation to their children—when no personal revelation hath been made to them ?

O, yes. They may certainly calculate on difficulties **and** trials for their loved ones. The character of their young people must be tested, and their hearts will probably be wrung with grief in the process.

Was Manasseh speedily restored to his throne on his repentance ?

Yes. Esarhaddon, for political reasons, saw meet to restore him to his throne, and God's purpose of mercy **was** accomplished in this matter.

Did Manasseh give himself to the work of reformation **on his** return ?

Yes, but not with great results.

How is he now remembered ?

Simply as a memorial of mercy and not as a great reformer.

What is the truth which his history impresses on our minds ?

The extent and greatness of the divine mercy.

If Manasseh failed as a type of the coming Son of David, may he not be regarded as an embodiment of Israel ?

We think he may : His individual follies were all repeated and amplified in the history of his nation, and his captivity was but a precursor of theirs.

But did they find deliverance and return like him ?

Yes indeed : Cyrus did for them under God, what Esarhaddon had done for Manasseh.

What was the song appropriate to their return from Babylon ?

The national and ever recurring chorus—"The Lord is God: His mercy endureth forever."

Is there not a yet larger illustration still of the divine mercy yet to be given in the history of unbelieving and apostate Israel ?

Yes. When they shall be brought into the church with the fulness of the gentile nations.

And can it really be that the Gentile nations, who have so long insulted God by their idolatries, and debased themselves by their immoralities, can it be, I say, that they **shall** yet find mercy—and that on a world-wide scale ?

So we expect as though by God's promises and provisions. His mercy is from everlasting to everlasting as to duration. It is above the heavens as to altitude, and it is wholly inconceivable as to tenderness and power.

Is there not encouragement in this for the awakened and the trembling ?

Certainly : None need despair **if** only willing to accept of God's mercy in His own righteous and wonderful way.

What is the imperative duty and great interest of each of **us** ?

To avail ourselves of this mercy if we have not already done so, and to give ourselves to the grateful acknowledgement of the same.

XVI. AMON.

"Amon was two and twenty years old when he began to reign, and reigned two years in Jerusalem. But he did that which was evil in the sight of the Lord, as did Manasseh his father, for Amon sacrificed unto all the carved images which Manasseh his father had made and served them. And humbled not himself before the Lord, as Manasseh his father had humbled himself; but Amon trespassed more and more. And his servants conspired against him, and slew him in his own house. But the people of the land slew all them that had conspired against King Amon, and the people of the land made Josiah his son king in his stead."—II. Chron. xxxiii. 21-25.

IN AMON, we come again to a wicked prince. It is grievous to see how constantly these wicked princes recur in the family of David. Nay, how they preponderate even in the annals of the sacred royal family. A good one arises occasionally, but the majority are bad. Could David have witnessed or anticipated their history how his heart would have bled.

This Amon now before us, is not in himself worthy of remark. There is nothing respectable or amiable about him so far as appears. His brief reign is not illumined by any military achievement or daring exploit. He reigns, and that is all; and there is really nothing about him on which admiration can fix.

Still we may find warning against evil, if not incitement to good in his brief story: and it is as important that we should be warned against the one as invited to the other. We are encompassed with temptation, and our own hearts are deceitful. We are all liable to the very faults which marked the life of Amon, and it is well that we should be reminded occasionally of the evil and destructive tendency of these faults, and also that we should be warned against tolerating them in ourselves.

Notice then, concerning this unworthy prince, his **impenitence**, his assassination, and the dishonour that **rests upon his** memory.

His Impenitence.

Here is the brief account of his character and reign—
"He did that which was evil in the sight of the Lord, as did Manasseh his father, for Amon sacrificed unto all the carved images which Manasseh his father had made, and served them; and he humbled not himself before the **Lord, as** Manasseh his father had humbled himself: but **Amon** trespassed more and more."

We wonder **how, in** his brief reign, he could have **gone so far astray,** considering **the state** of things from **which he must have** started. **His father,** Manasseh, must have **left the** worship **of the true God in** the ascendant in Jerusalem when he **died. We** know that, on his return from Babylon, "Manasseh took away the strange gods, and the idol out of the house of the Lord, and all the altars that he had built in the mount of the house of the Lord, and in Jerusalem, and cast them out of the city," and we know "that he repaired the altars of the Lord, and sacrificed thereon peace offerings, and thank offerings, and commanded Judah to serve the Lord God **of** Israel." And this must have been the state of things **when** Amon mounted the throne. How then could **Amon** so suddenly give himself, and his royal influence, **to the** overthrown idols? We would have supposed that, even though his leading were to idolatry, it would have taken more than the entire period of his reign to wear the ship of state into a new course! We would scarcely have expected him to be as prompt and decided in the service of error as his grandfather Hezekiah had been in the service of truth. Error and corruption usually creep or steal over the community. They cannot have the bold and uncompromising front of the heaven-sustained. **But** the fact would seem to be that Manasseh's reforms were forced by the royal authority on **an** unwilling community, and that that monarch was no sooner numbered with the dead than the repressed idolatries revived, and Amon willingly placed himself at the head of the unwise and un-Israelitish movement. Be this as it may, Amon gave himself forthwith to the service of false gods and to all manner of wickedness. And he did **so** without any relentings of heart, or aught of penitential regrets. In many cases bitter thoughts and compunctions mingle with the false pleasures of the young who forsake God, but **none** such seem **to** have troubled Amon. His heart **was** fully set in him to do **evil.** Though he had heard of the piety of his grandfather Hezekiah, and though he had seen and known the penitence of his father Manasseh, he acted as if no such things had ever crossed the line of his mental vision. He unhesitatingly renounced the ways of Hezekiah, and " he humbled not himself as his father Manasseh had humbled himself." In one word, he was at once impious and idolatrous, impenitent and unhumbled !

Now, mark what is implied in this state of mind in the case of Amon. It is implied, in the first instance, that he was wholly unmindful of, and unconcerned about, the great things that God had done for his nation. He thought not of the deliverance from Egypt under Moses, not of the mighty demonstration given on that occasion of the supremacy of Israel's God as compared with the idols of Egypt. He thought nothing of the wonders of the wilderness, nothing of the pillar of cloud and of fire, nothing of the majesty of Sinai, nothing of the two tables of stone, nor of the laws inscribed thereon, nothing of the manna, nor of the marvellous preservation of so large a multitude in a desolate territory for so many years. He thought nothing of the story of Joshua, nor of the settlement of Israel in Canaan in spite of **the** wicked and warrior possessors of that region, and nothing of the truth connected with the building of the Temple of Solomon, which still remained in his time as a monument of more glorious years. All these things he ought to have known, all these things he ought to have remembered with grateful joy; and if he had done so, **it would have been impossible for him to be, or to remain, unhumbled or perverse in relation to the true God.** But **he** remembered them not. **He** treated the history of his people as a fable, or **as a** series of fables, or, **at** any rate, as of no account. He **had** ears for the unfounded and **empty** declamation of idolatrous priests, but none for the veritable records **or** announcements of heaven. As king of the sacred people **he** was under obligation to study the writings of Moses, but these he seems entirely to have overlooked. It is possible that these writings may have been lost sight of in his day, by reason of the general ignorance and ungodliness, but had Amon been as earnest after the true and the good as his son Josiah **was, he** would **have** anticipated the discovery of that prince, **and** brought **the sacred** oracles again to light under **his** own reign. **This,** however, was no concern of Amon's. His affections **were** elsewhere than in the truths and claims of God.

Then in the second place, Amon **was** wholly indifferent to the purposes of God in his dynasty. It mattered not to him that God had made a covenant with David, and his sons after him. It mattered not to him that **a** prince was to arise **in** the line of his family **who** was to rule over the house of Israel for ever, and be a light to lighten the Gentiles as well as the glory of the sacred people. The hopes of **the** world and the magnificent outcomings of the divine benignity were nothing to Amon as compared with his own momentary and wicked enjoyments. Though a son of David, he was wholly alien in spirit from his great progenitor. Though an ancestor of Messiah, he had neither perception nor desire in relation to the world's ineffable and transcendent benefactor! Hence his unhumbled and impenitent state of mind. **How** different, had he entered into the purposes and grace of God, and cherished the hopes of his distinguished ancestors. He would then have humbled himself as his father Manasseh had humbled himself! Instead of joining the idolatrous and increasing their influence by his authority, he would have wept for their perverseness and used his royal influence to arrest them in their mistaken course. But his sympathies were not with the believing and the pious! He delighted rather in the companionship of those who overlooked the operation of the divine hand in human affairs; and his heart was unhumbled and impenitent accordingly! He cared neither for the past nor for the future as connected with God.

But though thus unmindful of God's interpositions in the history of His people and indifferent to God's purposes in the dynasty of David, it is just possible that he might mean to become a different man at some future period. His father, he knew, had run a self-pleasing course for many years, and then gave himself to penitence; and he might fancy that he would do the same. Besides, he might consider, as very many do, that youth is a time for gaiety and gratification, and that it would be soon enough some twenty or thirty years after his accession to turn to serious thoughts and uninviting austerities. If he thought so, he was entirely disappointed; the remote opportunity to which he looked forward was never his! The more favourable conditions for sober thoughts which he expected to arise never surrounded him. He was swept away without warning, and without respite. The time for repentance he failed to improve, and the retribution of eternity confronted him with a most undesirable suddenness. Probably, he never would have repented though he had lived or reigned as long as his father. It is much more likely that he would have gone on from bad to worse. So long as he did live he only grew more and more hardened against God and true goodness. But we need not speculate about possibilities. We know certainly that he lived wickedly, and died in the flower of his years, unhumbled and impenitent, and estranged from all that was peculiar and heavenly among the people over whom he reigned.

v

Think then, this unhumbled and impenitent state of mind is a most undesirable state in which to live, and a most unsafe state in which **to** die. Apart from the ingratitude of **it**, it is both unsatisfactory and dangerous. To be thus, is to be estranged from the true and the good! **To** be thus, is to be unenlightened and indifferent as **to** the grand purposes of heaven in human history! To be thus, is to be blind to the operation of God in the spirit world, and to stand exposed to God's irresistible displeasure! God resisteth the proud and **the** unhumbled; and no wonder. Why should He, the supreme authority, be defied by the dependent and the obligated? Why should the ways of God be disregarded or contravened by the impotent and insignificant, or why should the impenitent or unsubmissive expect impunity in their presumption? If God has spoken, surely men are bound to listen! **If** God has communicated His purposes, surely men ought to consider them, and to concur in **them!** If they do not; if on the contrary, they harden themselves against God, live unmindful of His words, contravene His purposes, defy his power, defame his justice, or impeach his wisdom; surely then, they need not wonder if he whet His glittering sword, or awaken against them the agencies of destruction! **O,** would it not be a matter of regret if any of our contemporaries were thus, like Amon, impenitent and hardened against God? And yet, alas! it is ever thus with very many,— and you know it—hundreds and hundreds more despise in effect, the words of the Most High God, and are content **to** live for other purposes than His; and they will not believe that God is angry with them, or that they have any need to dread His displeasure, and if any attempt to convince them of their danger, they account such as no better than gloomy enthusiasts. But, whether they will believe it or not, God's eye is upon them for evil, and if they turn not **to** him in penitence and faith, they must ere long feel the weight of His avenging arm. Who that should see a multitude of persons enclosed, like **Baal's** priests, and unconscious of their impending fate, would not pity them? **Yet,** here are millions **of** immortal souls soon to be summoned into the presence of their Judge, and setting at defiance the doom that so certainly awaits them. Should not rivers of tears run **down** our eyes for them? Yes, verily, as our Lord wept over Jerusalem in the view of the destruction that awaited it; and as the Apostle Paul had great heaviness and continued sorrow in his heart, on account of his unbelieving brethren, **so** should we mourn bitterly for those who are, like Amon, unhumbled towards God, and who will not mourn or be in bitterness for themselves!

And we should, each of us, be careful that it is **not so** with us. We should be jealous over ourselves **in this** matter. Though not **so** openly impenitent **as** Amon, we may still be self-pleasing and God-forsaken in heart. Even professing Christians ought to look to themselves, lest there be in any of them an evil heart of unbelief in departing from the living God. There is danger that it may be so, and professors should bring themselves **to** the test from time to time. "Examine yourselves, says the apostle, whether ye be in the faith." Examine yourselves each of you, with such questions as these: Am I unmindful of what God hath wrought in the history of His church?

Am I indifferent to God's purposes as unfolded and prosecuted in and by Christ Jesus—the Son **of** David and Saviour of the world? Can I live for days and weeks without meditation and prayer? And am I solicitous rather for worldly pleasure, or worldly profit than for divine grace and divine fellowship? If you must answer **such** questions **in** the affirmative, then you are in **a** state of impenitence and hardness in relation to God, and culpably insensible to His claims. It is the humble-heart that God delights in. It **is** the broken-heart that is the best sacrifice on God's altar! And the broken-hearted necessarily live in the light of God's throne, and under the influence of his love, while the unhumbled and impenitent are estranged and ungrateful, and wholly unawake to the glories and the obligations of the divine! **Be** sure that it is not **so** with you. O, fear an unhumbled

and unsoftened state of mind in relation **to** God! If you **abide** in impenitence all the bright issues and possibilities **of** existence are closed against you! And dark judgments are on **your** track, yes, dark judgments!

Many, **we** know, doubt of these judgments. They could not **be so** indifferent **and** unconcerned as they are, if they did not. They cannot see how these judgments can fall upon the *distinguished*, and they cannot under**stand** how they can fall on *so great a multitude*; and they cannot believe that any judgments from the merciful heaven can **be** as *terrible* as represented. But we can appeal to facts. As to the distinguished, angels confessedly are a far more exalted race of beings than men. Yet not even angels were spared, when once they had sinned against God, but were cast headlong from heaven into the bottomless abyss of hell! But will God proceed against so many? Look **to** the old world, where not one human being, except Noah and his family, was saved! But shall **it** indeed be so terrible? Look **at** the cities of the plain, and see what overwhelming destruction was brought upon them! And bear in mind that these very judgments were intended "for an example (and warning) unto them that should thereafter live ungodly." Look, I say, **at** these things, and then doubt whether the judgment which is threatened shall be executed? "God will rain down upon the wicked snares, **fire** and brimstone, storm and tempest; this shall be their portion. If, after seeing such proof of the divine indignation—we will not believe, we shall be constrained to believe when our own bitter experiences shall leave no room for a possibility of doubt. The judgments may be delayed, even as the deluge was, but, at the appointed season, the vengeance will come, and will not tarry!" It came speedily, you see, in the case of Amon, even in relation **to** human measurements, and it will not be very long deferred in the case of any persistently impenitent ones! But this leads me to notice concerning the unwise and unhumbled young king.

II. *His assassination.*

That may be regarded as the judgment of the Holy against him, and because of his presumptuous wickedness. His opportunity was brief, and his punishment signal. We cannot explain how it is, that some wicked men have long respite, while others are taken short up, and driven suddenly from the stage of opportunity and hope. No doubt, there are good and sufficient **reasons** in every case in the presence of God. Any way, **we can** see that Amon had no reason to complain. He **was** of sufficiently mature faculties when he came to the throne, and he was not unacquainted with the story of his father, to say nothing of his grandfather. He had ample materials for a right decision, and, if disposed to be faithful, he had only **to** continue the administration as he found it. If, in these circumstances, he threw himself, heart and soul into the ways of disobedience, and had two years allowed him **to** reconsider his foolish decision, he had no right to complain, that the thunderbolt fell without warning and beyond recall. Supposing that he promised amendment to himself at some future period, (and too many of the young and pleasure seeking do, as you know,) what a terrible discovery he awoke to, on the further side of death, when he found himself in the hands of justice, without a chance of reversing his course, and without a possibility of escape! Pity that the young and God-forgetting will not take warning, but will persist in calculating on a future that may never come for them, and that though it should come, will only find them more indisposed than ever to repentance and reformation! "We know not what a day may bring forth**!**" The youngest among us may be with the unseen before another year, or before another month, or even another hour! How silly then to go out of the way of safety when the agencies of destruction are so numerous and so active around **us**! Let the young keep by the true, by the divine, by the redeeming, and then, if early death should overtake them, heaven-born hope will sit and sing on their silent tomb, but, if they wander into devious **and** unworthy ways, and death overtakes them ere they **have** had opportunity to return, then darkness and grief is the only legacy **they** can leave **to survivors.** O, how many hearts are **even** now breaking for **those** who are gone beyond recall, and who were overtaken like Amon, by the dark enemy while yet in eager pursuit of the delusive and the destructive! If there be who have ears to hear let them hear!

But the assassination and **fall of** Amon **was** not only **a** sudden **and** admonitory judgment; it also furnishes in**struction** when viewed in relation **to** its agents. Who **were** these agents? **Were** they **of the** idolatrous party **into** whose ranks the king had thrown himself, and at **the** head of whom he stood? Probably they were, but they acted not as the agents of that party. Their deed **was** recognized, **not** approved by that party. Instead **of** this, the **people** of the land (who constituted that party) **slew the** assassins of their king and leader. Were these assassins then **the** agents of the small and uninfluential party of the pious? Not **at** all. Assassination is not the manner of the good. However much they disapproved of the administration of Amon, they would **never** have thought to mend matters in this way. The truth seems to be, the assassins acted not for either **party.** They acted of and from themselves. And **who were** they? They were the servants of the king, the inmates of his palace—the recipients of his bounty, and the witnesses **of** his private life! And why should they slay **their** master and king? Not from a feeling of ambition apparently. It **was** not that any **of** them wished to **oc**cupy his throne. **It** must have been from a sense of **pri**vate and very great wrong. A slight matter would not lead **to** such a catastrophe. What the particular wrong or wrongs might be we cannot say, but the general principle from which they sprang we may easily imagine. It was *pride* in Amon, we well believe, which led to his speedy destruction: pride of station—pride fostered by the flattery of the idolatrous—and pride that was little scrupulous concerning the rights **or** the feelings of those who were in contact with **him**. **Pride**, you know, is another word for selfishness and lawlessness. The proud and self-centred care not what injury they inflict. They scruple not to do the most cruel things if only they can thereby advance their own wishes or pleasures. It never seems to enter into their thoughts that others have rights and feelings which ought to be respected. All must yield to them. Especially if socially exalted, if royal or imperial in station, they think every thing becomes them. It matters not whether it be shameless profligacy, or tyrannical exaction or cruel tortures, they allow nothing to stand in their way, and they resent every opposition to their will.

Now this, **we fear, was the** case with Amon. He was wicked, impenitent, and unhumbled in relation to God; And pride and haughtiness toward men we know also naturally ally themselves with such a state of mind. He might be popular enough with such of his idolatrous sub-subjects as were not in immediate contact with him. They felt not his caprice, his unreasonableness, or his spirit of exaction and selfishness. But it was otherwise with his servants. They were troubled and exasperated by his daily doings. They kept down their indignation for a time, hoping improvement on his part, and not daring to remonstrate or resist. But matters grew no better; as he grew worse and worse in relation to Heaven, his conduct became more and more intolerable in relation to his servants. They first scorned himself and his conduct in secret. They then complained to each other, and denounced their tormentor, but were slow to breathe ought of vengeance or of death. Not that they disapproved of their master's ungodliness. They were almost certainly ungodly themselves, but they could not bear his proud and lawless ways. For two years this smouldering resentment was kept under, but at the end of that time they could restrain it no longer. At the risk of their own lives, and in the face of every inducement to a different course of action, they arose against him and slew him in his own house! How intolerable his pride must have been, and how offensive his conduct to have prompted such a deed by such parties. Why domestics usually stand by their master and chief. If there be not some deadly cause of displeasure against him, they will defend his life, and not assail it; but the servants of Amon were so disgusted with him, and so bitterly exercised under his capricious and proud conduct, that they actually combined for his destruction!

Oh, how sad to think of it—that one so young (only twenty-four) and so exalted in station, and so privileged as to ancestry and relationship, should have brought upon himself such a fate! " Wearied with one day's sin, and intending to rise afresh to begin another, he lay down that night in fancied security." But the hand of vengeance was near! " He lay down in time and awoke in eternity?'" It is well that our eyes cannot follow the guilty soul to the judgment seat of God. The sight would be too dreadful. It would overwhelm us. A vail hath been thrown over that awful scene. God has kept its secrets to Himself. " The wicked are like chaff which the wind driveth away!"

If, however, we cannot follow Amon to the unseen, we can be admonished, not only of the impenitence which challenges judgment, but also of the pride which rouses the agents of destruction. We would do well to walk humbly. We cannot walk safely otherwise! Every step of pride awakens an echo of retribution. Every look of pride awakens a reaction of evil toward the proud one. "God, the ever present, and the irresistible, resisteth the proud!" And how think you, will the proud and self-willed gain any true advantage or lasting good with such resistance to be overcome? It is impossible. The proud but act to their own undoing, and awaken, by their presumption influences or agencies to react, with overwhelming effect, against themselves!

And need I remind you that this evil principle of pride hath place in every human bosom. It develops itself in earliest youth, and it clings to the heart even to the latest hours of life. Under the most favourable conditions, it needs perpetual watching, and repression. Even the believing and the heavenly-minded have to grieve for its presence, and inflating influence within them. The humblest are scarcely free from it. Were **it not** unwise, then, **to** give this evil principle any advantage? Were **it** not unwise to remove necessary restraints from it and **to** give it free and unobstructive scope for development? Most assuredly! Then what **do** they do, who, like Amon, turn away **from God**, and from **the** great redeeming Son of David? What, my friends, **but** this? They withdraw themselves from the indispensable restraints on pride, and leave that evil principle free to enlarge itself in the heart, and to dominate in the char**acter**. Assure yourselves of the fact, you cannot balance your own nature, and **no** influence known among men can supply the place of true piety in this matter of mental equilibrium. Withdraw yourselves from God, as Amon did, and from the knowledge of His goodness, and renounce all hopes from the Son of His love, who is also the Son of David, and your mental equilibrium, or mental well-being becomes an absolute impossibility. You cannot be ungodly and truly humble at the same time. Pride will take advantage of your alienation from God, and distort and disfigure your character, and challenge or awaken at the same time the agencies of your ruin. I need not tell you what calamities pride, unchecked and unrestrained by **the** fear of God, hath brought upon families and localities, even where it had not gone the length of provoking to assassination. You must know yourselves, (if indeed you consider your mental states, and observe the mental habits **of** others). You must know yourselves how pride embitters and tumultuates the heart in which it reigns, **or** in which it gains temporary ascendency! And you must know how it divides those whose interest it is to be fast friends—how it inflames society—how it irritates, enrages, rouses to resistance and reprisals, and often leads to fatal quarrels and revenges! The truth is, we cannot be peaceful in history, **or** serene in spirit, or harmonious in association, or stable in habits, if pride have a commanding position in our hearts!

Our wisdom then is, to turn from every thing favourable to **pride, and to** cultivate every thing favourable to humility. Our wisdom especially is to turn from all inferior **and false** gods, and to give ourselves fully to the knowledge of the true. The service **of** the false inflates and debases, furnishing no adequate pressure of superiority **and** goodness **to** repress inflation, while the **knowledge** and the service of the true elevates and refines and represses **vanity** at the same time. No creature can feel otherwise than insignificant in the presence of the Infinite and the Unsearchable. Had Amon served the God **of** Israel as fully **as** he **served** idols, he would have walked less proudly, **and** the unchallenged indignation of his servants would have left him free to live and reign during **the term** of his natural life! It **is** not essentially otherwise **with** ourselves, we must know God, if we are **to be** rightly adjusted **in** character and sentiments. More especially, **we** must give ourselves to the discipleship and the guidance **of** His Incarnate Son, if we are to be truly humble, truly equalized in spirit, and truly happy **in** the divine friendship. Jesus, you know, was meek and lowly **in** heart, and He promises rest, and mental equilibrium to those who take upon them His yoke of meekness, and follow Him in lowliness and truth! If only consistently **His, we** shall be saved from much mental agitation and suspense! If only consistently His, we may incur the hatred **of the** wicked because of our fidelity and unbending rectitude **; but** we shall never incur the hatred or the domestic revenges of injured and irritated servants. We shall conciliate their love and confidence rather. If only consistently and humbly His, we may in the world have tribulations, but in Him, and in the meekness and humility which He teaches, we shall have peace! Under Him, pride will lose its power over us, and all the misery which pride occasions will disappear from our personal experience!

We come **now to** notice concerning Amon

*III. The dishonour that rests **upon** his memory.*

And first here. He hath **small** place in the history of the royal family to which he belongs. While every king that preceded him from David downward, has at least a chapter of many verses assigned to him (some having two or three chapters). Amon is dismissed with five verses. The truth is, there is nothing worthy to record of him— no worthy deed—no noble aspiration—no effort, however feeble in the right direction. His existence is recognised as a link in the sacred family, but that is almost all. His character and his fate are touched, but with **as** brief a hand as possible. He is regarded as of **no** account, and passed with the smallest possible notice.

Now, this itself is dishonour. A king has an opportunity of making his mark in history, and, if he fail to do so, he is in so far dishonoured. A poor man may die unknown to fame, and unnoticed **by** the historian, and yet not incur dishonour thereby. **Not so** a king; he is the representative of the nation over which he rules; and if the history of that nation is written, his name ought **to** fill an important space in the record. If **it** does not, **he** hath failed to fill his office worthily, and to illuminate his age. His name may survive, but it survives without honour. And thus it is with Amon, he proved himself to be unworthy of his high office! Nay, he abused and misused his trust, and was indeed a blight upon his people instead of **a** blessing. He can be remembered only as **a** vain, presumptuous and unfaithful occupant of the most illustrious throne in the world's history! Thus, while he occupies the smallest possible space in the gallery of the kings of Judah:

He hath, secondly, no place whatever among the worthies whose lives illumine the stream of time. He ranks not with Abraham, and Moses, and David, and Jehoshaphat, and Hezekiah. The light of heaven rested on the heads and flashed from the history of these; but no such light rests on the name or flashes from the history of Amon. These holy men anticipated **or** foreshadowed, less or more, the great Prince of the house of David, who was then to arise to enlighten the world, and to fill the ages with holiness and joy; but Amon neither anticipated nor foreshadowed Him. Amon ought to have done so, as a member of the house of David, and king of the sacred people, but he failed to realize the honour. He sunk instead, out of the brilliant line of types and hope enkindled expectants. He descended to a far inferior level, where the light of heaven was unknown, and where only the passing and delusive sparks of selfish enjoyment relieved the deep and painful darkness! He belongs not to the catalogue of those who through faith subdued kingdoms, wrought righteousness and conquered Satan, and who shall yet shine as the sun in the kingdom that is immortal. He belongs rather to the Satan-conquered and shame covered! More particularly,

Thirdly, *He belongs to the idolatrous, the dishonoured, the debased, and the castaway*. He takes rank with Jehoram, the wicked and ill-fated son of Jehoshaphat, and husband of Athaliah—and with Joash, the unworthy and ungrateful murderer of Zedekiah, the son of Jehoiada, his benefactor!—and with Ahaz, the pre-eminently wicked and presumptuous son of Jotham, who refused the sign of Heaven offered by Isaiah! Nay, more, he ranks with the Canaanites who were cast out before the children of Israel because of their abominations! And with the debased Phenicians and Carthaginians, who might not stand before the Romans because of their sanguinary superstition! And with all the modern pagan nations, who even now walk in darkness, and wallow in immorality! For a prince thus associated and that by his own foolish choice, when he had the opportunity of a higher companionship, there can be no true honour. Heaven will not honour such, and men though they were trying it, would fail in the attempt. The truth is, dishonour instead must rest on the head of such—the dishonour of self-chosen degradation—the dishonour of rejection by the holy and the exalted, and the dishonour of the vilest companionship! Nor will the future remove the cloud of dishonour from the name of **Amon**. Many of the good sink in apparent dishonour among men, but the future will reverse the decision and pour light and glory around their name! But small hope there can be that thus it will be with Amon. Rather we have reason to fear, he will rise at the last to shame and everlasting contempt!

And all this comes by his impenitence. He humbled not himself before the Lord. There were **two** ways open to him, (as there is to all of **us**). Either he must humble himself before God, or turning away from God serve self and idols. Had he taken the first way, God would have lifted him up, and made his name illustrious in the **next** world, if not in this ; but he took the second, and he was left accordingly to sink with his idols, to the unilluminated courses of dishonour and dispeace !

And thus he furnishes my friends a lesson and an incitement to you. The lesson is ;—See that you choose the service of God, and not of self or idols . See that you humble yourselves under the mighty hand of God, and wait for such uplifting and honour as God may see meet to vouchsafe. Amon thought to secure honour as well as pleasure, by conforming to the fashions of the idolatrous nations around him, but he found dishonour and sudden death instead. You will not fare better by conforming to the ungodly fashions of the age in which you live. O, be persuaded and choose the knowledge and service of God before all the honours and prizes of **time** ! More particularly give your best affections and persevering thought to the great Son of David, who was only promised in the days of Amon, but who is now long since revealed ! He is the great medium of divine knowledge, and the great depository for the sons of men, of wisdom, righteousness, sanctification and redemption ! had Amon lived in the hope of the coming of this great and announced One, he would not have made the mistakes and the shipwreck he did ! And so, if we live in the light of the advent and incarnation of this same great One, and under the influence of His mediatorial throne, we shall escape the errors and the fate of Amon, and enjoy participation with all the ransomed, and **all** the sanctified of all the ages! Yes, " Believe in the **Lord** Jesus Christ and thou shalt be saved!" He that hath the Son hath life—he that hath not the Son hath not life: and "The gift of God is eternal life, and that life **is** in *His* **son** !"

The believer in Jesus may be injured among men, **but he** cannot be dishonoured in eternity! The believer in Jesus may **be** maligned to posterity, but **he** cannot be misrepresented in the presence of angels. The believer in Jesus may **even be** assassinated by his fellows, but he cannot be permanently obscured **or** overlooked, or scorned **in the** world to come!

QUESTIONS ON AMON.

Did this prince carry forward the reform of his father Manasseh?

  Not at all. His father was no sooner dead than he and the majority of his subjects gave themselves again to idolatry.

How came it that he found so ready **a** concurrence on the part of his people?

  Because, it is to be feared, they had never been truly devoted to good. They had given **a** constrained attention **to** the divine service, because Manasseh, the king, wished it; but they were still in heart idolators, and ready like **a** bent bow when the force is removed to spring back again to their normal position **so** soon as opportunity offered.

What two things were implied in the idolatrous and impious conduct of Amon?

  First—That he was wholly unmindful of the great things God had done for his nation, and secondly—That he was wholly indifferent to the purpose of God in his dynasty.

But were these things worthy of his attention?

  Indescribably so : and besides there were obligations resting on him to attend to them : further still, his own happiness and the happiness of his people required such attention.

Is it possible that his non-attention was simply postponement, and that he purposed to repent as his father had done **at** some future day?

We think it is. We can scarcely think that, with his knowledge of Hezekiah and Manasseh, he was wholly insensible to the claims of Heaven.

Is it a safe or satisfactory state for a man to live in—to be indifferent concerning the operations of God in the past, or to His purposes in the future—or even with a secret purpose of future amendment?

No. It cannot. There is in such a state criminal ingratitude and insulting neglect, and liability to sudden and irreparable evil as well.

Are there not too many thus?

We fear there are.

Should we be content that it should be so with us?

No, we should examine ourselves whether we be in the faith—in the faith of the divine of the past—and in the faith of the divine of the future.

But what if we should continue indifferent?

Why, the bright issues and possibilities of existence must then be closed against us, and dark judgments must be on our track.

Are there not many who disbelieve as to these judgments?

Yes: they willingly forget the deluge, and other calamitous dispensations, and they persuade themselves that a vague mercy will still be exercised to them.

What sudden and irremediable judgment overtook **Amon** while yet young in history, and unrepentant in **sentiment**?

He fell by assassination.

Why should he have been taken so short while many wicked men have long years of opportunity allowed them?

We cannot tell; but we can see that he had no reason to complain.

Supposing that he had a secret thought of future repentance, what would he think of his postponement on the further side of death, when he found his opportunity for ever gone?

That it was the most consummate folly certainly.

Should young people take warning by his case?

One would think so. They should postpone the unimportant to the eternally important, and not the eternally important to the passing frivolities of time.

Who slew Amon?

His own servants.

What is implied in this fact?
That he had been haughty and unjust in his domestic administrations. It was not as partizans, or **as** prejudiced **strangers** that they slew him, but because of personal **wrongs.** The idolaters, as such would have **no quarrel with him,** and the pious, as such, would not slay **him,** however much they disapproved of his conduct. **His** death, therefore, was probably but the reaction of **his own** pride and unreasonableness.

How should **we** regard such a death?
With sadness and deep commiseration.

Is that all?
No. It **should** put us on our **guard** against pride—pride **which** springs **so** readily in every human heart, and which awakens **as** certainly resistance and revenge in those who feel themselves aggrieved by it.

How is it that we are to attain to true humility?
Only in the service of God and discipleship of His Son. The yoke **of** Jesus is meekness and lowliness.

What will **be** the effect of uniform meekness and lowliness in relation to our safety?
There will then be awakened no domestic revenge against us, and assassination, if it overtakes us, will come from some outside and prejudiced hand—not from those who know us.

What dishonour rests on the memory of Amon?
First—He hath **a** small place in the history of **the David Dynasty.**
Secondly—He hath no place whatevever among the worthies whose lives illumine the stream of time.
Thirdly—He ranks with the dishonoured and the **castaway.**

Tell the reason of his dishonour?
He renounced God who lifts His people, and he chose idols, which drag their adherents down in their own downfall.

Does this **furnish a lesson to** young people on the subject of decision?
Certainly. There are still two positions in society, even in these Christian times—the godly and the ungodly—and every one who would be wise should cast in his lot with the godly and not with the ungodly.

Say who is the leader and the hope of the godly?
The Incarnate One already referred to.

What shall be the fortunes of those who believe and follow this Incarnate One?

They may be injured, misrepresented, **or** even assassinated among men, but shall find honour, complacency and gladness in the realms of beauty **to** which they **are** going.

What is the imperative duty and the eternal interest of every **one** who hears the gospel?

To believe **on the** Son of David who is also the Son of God.

XVII. JOSIAH.

Josiah was eight **years** old when he began to reign, and he reigned in Jerusalem one and thirty years. And he did that which was right in the sight of the Lord, and walked in the ways of David his father, and declined neither to the right hand nor to the left.—II. Chron. xxxiv. 1, 2.

MON, **to whom in the** line of David **we** last turned attention, was a man hardened in heart, **and** unhumbled in spirit **as** you will remember. **He cared** nothing for the demonstrations of Heaven **in** the former history of his nation. He was unmoved by the repentance and representations of his father Manasseh, and he spurned the remonstrances of the faithful **few** among **his** courtiers who would **have** led him into **wiser** ways. Instead of listening **to** the Heaven-taught, and reining himself in that career of idolatry and folly on which he had entered, he trespassed yet more and more. Every **effort to** bring him to reason and righteousness only confirmed him in his self-willed and unworthy ways.

And he was proud and lawless in relation **to his** servants **and** dependents, as well as disobedient **before God.** Some ungodly men conciliate for a time **the** good **will** of their domestics at any rate, but not **so** Amon. His immediate attendants were embittered against him, and that in no ordinary degree. So far indeed did their hatred carry them, that they rose against him and slew him **in** his own house.

It was sad, that one so young, and one **so** sacredly connected should die in such a way. He was king in Jerusalem, of the line of David, and grandson of the good and honoured Hezekiah. Yet he died by violence in his twenty-fourth year. **Two** years of royal life and license, and then—the silent grave. How sad, I say, and yet what could he expect, unhumbled, proud, and self-willed as he was? And is it not a fact, alas, that too many are like him still? Yes, too many are unmoved by the written communications of God. Unhumbled under the providences of God—undismayed by the sad experiences of ancestors, and unaffected by the remonstrances and representations of the loving servants of the truth. What can such expect? They harden themselves against Heaven! They refuse to be instructed—they rush in effect against the thick bosses of the Almighty's buckler! And how is it possible that they should escape rebuke and destruction? O, beware how you become hardened like Amon through the deceitfulness of sin! Rather imitate Josiah, to whom we now turn your attention, and who was a person of a very different spirit from Amon his father.

"Josiah was eight years old when he began to reign, and he reigned in Jerusalem one and thirty years. And he did that which was right in the sight of the Lord, and walked in the ways of David his father, and declined neither to the right hand nor to the left."

Concerning this prince we shall notice his early and sincere piety; his conduct under the testimony of the discovered books of the law; and his premature death.

I. His early and sincere piety.

That was very remarkable; so much so that it hath been a theme of interest to all subsequent generations, even to the present time. For more than two thousand years the early piety of Josiah hath been an ever-recurring and an ever-pleasing theme with sacred teachers and faithful parents. And that piety is the more remarkable, that he was the son of a very wicked father, and still more so, that he was early left to the seductions of a lofty place in society, as well as to the flatteries of an idolatrous court and people. Is it not wonderful that a young king, between the years of eight and sixteen should be able to avoid the dangers of such a position, and should be found at the latter age (that is sixteen) prepared openly to take the unpopular and self-denying course of obedience and piety? It is something surprising and unusual. How different with his grandfather, Manasseh, when he became king at twelve! And how different even with his own father Amon! The fact can be accounted for only by the special grace of God! At the same time there were no doubt proximate agencies contributing to the result, but we are not informed what these agencies were. Possibly, his grandfather Manasseh, may have been instrumental in giving this direction to his heart and history. We may easily suppose that the great penitent, grieved for the confirmed ungodliness of his son Amon, was careful to instruct, or to have instructed, his youthful grandson Josiah, in the sacred peculiarities of his people. We may even suppose, that he sadly recounted to the little listener (and with a view of fortifying the opening mind against error and idolatry) his own sad story. He would tell him of the inexcusable folly of the early part of his reign, of his dethronement and exile in Babylon, of his distressing convictions and experiences there—of the mercy of God in his unexpected restoration. And no doubt, he would urge his little grandson when his time to reign arrived, to avoid idolatry and to abide by the temple of God. He might tell him, too of David, and of Moses, and of the wanderings in the wilderness, and of the giving of the law. If so, you can very well understand how the mind of the youthful Josiah might be preoccupied with truth, and thus be fortified against the influence of idolaters even in his immature years, and then, the blessing of God on these instructions will amply account for the wonderful results. Any way, Josiah early learned to fear God, and to desire the re-establishment of His worship in Jerusalem.

Accordingly at sixteen he began to be known as an earnest inquirer after God. At an age when very many young people think only of fashion and self-gratification, Josiah was exercised about the favours of God and the interests of religion. He had thought seriously long before, but then he began to seek out and to consort with those in Jerusalem, who truly feared the most High.

Many influential individuals around him sought, **no** doubt, to draw him into fashionable and evil associations, and earnestly the priests of idolatry would seek his royal countenance, but in vain. Like Moses, he would rather cast in his lot with the people of God than enjoy the pleasures of sin for a season. Many of his contemporaries, we may well believe, wondered **at** the royal youth, but the royal youth held on his way notwithstanding. He became more and more attached to the few faithful—more and more satisfied that idolatry was the bane **of** his kingdom—and that he ought to use his royal authority to put an end **to it.**

Four years of thought and careful consideration confirmed his views, and nerved him for action. When twenty, he became openly a reformer; and it is difficult to say, how very decided and sweeping his reformation became. The matter is briefly reported in the verses following our text thus: "For in the eighth year of his reign, while he was yet young, he began to seek after the God of David his father; and in the twelfth year he began to purge Judah and Jerusalem from the high places, and the groves, and the carved images, and the molten images. And they broke down the altars of Baalim in his presence, and the images that were on high above them he **cut** down; and **the** groves and the carved images and **the** molten images he brake in pieces, and made dust of them, and strewed **it** upon the graves of them that had sacrificed unto them. And he burnt the bones of the priests upon their altars, and cleansed Judah and Jerusalem. And so did he in the cities of Manasseh, and Ephraim, and Simeon, even unto Naphtali, with their mattocks round about. And when he had broken down the altars and the groves, and had beaten the graven images into powder, and cut down all the idols throughout all the land of Israel, he returned to Jerusalem."

But his operations are more fully reported in II Kings xxiii. There we see how thorough his procedure was. He was not like too many reformers who are afraid to go all lengths, and who rest in half measures. He spared nothing **connected** with evil, or that was calculated to lead his people to evil, neither elegance in altar, nor antiquity in buildings, arrested his destructive hand. The bones of the priests of idolatry of former years he burned and sought thus to purge the very atmosphere, and **the** very memory of the people from the pollutions **of the past.** But read II. Kings xxiii, 4-20.

So far, he might **seem** to be animated only with a spirit of destructiveness. Some men have **a** pleasure in pulling down, but are unable or disinclined to build up any thing **in the** place of the things they demolish. It was not so **with** Josiah. Having completed the preparatory work **of** demolition, **he** was now prepared to advance upon the **work of** reconstruction and rectification. In his twenty-**sixth year** he began to repair the temple, and to prepare **for the** re-establishment **of the** worship of the God of **Israel in** Jerusalem. **In** the prosecution of this work, his servants discovered **a** copy of the law of Moses—whether the autograph copy of Moses, **as some** suppose, **or** the only complete copy **then** known in Jerusalem, as others suppose, it is not necessary for us to determine. Enough that we know (and this is the point of special interest in the matter) that the discovery **was** most opportune for Josiah, and that it gave a new impulse to his reforming zeal. Heretofore his knowledge of divine things was imperfect, now he saw the truth in its length and breadth, so far as it was then given **to** believers **to** know it. Here-**tofore, he hated** idolatry as opposed to the purposes **and** interests of his nation—now he **saw** the evil case into which idolatry had brought his nation—exposing it to the righteous and overwhelming judgments of Almighty God. No wonder that his spirit was moved by the reading of the authoritative book. The insincere and the hardened can listen to words **of** terror without alarm, but not so Josiah. He was too honest in his convictions, and too sincere in his desires to treat the word of God with indifference, or meet its threatenings with unconcern. But we shall notice this more particularly immediately. In the meantime we would wish you to observe, that the piety of Josiah suggests two things which it is important for us to recognize and to consider.

The first of these is, *the progressive character of the piety that is true and sincere.*—True piety cannot be stationary. It is a life, and life grows and advances, artificial rose-buds remain for ever rose-buds. They cannot expand or develope into full grown flowers. But let the rose-buds be living and true, and they will ere long spread forth their leaves, and drink the sun-shine, as well as fill the surrounding space with fragrance. You expect no fragrance from the artificial flower ; but the living must shed forth its pleasing perfume. It is thus with the true child of God. He goes from step to step in his advancing and beautiful life. He acquires strength and confirmation amid the agitations that surround him. He resists temptation with ever increasing ease, and becomes luminous in the heavenly atmosphere which he habitually breathes. From a seeker after God he becomes a reformer among men. From a timid disciple of truth, he advances until he is known as a fearless advocate of truth ; and if he have power or authority in society, he makes that power and authority felt on the side of Heaven, and in opposition to the ungodly fashions and customs of society.

You see this progress distinctly in the case of Josiah. Up to his sixteenth year, as we have seen, he but yearned for the right in his own heart. He dared not yet make any outward demonstration. The divine life within him, was only then in its incipient stage. At sixteen, however, he began openly to seek after God, and to consort, as we have also seen with the truly pious. At twenty he came out as a reformer, and he advanced in his career as a reformer, from that time overturning idolatry in Jerusalem, in Judah, and in Samaria. And then at twenty-six, he began to repair the temple, and to prepare for the national celebration of the temple worship.

It is not thus I repeat, with mere formalists—men whose piety is merely apparent or assumed. They are stationary, if not retrograde. They may keep up appearances before men for years, while in heart and reality they are really going backward. But say they are simply stationary, that itself proves they have no true life in them, if they go the round of apparent piety from week to week, for a year, or for five years, or for ten, and remain at the end of any of these terms merely where they were at the beginning, they have reason to doubt the sincerity and reality of their profession. It is not in the nature of things that a man can be in living converse with the divine, and yet not acquire greater appetency for the divine—and more robust loyalty in relation to the divine—and more earnest and more intelligent regard for the purposes of the divine. "The path of the just is as the shining light which shineth more and more unto the perfect day," and "he that hath clean hands will certainly grow stronger and stronger."

Here then is a test by which you may try your own profession. Endeavour to compare your life and sentiments as professing Christians now with your life and sentiments as professing Christians nine or ten years ago, and ascertain whether, during that period, you have made any progress in enlightened conviction, in courage, in disinterestedness, in devotedness, in love for God, or in love for his saints? Have you gone, like Josiah, from one degree of strength to another? Or are you just where you were? If you find that you have made any advance, however small, take courage and press forward; but if you are conscious of no improvement, then hasten to the throne of grace, and seek a new heart, and the divine adoption to which, you have reason to fear, you have heretofore been strangers!

But the second thing suggested by the early piety and experience of Josiah which you would do well to consider is this:—*The divine Friend of humanity is ever ready to step in with new facilities for those who honestly use and improve the facilities which they have*, or, in other words, *who honestly act up to the light which they possess*. It was while acting up to his knowledge that Josiah was brought into contact with the records of Heaven. Had he, conscious, in some degree, of the claims of the temple, left the sacred edifice as he found it, he would never have met with the book of the law. Had he been indolent or indifferent in relation to the claims of God, he would never have walked in the higher and more perfect illumination into which he **was** introduced by this discovery. But, because he acted up to his knowledge, *and by acting up to his knowledge,* he found the sacred directions which revealed to him his true position, and the **true** position of his people, and which enabled him to determine wisely and accurately as to his future course. And thus it is, and thus it hath been, with many besides Josiah. The wise men from the East, for example, seeking the **new** born Saviour found unexpected facilities and aids in their way, and were led to the presence of Him they sought; and the Ethiopian Eunuch, who, according to the best of his knowledge, had gone to Jerusalem to worship and, who, returning still unenlightened, read the prophecy of Isaiah, found, in his bewilderment, a teacher in the wilderness, and was by that teacher ushered into the light of peace and salvation. And so Luther, when mourning and yearning after God, and following that which is good so far as he knew, was led, like Josiah, to the discovery of a Bible, and by it to the further discovery of the true way to salvation.

Here then is encouragement for those **who** honestly walk up to the light they have. Their case is not unknown in the courts of Heaven. They will not be left unsatisfied or unassisted while they follow on to know the Lord, they shall find new facilities or helps in their way. A pious friend or a book suited to their case, or a new light thrown by **the** spirit of truth on some appropriate passage of scripture, will lead them into higher illumination or hope. "Unto the *upright* light shall arise in the darkness:"—an angel was sent to Cornelius, directing him to Peter, the disciple of, and the witness for Jesus, and angels are still ministering spirits for them who shall be "heirs of salvation." They will not leave the honest and humble inquirer unaided. They will lead him (though himself all unconscious of their guidance) to some discovery or to some divine oracle, which shall testify to him of the great and divine Saviour, and which shall be to him, it may be, the occasion of his receiving the Holy Ghost, or preparing him for that blessing!

Be reminded then, my friends, of the early piety of Josiah, and of those two suggestions furnished by the first years of his life, viz:—First, That true piety is progressive, and secondly, that they who rightly use the knowledge they have, will be led, in the Providence of God, to higher, and yet higher, and more satisfying illumination still! "To him that hath shall be given, and he shall have abundance." That is, if he rightly use and improve that which he hath.

But we come now to notice concerning Josiah.

III. His conduct under the testimony of the discovered books of the Law.

It was not that of the antiquary who is chiefly concerned about the relics and memorials of the past. Such parties too frequently deal with the material rather than the spiritual, and in the case of a recovered manuscript of the book of God, they would be far more interested in the antiquity of the manuscript than impressed with the solemn import of its contents.

Neither was the conduct of Josiah, when he heard the denunciation of the book of God, that of *the critic*, who is ready to explain away the direct meaning of the writing rather than submit to humiliation and penitence under it. We have too many such in our own day. You need not be told, that critics abound now as well as antiquaries and so powerful is their critical acumen that they can weaken, for themselves, and for those who are willing to be misled by them, the force of the most direct and unequivocal language. Many thus neutralize the whole volume of revelation, while others, not quite so daring, are content to explain away such portions of the book of God as are unpalatable to themselves, or to the party to which they belong. **There** was, however, no such dishonesty with Josiah.

Neither did he attempt **to weaken the** force **of the** divine testimony by considering **it as** *inapplicable to the ideas of his age.* He did not think, **as so** many do, that himself, or his generation, had outgrown the legislation and authority of Heaven. He had among his contemporaries and subjects, many advocates of the more liberal order of things, **as** they supposed, many who could not see the propriety of the men of Israel binding themselves up to their own national peculiarities, and thus cutting themselves off from free and easy communication with surrounding nations. They considered such conduct as unworthy of a liberal age, and were prepared, accordingly to set Moses aside, that they might mingle upon more equal terms with the fashion of contemporaneous and more powerful states. Like too many of our own time, **they** preferred conformity **to the** fashions of the many in **error,** to sympathy with the few **in** fidelity to the truth. But Josiah was not of that number. He held himself ready to receive the word of **God** in all its integrity. He neither sought to evade it by criticisms, nor to neutralize it **by** referring it **to** a previous age. He was prepared attentively to hear, and honestly to interpret, the words **of** the most High. And what was the result **when** the book **was** read before him? **It was** penitence and fear **and** *earnest further inquiry*—a renewal **of** the covenant **with** Heaven, and **a** great national passover.

First, penitence and fear. His heart was made tender, and **he** humbled himself before God. Nay, he rent his clothes and wept before the most High. He saw that evil **was** determined against the sacred city, and the sacred people, because of contumacy and long continued disobedience. He knew well the state of the public mind, and he felt well assured that, though there were some faithful, and though many were content to conform externally to the true worship, yet the nation, as a whole, **was** idolatrous **at** heart. He saw perfectly well, that the **true** God was not really the God of Israel, and that **the** immoral fashions of the idolatrous nations had more charms for the people over whom he ruled, than the holy law of God. He could not but dread the consequences. He believed the denunciations of God, being fully assured of the power and faithfulness of Him whose denunciations they were. Heretofore he had been trying to rectify what was wrong, but now he saw the gathering cloud of judgment about to descend and overwhelm the chosen people. No wonder that he should weep, and rend his clothes. It was altogether in keeping with the sincerity and earnestness of the former part of his history.

But secondly,—He hastened to inquire of the Lord concerning this dread prospect. Not content with weeping, he must needs have directions or encouragement from God in the circumstances. Accordingly he sent some of his servants to Huldah, the prophetess. He could not enquire at the temple by Urim and Thummim for the house was out of repair, and the High Priests had been long unused to this part of their office. But he sent to one who was known and recognized in that day, as an exponent of the will of Heaven. Even as Hezekiah had sent in his perplexity to Isaiah, so Josiah sent to Huldah, and he received in anwer, from this prophetess, some personal acknowledgments and encouragements, together with the assurance that the dreaded judgments would certainly overtake the community. Accepting this assurance, as he must, Josiah did not lie down in indolence or despair, but set himself about confirming the few faithful, and also limiting or postponing the coming judgments, as far as might be, by a return to God. For

Thirdly, He renewed the covenant with God, which his people ought never to have broken or forsaken. He gathered together the elders of Judah and Jerusalem, laid before them the book that had alarmed himself, read to them the threatenings of the Holy, and engaged them anew in the covenant of the Most High. Then still acting under the testimony of the law,

Fourthly, He summoned his people to a national passover, and then he renewed on that occasion with all exactness, the order of the temple-worship, manifested princely munificence in the matter of sacrifices, set the musicians in their places, according to the commandment of David, and Asaph, and Heman, and re-established the songs as well as the sacrifice, in honour of the true God —the God of Israel. By this ordinance, he drew the people again under the wing of Omnipotence, revived the memory of their national history, and increased the power of piety in the land, and of this solemnity we find it said: "There was no passover **like to** that kept in Israel, from the days of Samuel the prophet, neither did all the kings of Israel keep such a passover as **Josiah** kept!" And such was **the** spirit of his administration during the years of his reign. The people, it is said, "departed not during all his days from following the Lord, the God of their fathers!"

Such was the effect of the words of God, honestly heard on the part of Josiah. **It** filled him with penitential sentiment, it prompted him **to** enquire of the Lord by an accredited prophetess, it prompted him further to renew the covenant which bound his nation to God, and it incited him **to** seek to draw his people under the wing of the Almighty by obedient **and** humble passover celebration!

Thus, I say, it was with Josiah; and thus it **was** in a long subsequent age, in the same city of Jerusalem, at the commencement of the Christian dispensation. The spirit being given at Pentecost, Peter preached, as you remember, to the assembled multitude and that with demonstration and with power. Like the recovered book of the law to the heart of Josiah, were the words of the Spirit-taught Apostle. In the light of these words sin and danger became apparent to thousands:—the awakened and enlightened ones were cut to the heart. They, in effort, rent their clothes, like Josiah, and wept before God. Then they applied to the accredited messengers of Heaven, demanding of the Apostles. "Men and brethren, what shall we do?" and the analogy advances. Instructed by the Apostles, (if they did not renew the covenant of Sinai) they gladly embraced the covenant of grace, ratified by the blood of Christ, and forthwith gave themselves **to a** life of passover celebration. They recognized the great truth, that Christ, the passover for humanity, had been sacrificed, **and** they brake bread in remembrance of the **fact, from house** to house, and ate their meat with gladness and singleness of heart.

Nor let it seem **a** peculiarity of Pentecostal days, that men were thus exercised in mind under the words of God. The same result is known **even up** to our own days, not indeed, in the case of the many, **who** hear the words with preoccupied or prejudiced hearts, **but ever** with some. Now one, and then another, **is** known to recognize the dangers of a sinful and God-forgetting state. They are smitten with sorrow in consequence—a **sorrow** deeper and more painful **than the** sorrows **of** the **world** ; and, if within reach of an accredited agent of **Heaven,** they inquire concerning **the** judgments **of** God, and whether there may not be a way of escape. **If** rightly instructed, they forthwith embrace the **covenant** of God's grace in Christ Jesus, and thenceforth rejoice to live under the overshadowing and permanent passover of New Testament times. There, they find shelter against merited and dreaded condemnation (there being **no** condemnation to them that are in Christ Jesus), and there they find consolation and hope that associate them with the divine and immortal! Be reminded of this fact, my friends, the *permanent elements of the Christian character* are those now before us, and exemplified in the history of Josiah, as well as **in** the converts at Pentecost, viz: *Penitence, prayerful inquiry,* and *supplication before God ; Faith in the covenant of grace,* **and** *Passover exercises !* Associated **as** we are with the sinful, and ourselves sinful, we cannot live in the light of God's law and God's throne without penitence! Exposed to dangers and dread liabilities, **we** cannot, when awake to our circumstances, live without prayer! Without merit, and without strength, we can find no resting place but in divine grace ! And when the divine provisions of that **grace** are once apprehended, we can have no greater privilege, no greater desire than to accept of and to enjoy these provisions! How gladly the heart recognizes the mighty and availing passover, provided of God! How perfect the security that passover affords! And how quickening and purifying the sentiments which it awakens! If Josiah's passover was distinguished, how much greater the distinction of the New Testament passover. That (the New Testament passover) spread through the ages, needs no repetition, accomplishes really what the Old Testament passover only did ceremonially, **fills the heart with peace and love, separates** those who keep it **from** evil, and binds up their energies for the heavenly pilgrimage! See that your life and experiences **are** passover life and passover experiences. Or more fully see that you walk *under the divine testimony*, like Josiah of old, in penitence, in tenderness of heart, in humility, in prayerful inquiry, **in** unquestioning faith, and in passover exercises and excellences! Or more briefly and more memorably, in *Penitence Prayer*, and *Passover Remembrances*. We come now to the notice concerning Josiah.

III. *His Premature death.*

This seems wonderful at first sight, **that one so devoted** and so useful should be so suddenly and so prematurely cut off! Yet it is explicable to a certain extent. We cannot of course understand all the reasons and influences that brought it about, but we can see enough to satisfy us in relation to its fitness.

See it first, in relation to his people, they were unworthy **of such** a king. They had not improved under his administration. Some few were like minded with himself, but the people, as **a** whole, were still idolaters. Many had conformed externally to the wishes and arrangements of the king, but they had not become thereby any better subjects of their true and heavenly king, the God of Israel, I mean. The readiness with which the nations returned to idolatrous ways under **the** successors of Josiah, and immediately after his death, shows clearly that his influence had only been superficial. The strong current of the national mind was still away from God. Josiah stemmed it for a time, but he could not really turn it, some surface waves seemed, under his influence to roll toward the Temple, but the depths of the national **heart underneath** had no such tendency. For twenty years Josiah laboured in the work of reformation, but he laboured with small result; and God, who had given him to the nation **in** kindness, saw meet, (after this lengthened and unsuccessful effort **to** bring His people back to Himself) saw meet, I say, to remove the devoted agent. In judgment he took him away (*i.e.*, so far as the nation was concerned) saying, in effect, by doing so "they are joined to their idols, let them alone!" And accordingly, once the faithful king was removed, matters went on in Judah and Jerusalem **as** the idolaters would have them, without further national check from God, the remonstrances of Jeremiah alone excepted. The result **was** that, **in** less than thirty years after, the sacred city was burnt, the temple was overthrown, and the infatuated inhabitants were weeping captives by the rivers of Babylon. All Judah and Jerusalem, it is said, mourned for Josiah, but their lamentations in relation to him were rather for a fallen king, than for an unsuccessful reformer! Had they mourned for their own want of improvement under his administration, things would have looked more hopeful. But **it was** not so. They were content to commit his remains to the tomb with some burning tears, and then to go on in their chosen way of self-pleasing and folly. They dreamt not that their stubbornness and perverseness had been the occasion of his removal, and if any one had assured them of the fact, it would not have altered their downward progress. They had taken their place definitively on the side of idolatry. The approaching judgment could not now be much longer arrested, and Josiah must **be** removed to make way for it. Had the **people as a whole** been willing to yield to holy influences, the life of the faithful king might have been prolonged, but since their preferences were wholly ungodly, even after all that Josiah had done, God saw meet to cut short the experiment, and to remove His servant from the thankless service! Pity for those who improve not the presence of the faithful servants of Heaven! God **is** constrained, after a time, to remove them, and their removal only opens the way for the coming retribution!

But *see* the premature death of Josiah, secondly in relation to himself. He was taken away from evil **to** come. Had his years been prolonged to the ordinary term of human life, he would have seen the ruthless legions of Nebuchadnezzar encamped before his capital; he would have heard the wild shouts of the enemy while the city was in flames, and seen the miseries of his people in the presence of sword and captivity. God saw meet to spare him the agony. As a mother, forseeing a storm, draws her little **one** under shelter before the storm falls, so the gracious **and** mighty one who watched over his servant Josiah, saw meet to deal with him. The manner of his death we shall notice immediately, but the fact of his death was to him a blessing in disguise. He was removed from a position of honour and usefulness indeed, but that position was irritating and disappointing in no small degree, and he **was** taken away from it to a more congenial association, where irritation and disappointment are forever unknown. For a premature death, in the case **of** the ungodly, there is no compensation, but for a premature death in the case of the godly, there is ample compensation in Heaven. Better live in harmony and gladness before the throne **on** high, then contend unsuccessfully with the disloyal and disobedient upon a throne on earth!

Thirdly—God's faithfulness too was made good by this premature death of Josiah. "Behold (said God) by Huldah, the prophetess (when consulted by Josiah,) I will gather thee to thy fathers, and thou shalt be gathered to thy grave in peace, neither shall thine eyes see all the evil that I will bring upon this place, and upon the inhabitants of the same." God had not forgotten his promise; **and**, when the proper moment arrived, Josiah was caught away from the confusion and **annoyance of an** unprofitable contest. His death might **seem to** his contemporaries fortuitous, **or mistimed,** but there was neither chance nor **mistake** about it. The eye that takes in all conditions **and all** circumstances decided **the** eventful moment, and **brought** about the combination **that** secured **it.** The actors each and all acted on their own responsibility, and according to their own views, but God determined the result, and made good His assurance to His servant by doing **so**!

You see **then, that** this death, apparently premature, was really significant **and** seasonable; **it** was a judicial punishment to **an** indocile **and** disobedient people! It **was** kindness to **a** faithful servant! And **it** made good a **divine** announcement, indicating the **care** and watchfulness of the Supreme **over his** faithful and humble worshippers!

And **now a word** about the manner of his death. It **reminds us** somewhat of the death of Abraham Lincoln; **he met it where** he ought not to have been. He ought **not to have** mingled himself up with the contest between Egypt and the Medes and Babylonians. The king of Egypt himself dissuaded **him** from meddling in the matter; **and,** as king of the sacred people, he ought **to have** held himself aloof from **the** quarrels of the rulers of those **idolatrous** nations. We grieve that the amiable president just mentioned, should have met his death in a theatre, and in like manner **we** grieve that the devoted Josiah should **have** met his death on the battle field, and **in** the quarrel of **the ambitious** and tyrannical. The fact reminds us of another deplored death in circumstances not very dissimilar from those of Josiah. I refer to Zwingle, the great Swiss **reformer.** He, too, fell in battle, where he ought **not to have been,** but he mistook the path of duty—not in a spirit **of** disobedience, but amid the confusion **of** clashing elements. He mingled up his faith and career as a preacher with worldly politics, (he could scarcely avoid doing so) and his heavenly Father overruled his very mistake for unmoving him from the confusion and misrule of the times. So Josiah mistook, and so he found his death by his mistake; **and so** God overruled his mistake for the accomplishment of his own gracious purposes concerning him. God was not taken by surprise in the affair. The combination of circumstances was indeed from Him, and Josiah disappeared from the stage of human history just at the right time, though not in a way honourable to his own wisdom. There might be reasons for his course which we do not see, but still we think it was clearly a mistake in him to join any of the contending parties, and further, it was eminently unwise in him to join battle with the party opposed, without waiting for the support of the party joined.

What then is the lesson which we may learn from the early removal of this devoted servant of Heaven? Just this, that the faithful may fearlessly commit their way to God—assured that he will not overlook or forget them—assured further, that their times are in His hands—and that His purposes of love concerning them shall not be disappointed. Let them, like Josiah, be earnest in the service of God, and earnest in the support of His cause in human society. And let them avoid the error of Josiah, viz: that of mingling themselves up in the contests of the ambitious, the corrupt, or the selfish. Let them remember whose they are, and whom alone they ought to serve; and fearlessly commit their fortunes to the wisdom and watchful love of their Heavenly Father. His purpose shall stand and He will do all His pleasure. Though His people mistake in judgment, while faithful in heart, He will overrule their very mistakes to the accomplishment of His own purposes concerning them. *Better that they should* **not** *mistake;* but where views are confused, and when uncongenial elements are mixed up together, mistakes cannot always be avoided. Nor need this discourage the conscientious, for their Heavenly Friend is able to check, to overrule, or to unravel, what may seem only inextricable or irremediable in their eyes. *Only let them abound in penitence and prayer, and in passover remembrances, and all shall yet be well!* Only let them walk in the divine Redeemer, whose death constitutes the great passover for humanity, and *no fatal* evil shall touch them! They may die unexpectedly in early youth **or in early** manhood, but their death will prove a blessing to **themselves** at any rate. They may leave their circle **in sorrow** and darkness, but they themselves shall find only **sweeter** and higher illumination and joy! Their death **may** even be in judgment to others, who **have** failed to **improve** their life and example, but it will **be a** relief and **a** reward to themselves! Their removal may seem mysterious **to survivors, as** Josiah's was, but they themselves **will have no** difficulty concerning it **as** they emerge from **the dark** rapids of death into the light and stable beauties **of** a **holier world**!

O, **for** grace to follow the example **of** Josiah! O for enlightenment to embrace and abide in the New Testament passover all the days of **our** lives! And O for faith to sing with the rejoicing apostle. "**I am** persuaded that nothing shall be able to separate me from the love of God, which **is** in Christ Jesus **our** Lord! Not faithless contemporaries—not untoward combinations, **nor** mistaken decision on our part, nor even early and apparently premature death! Happy, happy they who have such **a** conviction, and who, in the strength of it can add :—

> Goodness and mercy all my life,
>   Shall surely follow me,
> And in God's house for evermore,
>   My dwelling place shall be.

Let every one look to himself in this matter! **Let** each ask himself, is it thus with **me**?

QUESTIONS ON JOSIAH.

What was remarkable in the youthful son of Amon?
  His early and decided piety. Every thing in the courts of his father was favourable to a contrary result, yet he gave himself heart and soul to the ways of wisdom.

Who may we suppose to have been instrumental in giving this bias to his character?

We hope and fancy it might be his grandfather Manasseh, but cannot tell.

How old was he **when** first known as an earnest inquirer after God?

About sixteen.

Did he rest with inquiries?

No, when twenty he became an open and decided reformer—breaking and destroying all the symbols of idolatry.

Did he content himself with breaking down the idol altars?

No, at twenty six he began to repair the temple of God.

What happened in the course of these repairs?

The workmen found a copy of the writings of Moses.

What was the effect of the reading of these writings on **the** mind **of** Josiah?

A deep conviction of **the** danger of his nation **in** consequence of the prevalent idolatry.

What two important truths does the history of Josiah thus far illustrate?

1st. The progressive character **of true** and sincere piety. He was first an inquirer, then **a** reformer destroying the altars of idolatry—then a repairer of the temple, and an obedient servant of divine ordinances.

2nd. His story illustrates the further facilities for good that will be found to lie in the way of the truthful while living up to the light; we refer to his obtaining possession of the writings of Moses while repairing the temple.

Is there any encouragement for inquirers of our own day in this?

Certainly. They have but to press on so far as they know the right, and they will find guidance and direction by the finger-post of revelation or by means of unseen ministrations when their way becomes dark or uncertain.

Did Josiah regard the recovered writings of Moses as an antiquarian or as **a** critic?

O, **no!** He had them read before him as an inquirer—ready to bow to the authority of the God of Israel.

How did he feel as the sacred writings were being read?

Deeply penitent and alarmed.

Did he make any inquiry at the living and recognized servants of Heaven concerning the dark prospect before his kingdom?

Yes, he sent to the prophetess Huldah, who gave him appropriate encouragement and assurance.

What **his** next step?

He convened the elders of Judah and Jerusalem—laid before them the book that had alarmed him—read to them the threatenings **of** the Holy—and engaged them anew in the covenant of the Most High.

Did this content him?

No, he summoned the people to a national passover, desiring thus to draw the people again under the wing of Omnipotence.

Was there anything analogous to this at the commencement of the Christian dispensation?

Yes, many were aroused to address themselves to the **Apostle** of the Lord, crying "men and brethren what shall we do?" And three thousand **of** these awakened ones, when instructed by the Apostle, accepted of the new covenant of God, and gave themselves to a life of pass**over** celebration.

Were such things peculiar to the apostolic age?

Not at all. They occur frequently though less obtrusively in **our own** day. Now **one,** and **then** another is awakened **by the** words **of** God **to** the dangers of a sinful and God-forgetting state, and is led **to embrace** the divine covenant, and to live under the overshadowing and permanent **passover of the New** Testament times.

What by **the** way **are the** permanent elements of the **devout** character **as** illustrated in Josiah **as** well **as in the** Pentecostal covenant?

Penitence, prayer, and **passover** exercises.

What should be **our** desire **in the** light of this conduct of Josiah and **the** Pentecostal covenant?

That we may be enabled to receive the Word of God as they received it, and to follow **it** out to covenant and passover experience as they followed it out.

Was this noble prince, Josiah, a long liver?

No, as he was early called to reign, **so** he was early relieved of the cares of Government.

How are we to regard his premature death in relation to his people?

As a sign of God's displeasure **at** them. They had not improved the blessing of his pious example and influ**ence,** and God saw meet to withdraw the blessing.

And how are we to regard his early death in relation to himself?

As a paternal kindness. **He was** taken **away** from evil to come.

Was there any divine promise fulfilled by his early death?
: Yes. God had promised by Huldah that his eyes should not see the evil that was about to fall on his idolatrous capital and kingdom.

But what about the manner of his death?
: Why, he met it where he ought not to have been. He should not have interfered in the quarrels of the ungodly and the tyrannical. This as we think was his mistake, but God overruled his mistake for bringing about His own purposes.

What are we to be reminded of by this early removal of Josiah?
: The perfection of God's promises, and the unfailing love that encompasses the faithful in life and in death.

What should be the grand solicitude of the believing amid the dangers and fluctuations of life as suggested by the story of Josiah?
: To be found in the way of penitence, prayer, and passover remembrances.

XVIII. ZEDEKIAH.

Zedekiah was one and twenty years old **when** he began to reign, and reigned eleven years in Jerusalem. And he did that which was evil in the sight of the Lord his God, and humbled not himself before Jeremiah the prophet, speaking from the mouth of the Lord. And he also rebelled against Nebuchadnezzar, who had made him swear by God; but he stiffened his neck and hardened his heart from turning unto the Lord God of Israel. Moreover all the chiefs of the priests, and the people transgressed very much after all the abominations of the heathen; and polluted the house of the Lord which he had hallowed in Jerusalem. And the Lord God of their fathers sent to them by his messengers, rising up betimes and sending; because he had compassion on his people, and on his dwelling place: But they mocked the messengers of God, and despised his words, and misused his prophets, until the wrath of the Lord arose against his people, till there was no remedy. —II. Chron. xxxvi. 11, **16.**

WE have **now** turned your attention to all the kings **of the** line of David up to Josiah, there remain yet the four successors of Josiah: **three of** them the sons, and one the grandson of that prince. It shall not be necessary to rest on these four individually. There is no striking **or** noticeable dissimilarity among them. They are **all** only too much alike. They all did evil in the sight of the Lord and in similar circumstances, and with similar privileges. Then, two of these occupied the throne **only** three months each, while the remaining two reigned **each** about eleven years. We may therefore, without detriment pass over the reign of Jehoahaz, the first of the four, and Jehoiachin, the third **of** the four, because of the brevity of their rule, to say nothing of their wickedness, and we may also leave out Jehoiakim, **as** being so similar in character to his brother Zedekiah, that they scarcely admit of separate remark. They differed only in **two** particulars—First,

Jehoiakim was made king by the sovereign of Egypt, while Zedekiah was the creature of Nebuchadnezzar; and secondly, Jehoiakim **cut** with a penknife, and burnt in **the fire,** the roll of Jeremiah's denunciations, while Zedekiah only refused to listen to the Heaven-sent prophet. Jehoiakim was thus even **more** daringly impious than Zedekiah himself. We shall pass therefore from Josiah to Zedekiah, and notice concerning this prince his unimproved privileges, his undesirable distinction, his unhappy fate.

I. The unimproved privilege.

He was contemporary with a distinguished and inspired servant of Heaven. Jeremiah was a prophet of established reputation when Zedekiah ascended the throne. It **was** not as if there had been dubiety as to the inspiration **or** authority of the prophet; then Zedekiah might have **had** excuse for disregarding him—but there was none such. Before Zedekiah was born, Jeremiah had opened his commission, and been recognized by Josiah! Nay, before Zedekiah was born, Jeremiah had caused the striking remonstrance of the God of Israel to sound through Jerusalem: "Be astonished, O ye heavens **at** this, and be horribly afraid. Be ye very desolate, saith the Lord: For my people have committed two evils, they have **forsaken** me—the fountain of living waters, and hewed them out cisterns,—broken cisterns, that can hold no water." About the time of the accession of Zedekiah to the throne, again Jeremiah uttered forth his soul thus:—O that I had in the wilderness a lodging place of wayfaring men, that I might leave my people and go from them; for they are all adulterers, an assembly of treacherous men!"
* * * "Why have they provoked me to anger with their graven images, and with strange vanities? The harvest is past, the summer is ended, and we are not saved. For the hurt of the daughter of my people am I hurt. I am black: Astonishment hath taken hold on me. Is there no balm in Gilead? Is there no physician there? * * * * Oh that my head

were waters, and mine eyes a fountain of tears, that I might weep day and night for the slain of the daughter of my people." Thus at the accession of Zedekiah—and then, during all the years of Zedekiah's reign, Jeremiah put forth his plaints, and remonstrances, and denunciations and warnings. Not content with words merely, he employed impressive types and representations, to show the difference between the good and the bad, and to indicate the coming captivity of idolatrous Judah. So persistent and so fully felt were his ministrations and rebukes, that he incurred the enmity and persecution of the influential and the powerful, both at Anathoth and Jerusalem. But this mattered not to Jeremiah. His zeal was not abated, nor was his voice hushed. He still sought to keep alive the public conscience, and to awaken the slumbering and misguided inhabitants of Jerusalem. He even approached Zedekiah himself personally—assuring him from God, that the city would be given into the hands of the king of Babylon—that it would be burnt with fire—and that he, the king himself, would certainly be taken by the mighty invader. He denounced the princes also, under whose influence the king usually acted, for their cruelties to the defenceless, as well as for their unfaithfulness to God—assuring them that they should all be given into the hand of their enemies, and that their dead bodies should be meat to the fowls of heaven, and to the beasts of the earth. Zedekiah was not left to grope his way in the dark you perceive. He had a ready monitor ever at hand.

Here then was a privilege and an opportunity for Zedekiah. He had near him one who could inform him of the wishes and purposes of the most High. True, he had around him prophets and princes of a different stamp, but he might have known the true from the counterfeit, and he ought to easily have known the true from the counterfeit, if only he had been honestly desirous of walking in the right way. He ought to have attached himself to Jeremiah. O, he ought to have felicitated himself on the presence of such a man, a man whom he knew to be the agent of the Holy and the All-knowing. He needed not to send expensive embassies to distant and doubtful oracles, as heathen kings were wont to do, he had but to listen to the unambiguous teachings of the prophet of Heaven, and his way would have been made clear before him. If Urim and Thummim was now unusual as a means of ascertaining the divine mind, Zedekiah might well rejoice to have so easy and sufficient a substitute in the ready responses of the prophet. With such a privilege, he had no excuse for misjudgment or mistaken action. How happy a traveller is when uncertain of his way, he finds an adequate and trust-worthy guide! Not so Zedekiah. It was to no purpose that God had granted him such a privilege: for "neither he, nor his servants, nor the people of the land, did hearken unto the words of the Lord, which he spake by the prophet Jeremiah."

Zedekiah, however, was not wholly without some leanings toward the prophet. He even consulted him in private at the crisis of his fate—as to whether he should submit to the Chaldeans, or maintain the contest to the last? Jeremiah gave him a clear answer, and unmistakable advice; but he could not bring his mind to act upon it. He wished the safety of the city, and he wished the safety of his own person, but he could not submit to the conditions. He could not and would not lay down his arms to the Chaldeans, while God would not grant him deliverance on any other terms. He wished a deliverance like that enjoyed by Hezekiah, when the hosts of Sennacherib were smitten before Jerusalem, but God would not vouchsafe such a deliverance to an idolatrous prince. Had he been of like character with Hezekiah, his experience and mercies might have been similar to those of that prince; but his heart was not with God. He would willingly have had the miraculous deliverance of a true son of David, but he wished it in connection with the liberty and license of a lover of idols; and this, God would not grant. Still, because he was a son of David, God would secure his life and his metropolis if he would submit himself and follow the divine directions. But he would not. He persisted in the way of evil and disobedience, and "humbled not himself before Jeremiah, speaking from the mouth of the Lord." Here is an account of his last interview with the prophet.—Jeremiah, xxviii, 14–24.

See the folly of Zedekiah :—He was ashamed even to have consulted Jeremiah. And he would not be guided by Jeremiah, that is to say, he would not be guided by God, speaking by Jeremiah. His princes held one style of language, and God, by Jeremiah, held another. Zedekiah must attach himself to the one side or to the other. That of the princes was more in harmony with his own heart, and it prevailed accordingly. He would not humble himself either to God or to Nebuchadnezzar, but resisted to the last, and thus brought about the mournful catastrophe which Jeremiah was so anxious to avert.

This catastrophe, as it affected both Jerusalem and himself, we shall notice immediately. In the meantime, let us notice the lesson which his conduct teaches to us. And what is that lesson ? It is, the folly of turning from a divine messenger, and rejecting divinely-fixed conditions of safety. Stated in words, you admit this at once, and as seen in the conduct of Zedekiah, it is irresistibly evident. Had he but listened to Jeremiah, and followed Jeremiah's directions his life and capital would have been preserved, but he preferred the counsel of those who hated Jeremiah (for this counsel was in harmony with his own blind pride) he preferred I say, the counsel of those who hated the prophet, and he lost all in consequence. You see *his* error. Then, mark, it is for us to be warned of a like error.

We too are in danger. If not besieged in a material fortress by human and ruthless soldiery, if not liable to the vengeance of a fierce and powerful tyrant at the head of a resistless army—we are still in danger—and the danger is more serious and more awful than any merely earthly exposure can be. The powers of darkness are around us—the snares of evil are spread thick in our path, besides the officers of a righteous and all powerful government have, if I may speak so, a warrant against us. We may, if still unforgiven, be caught and cast into prison at any moment, and if once there, execution and eternal disgrace will surely follow. The rebellion of Zedekiah against Babylon, brought the hosts of Nebuchadnezzar around Jerusalem; so, our rebellion against Heaven hath laid us open to the judgments of the Holy. Besides, by **our** rebellion and estrangement from Heaven, we have associated ourselves with, and are greatly in the power of, the god of darkness of this world, who seeks more and more to blind our minds, and to confirm us in our rebellion. We are really in an evil case by nature although very many of **us** are little aware of this danger. Events press upon **us,** even as the Chaldeans pressed Zedekiah. The days fly; **the** catastrophe may be near. Death may overtake us at **any** moment, and we may then, and thenceforth **be** overwhelmed with righteous indignation on the part **of** Heaven, **or with** unrelieved remorse by the testimony and terrors of **our** own conscience.

In these circumstances it **is** important to know that there is a great Prophet near, greater by far than Jeremiah. This great prophet **is** prepared to counsel us in our pressing exigence: nay, **He** is prepared to shelter us from the consequences of **our** own rebellion; He is able to deliver us from our dark spiritual adversaries,—to secure our acceptance **at** the court of Heaven—and to compass us about with songs of deliverance, you know **to** whom I refer—Jesus, the prophet like unto Moses, and like also unto Jeremiah in some respects, and the Saviour of sinners. Far beyond Jeremiah in qualifications and competency. He is the prophet **of** the ages. He is the same yesterday, to-day, and forever: He is able to save to the uttermost **all** them that come unto God by Him. We have but to seek to Him, obeying Him and confiding in Him—and all shall be well. Himself hath made reparation to Heaven on our behalf: "He is the propitiation for the sins of the world," and He is at once the Wonderful Counsellor and the Prince of Peace. And His directions to those who seek His guidance, and are willing to trust in Him are similar to those of Jeremiah to Zedekiah. We must go forth to Him against whom we have rebelled. We must cease resistance to the government we have defied, dishonoured and overlooked. We must acknowledge the claims of our divine king, and that king will forthwith forgive all. The great Prophet assures us of it and pledges Himself that it shall be so. There may be those around us, (as in the case of Zedekiah,) who would discredit the teaching of the great Prophet, and who would have us continue in our rebellion and self-will, but we will only hasten and render inevitable the catastrophe by listening to them. It is submission or ruin with us (just as it was in the case of Zedekiah) submission under the directions and mediation of the great New Testament Prophet—or ruin in connection with those who counsel a contrary course!

The choice then, before each of you is, the righteous Mediator, or the rebellious and ungodly world—submission to God under the Saviour Prophet, or everlasting ruin in connection with Satan and his followers! And will any of you repeat the folly of Zedekiah? Will you disclaim the Redeemer, and abide in your rebellion? Will you really be so foolish? You cannot approve of Zedekiah's course in the crisis of his fate, and will you, in effect, repeat it in a crisis of far more tremendous significance in your own? Many, it is true, do so, and they will have long repentence for their choice; but you cannot surely decide so. O see that you disregard the dictates of pride, and the counsels of the hardened, and the apparent advantages of a course of self-pleasing, and listen to the great New Testament Prophet, and go forth in penitance, and under His guidance, to the righteous and merciful throne which you have dishonoured by sin, and accept (before the thunderbolt descends) of the grace and forgiveness that God is ready to extend to you in Him. This, then, is the lesson we ought to learn from the story of Zedekiah,—we must neither overlook nor disregard the advice of the great Saviour Prophet! We must listen to, and obey Jesus, if we would not perish!

Remembering this lesson, viz., **that Jesus** is to us what Jeremiah was to Zedekiah (and far **more**), and that **our** eternal safety requires us to abide by the instruction **of** Jesus, while at the same time we trust in His merits and good offices, let us attend now, concerning this **unworthy** Zedekiah, to.

II. His undesirable distinction.

And that is—that his name is forever **associated** with the overthrow of the city and temple **of God**, and that the typical throne of the dynasty of David disappeared from among men with him. It **was the** honour of David to found that throne. **It was the** dishonour of Zedekiah to make **an end of it— so far, at least, as it was preparatory and typical.** David loved the Lord, and the Lord made a covenant of loyalty with him **and his house**; Zedekiah turned from the Lord, **and** his royal honours, **and** the royal honours of his house, were abrogated and put aside, so far as natural descent was concerned. The throne which descended **to him** from a long line of kings, fell with **him and** was not again restored. His descendants henceforth mingled with the mass of the people, and were undistinguished **and** unhonoured. True, the symbols of **government were** still preserved in Judah **for** hundreds **of years after the** captivity, but in very inferior guise, **and only by** High Priests or patriotic warriors, **or subordinate governors.** The throne of David in its independence **and earthly** glory became permanently obscured; and **Zedekiah was** the last **of** the kings. He received **a throne from his** ancestors, **but** failed **to** transmit the same to successors!

Inferior calamities had fallen **out in** the reigns of other kings Judah, but this crowning calamity fell out in the days of Zedekiah. Rehoboam saw five-sixths of his subjects turn away from him, but his **capital and his** throne remained **to** him still; Zedekiah lost capital, **and** throne, and liberty, all at once. Asa saw his kingdom invaded by "Zerah, the Ethiopian, with an host of a thousand thousands and three hundred chariots," but "the Lord **smote** the Ethiopians before **Asa,** and Judah," and Asa's reign was not seriously interrupted; Zedekiah had no such deliverance from the hosts of Nebuchadnezzar, nor did his throne **survive** the invasion of that monarch. Amaziah **saw** the conquering hosts of **Joash** of Samaria enter Jerusalem and break down the wall **of** his capital, but Judah retired **and** left him though humbled and dispirited, **still in** possession **of** his royalty. Not so with Zedekiah. **His** conquerer having destroyed his capital, carried him, **or sent** him, into **an** unreturning captivity. Hezekiah too saw his capital surrounded by the armies of the proud Sennacherib, **and** had no power in himself to resist, but God laid low **the** invaders and Hezekiah **and** Jerusalem **were** safe! Zedekiah had no such relief; the storm burst over him, **and over** his capital, without restraint, and with overwhelming **effect.** Even Manasseh dethroned and carried into **captivity for** his wickedness, was in the wonderful **providence and** grace of God liberated and restored to **his** government, but no such liberation **or** restoration occurred in the fortunes of Zedekiah. In one word, other kings of the **sacred** line had met with calamities and disasters, but these were checked, or limited, or put aside, while Zedekiah fell from his throne without help, and without recovery! In the history of his **ancestors,** the succession, though interrupted **or** darkened for **a** time, had still been maintained, but **with** Zedekiah, the *royal* succession ceased and the *earthly* ***throne*** of David **was** permanently shrouded and overborn! **Besides** sufferings great and unspeakable accompanied this overthrow. You may well believe that a city besieged for nearly **two** years, and taken by storm at last and burnt by **its** conquerors, as to its leading and public buildings—you may well believe, I say, that this city **was** a scene of much suffering. To say nothing of the personal experiences of Zedekiah in the meantime, you can imagine, though but feebly, what the people endured from famine, **from** violence, and from cruelty.

The cruelties suffered by the inhabitants, (it hath been said,) especially during this last siege, were frightful.

The Lamentations of Jeremiah present us with vivid pictures of these. Enraged by their rebellion and vigourous opposition, Nebuchadnezzar, when he took the city, "had no compassion on young man or maiden, old man or him that stooped for age." Famine had done its work before the conqueror entered ; and children swooning in the streets from hunger, princes raking dunghills for a morsel, and other hideous and affecting sights, showed the extremities to which the people were driven. When the Chaldeans rushed through the breach, the usual brutalities were perpetrated by the licentious soldiery. The famished fugitives were pursued with relentless fury. The Chaldeans were hounded on by the Edomites and other neigheours of the Jews, who knew the country well, and, like blood hounds, tracked to the holes and caves such as had escaped from the city. Dead bodies lay piled in heaps upon the streets. Multitudes of these were mere boys and girls. Princes were hanged by their hand—enduring the slow horrors of crucifixion. Some seem to have been consigned to subterraneous dungeons —perhaps on the shores of the dead sea where " water flowed over their heads."

Never had so terrible a proof been given of Gods hatred of sin. "For the sins of her prophets, and for the iniquities of her priests, that shed the blood of the just in the midst of her," the daughter of Zion lay covered in a very cloud of wrath !"

And all this for the pride and self-will of Zedekiah, as the immediate and proximate cause. Had he listened to God by Jeremiah, the evil would have been postponed, if not turned aside. How painful the position for him ! To have completed the rebellion of many generations—to have finished the last and crowning reason for such an overthrow and to have been the immediate occasion of so much misery to his people ! And how undesirable the distinction, which links his character and his name with the heaviest disaster that had then fallen on the house of his father, or on the subjects of his kingdom !

And the world had reason to mourn the disaster, (if

had been enlightened enough,) **as** well as the people of Israel. Remember the overthrown temple was the only temple of the **true** God on earth, **and** the city of Jerusalem was the only centre of **peace** and hope for mankind in all the world. The **light of** truth, and coming good, had been kindled, by a gracious God, on the heights of Mariah and Zion. All the nations besides **were** in darkness. To extinguish the one light was **to** injure the whole of mankind. Evil became thus more oppressive and more irresistible, while the means of good became less influential for the recovery, or the help of the bewildered and the wandering sons of men. True, the embers of the Zion fire of purity and enlightenment were scattered **in** the region of the captivity, and were not unuseful in preparing the world for brighter and better days, but the central fire and beacon blaze were extinguished. It was as when a party of travellers are treading their way through an intricate country amid the darkness of night, and their one single light is extinguished. The condition of such is pitiable, as you may well conceive. They must then grope their way amid unknown dangers, and they can find only disaster at last if no help or guidance be furnished to the**m**. How grieved the party would be at the individual who had extinguished their one light, or who was the immediate occasion of its extinction! And thus it was with Zedekiah and humanity. He by his obstinacy and pride, caused the overthrow of the only light-house of mankind. For seventy following years the darkness **was** complete. At the end of that period, the liberated captives from Babylon endeavoured to rekindle the light on Mount Zion; but they succeeded only very partially, and for nearly six hundred years from the time of Zedekiah, the power of truth was all but unknown among men, while the demons of darkness and defilement revelled in every region and hurried generation after generation to the shades of hopeless woe. O, if the world had but seen the matter in the true light, how they would have denounced the folly of Zedekiah, and mourned his wicked obstinacy! But for the **grace** of God, (who kindled again, in a subsequent age, and on the same Mount Zion the fire of truth and righteousness, and that on a far grander scale than before) but for the grace of God, I say, this world could never have recovered the overthrow of Jerusalem and the burning of the one true temple. It must have yielded itself wholly and hopelessly to the tyranny and to the cruelty of Satan. Every succeeding generation must have seen the degradation of mankind increased, and the possibility of recovery made more and more hopeless. O, but Zedekiah thought not how much depended on his decision when called on by Jeremiah to submit to the conqueror! Had he guessed the thousandth part of the evil he was about to bring upon mankind by his refusal to submit, he would certainly have been appalled. True, he had not himself alone brought matters to such a crisis with Jerusalem and the temple, but he held the balance at the moment of fate, as it were. He might, by a different decision, have saved the sacred city, and the sacred temple for the time being, at least. He might have broken the fierce determination of the conqueror, and secured the power of Omnipotence for the preservation of his capital and its temple, *but he would not.* He preferred to disobey God, and to defy and enfuriate the earthly power which he could not resist, and which only wanted his vain and foolish resistance to wreck itself on the sacred city and temple with which his royalty was associated. Sad and undesirable distinction!—to furnish occasion, and that by unexcusable obstinacy, for an incalculable evil to all the nations of the earth. Sampson destroyed the idol temple of the Philistines, to the injury of some thousands of that people, but Zedekiah, in effect, destroyed the temple of the true God, to the injury of millions of mankind! Sampson's name must have been held as execrable among the people he so deeply injured, and so Zedekiah's name (if the world were enlightened enough) would certainly be held in perpetual disesteem by all the populations of subsequent times! And no thanks to him, that Heaven hath rekindled the light of truth on Mount Zion, his conduct did nothing to bring that blessing about. On **the** contrary, he did all he could to prevent it. In fine, Zedekiah plunged the world in darkness, and for anything he could do, **or** desire to do, it would have been in darkness even to the present hour! I should fancy that such distinction is any thing but desirable!

But notice concerning this Prince:—

III. His unhappy fate.

That was remarkable and mournful, and as announced beforehand by the prophets, apparently contradictory. That apparent contradiction was, that he was to be taken to Babylon, and yet, that he was not to see Babylon, Jeremiah said the one and Ezekiel the other. It is explained, as you well know, or will perceive, by the fact of his blindness—by the **fact** that Nebuchadnezzar, who took or sent him to Babylon, deprived him beforehand of the power of seeing Babylon. His sufferings were both great and manifold. He suffered **as** a king; he suffered as a father; and suffered as a man.

1st. *He suffered as a king.* He was constrained to leave **his** throne and his capital, **and** to seek safety in flight; and his flight was both hopeless and useless. He could not possibly escape the agents of Nebuchadnezzar, aided by the vigilance and enmity of the surrounding people; whither could he flee? His enemies were everywhere, and his friends, if he had any, powerless. There was no neighbouring people able to protect him even if they had been **so** disposed; **and** he had no means of supplying his necessities if he had betaken himself to some hidden and unknown cavern. He was taken in the plain of Jericho, and if he had not been taken then, he must have **been** taken soon in spite **of** all disguises, and in spite **of all** expedition. The truth is, *there was* **no** *escape for him.* The very royalty which he had abused and lost necessitated his capture. Nebuchadnezzar was not the man to allow him either time or advantage. And this of itself was grievous even though there had been nothing to distress him. He was dethroned and captured, and carried into the presence of his incensed conqueror. O, but this was bitterness to the proud and rebellious Zedekiah, who would gladly have escaped an interview with Nebuchadnezzar. But no, he must meet the stern and haughty monarch, and bear as best he might, the scorn, the reproaches, and the bitter taunts which that monarch was prepared to heap upon him. Already wounded by the burning of his palace, and the loss of all his royal accommodations, and also disappointed and grieved by the loss of his liberty, he must have felt the wrath of the king most keenly. Nothing more was needed, one would think, to make him wretched and miserable in the highest degree. His crown trampled in the dust—his capital overthrown—and himself a helpless captive, and that in the presence of one who knew nought, either of pity or of moderation, he may well excite our compassion as we think of him standing before his conqueror at Riblah. But other, and even deeper griefs, awaited him, for

2nd. *He suffered as a father.* His sons were slain by command of Nebuchadnezzar, and that before his eyes. An ordinary conqueror, if he wished to execute his vengeance on the children of a rebellious vassal, would have spared the agonized parent the sight of sufferings which he could do nothing to relieve. He would think it punishment enough for the parent to know that his children had been slain, without adding to the distress the sight of the execution. Not so with Nebuchadnezzar! His vengeance and displeasure could not be satisfied with half measures. His rebellious vassal must be wounded in his paternal feelings by the death of his children, and the wound must be intensified by the execution taking place in his own presence. Unworthy as Zedekiah was in relation to God, you cannot conceive him indifferent to the safety or to the sufferings of his children. What then must his feelings have been when he saw these butchered in their bloom, and laid lifeless and mangled at his feet! And they born to rule too, and brought up in elegance and in ease! Any father would have wept at such a sight, but especially a royal father! Zedekiah had been wont to see his children treated with honour; but now he must look upon them in the hands of the ruthless, and see them treated **with** indignity, with revolting cruelty, and with **unusual** barbarity. Pity for Zedekiah. Had his **sons died as** heroes, and been buried with honour, **he would** have grieved for their fate; but to see them slain in cold blood, and treated as dogs; O, this was terrible for a father's heart! No doubt he thought of their tender and happy infancy, and bitterly reproached himself for their unhappy fate, while **he** internally wept because of it! This then, might have sufficed surely—himself dethroned, and captive, **and** his children slain **before** his eyes—but no; his conqueror must have further vengeance still.

3rd. *He suffered* **as a** *man and in his own person.* **The** eyes, which had gazed upon the execution and sufferings of his children, were forcibly put out. He was subjected to pain of the most excruciating kind, and deprived at the same time of the precious capability of vision. Already driven from his home and deprived of his children, he must now **be** shut out from the visible and beautiful world. Long accustomed to royal gardens and exquisite sights, he must now look **on** loveliness no more. He is thrust into darkness, and rendered incapable **of** ever again revisiting or enjoying **the** day. It had been humiliation enough to his proud spirit simply **to** have been led captive in the train of the conqueror; but O, to be so led, childless, sightless, and hopeless, who may imagine the grief? Or who may imagine the gloom and the misery of his thoughts and memories, while his busy brain, driven in upon itself, reviewed or ruminated upon the past. Jeremiah, we may well believe, occupied **no** small space in the dark chamber of his remembrances. He thought, no doubt of the treatment which the prophet had received under his government; of the advice and assurances which the prophet had given, and of the terrific consequences of disregarding that advice and these assurances, and his remorse was keen and bitter beyond description. His heart was a scene of disorder and tumult. As he awoke every day to a dark world, he would grope in vain for anything fair or pleasing to rest upon: but nothing of such could he find. His idols could not help him, and his flatterers were far away from him! A good man can find comfort even in captivity, aye, even in blindness; but an ungodly man, when reverse hath overtaken him, can find nothing comforting or satisfactory to rest upon. His heart is like the troubled sea; it cannot rest. How long Zedekiah lived in blindness and captivity, we cannot tell; he is left by the historian in the obscurity to which his folly reduced him. He would not listen to God by Jeremiah, and he is cast away, as it were, into the wilderness or into the lumber-room, to be forgotten, uncared for and unsung. When a worthless rag is put aside, no one inquires further about it; and such, at best, is the fate of Zedekiah! Pity, O pity for Zedekiah! He shall never return to Jerusalem! He shall see the sacred land no more.

We have already reminded you of the analogy between our circumstances and those of Zedekiah. We have a prophet-teacher as well as he; and our Prophet-Teacher is far more exalted than his. See then in his fate the prospect of those who disregard the divine and Prophet Guide of these New Testament times! Zedekiah, because he would not listen to God by Jeremiah, was driven from his capital—driven in effect from his domestic comforts and family endearments (by the destruction of his sons)—driven again, in effect out of the illuminated world (by the loss of his eyes), and finally cast into darkness and forgetfulness. And it shall be so, in like manner, with the ungodly and unforgiven who refuse the instruction of Jesus, and in a yet higher and more awful sense. They shall be driven away in their unbelief; driven away from their possessions, driven from their family display and family plans; driven from the bright world, and cast into darkness and woe! Hear the words of the Saviour Himself: "Whosoever heareth these sayings of mine and doeth them, I will liken him to a wise man which built his house upon a rock; and the rain descended and the floods came, and the winds blew and beat upon that house and it fell not, for it was founded upon a rock. But every one that *heareth these sayings of mine* and *doeth them* not, shall be likened unto a foolish man, which built his house upon the sand; and the rain descended, and the floods came and the winds blew, and beat upon that house, and it fell: and great was the fall of it!"

Yes, *great was the fall of it*; and whither, I should like to know, shall the ruined man flee! He cannot remain in his overthrown house—he is driven thence. The agencies of death have prevailed against him. He must pass into the spiritual and the unseen: but in what direction shall be his flight! He has failed to find shelter with the Redeemer; and who else is there to protect and receive him? Like Zedekiah driven from Jerusalem, he has no refuge to which to betake himself! And as for escape from the agencies of vengeance, the thought is absurd. All the laws of the universe are against him as unbelieving and unforgiven. As surely as that the agents of Nebuchadnezzar arrested the fugitive Zedekiah (and far more surely), the agents of retribution will arrest the disobedient when once disembodied. Earth rejects them. Heaven disowns them. Every holy planet and system in the wide universe bars its portals against them. There is nothing for them but the gulf of darkness, and the affinities of their nature will draw them thither. Heaven having had no admission into their affections (they having rejected or disregarded the words of the great Prophet-Teacher), their hearts are hard and heavy, and incapable either of floating or ascending and they necessarily sink to their own unpleasing and awful place! And there they shall be forgotten, and left to their own remorseful memories. Like the captive and blind Zedekiah in Babylon, their record shall cease. The historian of the universe will no longer burden the page of history with their names. Their blasphemies and bitter execrations, if recorded, would contribute nothing to the edification or the comfort of the holy, and therefore the pall of forgetfulness shall be spread for ever over them. They have no longer inheritance in the halls of light and happy cognition, but pass their weary and wretched existence in the dark dungeons of unimagined grief. Are you prepared to meet such a fate ? Are **you** willing to hazard such a condemnation ? Then do **not** abuse the mercies of God, nor leave, Zedekiah-like your privileges unimproved. Do **not** turn **away from** Him that speaketh from Heaven. **Do** not allow **the** Saviour-Prophet to counsel you **in vain** ! O, do not allow the chariot of salvation to pass by you, without your attaching yourself to it, **or** to the throng that follows it. Be not like Zedekiah, of **a** proud and disobedient temper, but obey the heavenly Prophet, and humble yourself under the mighty hand of God, accepting His grace and His saving arrangements in His Son Jesus, and fearing the forfeiture of all. Remember God, who at sundry times and in divers manners spoke in times past, spake to the fathers by the prophets (to Zedekiah, for example, by Jeremiah) hath in these last days spoken to us by His Son ; and if we prove disobedient (as Zedekiah), the last of the merely human kings of the House of David did, we will find, like him, that there is for us, that indeed there *can* be for us, *no escape !*

QUESTIONS ON ZEDEKIAH.

What privilege did this prince enjoy ?
   He was contemporary with Jeremiah, an inspired **servant** of God.
How should **he** have conducted himself in relation **to** this servant of Heaven ?
   He should have listened to him surely, and conformed himself to his advice.
Have other princes shewn a desire to enjoy the guidance or advice of supposed superior beings ?
   Yes. In the case of heathen oracles. They sent on special occasions, expensive presents and embassies to these

oracles. Zedekiah had no need to apply to such oracles, **when** the accredited servant of Heaven was ever ready to point out to him, and that with unambiguous words, the way of duty or of safety.

Did Zedekiah manifest any **disposition to** listen **to the** prophet?

Yes. He consulted him privately **in** the crisis **of** his fate.

And why did Zedekiah not guide himself by the advice **of the** prophet?

Because that advice was distasteful to himself and to his ungodly counsellors.

What was his mistaken wish and expectation?

A deliverance from Nebuchadnezzar, similar to that enjoyed by Hezekiah from Sennacherib.

And why did God withhold such a demonstration **in the present** case?

Because Zedekiah, his princes, and **his** people had neither wish nor intention to walk in the covenant of God. They wished to enjoy the privileges of Israel without submitting to the laws of Israel—a wish which was wholly inadmissible and unreasonable.

What is the great lesson taught **us** by his conduct **on** the occasion?

The folly of turning from a divine messenger and rejecting divinely fixed conditions of safety. Had he (Zedekiah) but listened to Jeremiah, his life and capital would have been preserved.

Are **we** like Zedekiah, **in** danger, and do we need both advice **and assistance**?

Certainly **we** are, **as** moral and accountable **creatures.** The agencies **of** darkness and condemnation **are** pressing around **us, as** the Chaldeans around Jerusalem, and death may determine for us a sad fate at any moment.

Is there any heavenly prophet to whom we may apply for direction and help in these critical circumstances?

Yes. A mightier Prophet who is also the propitiation for the sins of the wolrd, and who is able to direct infallibly, and to save absolutely **all who** listen to and trust in Him.

And what are His directions to the condemned and death-doomed?

To cease opposition to God, and **to** cast themselves on the divine mercy. It was submission or ruin with Zedekiah. It is in effect the same with **us.**

And shall we allow pride and disaffection to ruin us as they ruined Zedekiah?

I trust not. We can see the folly of this son of Josiah in rejecting the counsel of Jeremiah, and we cannot but determine, if in any degree wise with heavenly wisdom, that we will not repeat the folly. "Believe in the Lord Jesus Christ and thou shalt be saved."

What was the undesirable distinction of Zedekiah?

His name is forever associated with the overthrow of the city and temple of God.

Had any calamity equal to this in magnitude overtaken the dynasty of David before the time of Zedekiah?

No. Other kings of this sacred line had met with calamities and disasters, but none so great as this. Other calamities had left the throne and the temple untouched, but this obscured the temple and made an end of the typical royalty of the house of David.

And did the people of Jerusalem suffer when Zedekiah fell?

Yes. To a frightful and indescribable extent. "The daughter of Zion lay covered in a very cloud of wrath"—and all for the pride of Zedekiah as the proximate cause.

Had the outlying nations any reason to mourn the downfall of the temple?

Certainly. It was the out-putting of the only light of the world. The nations were indifferent indeed, but it was because they knew not the importance of the suspended ritual.

To what were the nations indebted for the re-kindling of the light of Zion.

To the grace and interposition of God.

What would have been the consequence if Zion had remained unvisited and unrenewed?

The reign of Satan and of misery must have remained unbroken in all generations.

How must these subsequent generations regard the name of Zedekiah?

With unqualified disesteem. He plunged the world in darkness, and for any thing he could do or desire to do, it would be in darkness even to the present moment.

What was the experience of Zedekiah on the taking of Jerusalem by Nebuchadnezzar?

Mournful and sad.

What was the apparent contradiction of Jeremiah and Ezekiel in relation to him and Babylon ?
  The one said he would be carried to Babylon, while the other said he would never see that city.
How were these prophecies fulfilled ?
  By having his eyes put out before coming to Babylon, so that though in it he could not see it.
How did this ungodly prince suffer as a king ?
  By the loss of his crown, and by his humiliation in the presence of his angry conqueror.
How did he suffer as a father ?
  By being constrained to see his children slain in his presence.
How did he suffer **as** a man ?
  By having his eyes put out and himself thus thrust into permanent darkness.
And what of his subsequent life ?
  There is no report concerning it, he was unworthy of further notice.
All this evil happened to him because he would not listen to God by Jeremiah. How then think you will it be with those who persistently turn away from the New Testament and divine Prophet ?
  They shall be driven away in their unbelief. They shall be driven from their family-displays and sordid pursuits. They shall be driven from the bright world and cast into darkness and woe.
And what of their history in that dark world ?
  It will probably be unrecorded. It were not meet to burden the page of history with their story. Their blasphemies and bitter execrations would contribute nothing to good, and therefore **the** pall of forgetfulness may be thrown over them.
Are you prepared to incur such **a** fate ?
  I should suppose not. Then you must renounce pride and yield yourselves to the guidance and mediation of the heavenly Prophet and Saviour. See in Zedekiah a type of the terrific fate of those who act otherwise.

XIX. IMMANUEL—JESUS.

> And, behold, thou shalt conceive in thy womb, and bring forth a son, and shalt call his name Jesus. And he shall reign over the house of Jacob for ever; and of his kingdom there shall be no end. Luke i. 31-33.

WE have recently turned your attention to the kings of the dynasty of David in succession. Of Zedekiah, the last of the purely earthly members of the dynasty, we spoke recently. We might now leave them, but we think that the list will not be complete without a notice of Him who is the glory and the end of the dynasty. We have had frequent occasion to refer to Him in our remarks on the successive kings, but we would now ask your attention more fully and exclusively to Him. And we shall remind you, as guided by these verses from Luke, of His characteristics, of His subjects, and of the perpetuity of His kingdom.

I. *His characteristics.*

The first of these is **His** *name*. That was determined in Heaven, and was meant to be significant. It is often a matter of perplexity with parents to name a child, and it would be still more so, if they had to find a name descriptive of the child's future career or distinguishing character. This difficulty was obviated in the case of the wonderful party before us. The angel announcing His birth said, "thou shalt call His name *Jesus*:" And as reported by Matthew it is added, "for He shall save His people from their sins."

And I need only **remind** you that He justifies His

name. He does save his true disciples from their sins. He hath saved myriads, and He still conducts His saving operations among men. All the kings of the dynasty to which he belongs had significant names, as you know, but many of them failed to be, or to do, what their names indicated. Not so did this most interesting of David's sons. He is indeed a Saviour, as many a ransomed one in heaven can tell, as well as many a humble and grateful one on earth. Would that every one of us might know, in his own experience, the power of Jesus to save, and the preciousness of the salvation which He secures!

We seem familiar with the expression, "He shall save His people from their sins," but we often attach comparatively small importance to the statement. This however is our mistake. Sin is a malady affecting the soul, and far more intractable than any disease that can affect or afflict the body. It poisons all the springs of thought and volition, and all the outflowings of affection. No human skill can arrest or rectify it. Only He who made the being can effectually deal with it. And even He must deal with it in a way of skill and complicated arrangement. It requires special preparations to allay the fever which sin produces, and preparations which only God can make. And it requires special influences to apply the remedy provided, and expel the subtle poison from the system of the patient altogether. The truth is, to achieve a perfect cure from this disease of sin, in a single instance, is one of the greatest and most gladdening wonders in the history of intelligence. How great then the skill of the Saviour-Physician who secures the result in millions of cases! The light of eternity alone will enable us to judge worthily of this matter. David though honoured to free the sacred territory of intruders, still left the people under the power of this disease of sin; and Solomon, though honoured to build the temple, still did nothing effective in the way of subduing or removing the malady of sin from his subjects; and Hezekiah, though honoured as an intercessor for the unprepared who kept the passover, still left sin unsubdued in Israel; and Josiah, though distinguished for his zeal and passover observance still left the fatal disease rankling in the national mind; but Jesus, more penetrating in thought, and more thorough-going in purpose, and more ample in resources than any of His predecessors in the sacred dynasty, effectually saves his people from their sins. He saves them from the power of sin, and from the defilement of sin, and from the eternal condemnation and consequences of sin. The achievement is wonderful, and wholly beyond the sphere of human action and human accomplishment. He who truly bears the name of "the Saviour from sin," is something more than a mere human physician, and must be entitled to universal consideration and attention on the part of men! And this, His claims on attention more distinctly appears when you think of His second characteristic, **as** announced by the angel:—and that is, *His greatness.*

"*He shall be great,*" says that heavenly messenger. And who may declare, or who may imagine His greatness, or the thousandth part of it? He is great, as we have just seen, as **a** Physician and Saviour. He achieves a work which nothing short of divine power can accomplish. He is great too, as compared with all the other kings of the dynasty to which He belongs. David, with all his distinctions, is but **a** small forth-showing of the transcendent excellences of Jesus; Solomon with all his glory, as compared with Jesus, is lost in the blaze of **a** finer and more magnificent effulgence; a greater than Solomon is here. And all the subsequent kings of the dynasty but prepare the way for the manifestation of Jesus. It was indeed with a view to the coming of Jesus that the dynasty of David was set up; and Jesus fulfils all its purposes, and gives meaning and beauty to all its peculiarities. He is, by way of eminence, the son of David; nay, He is more truly David than David himself—seeing that He is the beloved in the presence of the great Unseen (*David,* you know, means the beloved) in a far higher sense and in a far purer and more perfect sense, than even David was, or ever could be! He is also *great,* as compared with all that is great in human history. Emperors, and conquerors, and legislators, all dwindle into insignificance before Him. His advent was the centre and the fulness of time—shedding light retrospective on all that went before, and pouring light divine and beautifying through all the ages that follow after! Nay, He is great compared with the hierarchies of heaven. He is even now set down on the right hand of the Majesty on high—far above all principalities, and powers—His name is above every name—and His authority is supreme. All power in heaven and on earth hath been committed to to Him, and for good reason. "The Father loveth the Son, and hath given *all things* into His hands." And His greatness will yet effulge on all humanity when He comes in the glory of His Father, and of the holy angels, to judge mankind, and to determine the eternal destiny of all. O, how great the greatness, and how unrivalled the greatness, of Him, who, through all time, is ever supreme, and ever the same, and of whom it is said, that the very angels of heaven are the ministering spirits of His gracious government!

But the third characteristic of this wonderful one is *His double Sonship*. That is distinctly set forth in the announcement of the angels. "He shall be called," said that heavenly messenger, "the son of the Highest, *i.e.,* He shall be known to be the son of the Highest," and then, the angel adds, "the Lord God shall give unto Him the throne of *His Father David*. Mark, He is the son of the Highest and also the son of David; or in the language of Paul, at the beginning of Romans, "He was made of the seed of David, according to the flesh, and declared to be the Son of God according to the spirit of holiness, by His resurrection from the dead."

Here, then, we have a characteristic in Jesus that is wholly unique, and wonderful beyond thought. There is nothing like it in any other member of the dynasty to which he belongs. There is nothing like it indeed in all human history. True, His disciples receive from Him power to become the sons of God, and they therefore may be said to have a double sonship as well as He,— they are at once the children of men and the children of God. But their sonship in the divine family is very different from His, as you may well believe. "He is the only begotten of the father." Their sonship is by adoption; His is by right! Their sonship is acquired by connection with him; His is eternal and independent of them! Their sonship is the distinction of many; His the distinction of himself alone!

In this we have a mystery that is beyond all solution. It is in vain that men attempt an explanation of it. And it were wise in us to accept it as a glorious truth, though wholly inexplicable and irresolvable. Only the Father knoweth the Son truly and adequately and in all the mystery of his mediatorial person. Only the Father knows Him, if I may speak so, from the divine side, and He must be known from the divine side to be known fully. Men know Him from the human side, but the human side is unfitted for a complete revelation of His glory. The divine light is there, and the divine light shines through the human, and the divine light glorifies and transfigures the human, but still the manifestation is limited, and walled in, as it were, by the limits that appertain to the human. The truth is, the manifestation was arranged in this way, to suit the limited faculties of men. The unclouded and unbounded forthbursting of luminous deity had been unsuited by its splendour, and even destructive by its intensity to our faculties and capabilities. We have reason therefore to be glad and grateful for the very mystery in the person of Jesus which challenges our wonder and curiosity. And the more so when we remember that this double sonship, which we cannot understand, fits Him for the mighty work and government which He has undertaken. But for His human descent, He could not have saved His people from their sins. (It was in His human nature that He must bear in their room and stead the penalty of the broken law.) And but for His divine sonship, His substitutionary death had been of no avail. His divine nature was, as it were, the altar which sanctified, ennobled, and rendered available the offering. His humanity again, is the point of knowledge and concentration for the ransomed, while His divine power enables Him to make good all that they desire and expect from Him as a Saviour. But for His humanity we could not have known God, nor have been reconciled to God, and but for His divinity, we could never have been brought again into character harmony with the Holy one.

Here then we see meaning in His double sonship, if we cannot explain it; and we may well leave the mystery unexplained, if only we may realize the salvation intended. O, but we may rejoice, and that daily, in the combined divinity and humanity which secures such a salvation, though we are wholly unable to understand how the divine can inhere in the human, or how the human can fitly work the works of the divine! Enough that this union of natures enables Him to save His people from their sins, and amply explains His unequalled greatness.

But a fourth characteristic of this wonderful prince of the dynasty of David is:—

The manner of his enthronement. This is announced by the angel thus: The Lord God *shall give* unto Him the throne of his father David. It was not by force of arms you perceive, nor yet by ambition on His part, nor yet by what the world calls happy accident, or a fortunate combination of circumstances, that he mounted the throne, but by the determination and interposition of the supreme authority in the universe. As Solomon in his day was placed upon the throne of David by anterior and unrecognized authority, so Jesus was in due time placed upon the same throne of David by anterior and supreme authority. There was no want of opposition to the enthronement of Jesus, as in the case of Solomon, but the opposition was vain and powerless. Spite of it all the Lord God hath set His Son, who is also the son of David, on His holy hill Zion!

And there was every propriety in this elevation. It

was the right of Jesus *by descent*. True, the family of David had fallen into poverty and obscurity, but this destroyed not the right of that family to royalty when the Lord God saw meet to reinstate it in the person of any one of its members. And then, it was the right of Jesus *by merit*. For He so subserved the purposes of the divine government by self-sacrifice and magnanimous service, that the Lord God saw meet to restore in Him the fallen throne of his father David: and further, it was proper that Jesus should be so exalted, because of His combined competency and willingness to accomplish the purposes for which the throne of His great ancestor was set up. Why did God choose David, and take him from the shepherd's fold? Was it not to feed Jacob, His people, and Israel, His inheritance? Was it not to lead them in the pastures of heaven, and to strengthen their attachment to the Holy? Was it not to guard them against the inroads of error and unrighteousness, and to keep them near to the temple of truth and divine intercourse? And who so fit for this service as He, who being the son of David, and also the Son of God, is the good shepherd—the righteous one—and the zeal-consumed servant of the divine government? It was right then, that the Lord God should give unto Jesus the throne of His father David, and we can see that it was so. God's ways are not unfrequently inscrutable to us, and wholly inexplicable, but the enlightened cannot but understand and approve of His counsel and His gift, when He gives unto Jesus the throne of His father David!

One other remark we think it desirable to add as characteristic of this great son of David, although there is no foundation for it in our text, and that is as to *the seat of His government*. He is set indeed on the holy hill Zion, but it is in the heavenly form, or development of that hill. The earthly Mount Zion were unsuited at once to the spiritual nature of His rule, and to the intended extent of His kingdom. It was needful that He should occupy a more commanding position than any earthly centre could furnish; and therefore, the Lord

God hath **set** Him at His own right hand, far above all principality, and power, and might, and dominion, and given Him **a** name above every name. Though wearing the form of humanity, He is not (on His throne in the the heavens,) subject **to the** decay and vicissitudes of human things. Kings **on** earth die, and give place to their successors, and empires rise and fall among men, but King **Jesus** dieth no more—death hath no more dominion over Him. His empire is **as** lasting **as** time, and it is all-controlling as well. He **is** made head over all things to His church, and "He is the same yesterday, to-day and forever!" The change of capital **of** the Roman empire under Constantine, from Rome to Constantinople, was a step toward the downfall of the empire itself; but the changes of capital on the part of Jesus, from the earthly Jerusalem to the heavenly, was but a part of an extended plan, rendered necessary by the ample operations contemplated, and it will certainly prove conducive in the end to the establishment and success of the mediatorial and restorative kingdom of the house and dynasty of David in all the earth!

See then, in brief the characteristics of Immanuel Jesus, *His name is significant—and He makes good its significance.*—His greatness is unrivalled—His descent is gloriously mysterious—His enthronement is honourable—and the seat **of** His government is heavenly—all untouched by decay, and all unhampered by **the** limitations of earthly rule!

Now **is** it possible that we, or that any people made acquainted with the facts, can be inattentive or indifferent to such a potentate? Why, even though we had no personal interest in Him at all, He is supremely worthy of attention—and that on the part of all nations, and through all time. There is no one to compare with Him among the kings of the earth as we have already observed. There is no one to approach as to dignity and glory —**no** not by thousands of degrees! And then, His is just as suitable to our circumstances, and as necessary to our safety and happiness, as He is transcendent and unrivalled in Himself? Are we not oppressed by sin? And is it not He, and He alone who saves from sin? Are we not formed to admire greatness, and to have pleasure in admiring it? And where will you find greatness like the greatness of Him whose name is above every name? Are we not formed to wonder in the presence of the gloriously inexplicable? And where will you find mystery more glorious, or more inexplicable than the double sonship of Immanuel Jesus? Have we not been gifted too with moral sensibilities—enabling us to rejoice in the honours of the meritorious and self-sacrificing? And where will you find merit and self-sacrifice like that of Jesus, or rewards more exalted or more inconceivable than His? And further, are we not formed for the Immortal? Are we not restive under the limitations of *this* earthly and decaying life? And is not the throne of this King heavenly? And is He not preparing His true subjects for an inheritance that is incorruptible and unfading? O, where will you not find a king or a friend like Immanuel Jesus? And will any of you be so untrue to the necessities and the interests of his being as to withhold his attention from this divine Saviour, or willingly remain outside His kingdom and unanimated by the hope of His subjects?

But this leads me to notice:—

II. *His subjects.*

These are briefly described in our text **as** "the house (or household) of Jacob." But this expression we know does not mean merely the natural descendants of Jacob. If it did so, then the subjects of Immanuel Jesus, would be simply the Jews, and all of that nation of course. But what says Paul concerning this matter? Why this, "that they are not all Israel which are of Israel." And again "they which are the children of the flesh, these are not the children of God, but the children of the promise are counted for the seed." And as, on the one hand, they are not all of Jacob who belong to the tribe of Jacob, so neither on the other hand, are they all excluded from this honour who are sprung of another lineage. To the Gentiles of Ephesus, Paul writes : " Now, ye are no more strangers and foreigners, but fellow-citizens with the saints, and of the household of God." Remember " the house of Jacob," and " the household of God " are convertible terms, and the privilege of belonging to this association is as open to the Gentiles as it is to the Jews. In other words, the circumcised in heart may belong to any people. And so of faith, Abraham is the father of all them that believe, whether they be Jews or Gentiles. In one word, the spirit of love, which is the spirit of God, is confined to no nationality ; and the house of Jacob is co-extensive with the reign of love among man. More particularly, Jacob was a child or son of God ; and all of like characteristics with him, as such, belonged to his sacred and God-loved, and God-animated house. And these constitute the subjects of that special kingdom over which the Immanuel son of David reigns. "He shall reign over the house of Jacob for ever!"

Now, by paying attention to the characteristics of Jacob, as a son and servant of God, we shall learn to know who they are that belong to his house, or household. You are familiar with his story, and you will readily recognize the following traits in his character, or facts in his history :—

First. He was loved and chosen of God : **"Jacob have I loved, and Esau have I hated."**

Secondly. He set store by the *birth-right*, that is, by the right and privilege of transmitting the promises of God to coming ages. He seized the first opportunity of obtaining the relinquishment of it from Esau in his own favour. We do not say he acted generously in this ; but we see, in the transaction, at once his desire for the distinction, and Esau's indifference to it, or slight estimation of it.

Thirdly. He humbly and gratefully accepted the divine covenant at Bethel. When God declared His gracious purposes concerning him and his, he devoutly devoted himself to the service of God, and consecrated a tenth of his increase to the divine service.

Fourthly. He was a man of earnest prayer. See how he agonized and wrestled with the Divine through the night at Penuel, when in danger from the approach of Esau. Then, his hope was in the great and coming Shiloh-centre for the nations. You remember his language concerning Judah on his death bed : " The sceptre shall not depart from Judah, nor a lawgiver from between his feet until Shiloh come, and unto him shall the gathering of the people be !" And to crown all, he died in the faith of the promised inheritance—taking an oath from Joseph in his last hours, that he would bury him in the sacred territory.

Such were the characteristics of Jacob, and such are the characteristics of all the true members of Jacob's house. The association with which Jacob's name is so strikingly linked is not heterogeneous, you will observe, but homogeneous. The same spirit and the same sentiments belong to them all. They breathe, if I may so say it, a common atmosphere; nay, like the sons of Adam among themselves, they have common features—modified indeed as to proportion, and ranging pretty widely from each other in particular cases, but all radically and essentially alike ; and by that likeness they may all be known, to the enlightened and interested, as belonging to the house of Jacob, and to the kingdom of Immanuel Jesus. " For He shall rule over the house of Jacob for ever." Let us think for a moment of these characteristics ; as found among the members of Christ's kingdom.

First. The subjects of *Immanuel Jesus are all loved of God.* They have all been chosen in their glorious king from before the foundation of the world, with a view to their being holy, and without blame before God in love. They have all been predestinated to the adoption of children by Jesus Christ unto the Father himself, according to the good pleasure of His will. They are all elect, according to the foreknowledge of God the Father, through sanctification of the spirit, unto obedience and sprinkling of the blood of Jesus Christ. As with Jacob, so with all who are of his house—they are loved of God, and chosen by God to their ineffable felicity and very great honour. I am aware that the unsubdued heart of humanity objects to this as unjust in relation to the unchosen, and inimical to the interests of morality in the Church; but this is their mistake. I cannot explain the matter to the satisfaction of objectors, and it is noticeable that Paul himself, in the ninth chapter of Romans, does not attempt to **explain** it. The difficulty is founded **on the** divine sovereignty, and must **be acceded to in** the meantime without **explanation.** God Himself affirms it by His servant, and remonstrates with **the** objector thus:—"Nay, but, O man, who art thou **that** repliest against God?" There then, the matter must **rest,** but with this observation:—The divine election is known only to God Himself, until the appearance of the other characteristics of the Jacob household in the heart and history of any given individual reveals it. The election, therefore, cannot be a ground of action or of non-action, in the first instance, but only a fact for subsequent and grateful recognition on the part **of** the believing. The other characteristics of the house of Jacob are more within the range of human recognition and observation. Let us notice them then and commence the enumeration from this point.

First. *The subjects of Immanuel Jesus are all desirous of the birth-right in relation* **to** *a brighter life.* They are not, like Esau, chiefly concerned about present gratification. They are not **willing to** sell the future for a mess of pottage **as** he did. And **they are** not willing, like him, to cast in their lot with the ungodly and the idolatrous world around them. They have heard of brighter things, and they yearn after these brighter things! They are willing to sacrifice **the** little and defiling present for the glorious and undefiled future. Like Jacob, they prefer the prospects which God hath opened up to humanity to all the pottage and privileges of earth. While the ungodly are indifferent to the divine announcements and purposes the men of the house of Jacob dwell apart, and ruminate upon these announcements and purposes. While the ungodly, Esau-like, have no scruple in sacrificing their heavenly prospects to their earthly gratification, the subjects of Immanuel Jesus, Jacob-like, readily sacrifice their earthly gratification to their heavenly prospects. By this alone you may very well know who are the subjects of the great king; and whether you yourselves are **so**: But further

Secondly. *The subjects of Immanuel Jesus willingly and gratefully accept the covenant of grace in Christ Jesus, as proposed in the sacred volume.* What the vision of Bethel was to the birth-right loving Jacob, that the communications of the New Testament are to the heaven-preparing souls of our own time. Reading and apprehending the truth—the salvation-desiring are filled with wonder and with awe. For a time the condescension, and provisions, and promises of God may seem to such like a dream, but ere long they are seen to be all reality; and the awe-stricken and the awe-filled soul rises, as it were, exclaiming, "this, this indeed *is* the house of God—this *is* the gate of heaven!" Forthwith the entranced one raises, if I may say **so, a stone** of remembrance, and, pouring forth the oil **of its** grateful worship thereon, it responds to **the** gracious Eternal, saying, "since God will be my God, in Christ I will be His servant, and I hereby dedicate myself and my possessions—whatever He in His love and wisdom gives to His honour and service." Then having thus accepted and entered into the covenant of heavenly grace the believer goes on his **way** rejoicing. But

Thirdly. *The subjects of Immanuel Jesus are all men of Prayer.* Their safety and their peace is with Him into whose covenant they have entered, and they seek Him daily for supplies or encouragements as they need. In special duties they seek special aid; and when appalling dangers threaten, they seek shelter or deliverance, as the case may require, from Him who hath revealed Himself to them, and enabled them to accept of His friendship. Jacob's wrestling with the angel of the Lord at Penuel is but the type of the habit of the men of his house. They are all of them men of prayer. They pray daily; they pray in all languages; they pray in all circumstances; they pray in the spirit; they pray for themselves each of them; and they pray for the church; and they pray for the world, and for the fulfilment of the divine purposes in relation to it, the world. They are clearly distinguished by this habit from the ungodly and sense-wrapped world. They cannot but pray, and they seek fellowship and sympathy with the unseen by means of the exercise, while the unilluminated and unquickened around them cannot rise to such exercises and such intercourse. Of this habit of theirs it hath been said:—" All good men from the beginning of time have practised it. Not one of them now in a better world but did. On every spot where there has ever been a good man, there has been prayer. With all good men it has been the primary expedient in seeking to be happy. It has been the grand recourse in seeking truth—in performing duty—in resisting temptation—in bearing afflictions—in preparing to meet death. What a delightful and solemn, and magnificent vision, back in thought, is that of all who ever prayed habitually on earth!"

And these are the subjects of Immanuel Jesus. It is through Him that they have the spirit of prayer; and it is because of His mediation that their prayers are heard and answered. They are of the house of Jacob, (who was a prince in prayer,) because of this habit; and they are known to be the subjects of Immanuel (who is the sole centre and medium of acceptable prayer) by means of the same habit. But

Fourthly. *The subjects of Immanuel Jesus all gather around Him as the Shiloh-centre of the nations.* He is, with them, the worthy Ruler of the nations, and the adequate centre of union and authority. Human-built thrones may serve local and temporary purposes, but Jesus, they know, is a divine king, and able to meet the requirements of a universal dominion. The prayerful rejoice in His competency, and are happy to know **and to** obey the laws of His kingdom. While the unbelieving and the self-seeking are running in every direction—seeking **each** some unsatisfying or injurious vanity, the prayerful men of the house of Jacob crowd the banners of Messiah—wait the evolutions of His providence—glory **in** His yoke of meekness and patience—and look rejoicingly forward to His second coming. Meantime, they willingly lend themselves to His purposes, so far as they have ability or opportunity **to** serve them. O, **but** they congratulate themselves continually, to have found, in finding Him, **the** true and blissful centre of excellence, and they account all things but *loss* for **the** excellency **of** the knowledge **of** Him. And

Finally. *The subjects of Immanuel Jesus live and die in the hope of a heavenly inheritance.* They have been begotten to this hope by the resurrection of their Lord from the dead, and by His ascension to heaven, and His enthronement there. The seat of His government is on high, as we have seen, and they hope to join Him in that blissful region. He is set down at the right hand of the divine majesty, and their life is hid with Him in God. Jacob thought much of the earthly and typical inheritance, and gave orders that his bones should repose there with those of his honoured ancestors; but the prospects of his house have been enlarged and exalted since then, and the **members** of it look for a higher inheritance—an inheritance no longer typical, but heavenly—no longer corruptible, but incorruptible—no longer decaying or alienable, but undecaying and inalienable! They hope **that,** when their Lord and king re-appears, they will appear with Him **in** glory:—They hope that, instead of causing their bones to be carried **to** the heavenly Canaan, He will change their vile bodies, and fashion them like **to** His own glorious body, and introduce them, in their renovated and completed being, into the companionship of the living and immortal. Jacob in dying, would sleep with Abraham and Isaac in Machpelah, but the men of his house now, when summoned from earth, think chiefly of joining Abraham and Isaac, and all the believing and prayerful ones, in the golden city!

Such, then, is the house of Jacob **over** which Immanuel Jesus reigns. Its members are all loved of God—all desirous of **the** heavenly birthright—all willing and glad to **embrace the** divine covenant of grace—all prayerful— all **Shiloh-centred—and all** hopeful in relation to the **heavenly** inheritance! **And you** ought to notice, that **the first** peculiarity, **viz, that they** are **all** like Jacob, **loved of** God, though **properly placed** first **as** read **from** heaven, ought **to be placed last as read** from earth. No man can know his **election of God, but** by his faith, prayerfulness, and **conformity** to **his Shiloh** king. And **no** man has **a** right **to make** the hidden counsels of God the ground **of** his action as we have already observed. **No man, indeed,** hath the power of doing so; and **where there** is no power there **can** be no right. And no man has a right to quarrel with God's decisions! God does injustice **to none,** and He may **surely** be allowed **to** show mercy where He will. If He exercises sovereignty in relation **to** men, it is ever **on** the side of mercy—never on that of injustice. If He depart in the case of some from the strict line **of** retribution, it is not to inflict unmerited wrong, but to confer unmerited kindness; and even this He does not do, without making adequate reparation to the law whose sentence has been in so far cancelled! Leaving, then, the first characteristic of the house of Jacob to be taken up and recognized at a subsequent stage, **see** that **you** examine yourselves as to the other five, if indeed you wish **to** be subjects of the Immanuel king! And see that you exercise yourselves on these five yet more and more, if you would be prepared for the consumations of His kingdom: That is to say, set your heart on the *birthright* for immortality. Embrace the New Testament *covenant of grace*—abound in *prayer*—gather to the *heavenly centre of the nations* (that is to Messiah Jesus), and cherish the *hope of His heavenly kingdom*. If exercised thus, it matters not what be your earthly nationality, you belong to the house of Jacob, and therefore to the kingdom of Immanuel. Then, belong to that kingdom you have friends and brethren in all regions of the earth. And you will yet be gathered with all the prayerful and believing from all generations into the heavenly kingdom of your prince!

But this leads me to **notice** concerning this:

III. The perpetuity of His kingdom.

"**And of** His kingdom," **it** is said **in** our text, "there shall be no end." Earthly kingdoms grow and decay, but the kingdom of Immanuel Jesus knows no decay. The mightiest empires known in history seldom exceed **one** thousand or twelve hundred years **in** duration; and many of these never reach that term. The causes of their decay grow with their growth, and necessitate their downfall. Pride, luxury, oppression, and immorality ever go hand in hand with earthly greatness, and these being in operation in any community render permanence in its power or **in its** glory, wholly impossible. Besides, no earthly community **can secure a** succession **of able** rulers, so that what is gained in one reign **is very** often lost **in an**other. Further, no earthly empire **can be** secured against the upspringing of a rival kingdom—more powerful than itself, and in this event its prestige, and its power must be lost and overthrown. No such contingency, however, **can** arise in relation to Immanuel's kingdom. Himself wields the sceptre through all generations, and He cannot be restricted by the exercise of power. Nothing can be lost by the incumbency of **a** weaker prince **on** His throne; for He never **vacates** it, nor transmits it to another. And no rival kingdom **can** arise to dispute with **Him in** His dominion—seeing **He** is made head over all things **to** His church. And no pride or oppression, or immorality is or can be tolerated among His subjects, so **that** there can arise no cause of disunion or disruption **in** this kingdom. All the elements of dislocation **or** revolution are thus excluded from it, and only harmony and stability can be the result. Demagogues and agitators, if it were possible that any such should arise in this kingdom, (which it is not) would have no grievance to work upon, and no plausible excuse for change. Besides, the throne is the throne of the immutable—the throne of the divine, and even the gates of the grave, which prevail against everything human, cannot prevail against it. Already this kingdom hath lasted twenty centuries (to say nothing of its preliminary existence even from the beginning). And it hath about it no symptom of decay at the present hour. It is even now sounding its trumpets and sending forth its agents for further conquest. It hath mighty interests and enmities to contend with, but it knows neither trepidation nor doubt. Its prince hath all power in heaven and on earth, and its subjects have all confidence in the faithfulness and purposes of their chief. He is the light of the world, and in Him it is, that all the nations of the earth are yet to be blessed. "All the ends of the world, says the inspired psalmist shall remember and turn unto Him—and all the kindreds of the nation shall worship before Him: For the kingdom is His, and He is the governor among the nations!"

And this, my friends, is the consummation of the dynasty of David—this the centre of righteousness—this the conquering king—this, spiritually speaking the temple-reigning prince of peace—this the world-instructing sovereign—this the unity-restoring Mediator and Intercessor—this the passover-furnishing High Priest and Redeemer! He is thus in Himself you perceive, at once, the David, the Solomon, the Jehoshaphat, the Hezekiah, and Josiah of New Testament times; and far more honoured and far more worthy than any of them! He is more beloved and more successful than David! He is more royal, more pacific, and more enlightened than Solomon! He is more devoted and more persistent in the matter of instruction than Jehoshaphat! He is more influential as an intercessor than Hezekiah! And He is more distinguished as to passover-observance than Josiah. The millenial age indeed, will yet keep passover under Him for a thousand years. He is the last of the kings of this dynasty—as He can have no successor. And

He is the glory of the dynasty, the origin and the spring as well of all that is excellent in it. He fulfils and intensifies all that was bright and honourable in the worthy members of the dynasty. And as for the unworthy or inconsistent members thereof, they receive no excuse or countenance from anything in His government. There is with Him no unfaithfulness, as in the case of Solomon! No impotent pride as in the case of Rehoboam! No hypocrisy as in the case of Abijah! No sinking from the divine life, as in the case of Asa! No misjudgment or misalliance as in the case of Jehoshaphat! And no renunciation of truth in favour of idolatry as in the case of Jehoram, Joash, Ahaz, Amon, and Zedekiah! He is, at once, faithful, true, faultless, and wonderful! The truth is, all that was worthy or illustrious in His David ancestry, but foreshadowed and intimated His coming, and all-eclipsing glory! He is, in relation to His dynasty, the first and the last—the beginning and the end. It was with a view to Him that the covenant was made with David and his family at first. And now that He has been manifested, no other son of David can or will dispute with Him the sacred throne. He must reign, and He must increase! And, while He is the glory of the house of David, He is also the hope of the entire world.

His disciples gathered from among all nations, are all dignified and consecrated by their subjection to Him. They are all Davids, all beloved and all accepted in Him as the great beloved! And all made priests unto God as well, and all members of His undying and unending kingdom.

O, but we ought to rejoice that such a king hath been enthroned! And how earnestly we should desire, every one of us, to be subjects of His government! Let us forsake and renounce all evil that we may seek and find in Him divine favour, royal existence, and immortal peace!

QUESTIONS ON IMMANUEL—JESUS.

Will you mention the characteristics of Immanuel Jesus, as set forth in the verses of Luke?
  His name, His greatness, His double sonship, the manner of His enthronement and the seat of government.
Is He able to realize what his name imports?
  Yes, certainly. He is able to save to the uttermost all them that come unto God **by** Him.
What is the extent of His greatness?
  It is unrivalled. His name is above every name.
What do you mean by his double sonship?
  That he is at once the son of God and the son of David.
Is this double sonship explicable?
  No. It is beyond the reach of human intellect and investigation.
What is the value of this mystery to us?
  Though wholly inexplicable, it yet enables us to see **how** this son of David can be truly the Saviour from sin.
What is noticeable concerning the manner of His enthronement?
  It was not by violence, or because of ambition on His part that he obtained the throne, but by anterior and adequate authority. "The Lord *gave* Him the throne—gave it Him not only because of His lineage, but also because of His merits."
And where is the seat of His government?
  In the heavenly Mount Zion, at the right hand of the Majesty on high.
What rendered it needful to change the scene of His rule from the earthly Mount Zion to the heavenly?
  The universal and spiritual nature of His government.
And is he just such a Saviour as the fallen and dying sons of men **need**?
  Yes. He meets in Himself all their wants, capabilities and aspirations.
What should be the first solicitude of every young person?
  Truly to know this mighty son of David.
But how are the subjects of this wonderful prince described?
  As "the house or household of Jacob."
Is this house (or household) confined to the natural descendants of Jacob?
  No. "They are not all Israel that are of Israel."
Who then constitute this household?

They that are of like character with Jacob, no matter what their earthly nationality may be.

What were the peculiarities in the life and habits of Jacob?
He was loved of God. He set store by the birth-right. He gratefully accepted the divine covenant at Bethel. He was a man of earnest prayer. His hope was in the coming Shiloh and He died in the faith of the promised inheritance.

And what about Jacob's house (or household) in relation to these peculiarities or habit?
They are common to all the members thereof.

What is that fundamental peculiarity in Jacob and **his household** which lies beyond or above the range **of human** agency or human understanding?
The sovereign love of God towards them.

Where then must we begin the enumeration of the peculiarities and habits of the members of Jacob's household?
In their desire after the birthright which stands linked with the ultimate inheritance. Under the influence of this desire, they are willing to sacrifice the present to the future, while they who belong not to the household, readily sacrifice the future to the present.

What next distinguishes them?
They willingly and gratefully accept the covenant of grace proposed by God in His gospel and dedicate themselves to the service of God accordingly.

What is the third peculiarity of the members of Jacob's **household**?
They are all men of prayer. Like Jacob, they wrestle with the divine and find comfort or victory by the exercise.

Mention the fourth characteristic of the members **of** this household?
They all gather around the Shiloh—centre of the nations—rejoicing in His fulness and transcendent excellences.

And what is the last characteristic of the members of this household?
They all live and die in the hope of a promised inheritance.—Not now a typical inheritance, but a heavenly and inalienable inheritance.

What is the difference concerning the sovereign love of **God** to the house of Jacob, when read from the divine side and the human side respectively?
When read from the divine side, it must be placed, first—When read from the human side, it can only properly be considered last: That is to say, it is by the existence of

faith, prayer and hope in the believer that the election of God is known in any case. The method of our procedure therefore must be—not to believe because we are elected; but by faith, prayer and hope **to** make our election manifest.

What is said about the kingdom **of** Immanuel Jesus, **as to** continuance?

That it will have no end.

What security for its continuance is there in **its** laws and customs?

The absolute right **of** these laws and customs. **It** admits of no pride, luxury, oppression or immorality.

And what security in the nature of its chief?

He is immutable—the same yesterday, to-day and forever, and his throne cannot be superseded or set aside by resisting or opposing authority.

What is the position of this kingdom at the present time?

Commanding and advancing.

What have you to notice of the crowning prince of the dynasty in relation to the entire dynasty?

That He combines in Himself all the excellencies of His progenitors, and that these excellencies in Him are all intensified. He is at once the David, the Solomon, the Jehoshaphat, the Hezekiah and the Josiah of the New Testament times.

But what of unworthy members of the dynasty in relation to this prince?

They have neither excuse nor countenance from any thing in His government.

How should we regard this crowning prince?

With great and inexhaustible gladness.

And what should be the supreme desire **of every one of us** concerning Him?

That we may be truly subjects of His government and sharers in His love.

What are the prizes to be obtained in connection with Him?

Divine favour, royal existence, and immortal peace.

FINIS.

www.ingramcontent.com/pod-product-compliance
Lightning Source LLC
Chambersburg PA
CBHW022145300426
44115CB00006B/346